Personal Course for Bankers

INTERNATIONAL TRADE FINANCE

Foreword to Sixth Edition

This book has been written for:

- students preparing for the *International Trade Finance* examination of The Chartered Institute of Bankers (CIB), London
- other students of international trade finance
  - on Business Studies degree courses
  - of The Institute of Export
  - of other banking institutes, such as The Chartered Institute of Bankers in Scotland

The syllabus for The Chartered Institute of Bankers, London examination entitled *International Trade Finance* covers the financial aspects of international trade and examines the problems of risk, and the management of risks often associated with overseas trade. There is comprehensive coverage of bank services and the many forms of support and finance available to bank customers. Readers should be aware of the competition which is - and will continue to appear - from other financial services groups, both within the European Union and beyond.

The book, which assumes no prior knowledge of the subject, is designed to be as practical and readable as possible. It is divided into fourteen lessons and broadly follows the scheme of work suggested by The Chartered Institute of Bankers.

The structure of the book makes it ideal for the student attending college as well as for the student who finds it impossible to attend a college and has to 'go it alone'. Past CIB examination questions are given at the end of each lesson as a guide to questions that have been asked in recent years. Each lesson contains a 'Know your ....' test which calls for short answers on the material that has just been studied. Spread throughout the book is a series of eight sets of 'Multiple Choice Questions'. Whilst such questions do not feature in the CIB examinations, many teachers and students like to use them as short tests by which progress can be measured.

Note that CIB examinations since 1993 have contained two 'scenarios', to which a number of questions are linked. In this book the scenario may be on a different page to the linked question: the page reference where the scenario can be found is given, and the scenario should be read to put the question into context.

Students will find that Appendix A contains exchange rate and calculation questions; Appendix B contains the answers! Appendix C contains suggested outline answers to the questions from each lesson which are indicated with an asterisk (*). Answers to Multiple Choice Questions are given in Appendix D.

Exchange rates quoted in past examination questions are 'as set'; in the text, rates are those of Summer 1994, which gave approximately USD 1.40 - 1.60 to the pound. With the considerable fluctuations over the last few years it is virtually impossible to show 'realistic' rates throughout the book: it is, of course, the principle that is important. In fact, in the 1860s, £1 was worth $12 and in 1980 it was $2.42 at one point; in early 1985 it almost achieved parity (i.e. £1 = $1), while just seven years later it almost reached $2.

It is important for students to be aware of the syllabus requirements, of the type of questions asked, and the format of the examination paper. However, this book should not be used solely as an 'examination crammer', but instead as a guide to this complex and ever-changing subject. It should form the solid foundation to further enquiry which should be enhanced by a regular reading of the financial press and of specialist banking magazines.

David Cox FCIB FCCA Cert Ed
Formerly Senior Lecturer in Banking
Worcester College of Technology

Acknowledgements

The assistance of the following organisations is gratefully acknowledged:

- The Chartered Institute of Bankers for kindly granting permission to use past examination questions

- Barclays Bank PLC, for permission to reproduce the specimen letter of credit from their booklet *Documentary Letters of Credit*

- Midland Bank PLC, for permission to reproduce their collection order

- National Westminster Bank PLC, for permission to reproduce the specimen tender bond and performance bond

- The Simpler Trade Procedures Board, for permission to reproduce documents from their book *Top Form*

- Norwich Union Fire Insurance Society Ltd, for permission to reproduce their marine insurance certificate

- The International Chamber of Commerce for permission to reproduce:
  ICC Uniform Rules for Collections
  ICC Publication 322
  Published in its official English version by the International Chamber of Commerce, Paris
  Copyright © 1978 – International Chamber of Commerce (ICC)
  Available from: ICC Publishing SA, 38 Cours Albert 1er, 75008 Paris, France
  And from: ICC United Kingdom, 14/15 Belgrave Square, London SW1X 8PS

  ICC Uniform Customs and Practice for Documentary Credits – 1993 Revision
  ICC Publication 500 – ISBN 92.842.1155.7
  Published in its official English version by the International Chamber of Commerce, Paris
  Copyright © 1993 – International Chamber of Commerce (ICC)
  Available from: ICC Publishing SA, 38 Cours Albert 1er, 75008 Paris, France
  And from: ICC United Kingdom, 14/15 Belgrave Square, London SW1X 8PS

FCIB, FCCA, Cert Ed

WITHDRAWN

NORTHWICK PUBLISHERS

Published by
Northwick Publishers,
14 Bevere Close, Worcester, WR3 7QH.
Telephone (0905) 456876/456529 FAX (0905) 454907

British Library Cataloguing in Publication Data
A catalogue record for this book is available from the British Library

ISBN 0-907135-79-X

Printed and bound by Ebenezer Baylis & Son Ltd.,
The Trinity Press, London Road, Worcester, WR5 2JH.

Contents

Introduction to International Trade Finance

❏ What is international trade finance?

International trade finance is about the way in which businesses, located in different countries, trade with one another. Principally, it covers

- terms of trade
- documents
- methods of payment
- credit insurance
- financing schemes

For all trading transactions there are a number of risks which may include: risk of non-payment, receipt of poor quality goods, risk of exchange rate movements. International trade finance attempts to minimise risks from the viewpoint of both seller and buyer.

❏ International trade finance - the UK perspective

Since the establishment of the single European market in 1993, international trade finance from the point of view of a United Kingdom business falls into two categories:

- trade with other members of the European Union (EU) – formerly known as the European Community
- trade with countries outside the European Union

Note, however, that trade within the *internal market* of the EU will still involve the use of foreign currencies until the use of the European Currency Unit – see pages 35/6 – becomes more widespread).

❏ International trade finance - the role of banks

Many services provided by banks can be used for international trade. These include:

- *payments* – documentary credits (see lessons 7 and 8), collections (lesson 9)
- *credit insurance* – provided by the private sector (see lesson 10)
- *bonds and guarantees* – see lesson 11
- *finance* – particularly forfaiting by means of avalisation of bills of exchange (see pages 225-228) and factoring, leasing, and instalment finance (see lesson 12)

Lesson One
Foreign Exchange and Forward Contracts

This lesson is concerned with all aspects of exchange rates, including operations in the foreign exchange market and the use of forward foreign exchange contracts by bank customers who export and/or import goods priced in a foreign currency. Lesson 2 continues the theme but is concerned with ways in which customers can avoid exposure to exchange risks.

❏ An introduction to foreign exchange

A rate of exchange is the price of units of currency of one country expressed in terms of units of currency of another. Most rates quoted in Britain state the amount of the foreign currency which may be exchanged for £1 sterling: this is known as a *currency rate*. For example, each day in Britain the television news states the rate at which the pound closed against the US dollar in the foreign exchange markets and a caption similar to the following:

£1 = USD 1.4865

Put another way round (as a *pence rate*) this means that one dollar equals £0.67 (£1 ÷ USD 1.4865). Let us see what happens when the rate rises to, say, USD 1.5285; one dollar now equals almost £0.65. We can see here that the dollar has *weakened* (i.e. is worth less) against the pound; put the other way round, the pound has *strengthened* against the dollar. If the rate falls to USD 1.4425, one dollar is now worth £0.69 and we can say that the dollar has strengthened against the pound, or that the pound has weakened against the dollar.

It is clear from the above that, when using currency rates, a foreign currency which is strengthening (or becoming more expensive) will fall when compared with the unit of the 'home' currency; conversely, when the foreign currency is weakening (or becoming cheaper), it will rise against the 'home' currency. In foreign exchange dealings there are always two ways of looking at a situation: from the point of view of the foreign currency, or from the point of view of the home currency. In the case just mentioned in this paragraph the home currency is weakening and strengthening respectively when compared with the foreign currency.

❏ Buying and selling

All products which are bought and sold have a buying price and a selling price: foreign currencies are no exception. When dealing with items such as stocks and shares, pairs of shoes, books, etc., it is easy to see the price at which those who deal in the product will buy, and the price at which they will sell. It is obviously a case of buy low, sell high, because the prices are expressed in the home currency. In the foreign exchange market, however, the buying and selling prices are usually quoted as currency rates, e.g.

USD 1.4865 - 1.4875

We have already seen that a foreign currency is worth more, in terms of pounds (or the home currency), when the currency rate is lower, and worth less when the currency rate is higher. Therefore those who are dealers in the market (e.g. dealers working in the foreign exchange department of a bank) will

✳ SELL LOW;   BUY HIGH

This is the 'golden rule' of foreign exchange transactions - from the point of view of the banks and dealers in the market. This rule applies provided that the foreign currency is quoted as a rate of £1 sterling (or the unit of the home currency) and that the deal takes place on the London (or home) market. In practice most examination questions fit these circumstances. It will be seen from the above rates for the US dollar that a bank's buying rate is on the right, while its selling rate is on the left: this is generally the case, although it is always as well to check.

The rate for US dollars quoted above is similar to that taken from the morning newspapers and, therefore, will generally be the market price at some time during the previous day. This rate should only be taken as an indication of market rates because transactions on the market will have taken place at differing rates during the day; furthermore the rate stated in the newspapers will have been ascertained by contacting a number - but not all - of the dealers. It is essentially an *interbank rate* for large (wholesale) amounts of currency, i.e. a bank dealer will sell to another bank requiring currency at 1.4865, while the dealer will buy from another bank wishing to sell at 1.4875. A bank customer who needs foreign exchange to pay for imports or has foreign exchange for sale as a result of having received a payment for exports will generally deal in smaller amounts. Accordingly a wider *spread of rates* will apply in much the same way that a food wholesaler works to a lower profit margin than a retail shop. Further, different rates will apply, with an even wider spread, for the purchase and sale of foreign bank notes. This rate, together with an even wider one, for buying and selling foreign coins are justified because of the costs in handling notes and coin. An example spread of rates for US dollars is illustrated as follows:

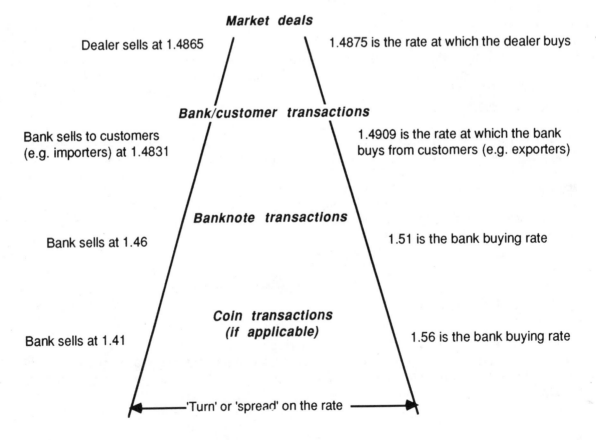

Usually these other rates are calculated with reference to the market rates. Thus the rate for bank/customer transactions might be market rate adjusted by 2‰ (2 per mille), i.e. two parts in one thousand. Using the market selling rate of USD 1.4865 from the example above, the bank/customer selling rate would be:

$$
\begin{array}{l}
\text{USD } 1.4865 \\
\underline{\phantom{\text{USD } 1.}0030} \text{ less } 2‰ \\
\text{USD } \underline{\underline{1.4835}}
\end{array}
$$

Note that as the bank is selling the adjustment is deducted from the market rate to follow the principle of 'sell low'. If the bank was buying the adjustment would be:

$$
\begin{array}{l}
\text{USD } 1.4875 \\
\underline{\phantom{\text{USD } 1.}0030} \text{ add } 2‰ \\
\text{USD } \underline{\underline{1.4905}}
\end{array}
$$

The adjustment is added because the bank will always wish to 'buy high'. (To calculate the adjustment, divide the market rate by 1 000 and then multiply by 2).

If you still have doubts about the rule of 'sell low, buy high' then imagine a very wide spread in the rate, e.g. USD 2.0 - 3.0. Remember that you should look at the rates from the point of view of a bank dealer: the bank will buy at the higher rate, i.e. one dollar equals 33p, and will sell at the lower rate, i.e. 50p per dollar, giving a profit (if the correct rates are used!) of 17p.

In an examination question there will not usually be a choice of different transactions rates: the correct rates for the types of transaction being considered will be given.

The rates we have considered so far are known as *spot rates,* i.e. the rate of exchange for an immediate foreign currency transaction, although settlement of market deals usually takes place two working days after the dealing date (the two days gives time for the transfer of funds to be made between the banks involved - see lesson 3).

❏ Forward rates and forward exchange contracts

Having just considered spot rates we will now look at forward rates which are quoted for all major currencies. These are the prices at which currency for delivery or supply at a date in the future are quoted. They are *not* predictions of future rates but mainly reflect the current interest rate differentials between the currencies involved. Other factors which may affect the position are economic and political considerations, including exchange control, and also the supply and demand in the forward market. Currencies which are stronger for forward delivery are quoted at a *premium* to the spot rate, i.e. they are more expensive forward than they are at spot; currencies which are weaker for forward delivery are quoted at a *discount* to the spot rate, i.e. they are cheaper forward than they are at spot.

Who buys or sells currencies forward? In the main it is business people and others who know that, having entered into a contract to sell goods abroad or buy from abroad, they will receive a payment in the future in a foreign currency, or have to make a payment in a foreign currency. (Note that not all trading transactions will involve settlement in a foreign currency as exporters may contract to receive in sterling - or their own home currency - and sometimes importers may be lucky enough to be able to make a payment in their home currency. The points to remember are that when payment has to be made in the currency of the seller, the buyer takes the risk of fluctuating exchange rates; when payment has to be made in the currency of the buyer, the risk is the seller's). When a business person knows that he or she will be involved in a foreign currency transaction, it is in his or her best interests to enter into a forward foreign exchange contract. This is defined as:

an immediately firm and binding contract between a bank and its customer for the purchase, or sale, of a specified quantity of a stated foreign currency at a rate of exchange fixed at the time that the forward contract is made, for performance by delivery of and payment for the stated foreign currency at an agreed future time, or between two agreed future dates.

The important thing to note is that such a contract is a legal contract which *must be completed:* if for some reason all or some of the contract is not used it will have to be *closed out* by the bank either buying or selling the balance on behalf of its customer at the spot rate ruling on the future date agreed in the contract.

Forward exchange contracts can be either *fixed* or *option*. Under a fixed contract, delivery of the currency is made on the date of maturity of the contract. Under an option contract, delivery of the currency may take place either between the date of the contract and its maturity, or between two specified future dates. The word 'option' does not give the bank's customer the choice as to whether or not to complete the contract, but refers to the choice of date of delivery.

A forward contract can be taken out to mature for any period more than two working days ahead, but most are for periods of one, three or six months. Such contracts are of great benefit to businesses that wish to insure against fluctuating exchange rates in the period between contracting to buy or sell goods from or to overseas and the date of making or receiving payment in a foreign currency. Forward contracts take the element of speculation out of trading transactions and allow the business to get on with the job of making a trading profit. Once a business has entered into a forward contract, it has eliminated exchange risks and knows the exact sterling equivalent that will be paid or received. The banks themselves do not take many risks on the foreign exchange markets by running 'open' (or uncovered) positions: they will generally try to match transactions so that each forward purchase of a particular foreign currency is 'married' to a forward sale for a similar amount and time span. (The same procedure takes place in connection with spot transactions.)

However, there are *risks in forward exchange contracts* and they are:

To the bank: that the customer may not, or may not be able to, honour his or her part of the contract (e.g. an underlying commercial contract falls through).

To the customer: that he or she will be unable to complete the contract because of a failure of the buyers/suppliers to complete the underlying commercial arrangements.

It can be seen that these are two sides of the same problem. The procedure is for the bank to *close-out* the contract in each case - this topic is dealt with on pages 14 and 15.

Liabilities under forward contracts

When a bank enters into a forward contract with a customer, it is providing a facility. As such, a percentage of the forward contract value is taken as being the equivalent of lending; this percentage varies from bank-to-bank, but is usually between 10% and 20%. Thus, a forward contract with a sterling value of £100 000 might be considered as utilising between £10 000 and £20 000 of the customer's facilities with the bank. The reason for this is that, in the event of a close-out (see pages 14 and 15) of the forward contract, the bank may face a loss.

❏ Forward rates - a worked example

The following rates apply on 1 February:

	SPOT		FORWARD
US	1.4865 - 1.4875 dollars	one month	0.11 - 0.06 c.pm.
		two months	0.55 - 0.50 c.pm.
		three months	1.05 - 0.95 c.pm.
Italy	2397 - 2399 lire*	one month	11 - 14 lire dis.
		two months	23 - 26 lire dis.
		three months	47 - 51 lire dis.

* Note that Italy is likely, before too long, to introduce a new (or 'heavy') lira by removing three noughts: thus 2397 will become 2.397.

We have already seen that the bank will buy these two currencies spot at the higher rates of USD 1.4875 and 2399 lire respectively, while it will sell at USD 1.4865 and 2397 respectively.

Earlier, we saw that strong currencies are quoted for forward delivery at a premium to the spot rate, while weak currencies are quoted at a discount. As far as fixed forward contracts are concerned, to calculate the rate we simply take the appropriate spot rate (buying or selling) and adjust the premium or discount for the date when the contract is to mature. If we are using a left-hand (selling) spot rate, the appropriate premium or discount will also be that appearing on the left-hand side. Premiums are deducted (making the currency stronger against sterling), while discounts are added (making the currency weaker against sterling).

A bank will therefore buy US dollars under a one month fixed forward contract at:

Spot Rate	USD 1.4875 (bank's buying rate)
Deduct Premium (cents)	006
	USD 1.4869

Take care to put the forward premium in the correct decimal place - it is 0.06 cents, i.e. 0.0006 dollars. Most currencies use a decimal system and the forward premium or discount is usually expressed in terms of the one-hundredth division (e.g. cents) of the main unit of currency. One exception is Italian lire, where this is the only unit of currency (until the new lira mentioned earlier is introduced).

A bank will buy Italian lire (ITL) under a one month fixed forward contract at:

Spot Rate	2399 lire
Add Discount (lire)	14
	2413 lire

As an example of a bank's selling rate, a bank will sell US dollars under a three month fixed forward contract at:

Spot Rate	USD 1.4865
Deduct Premium (cents)	105
	USD 1.4760

Questions

Calculate the rates for the following forward contracts using the above rates (answers are on page 28):
1. bank buying rate for US dollars under a two month fixed forward contract
2. bank selling rate for Italian lire under a one month fixed forward contract
3. bank buying rate for Italian lire under a two month fixed forward contract
4. bank selling rate for US dollars under a one month fixed forward contract
5. bank buying rate for US dollars under a three month fixed forward contract
6. bank selling rate for Italian lire under a two month fixed forward contract

Now that you have got those right there should be no further difficulty in calculating forward rates for fixed contracts. The only problem is that not all customers will want fixed contracts. Importers, especially, will not know exactly the date on which they will require (or, in the case of exporters, be able to supply) the foreign currency, but they will still want the exchange risk to be taken out of their hands. This problem is solved, as we have seen, by entering into an option forward contract with their bank. Here the currency will be supplied by the bank (or delivered to the bank) either between the date of the contract and its maturity, or between two specified future dates.

Let us consider the case of an importer in Britain who has today (1 February) ordered some goods from America. She has agreed to pay for the goods within a week of receiving the shipment but she doesn't know exactly when the goods will arrive. However, the contract with her American supplier does say that they will deliver the goods to her not later than 20 March. The payment is to be made in US dollars. She comes to you for advice about covering her exchange risk.

The problem here is that she does not know the exact date of payment, but she does know that it will be before the end of March. This customer needs an option forward contract for two months under which the bank will supply her with the necessary currency anytime between now, 1 February, (the date of the contract) and 1 April (the maturity of the contract). The second problem is the rate for the contract: the customer might need the currency anytime between 1 February and 1 April, and so, using the spot and forward rates, we need to calculate what the rates will be on these dates. The following diagram will illustrate this:

BANK SELLING

1 February --➤ **1 April**	
(date of contract)	(maturity of contract)

USD 1.4865		USD 1.4865
	deduct two month premium	.0055
		USD 1.4810

As the customer requires the currency at any time between these two dates, the bank will always look on the 'black' side and assume that the customer will request the currency at the worst possible time (in terms of rates) for the bank. This means applying the principle of *sell low; buy high* and, as the bank is selling in this case, it will quote the lower rate of USD 1.4810 and for this option contract.

(Note: until you are more proficient at calculating rates for option forward contracts, I thoroughly recommend that you prepare a rough diagram, as above, showing the time scale and the rates applicable at the relevant dates.)

Let us continue with the example of a customer seeking an option forward contract but, instead of being an importer needing dollars to pay a supplier, it is an exporter who is due to receive dollars at some time within the next two months. This time the bank will be a buyer of dollars and the diagram will be as follows:

BANK BUYING

1 February --➤ **1 April**	

USD 1.4875		USD 1.4875
	deduct two month premium	.0050
		USD 1.4825

Once again, the bank will assume that the customer will complete his or her side of the contract at the worst rate for the bank, i.e. that which applies on 1 February (the higher rate), and will quote a rate of USD 1.4875.

We have learnt a rule about option forward contracts where the forward rates for a currency are at premium to the spot rate. It is that, where a bank is a seller, the premium will be deducted from the spot rate to give the rate for the option contract; where a bank is a buyer the spot rate will be used. There is no need to learn this rule, the relevant rate can always be worked out in an examination, using a time chart (as above) if necessary.

Let us now see what happens when a currency is at a discount in the forward rates to the spot rate.

The importer mentioned earlier comes to you again on 1 February to say that she has recently ordered some goods from Italy and that payment will have to be made ten days after the arrival of the shipment. She does not know when the goods will arrive - it could be any time between now and 20 April. The currency of payment is to be Italian lire and your customer seeks advice about covering her exchange risk.

Again the solution is an option forward contract, except that this time it will have to be an option for three months, i.e. that the customer will require the Italian lire at some time between 1 February and 1 May. The time scale with the rates for the relevant dates will appear as:

BANK SELLING

1 February ---➤ **1 May**

ITL 2397   ITL 2397
                                                                       add three month discount ___47
                                                                                                      ITL 2444

Here the bank will apply the lower rate of 2397 lire, working on the assumption that the customer will require the currency at the worst possible time in terms of the rates.

If the customer were an exporter requiring a three month option forward contract, the rates would be:

BANK BUYING

1 February ---➤ **1 May**

ITL 2399   ITL 2399
                                                                       add three month discount ___51
                                                                                                      ITL 2450

As the bank is buying, it will wish to *buy high* and so the rate would be ITL 2450.

The rule for option contracts where the forward rates are at a discount to the spot rate is that where the bank is a seller, the spot rate will be used; where the bank is a buyer the discount will be added.

So far we have calculated fixed forward rates, and option forward rates with the option running between the date of the contract and its maturity. We will now consider contracts where the option lies between two specified future dates.

For example, to return to the importer buying goods from America and paying in US dollars. She may come to you on 1 February saying that she will have to make the payment sometime in March, but not before and not after. The contract required on 1 February is for *two months forward, option over second month*. Here we use the spot rates and forward premiums applying on 1 February but calculate rates at the beginning and end of the option period:

BANK SELLING

1 February -------------------➤ **1 March** ------------------------➤ **1 April**
(date of contract)   (beginning of   (end of option
                                      option period)   period)

                                      USD 1.4865   USD 1.4865
              less one month   less two month
              premium   011   premium   055
                                      USD 1.4854   USD 1.4810

As the bank is selling, the lower rate will apply, i.e. USD 1.4810.

Questions

Calculate the following, using the rates on page 10 (answers are on page 28):

1. bank buying rate for US dollars under a three month forward option contract
2. bank selling rate for US dollars under a three month forward contract, option over months two and three
3. bank buying rate for Italian lire under a two month forward option contract
4. bank buying rate for Italian lire under a two month forward contract, option over second month
5. bank selling rate for Italian lire under a three month forward contract, option over month three
6. bank buying rate for US dollars under a three month forward contract, option over months two and three

Premiums and discounts: a further point

You now know a lot about spot and forward rates. However, there is one slight difficulty which very occasionally occurs when calculating the rate for an option contract. The problem is easily solved by being aware of it and checking to see that a particular set of circumstances has not arisen. By way of an illustration of the difficulty, let us consider the following rates:

	SPOT		FORWARD
Italy	2365 - 2366 lire	one month	2 - 1 lire pm.
		two months	3 - 2 lire pm.
		three months	1 lire pm. - 1 lire dis.
		four months	2 - 4 lire dis.

Now calculate the rate applicable where the bank is selling under a four month option contract. The two rates to compare will be spot, i.e. 2365 lire, and that applicable at maturity of the contract, i.e. 2367 lire. From what you have learned so far you will say that the rate for the contract will be 2365 lire, i.e. the lower of the two rates. But this is wrong because the forward rates swing from premium to discount during the life of the contract. We already know that a bank will assume that a customer will require completion at the worst possible time (rate-wise) for the bank and this would, here, be after two months. Therefore the rate for this selling contract will be 2362 lire, i.e. the lowest possible rate that will apply during the life of the contract. In this example, there will be no problem in the calculation of a bank buying rate.

Although the circumstances outlined above, where a currency swings from premium to discount, or discount to premium in the forward rates, are fairly rare, it is a simple matter to study the rates and see if the circumstances are likely to apply. It is better to *think* about the calculations you make rather than to carry out mechanical calculations to a set of rules.

❏ Close-out and extension of forward contracts

We have already seen in our definition of a forward contract that it is a legal contract which must be completed at a certain date in the case of a fixed contract, or between certain dates in the case of an option contract. Where the bank's customer is unable to complete the contract it may, depending on the circumstances and the wishes of the customer, be either closed out or extended.

Close-out of forward contracts

Where the underlying commercial contract has fallen through, the customer will wish the forward exchange contract to be cancelled. This will involve the bank in either *buying* or *selling* currency at the spot rate on the day the contract is cancelled. As rates will have altered over the life of the contract there will be a profit or loss arising which will be passed to the customer's account. The prospect of a loss is the reason why banks often take a percentage of the sterling value of the forward contract - usually between 10% and 20% - and regard it as the equivalent of lending to the customer.

For example, a customer has entered into a two month fixed forward contract under which his bank sells him USD 10 000 at a rate of 1.5145. The underlying commercial contract falls through and, at the maturity date of the forward contract, the customer asks his bank to close out the contract. At this date the spot rate is USD 1.5305 - 1.5325. Calculate the net amount debited or credited to the customer's account.

The sterling equivalent of the forward contract is £6 602.84 (USD 10 000 ÷ 1.5145) and this amount would have been debited to the customer's account if the contract had been completed. As it is to be closed out the bank will have to buy back USD 10 000 at 1.5325. This has a sterling equivalent of £6 525.29 and would be 'nominally' credited to the customer's account. However, in practice only the net debit or credit will be passed to the customer's account - in this case a debit of £77.55.

The same procedure would be carried out where a part of forward contract remains unutilised and is to be closed out.

Questions

For the following close outs of forward contracts, calculate the amount to be debited or credited to the customer's account (answers on page 29):

1. A bank entered into a fixed forward contract to buy USD 100 000 from a customer at a rate of 1.5175. The customer is only able to supply USD 80 000 and, at the date of maturity of the contract, spot rates are USD 1.5415 - 1.5445.

2. A bank entered into a fixed forward contract to sell USD 20 000 to a customer at a rate of 1.5345. The underlying commercial contract has fallen through between the customer and his overseas supplier, and the contract is to be closed out. On the day of close out spot rates are USD 1.5105 -1.5150.

3. Here the fixed forward contract is for the bank to buy DEM (Deutschemarks) 50 000 at a rate of 2.5450. The amount to be closed out is DEM 10 000 and the spot rate at the date of close out is DEM 2.5175 - 2.5275.

Note that a forward contract can, in effect, be closed out before the maturity date by the customer asking the bank to enter into a *forward contra sale or purchase* which matures on the same date as the original contract. For example, a customer has entered into a three month fixed forward contract for the bank to buy USD 100 000. After one month, the underlying commercial contract falls through and, to reduce its exchange risk exposure, the company asks the bank to enter into a two month fixed forward contract for the bank to sell USD 100 000. In this way, the original contract has been closed out by a contra transaction for the same currency amount and maturity date. Inevitably, some exchange rate movement will have taken place, so that there will be a debit or credit passed to the customer's account at the maturity of the two contracts, but this is almost certain to be less than if the original contract was closed out at maturity.

Extension of forward contracts

Where there has been a delay in a commercial contract, etc., the customer might ask his bank to extend the forward contract for a further month or so. The bank can do this in one of two ways:

1. extend the forward contract, using the diagonal rule, or
2. close out the first contract and arrange a completely new one immediately.

Under (1) the rate for the new contract is calculated by finding the rate at which the contract would be closed out, i.e. spot rate. To this is added the discount or deducted the premium for the new forward period. For example, to extend a contract to sell currency to a customer, the bank will ascertain the close-out price, i.e. spot buying price (right-hand rate); to this price will be added the discount or deducted the premium *from the bank's selling side* (a left-hand rate). By using a close-out rate on one side, and a forward premium or discount from the opposite side, this method is known as the *diagonal rule*.

Under (2) the original contract is closed out at spot rate and a new contract taken out in the normal way. For example, a contract to sell currency to a customer will be closed out at the bank's spot buying price; the new contract will use the spot selling price with the amount of discount added or premium deducted for the relevant forward period.

Important note: In both cases the customer must be charged or credited with the sterling difference on the contract between the existing forward contract rate and the actual or notional close-out rate.

Example:
A customer entered into a fixed forward contract under which the bank would buy USD 20 000 at 1.5395. Upon maturity of the contract the customer requests his bank to extend the contract for one month, again on a fixed basis. On the day the extension is carried out the spot rate is 1.5245 - 1.5285 and the one month forward premium is 0.75 - 0.70 c.pm. Calculate the rate at which the contract will be extended and the net sterling credit to the customer.

Answer:
1. **Extend the forward contract using the diagonal rule**

The bank will:
Credit the customer with USD 20 000 at 1.5395
(i.e. complete the forward contract)   =   £12 991.23
Debit the customer with USD 20 000 at 1.5245
(i.e. spot selling price)   =   (£13 119.05)
Net debit to customer   =   (£127.82)

The contract is now extended at:
   spot selling price   1.5245
   forward buying premium   70 c.pm
                    1.5175

Thus, when the contract is finally completed the
customer will be credited with USD 20 000 at 1.5175   =   £13 179.57
Final net credit to customer   £13 051.75

2. **Close out the contract and arrange a new contract immediately**

The bank will:
Credit the customer with USD 20 000 at 1.5395   =   £12 991.23
Debit the customer with USD 20 000 at 1.5245   =   (£13 119.05)
Net debit to customer   =   (£127.82)

A new contract is now entered into at:
   spot buying price   1.5285
   forward buying premium   70 c.pm
                    1.5215

Thus, when the contract is finally completed the
customer will be credited with USD 20 000 at 1.5215   =   £13 144.92
Final net credit to customer   £13 017.10

Note: In the UK, the Bank of England expects banks to use method (1), i.e. the diagonal rule. It is, therefore, recommended that you use this in the examination.

Questions

Calculate (a) the cost of the close-out

(b) the rate at which the contract will be extended

(c) the final net debit or credit to the customer's account

(answers are given on page 29):

1. The original contract was for the bank to buy USD 50 000 at a rate of 1.4535. The contract is to be extended for two months fixed; on the day of the extension spot rates are 1.4375 - 1.4385, while the two-months forward premium is 0.95 - 0.89 c.pm.

2. The original contract was for the bank to sell Italian lire 7 500 000 at a rate of 2320. The contract is to be extended for one month fixed; on the day of the extension spot rates are 2355 - 2363, while the one-month forward discount is 2 - 6 lire dis.

Further questions (answers on page 29).

1. On 1 January a bank entered into a three month fixed forward contract to buy USD 50 000 at 1.5125. On 1 April the customer requests the contract to be extended for one month on a fixed basis. At this date spot rates are 1.4875 - 1.4915; the one month premium is 0.35c. - 0.25c. On 1 May the customer delivers the currency amount.

   Show the transactions on the customer's account, summarizing them as a final net figure.

2 (a) On 1 July a bank entered into a three month fixed forward contract to sell Italian lire 5 000 000 at 2305. On 1 October the customer requests the contract to be extended for one month on a fixed basis. At this date spot rates are 2350 - 2380; the one month discount is 5 - 10 lire. On 1 November the contract is completed.

   Show the transactions in the customer's account, summarizing them as a final net figure.

   (b) How would the transactions have differed if, on 1 October, the customer requested the contract to be extended on an option basis?

❏ Forward exchange cover expressed as a percentage

While bank customers can usually see the benefits of covering their foreign exchange commitments forward, one aspect of forward exchange contracts often causes difficulties. This is the problem of calculating, in percentage terms, the cost or benefit of forward exchange cover.

For example, US dollars are spot 1.5145 and the three month forward premium is 0.95 cents. The cost or benefit of forward exchange cover as a percentage per annum can be calculated by applying the following formula:

$$\frac{\text{premium or discount x number required to raise period of forward cover to one year}}{\text{forward rate}} \quad x \quad \frac{100}{1}$$

In this example, the percentage will be:

$$\frac{0.0095 \text{ x } 4}{1.5050} \quad x \quad \frac{100}{1} \quad = \quad \underline{2.52 \text{ per cent per annum}}$$

This represents, with the currency at a premium, a cost to a UK importer (who is buying foreign currency from the bank), or a benefit to a UK exporter (who is selling currency to the bank).

Points to note:

- If the premium or discount is, as in this case, quoted in a sub-unit, e.g. cents, of the main unit of currency, it must, for the calculation, be expressed in terms of the main unit of currency, e.g. USD 0.0095.
- When a currency is at a discount in the forward markets, this represents a benefit to an importer, or a cost to an exporter. This is because the forward rate is cheaper than the spot rate. A benefit is usually expressed by showing the answer as a minus percentage, e.g. -1.4 per cent.
- The Financial Times regularly quotes the cost of forward exchange cover for major currencies.

Questions

Calculate the cost or benefit of forward exchange cover to an importer as a percentage per annum for the following (answers on page 30):

1. Spot rate: USD 1.4560; one month forward premium 0.35 c.
2. Spot rate: BEF (Belgian francs) 49.50; three month forward premium 10 c.
3. Spot rate: ITL (Italian lire) 2400; three month forward discount 40 lire.
4. Spot rate: CHF (Swiss francs) 2.16; one month forward premium 2 c.

The importance of these percentages becomes more apparent when one considers a bank customer who wishes to know if it is cheaper to borrow in sterling (or the home currency) or in another currency. It may be that he is paying ten per cent per annum to borrow sterling, and that the cost of borrowing US dollars is seven per cent per annum. If the customer chooses to borrow US dollars for three months he will realise that, at the end of the three months, he must repay his dollar loan in US dollars. Although the lower rate of interest charged on the dollar loan will be attractive to him, he should be aware that movements during the three months could make the dollar more expensive so that when he repays the loan, at best the interest rate advantage is lost and, at worst, the rates will have moved so much against him that he suffers a loss on the transaction. The way to solve this problem is to arrange a *swap* transaction, converting the dollars into sterling at spot rate and immediately entering into a forward contract to buy dollars back at the end of the time, in this case three months. Thus, by means of a swap transaction, the exchange risks have been covered, but at a cost, illustrated as follows:

Borrowing cost of sterling		10.00% p.a.
Borrowing cost of US dollars	7.00% p.a.	
Cost of forward cover for three months, say,	2.52% p.a.	
		9.52% p.a.
Percentage benefit of borrowing in US dollars		0.48% p.a.

Generally, as in this example, any benefit of lower interes rates in a foreign centre is virtually eliminated:

- the currency of a country with lower interest rates than the home country will be at a premium in the forward markets
- the currency of a country with higher interest rates than the home country will be at a discount in the forward markets

As in the above example, any benefit is likely to be small and may not be worthwhile, even for large amounts. Other factors would also have to be taken into account, especially if there is likely to be a change in the cost of borrowing in either country.

❏ Cross rates

With the increasing use of foreign currency accounts there has been more widespread use of *cross rates*. These are simply exchange rates between two currencies, neither of which is the home currency. For example, if a UK customer of a bank has an account in US dollars and wishes to make a payment in Deutschemarks, there is no need to convert the dollars into sterling which, itself, is then converted into Deutschemarks. Instead the customer can go straight from dollars to Deutschemarks by using a cross rate.

For example:

	USD/DEM
Spot	1.7096 - 1.7145
3 months	5.00 - 4.83 pf.pm.

This shows that, like other currency rates, there are approximately DEM 1.71 to each USD. The usual banking 'rules' of *sell low: buy high* apply. Therefore a UK bank would sell DEM spot in exchange for USD at a rate of DEM 1.7096. Premiums and discounts work in the same way, and a UK bank would sell DEM three months fixed forward in exchange for USD at a rate of DEM 1.6596 (i.e. 1.7096 less 5.00 pf.pm.).

Questions

The cross rates between US dollars and Japanese Yen are:

	USD/JPY
Spot	107.85 - 108.34
1 month	2 - 1.75 Yen pm.
2 months	3 - 2.5 Yen pm.

Calculate the rates which will apply for the following transactions (answers are given on page 30):

1. Bank to buy Yen in exchange for US dollars, at spot rate
2. Bank to buy Yen in exchange for US dollars, two months fixed forward
3. Bank to sell Yen in exchange for US dollars, two months option forwards
4. Customer to buy dollars in exchange for Yen, one month option forward

❏ Reasons for fluctuations in exchange rates

By and large the foreign exchange market is a relatively free market which readily responds to demand and supply by fluctuations in spot and forward exchange rates. Factors which will affect rates of exchange include:

1. Inflation rates

These have a limited effect on exchange rates but are one of several factors giving an insight into the state of a country's economy. A large, unexpected, increase in the rate of inflation would have an adverse effect on exchange rates.

2. Confidence in a country's economy

Economic news usually has a more immediate effect on rates of exchange. In particular news about a country's money supply and the impact of world prices (such as oil) will often have a marked effect.

3. Balance of payments

The effect of a balance of payments surplus will create a demand for that country's currency which will increase in value in terms of other currencies in the spot and forward rates. The logic behind this is that, other factors remaining unchanged, there will be more money flowing into the country than comes out of it, hence there will be more overseas buyers seeking to acquire the currency to pay for their imports from the country. Such demand will cause the currency to increase in value and forward rates to go to a premium. Conversely, a country suffering balance of payments deficits will find that its currency weakens or falls in value, with forward rates going to a discount.

4. Interest rates

International investors are very conscious of interest rate differentials between countries. There is a natural tendency for their funds to be attracted to centres where high interest rates prevail, provided that the currency of the centre is thought to be stable or likely to appreciate. We have already mentioned that a major factor considered when forward rates are calculated is the difference in interest rates between centres. Generally investors who transfer their funds to an overseas centre will find that the cost of forward cover in the currency of the centre will rise to wipe out the advantage of the centre to those investors who are prudent enough to cover the exchange risk forward on their investment. This rise in the cost of forward cover will not deter those who move speculative *hot money* from centre to centre hoping to find a strong currency which will appreciate in value, because such funds are often not covered forward.

5. Central bank support and exchange control

Support for a particular currency may be given by the central bank of the country. This would normally be carried out by the central bank entering the foreign exchange market to buy the home currency and to sell foreign currencies from the country's reserves. The objective in doing this is to maintain the value of the home currency. Such action also works in reverse when a particular currency is appreciating too rapidly, the central bank of the country will sell the home currency and buy foreign currencies to add to the reserves. Central banks can intervene in this way in both the spot and forward markets.

Exchange control regulations can also affect exchange rates. The introduction of new regulations which restrict the free movement of funds will cause a reduction in demand for a currency; conversely the relaxation or abolition of exchange control regulations will make for a freer market in that country's currency and will usually lead to increased demand.

6. Other factors

Political events within a country, civil war and disobedience, a failure to pay interest on international loans, and a moratorium on commercial and other payments will have a marked effect on the country's currency in the foreign exchange markets.

The above factors will, to a greater or lesser degree, affect the standing of one country's currency against that of another. Some of the factors will cancel each other out but, in the long term, the market will reflect the views of the international financial community on the stability or otherwise of currencies.

❑ Effect on changes in exchange rates on exports and imports

1. Effect on exports

A weakening home currency makes exports cheaper and therefore more competitive so that more goods can be sold abroad resulting in an improvement in the balance of payments. This is perhaps a simplistic view! A full consideration of this is mainly outside the scope of a book on *Trade Finance*, but would be found in a book on economics.

An example will explain why exports become more competitive when the home currency is weakening. Suppose the rate of exchange between sterling and the US dollar is £1 = USD 1.50. This means that a US buyer wishing to purchase a British product costing £1 will need to pay USD 1.50. If sterling weakens to USD 1.35 then the same product will now cost the buyer USD 1.35. Thus the product has become cheaper on the US market.

Like most things in this subject the opposite is also true. A strengthening home currency will make a country's products more expensive on overseas markets and may, subject to other economic pressures, lead to a fall in demand.

2. Effect on imports

When the home currency is weakening, imports will become more expensive. As an example, consider a UK importer of Swiss watches, who buys each watch at a price of CHF 100. When the rate between sterling and Swiss Francs is 2.5, each watch costs £40. If the pound weakens to CHF 2.0, each watch now costs £50.

Again, conversely, a strengthening home currency will make imports cheaper, leading to increased demand for them, possibly leading to balance of payments difficulties.

❏ Specimen examination question

The following question is taken from The Chartered Institute of Bankers' paper of Autumn 1993:

Scenario

Telecom Exports Ltd

Telecom Exports Ltd is the UK subsidiary of a large UK corporate customer of your bank. It specialises in providing telecommunications equipment and software on a worldwide basis to major corporates and institutions like banks which have a network of offices.

Telecom Exports Ltd has a subsidiary in the USA to handle sales in North America and another in Singapore to cover sales in the Far East. The UK company looks after the rest of the world, for which they are willing to provide a full service including installation and training.

The office is capably organised by the export manager, Mrs Erin Daws.

Question

There was extraordinary turbulence in the foreign exchange market in 1992 and 1993, as demonstrated in the following rates:

4 November 1992	Spot US$	1.5375 – 1.5385
	One Month	1.5315 – 1.5327
	Two Months	1.5274 – 1.5286
	Three Months	1.5233 – 1.5246
Base Rates	£ 8% US$ $3\frac{1}{2}$%	
4 December 1992	Spot US$	1.5570 – 1.5580
	One Month	1.5527 – 1.5539
	Two Months	1.5486 – 1.5498
	Three Months	1.5445 – 1.5458
Base Rates	£ 7% US$ $3\frac{3}{4}$%	
4 January 1993	Spot US$	1.5020 – 1.5030
	One Month	1.4966 – 1.4978
	Two Months	1.4925 – 1.4938
	Three Months	1.4883 – 1.4896
Base Rates	£ 7% US$ $3\frac{3}{8}$%	

4 February 1993	Spot US$	1.4445 – 1.4455
	One Month	1.4408 – 1.4420
	Two Months	1.4378 – 1.4391
	Three Months	1.4345 – 1.4358
Base Rates	£ 6% US$ 3$\frac{1}{4}$%	

To compete on the world stage, Telecom Exports has to price its goods competitively and manage its exchange risk and cashflow effectively.

The finance director, Mr Winchester, asks you to meet him at his club to discuss how the company might conduct its exposure management in future.

He gives, as an example, the decision taken on 4 November last year to wait until the due dates shown below before covering the exposure for the four large transactions at spot rates:

1. Purchase of components from suppliers in USA for US$312,527.70 due 4 December 1992.

2. Purchase of spare parts from Hong Kong for US$127,452.67 due 4 February 1993.

3. Sale to subsidiary in USA for US$315,039.19 due 4 January 1993.

4. Sale to subsidiary in Singapore for US$140,284.66 due 4 January 1993.

Required:

Using the rates shown above, explain:

(a)   what methods Mr Winchester might have adopted on 4 November last year to cover the exchange risks in the four transactions above and at what rates.   [10]

(b)   with the benefit of hindsight, what would have been the best date for (i) buying and (ii) selling US$ during the period 4 November 1992 to 4 February 1993. Give reasons for your answers.   [4]

(c)   the reasons why in theory (i) the spot and (ii) the forward rates fell during the period 4 January to 4 February 1993.   [6]

[Total marks for question – 20]

Answer

(a)   *Fixed forward exchange contracts*
On 4 November 1992, the company could have entered into fixed forward exchange contracts with their bank:

- bank to sell USD 312,527.70 one month fixed forward at a rate of 1.5315
- bank to sell USD 127,452.67 three months fixed forward at a rate of 1.5233
- bank to buy USD 315,039.19 and USD 140,284.66 two months fixed forward at a rate of 1.5286

Currency borrowing and currency deposits (see also page 34)
As the company has a number of receipts and payments, all in US dollars, it should consider matching the transactions through the use of a currency account:

- On 4 November 1992, the bank sells to the customer USD 312,527.70 at spot rate; the company then puts the dollars into a USD deposit account at a credit interest rate linked to the US base rate of 3$\frac{1}{2}$%. On 4 December, the funds are used to make the payment of USD 312,527.70

- Alternatively, on 4 December 1992, the bank could arrange a one-month foreign currency loan/overdraft for USD 312,527.70 at a debit interest rate linked to the US base rate of 3$\frac{3}{4}$%. The payment for USD 312,527.70 can then be made, with repayment to come from the receipt of USD 315,039.19 on 4 January 1993.

- On 4 January 1993 the receipts of USD 315,039.19 and USD 140,284.66 are credited to the currency account. Sufficient funds are left on the account for one month (at a credit interest rate linked to the US base rate of $3^3/8\%$) in order to pay USD 127,452.67 due on 4 February. The funds not required for this payment are converted into sterling on 4 January at the bank's spot buying rate of 1.5030.

Note the higher level of base rates in the UK compared with the US. Wherever possible, it would be prudent for Telecom Exports Ltd to borrow in the US and deposit funds in the UK – subject to matching of receipts and payments. Remember that base rate is not the rate of interest that the company will pay on its loans or receive on its deposits: the actual rates will be higher and lower, respectively, than base rate.

(b) (i) *buying*

bank	USD 1.5580 ('buy high') on 4 December 1992
customer	USD 1.5570 (as many units of currency to the pound sterling as possible) on 4 December 1992

(ii) *selling*

bank	USD 1.4445 ('sell low') on 4 February 1992
customer	USD 1.4455 (as few units of currency to the pound sterling as possible) on 4 February 1992

(c) (i) *spot rates*

Between 4 January and 4 February 1993, UK base rate fell by one percentage point (from 7% to 6%); US base rate fell by $1/8$ of a percentage point (from $3^3/8\%$ to $3^1/4\%$). Investors are likely to have sold sterling in order to invest in other currencies with higher interest rates.

(ii) *forward rates*

The forward margin fell as the differential between UK and US base rates narrowed. For example:

	4 Jan	4 Feb
Bank's spot buying rate	1.5030	1.4455
One month	.0052 c pm	.0035 c pm
	1.4978	1.4420

As the spot rate fell, the amount of the forward margin also falls.

Appendix A contains a number of calculation questions which you should attempt. To answer some of them you will need knowledge from other parts of this book, so it is perhaps best not to try to work through them all just yet!

Questions which could, with care, be attempted at this stage are those set at the September 1987, May 1992, Spring 1993 and Spring 1994 examinations. Worked answers to all the questions in Appendix A are contained in Appendix B. Recent CIB papers have contained one question involving the calculation of rates. In some of the latest papers, the 'calculation question' has required some foreign exchange calculations, combined with a discussion of other aspects of the question. Thus the calculation element has been reduced - this would seem to be the trend for the future.

❏ International currency nomenclatures

The following are the SWIFT (Society for Worldwide International Financial Telecommunications - see pages 50/51) nomenclatures for the major currencies:

AUD	Australia (dollar)	HKD	Hong Kong (dollar)
ATS	Austria (schilling)	IEP	Ireland (punt)
BEF	Belgium (franc)	ITL	Italy (lira)
CAD	Canada (dolar)	JPY	Japan (yen)
DKK	Denmark (kroner)	NZD	New Zealand (dollar)
FIM	Finland (markka)	NOK	Norway (kroner)
FRF	France (franc)	PTE	Portugal (escudo)
DEM	Germany (deutschemark)	ESB	Spain (peseta)
GBP	Great Britain (pounds)	SEK	Sweden (kroner)
GRD	Greece (drachma)	CHF	Switzerland (franc)
NLG	Holland/Netherlands (guilder)	USD	USA (dollar)
		XEU	European currency unit

❏ Glossary of Foreign Exchange Terms

Close-out: The term used when a forward contract cannot be completed and the bank buys or sells foreign currency on the spot market for the purpose of fulfilling the contract.

Discount: When the forward rate is cheaper than the spot rate in terms of other currencies - add the discount to the spot rate.

Forward exchange contract: An immediately firm and binding contract between a bank and its customer for the purchase, or sale, of a specified quantity of a stated foreign currency at a rate of exchange fixed at the time that the forward contract is made, for performance by delivery of and payment for the stated foreign currency at an agreed future time, or between two agreed future dates.

Par: When the forward rate of exchange of any currency is the same as the spot rate.

Premium: When the forward rate is more expensive than the spot rate in terms of other currencies - deduct the premium from the spot rate.

Spot: The rate of exchange for an immediate foreign currency transaction, although settlement is made two business days later.

Strong: A currency which is becoming more expensive in terms of other currencies.

Swap:
- the purchase/sale of a currency in the spot market combined with a simultaneous sale/purchase in the forward market;
- an arrangement for matching two companies with matching and opposite currency needs.

Weak: A currency which is becoming cheaper in terms of other currencies.

❏ Examination hints

- All past examination papers have contained a foreign exchange calculation: therefore the material of this lesson is very important; it seems likely that some calculation element will remain in future papers.

- Many calculation questions ask the examination candidate to determine either the sterling profit on a foreign currency transaction, or the cost of such transactions, and often a partial close-out or extension is included.

- Other calculation questions require a comparison of interest rates in a foreign centre with those obtainable in the UK.

- It is essential to know the definition of a forward contract, and to be able to explain its benefits to a customer.

- Other foreign exchange terms, such as premium, discount, par, etc. should also be known.

- Some questions have taken on a 'marketing' aspect, e.g. by asking the benefits of pricing goods in the currency of an overseas market; the disadvantages and the way they may be solved should also be considered.

KnowYour .... Foreign Exchange and Forward Contracts

1. Distinguish between a currency rate and a pence rate.

2. Will rates for large transactions be the same as for small transactions? If not, explain why not.

3. What is the 'golden rule' for foreign exchange dealings from the point of view of the bank?

4. What is meant by the term 'spot rate'?

5. Define the following:
   (a) Par
   (b) Premium
   (c) Discount

6. The following spot rate applies: USD 1.4295 - 1.4365
   (a) A bank will buy the currency at .... and will sell at ....
   (b) The customer of a bank will buy at .... and will sell at ....

7. Define a forward exchange contract.

8. What is meant by:
   (a) a fixed forward exchange contract?
   (b) an option forward exchange contract?

9. When a forward exchange contract cannot be completed, either in full or in part, and the bank buys or sells foreign currency on the market to fulfil the contract, this action is known as
   ....

10. The following spot rates apply:

	SPOT	FORWARD	
	USD 1.4470 - 1.4480	1 month	0.05 c.pm - 0.05 c.disc
		3 months	0.23 - 0.33 c.disc
		4 months	0.30 - 0.40 c.disc

   Quote rates for the following:

   (a) bank buying rate for one month forward fixed
   (b) bank selling rate for one month forward option
   (c) bank buying rate for four months forward fixed
   (d) bank selling rate for four months forward fixed
   (e) bank selling rate for four months forward option
   (f) bank selling rate for four months forward, option over fourth month
   (g) bank buying rate for four months forward, option over fourth month

11. The following rates apply:

	SPOT	FORWARD	
	USD 1.4940 - 1.4960	3 months	0.43 - 0.33 c.pm
		4 months	0.97 - 0.87 c.pm

   Quote rates for the following:

   (a) bank spot buying rate
   (b) bank selling rate for three months forward fixed
   (c) bank buying rate for three months forward option
   (d) bank selling rate for four months forward fixed
   (e) bank buying rate for four months forward option
   (f) bank selling rate for four months forward, option over fourth month
   (g) bank buying rate for four months forward, option over fourth month

12. What are the advantages to an exporter who sells in foreign currencies of taking out a forward exchange contract to cover foreign currency commitments?

13. Calculate the percentage interest p.a. for the following:
    Spot USD 1.44; forward premium three months, 3 cents.

14. State the advantages to an importer of taking out option forward exchange contracts to cover foreign currency commitments. What is the major commercial disadvantage for an importer of taking out a forward exchange contract?

15. Are forward rates predictions of future spot rates?

16. List the factors that will affect the exchange rate of a currency.

17. What is the effect of changes in exchange rates on exports and imports?

18. What is a cross rate?

(Answers to numerical questions are on page 30).

Past Examination Questions

Notes: • See also Appendix A.

• Questions in this and subsequent lessons which bear an asterisk (*) against the question number are answered in outline form in Appendix C.

• Some questions require knowledge from other sections of the examination syllabus.

1.1*   Ivor Pylle is a very wealthy customer who has a large investment portfolio both in the United Kingdom and overseas. He calls to see you to discuss foreign exchange movements and advises you that he has plenty of surplus funds at the present time. He tells you he would like to invest a proportion of these funds in Italian lire, as it appears that he can obtain a higher rate of interest than is at present possible for sterling in the United Kingdom.

Mr Pylle produces a copy of the *Financial Times* which shows that the rate for 6 months lire is more than 2% per annum above the rate for 6 months sterling. He asks you to quote your rates for an investment of £500 000 for 6 months fixed either in sterling or Italian lire. Your rates at that time are:

Sterling 6 months fixed	11.5% p.a.
Lire 6 months fixed	13.875% p.a.

Apart from the interest rate difference, your customer indicates that he would be able to cover the exchange risk by entering into a forward contract and he believes the exchange risk must work in his favour as the forward lire is at a discount. The rates which your bank is quoting at the present time are as follows:

Spot	2695 lire
6 months forward	35 lire discount

REQUIRED:

Brief notes showing the points you would make when explaining the position to your customer. Use the spot and forward margins and interest rates shown above to illustrate your answer. Indicate whether the points made by Mr Pylle have any validity or not.

Note: Ignore any charges or commissions which the bank might make.

(question 9, April 1986)

1.2   Live-in-Hope is a small private limited company which is controlled and managed by a husband and wife team. For many years they have produced a number of consumer items which they have successfully sold in the United Kingdom, and recently orders have appeared from the United States.

During a recent business trip to the USA, the directors appointed an agent in New York who suggested that the goods should be invoiced in dollars as opposed to sterling, as this would help to increase the sales in the USA.

The company's directors call to see you to discuss these orders from the USA. They ask for your help and advice concerning the advantages or disadvantages to the company in quoting prices in dollars as opposed to sterling.

REQUIRED:

A brief explanation covering the following points:

(a) The validity of the agent's statement that it would be beneficial to quote in dollars as opposed to sterling. *[4]*

(b) The advantages and disadvantages to the customer in adopting the procedure described in (a) above. *[6]*

(c) The methods by which the possible risks you have identified in (b) could be overcome or reduced. *[10]*

[Total marks for question - 20]

(question 3, September 1987)

❏ Lesson 1: answers to numerical questions

Answers to questions on page 11

1.	USD 1.4875 deduct 0.50 c.pm	= USD 1.4825
2.	2397 lire add 11 lire dis.	= 2408 lire
3.	2399 lire add 26 lire dis.	= 2425 lire
4.	USD 1.4865 deduct 0.11 c.pm	= USD 1.4854
5.	USD 1.4875 deduct 0.95 c.pm	= USD 1.4780
6.	2397 lire add 23 lire dis.	= 2420 lire

Answers to questions on page 14

1.   Rate at 1 February: USD 1.4875;   rate at 1 May: USD 1.4780; therefore rate will be USD 1.4875.

2.   Rate at 1 March: USD 1.4854;   rate at 1 May: USD 1.4760; therefore rate will be USD 1.4760.

3.   Rate at 1 February: 2399 lire;   rate at 1 April: 2425 lire; therefore rate will be 2425 lire.

4.   Rate at 1 March: 2413 lire;   rate at 1 April: 2425 lire; therefore rate will be 2425 lire.

5.   Rate at 1 April: 2420 lire;   rate at 1 May: 2444 lire; therefore rate will be 2420 lire.

6.   Rate at 1 March: USD 1.4869;   rate at 1 May: USD 1.4780; therefore rate will be USD 1.4869.

Answers to questions on page 15

1. Sterling amount outstanding on forward contract (credit to customer)   £13 179.57
    Close out: sell to customer USD 20 000 at 1.5415 (debit to customer)   £12 974.37
    Net credit to customer in respect of close out only   £205.20

2. Sterling amount outstanding on forward contract (debit to customer)   £13 033.56
    Close out: buy from customer USD 20 000 at 1.5150 (credit to customer)   £13 201.32
    Net credit to customer   £167.76

3. Sterling amount outstanding on forward contract (credit to customer)   £3 929.27
    Close out: sell to customer DEM 10 000 at 2.5175 (debit to customer)   £3 972.19
    Net debit to customer   £42.92

Answers to questions (extension of forward contracts) on page 17

1. CR. £34 399.72,   DR. £34 782.61,   Net DR. (cost of close-out) £382.89.
    Contract extended at USD 1.4375 - 0.89 c.pm = USD 1.4286.
    DR. £382.89, CR. £34 999.30, Net CR. £34 616.41.

2. DR. £3 232.76,   CR. £3 173.93,   Net DR. (cost of close-out) £58.83.
    Contract extended at ITL 2363 + 2 lire dis. = ITL 2365.
    DR. £58.83, DR. £3 171.25, Net DR. £3 230.08.

Answers to further questions (extension of forward contracts) on page 17

1. 1 April   USD 50 000 @ 1.5125   =   £33 057.85 CR
                USD 50 000 @ 1.4875   =   £33 613.44 DR
                Net debit to customer   £555.59 DR

    Contract extended, using the diagonal rule, at:
             1.4875
    Less   025 c.pm
             1.4850

    1 May   USD 50 000 @ 1.4850   =   £33 670.03 CR
    Final net credit to customer   £33 114.44 CR

2. (a) 1 Oct   5 000 000 lire @ 2305   =   £2 169.20 DR
                 5 000 000 lire @ 2380   =   £2 100.84 CR
                 Net debit to customer   £68.36 DR

    Contract extended, using the diagonal rule, at:
             2380
    Add   5 lire
             2385

    1 November   5 000 000 lire @ 2385   =   £2 096.44 DR
    Final net debit to customer   £2 164.80 DR

    (b) If contract was extended on 1 October for one month on an option basis, the rate would be 2380 (i.e. bank will sell at lowest rate). This gives a debit on 1 November of £2 100.84 which, together with the close-out debit of £68.36, gives a final net debit of £2 169.20. Thus the option contract has cost the customer £4.40 more.

Answers to questions on page 18

1. $\dfrac{0.0035 \times 12 \times 100}{1.4525} = 2.89$ per cent

2. $\dfrac{0.10 \times 4 \times 100}{49.40} = 0.81$ per cent

3. $\dfrac{40 \times 4 \times 100}{2440} = -6.56$ per cent

4. $\dfrac{0.02 \times 12 \times 100}{2.14} = 11.21$ per cent

Answers to questions (cross rates) on page 19

1. 108.34 Yen
2. 105.84 Yen

3. 104.85 Yen
4. 108.34 Yen

Numerical answers to "Know your foreign exchange and forward contracts" (page 25)

6. (a) 1.4365;   1.4295

   (b) 1.4295;   1.4365

10. (a) 1.4480
    <u>05</u> c.disc
   1.4485

   (b) 1.4470
    <u>05</u> c.pm
   1.4465

   (c) 1.4480
    <u>40</u> c.disc
   1.4520

   (d) 1.4470
    <u>30</u> c.disc.
   1.45

   (e) 1.4470
    <u>05</u> c.pm
   1.4465   (best rate for bank during period)

   (f) 1.4470
    <u>23</u> c.disc.   (forward currency at discount therefore, when bank selling, add three month discount only)
   1.4493

   (g) 1.4480
    <u>40</u> c.disc   (forward currency at a discount therefore, when bank buying, add full four month discount)
   1.4520

11. (a) <u>1.4960</u>

   (b) 1.4940
    <u>43</u> c.pm
   1.4897

   (c) <u>1.4960</u> (spot rate will apply

   (d) 1.4940
    <u>97</u> c.pm
   1.4843

   (e) <u>1.4960</u> (spot rate will apply)

   (f) 1.4940
    <u>97</u> c.pm   (forward currency at a premium therefore, when bank selling, deduct full four month premium)
   1.4843

   (g) 1.4960
    <u>33</u> c.pm   (forward currency at a premium therefore, when bank buying, deduct three month premium only)
   1.4927

13. $\dfrac{0.03 \times 4 \times 100}{1.41 \qquad 1} = 8.51$ per cent per annum

Note: Answers to other questions (non-numerical) will be found at the appropriate point in the text.

Multiple-Choice Questions: Set 1

Read each question carefully. Choose the *one* answer you think is correct.
Answers are given on page 318.

1. Under which one of the following circumstances would it be prudent for your UK customer to arrange a forward foreign exchange contract?

    A   export of goods priced in sterling
    B   import of goods priced in sterling
    C   import of goods priced in a foreign currency
    D   export of goods priced in a foreign currency where the rate of exchange has been agreed in the sale contract

2. The spot rate for US dollars is 1.4545 - 1.4555; the two-month premium is 0.45 - 0.40 cents. What is the rate at which a bank would buy dollars under a two-month fixed forward contract?

    A   1.4595
    B   1.4515
    C   1.4510
    D   1.4580

3. An option forward exchange contract is where:

    A   the customer can decide whether to complete or not
    B   the customer must complete the contract within specified dates agreed with the bank at the start
    C   the customer must complete the contract at any time of his or her choosing
    D   the bank decides when the option can be exercised, depending on exchange rate movements

4. In Britain, the USD falls from 1.50 to 1.30:

    A   the pound has strengthened
    B   the dollar has weakened
    C   the pound has weakened
    D   the pound is firmer

5. Using the rates from question 2, what would a bank quote for a two-month forward option contract where the bank is buying?

    A   1.4545
    B   1.4595
    C   1.4515
    D   1.4555

6. US dollars are spot 1.4050 and the three month forward premium is 1.05 cents. What annual percentage rate does this represent?

ERRATA

Page 31, Multiple-Choice Question 6

Choices should read:

A 3.01%   B 2.99%   C 9.04%   D 0.75%

7.   The following rates are quoted by a bank to its customer:

Spot	USD 1.4060	DEM 2.4550
Three months forward	USD 1.4125	DEM 2.4505

Which one of the following statements is correct:

A   US dollars and DEM are both at a premium in the three-month forward market
B   US dollars and DEM are both at discount in the three-month forward market
C   US dollars are at a premium and DEM are at a discount in the three-month forward market
D   US dollars are at a discount and DEM are at a premium in the three-month forward market

8.   Currency X is at a premium against sterling in the forward markets, while currency Y is at a discount. A UK importer wishes to enter into three month option forward contracts in both currencies. Respectively, which rates will be applied by the bank?

A   three month; three month
B   spot; three month
C   spot; spot
D   three month; spot

9.   The pound strengthens against the Spanish peseta. To a UK citizen going on holiday to Spain this means that:

A   the cost of the holiday will increase
B   presents bought in Spain will cost more
C   she will have more money to spend in Spain
D   she will have less money to spend in Spain

10.   An option forward exchange contract was entered into by an importer to buy USD 10 000 from the bank at a rate of USD 1.4905. At maturity of the contract the importer asks for the contract to be extended for one month, again on an option basis. At this date the rates are:

Spot	USD 1.4865 - 1.4935
1 month	0.45 - 0.40 c.pm

What rate will the bank quote for the extension?

A   1.4890
B   1.4865
C   1.4935
D   1.4880

Lesson Two
Avoidance of Exchange Risks

In the last lesson we were particularly concerned with the use of forward exchange contracts as a means of avoiding the risk of fluctuating exchange rates. Exporters, importers and others, who are due to receive or pay amounts in a foreign currency are recommended to take out a forward contract because their main concern should be to make a profit on the trading transaction and not to speculate on movements in exchange rates. However, there are other ways of avoiding the exchange risk. These are considered in this lesson and are:

- the use of currency accounts

- the use of currency borrowing

- the use of European Currency Units or Special Drawing Rights; both ECUs and SDRs are 'baskets' of currencies and are less likely to fluctuate to the extent of an individual currency

- the use of financial futures contracts on the London International Financial Futures and Options Exchange (LIFFE); or the use of currency options, often known as pure options

It may also be possible for an exporter or importer who has not taken positive steps to avoid exchange risks to speculate on foreign exchange receipts and payments by means of *leads* or *lags*. These are, respectively, to make or receive payment as soon as possible, or to delay making or receiving payment in the hope that the movement in exchange rates will be favourable. These actions are, simply, a form of speculation which is no substitute for taking positive steps to minimise foreign exchange exposure.

❑ Currency accounts

The use of currency accounts is particularly appropriate where a trader has a regular flow of both receipts and payments in a given currency. By offsetting payments against receipts, the cost of buying and selling currencies is reduced and exchange risks are avoided.

Many companies operate bank accounts designated in world currencies where they have a regular two-way flow of funds. Such accounts are operated in exactly the same way as sterling bank accounts with the usual cheque and paying-in facilities. If the balance on the overseas bank account builds up over a period of time, then there is an exchange risk unless major currency payments are to be made in the future. However, the company can choose its own time for transferring surplus funds back to its sterling bank account, waiting until exchange rates are most advantageous.

A further benefit of a currency account is where a business receives a large quantity of low value currency cheques. These can be paid into the account held in the country in which the cheques are drawn at minimal cost when compared with the cost of its UK bank collecting the proceeds of each one. When a sufficient balance has been accumulated, any surplus not required for currency payments can be transferred back into sterling.

❏ Currency borrowing and currency deposits

Nowadays, with the ease in which foreign currency bank accounts can be opened, it makes sense for exporters to consider *currency borrowing* as an alternative to covering forward on the foreign exchange market. Importers, on the other hand, will need to make *currency deposits*.

For an exporter who is invoicing an overseas buyer in a foreign currency, it may be possible to borrow immediately from a foreign bank, in anticipation of the currency to be received, an appropriate sum in the same currency by way of a fixed loan. The amount borrowed is sold immediately to a UK bank, and the proceeds credited to the UK bank account. Interest will be charged on the foreign loan at the bank lending rates relating to the currency borrowed - they will not be linked to sterling base rates. If the exporter is normally in overdraft in the UK, sterling interest will be saved on the amount credited immediately. The foreign loan will be repaid from the proceeds of the foreign invoice, non-receipt of funds being the main risk of this technique.

For an importer who knows that, at a certain time in the future, a currency payment will have to be made, currency deposits can be an alternative to covering forward. The appropriate amount of foreign currency is bought at spot and placed on deposit in the overseas centre until it is needed to make the payment. Interest will be earned but, balanced against this, will be the fact that UK interest on a deposit account will be lost, or that overdraft interest will be incurred.

Both exporters and importers will need to consider carefully the various costs involved, comparing interest payable or receivable with the alternative costs of covering forward.

❏ European Monetary System (EMS)

The EMS was set up in 1979 to bring about a more stable framework of exchange rates between the currencies of countries of the European Community (now the European Union). It is the successor to the "snake" arrangements of the mid-1970s. The aim of the EMS is to develop European economic and monetary union and to stabilize exchange rates between currencies in the EU through the operation of the Exchange Rate Mechanism (ERM). For each currency a central rate is fixed in ECUs (European Currency Units). The Unit is based on a 'basket' of national currencies made up of all EU countries. The amounts of each currency going into the basket are based on the importance of each country in EU trade. Bilateral exchange rates are established on the basis of the central rate and margins of fluctuations around these rates must not exceed, at present, 15% (apart from 2.25% for Germany and Holland). Intervention points are fixed at 75% of their maximum divergence spread: upon reaching these points central banks are obliged to intervene to keep exchange rates within the agreed limit.

Each country participating in the EMS has placed 20% of its gold and dollar reserves into a European Monetary Co-operation Fund, and receives a supply of ECUs to regulate central bank intervention. Short-term swaps are available between central banks to enable countries with limited reserves to support their currency.

After much debate, Britain joined the Exchange Rate Mechanism of the EMS in October 1990 with sterling based on a central rate of DEM 2.95 and a 6% margin of fluctuation (at that time, the margins were 2.25% for most European currencies, with 6% for a few, newer, members of the ERM). Britain withdrew from the ERM less than two years later (in September 1992) after the pound weakened against other European currencies and the UK government chose not to raise interest rates to support the pound. At the same time, Italy also withdrew from the ERM.

A further currency crisis in the EMS in summer 1993 caused the margin of fluctuation to be altered to the current level of 15% (apart from Germany and Holland which remained at 2.25%). This means that, in theory, most currencies of the EU are floating freely and finding their own levels. However, in reality, it is unlikely that a government would allow its currency to fall by 15%, and so the exchange rate is still being managed (this is known as a *dirty float*).

Development of the EMS

Despite the setbacks with the ERM, major developments towards European Economic and Monetary Union (EMU) are still planned to take place in the remaining years of this century (subject to ratification by the national parliaments of EU countries):

- in 1994 a European Monetary Institute (EMI) is being established in Frankfurt; this will become Europe's central bank in 1998

- from 1994 there is to be a convergence of economic performance in EU countries in terms of inflation, interest rates, government deficits and exchange rate stability

- in 1999 EU countries will use the ECU as a national currency with fixed exchange rates (note that the UK Government has reserved the option to decide by 1996 whether or not to proceed with this stage)

- from 1999 monetary policy to be managed centrally on a European basis by the European Central Bank (ECB)

❏ European Currency Units (ECUs)

We have seen that the aim of the European Monetary System is to increase exchange rate stability between member currencies, and to promote greater co-operation in the conduct of members' financial and economic policies.

The currency denominator of the EMS is the European Currency Unit (ECU). This is, as we have seen, calculated by a formula based on a fixed amount of each member's currency, weighted according to the member's importance in EU trade. The ECU performs the following functions:

- denominator for the exchange rate mechanism
- denominator for operations in both the intervention and the credit mechanisms (see below)
- means of settlement between the monetary authorities of the European Community

Intervention points

Each currency in the Exchange Rate Mechanism (Britain and Italy withdrew in September 1992, Greece has not yet joined the ERM) has an ECU central rate. These rates determine a 'grid' of central rates between each member's currency. At present, each member of the EMS must ensure that its rate keeps within a band of 15% (2.25% for Germany and Holland) on either side of its central rate. If a member's exchange rate threatens to move outside its limits, it must intervene and take corrective action. Adjustments have been made to realign parities between currencies in the past; however, it is now proposed that the composition of the ECU should remain unchanged as the EU moves towards monetary union in the remaining years of this century. This means that any currency which devalues will see its percentage weight in the ECU diminish.

Credit mechanisms

As EMS members are expected to intervene by using their foreign exchange reserves to support agreed parity rates, a number of mutual support schemes are available under the EMS. These are a very short-term facility (VSTF), short-term monetary support (STMS), and medium-term financial assistance (MTFA).

Corporate use of ECUs

For companies, the use of ECUs is becoming more widespread. ECUs can be used as the denominator for invoices, bank deposits, payments to other companies, certificates of deposit, and eurobonds. Instead of denominating these financial transactions in, say, dollars or sterling, they are increasingly denominated in ECUs. Forward contracts to buy or sell ECUs are available in the same way as for major foreign currencies; in addition LIFFE offers ECU futures contracts.

The advantages of using ECUs in these ways are:

- there is no USD content in the ECU, so that ECUs do not follow the often considerable fluctuations of the dollar against European and other currencies

- the ECU is calculated solely on the basis of European currencies - this well suits those companies that trade only in Europe, because it reflects their currency needs, without the influence of currencies outside the EMS

- there is a well developed secondary market in ECU-denominated instruments, e.g. inter-bank ECU deposit market

- government securities are increasingly designated in ECUs (e.g. the UK government has issued ECU treasury bills since 1988)

- use of the ECU is made by European Union authorities in most of their monetary transactions

Personal use of ECUs

With the increasing corporate use of ECUs, further developments have centred around personal use. Already a large number of people working in Europe receive their salaries, either wholly or in part, in ECUs. Personal uses include:

- travellers' cheques denominated in ECUs (see also page 65), which can be encashed easily into local currency in most European countries

- credit cards offering monthly billings in ECUs

- ECU-denominated deposit accounts

- it is expected that, before too long, Eurocheques will be able to be drawn in ECUs

❏ Special Drawing Rights

While the ECU represents a European basket of currencies, Special Drawing Rights (SDRs) represent an international basket of currencies. They were first introduced by the International Monetary Fund (IMF) in 1970. Their purpose is to add to international liquidity, and to ensure that the total amount of liquidity available is sufficient to meet world trading needs. They are currency reserves which are added to a country's existing gold and dollar reserves. SDRs are, therefore, an international currency which can be used only between central banks, or between a central bank (and a few other specified holders, such as the Bank for International Settlements, and the World Bank) and the IMF.

SDRs are created by the IMF, following international agreement about the quantities to be created. The IMF then allocates SDRs to member countries, who add them to their official reserves.

The SDR gives its bearer the possibility of purchasing foreign exchange from the central bank or monetary authorities of another member country. If a country is faced with a balance of payments deficit, it can exchange its SDRs for a currency specified by the IMF, without any special economic policy conditions being attached. A country's deficit, therefore, is not financed by the SDRs themselves, but by the currency for which they are exchanged. Going along with the right to use SDRs is the obligation to purchase SDRs, if so instructed by the IMF. Here a country must supply its own currency, or that of another country, in exchange for SDRs.

The value of an SDR is based on a weighted 'basket' of the leading five international currencies - US dollars, deutschemarks, Japanese yen, French francs and sterling. The composition of the 'basket' is reviewed every five years. On the basis of the market value of the five basket currencies and their weighting, the value of an SDR is determined daily. Being based on a basket of currencies, the exchange value of the SDR against other major currencies tends to be relatively stable. The SDR thus provides additional liquidity with a relatively stable value.

Although SDRs were created as a medium for official transactions between monetary authorities, they have to some extent been adopted for commercial use, the reason in all cases being the desire to spread currency risks. Examples include:

* SDR-denominated deposits accepted by banks
* SDR-denominated issues in the eurobond market
* SDR-denominated certificates of deposit

Other uses are by IATA for its air fares and cargo rates; for calculating Suez Canal charges; and, on a number of occasions, the OPEC countries have considered setting oil prices in SDRs instead of US dollars. Payment of SDR-denominated items is in a foreign currency, at an appropriate rate of exchange between the SDR and that currency.

A member country of the IMF can buy SDRs from other countries without having to establish a balance of payments need. In this way, SDRs act as an international currency and can be used to settle financial obligations with other countries. A number of countries also use the SDR as a currency 'peg', so that the value of their currencies is fixed in terms of the SDR.

❏ The London International Financial Futures and Options Exchange

A financial future is an agreement to buy or sell certain forms of money at a future date, with the price agreed at the time of the deal. In a financial futures market, standard agreements (contracts) can be traded so that dealers can anticipate interest rate movements by trading interest bearing securities such as bank deposit certificates (Eurodollar or sterling time deposits) or gilts, or they can anticipate foreign exchange rate fluctuations by trading currencies.

The London International Financial Futures and Options Exchange (abbreviated to LIFFE) deals with the following currencies: Sterling (quoting USD per £), Deutschemarks (quoting DEM per $), Yen (quoting JPY per $), and Swiss Francs (quoting CHF per $). Unlike forward exchange contracts which are legally binding, a futures agreement does not have to be completed. Like forward contracts, a futures agreement may be closed out by entering into an exact opposite transaction for the same settlement date. Contracts on LIFFE are for set amounts of currency, e.g. in sterling the units are £25 000 each. Therefore, while LIFFE enables a dealer to 'lock in' to known rates of exchange in advance, it lacks the flexibility of forward exchange contracts because of a limited range of currencies and high minimum contract units. To many people, financial futures contracts are little more than a 'bet' by speculators in the way in which interest rates and exchange rates are likely to move. When an agreement is entered into, an 'initial margin' has to be paid of about £1 000 - £1 500 for each contract.

Another facility that is of benefit to companies at risk from fluctuating exchange rates is the *currency option* (often known as a *pure option*). Options are traded by both LIFFE and the Stock Exchange, and give the right (but not the obligation) to buy or sell specified currencies in the months ahead at a fixed price regardless of exchange rate movements. Thus, on payment of the option premium, a company can lock on to an agreed exchange rate, but does not have to complete the deal if rates move in the company's favour. As with financial futures contracts on LIFFE, traded options are in a limited (but increasing) range of currencies, for fixed amounts, and with a limited range of settlement dates. However, banks are in a position to combine the requirements of customers who do not wish to enter into the full amount of an option: thus there is considerable scope for a bank to offer a 'retail' service to customers.

Both financial futures agreements and currency options are rapidly developing as an alternative, in some circumstances, to the forward contract. Currency options are described in greater detail below.

❏ Currency options

In recent years, a technique for avoiding exchange risks has been developed by banks and other institutions: this is the *currency option* (also known as a *pure option*).

What is a currency option?
A currency option is defined as:

> *an agreement whereby the purchaser (the customer) of an option purchases the right, upon payment of a premium, to buy from or sell to a bank (the writer of the option) a specified amount of any underlying foreign currency at an agreed rate against delivery of a counter-currency either at any time during a given period, or on a fixed future date*

An option, therefore, gives the right, *but not the obligation,* to complete the deal; in this way it differs from a forward contract which is an 'immediately firm and binding contract'. An example of when a currency option could be used is a firm tendering for an overseas contract priced in foreign currency: it can take out a currency option and, if it is awarded the contract, it has already protected itself against foreign exchange exposure; if the contract is not awarded, the cost has only been the cost of the option premium - often 2% or 3% of the total amount of the option.

Who trades in currency options?
There are three main sources:
- Over-the-counter
- London International Financial Futures and Options Exchange (LIFFE) - see above
- The Stock Exchange, London

The *over-the-counter market* is available from major banks, and provides contracts which are tailor-made to suit the holder and cover a wide range of currencies. With LIFFE and The Stock Exchange, on the other hand, options are standardized with regard to contract amounts, currencies available, and option periods.

Features of a currency option contract
- Each option contract has a seller ('writer') and a buyer ('holder').

- Currency options are either 'call' or 'put' options: with a *call option,* the holder has the right to buy currency from the bank; with a *put option* the holder has the option to sell currency to the bank.

- The 'holder' pays a premium to the writer when the contract is entered into: the premium is a percentage, commonly 2% or 3%, of the option amount, but varying with the chosen rate (or 'strike price') for the option.

- The option period runs from the start date to the expiry date. With an *American option* the buyer can exercise the option at any time up to the expiry date; for a *European option,* the buyer can exercise the option on the expiry date only.

- Option periods of up to twelve months are available. Minimum amounts for contracts vary, with the over-the-counter market - available through banks - being the most flexible, with amounts from £12 500 (or the currency equivalent). LIFFE and The Stock Exchange both take standard contracts in parcels of £25 000 and £12 500 respectively.

- The currency options available through banks are available in any freely traded currency, with a spot and a forward market.

Using currency options

Currency options are appropriate whenever there is exchange rate exposure, in similar circumstances to the forward foreign exchange contracts. However, options contracts are particularly appropriate where there is uncertainty of amounts payable or receivable in foreign currency.

To illustrate the circumstances under which a currency option might be beneficial, we will consider two companies, A and B, both of which expect to receive USD 1 million in six months' time.

Company A enters into a forward exchange contract under which its bank will buy the dollars at a rate calculated as follows:

Spot rate	$1.4040
Less 6-month premium	135
	$1.3905

Six months later the dollars are received and the company's bank account is credited with USD 1 million at $1.3905 = £719 165.76.

Company B enters into a currency option under which the bank will buy the dollars at a rate of $1.3850. The premium for this is 2.5% of the sterling value of the option (i.e. 2.5% of [USD 1 million ÷ $1.3850]) = £18 050.54. When the dollars are received it is found that the dollar has improved against sterling and that the spot rate is $1.3445. The company has the choice of exercising its option to sell the dollars to the bank at the agreed rate, or it can ignore the currency option and sell them at spot rate. It chooses to follow the latter course and the company bank account is credited with USD 1 million at $1.3445 = £743 770.91. Taking into account the premium on the currency option, the company has received a net credit of: £743 770.91, less premium £18 050.54 = £725 720.37 (i.e. saving £6 554.61 over using a forward contract).

By using a currency option in the above example, company B has protected itself against exchange risks but, at the same time, has left itself in a position to take advantage of the strength of the dollar which it could not have done under the traditional forward exchange contract. The essence of the currency option is that it gives the right, but not the obligation, to buy or sell a stated amount of currency at an agreed rate at a chosen time in the future. The cost to the company is a single front-end premium payment.

Summary

Foreign currency options are available through banks, The Stock Exchange, London, and LIFFE. While traditional forward exchange contracts will continue to be used extensively, currency options offer another technique in the management of foreign exchange exposure.

❏ **Glossary of Currency Option Terms**

- American option
  - An option which can be exercised at any time up to the expiry date

- Call option
  - The holder has the right but not the obligation to buy currency from the bank

- European option
  - An option which can be exercised on the expiry date only

- Holder
  - Customer who purchases an option

- Option currency
  - Currency in which the customer wishes to hedge

- Premium
  - Price paid by customer of bank to purchase an option

- Put option
  - The holder has the right but not the obligation to sell currency to the bank

- Strike price
  - Fixed rate at which the customer can exercise rights to buy or sell currency under an option contract

- Writer
  - The party (bank, LIFFE, or The International Stock Exchange) which undertakes to provide a currency option in its name.

Questions (answers on page 45)

1. A bank customer enters into a three month call option for USD 100 000 at a rate of $1.5750. The premium is 2.5% of the sterling value of the option. In three months' time spot rates are:
    USD 1.5425-1.5450

    Calculate the sterling results of:
    (a) exercising the rights under the currency option,
    (b) using spot rates.

2. A bank's company customer expects to be awarded a contract under which it will receive USD 500 000 in six months' time. Rates are as follows:
    Spot   USD 1.4725-1.4750
    Six months' forward 1.45-1.35 c.pm

    A currency option can be entered into at a rate of USD 1.4525, the premium for which will be 2.5% of the sterling value.

    Advise the customer of the merits, or otherwise, of a currency option where there is doubt about whether the overseas contract will be awarded.

    In six months' time the spot rate is:
    USD 1.4835-1.4880

    Calculate the relative costs which would result if the customer had:

    (a) entered into a forward exchange contract, both on an option and a fixed basis,
    (b) entered into a currency option.

❏ Leads and lags

We have seen earlier that fluctuations in exchange rates largely reflect the confidence that those who deal in currencies have in a particular currency. In a similar way businessmen who have to pay amounts in foreign currencies will take an interest in the movements of rates of exchange. This is because those who have not covered their forward exchange risks will be able to minimise the amount they pay in the home currency by either paying their foreign currency debts as quickly as possible, or delaying payment for as long as possible.

These actions are known as *leads* and *lags* respectively, i.e. a rush to pay (leads), or a delay in payment (lags). Which action is taken will depend upon whether a currency is strengthening or weakening. To avoid losses there will be a tendency to pay off debts in strong currencies as quickly as possible (leads), while the payment of debts in weak currencies will be postponed for as long as possible (lags). Where a businessman is to receive foreign currency amounts, the opposite will apply, i.e. receipts of payments in strong currencies will be delayed for as long as possible (lags) in the hope of making an additional gain in the rate of exchange, while receipts in weak currencies will be converted at the earliest possible opportunity (leads). Note that all these assume there is no forward contract covering the exchange risks and therefore the businessmen are indulging in a form of speculation with their foreign currency receipts and payments.

Example of leads and lags:

A UK businessman has to pay $1 000 to a US supplier and receive $1 000 from a US buyer. He has not entered into any forward contracts, and we will ignore the possibility of him operating a foreign currency bank account in US dollars. The pound is weakening against the dollar: at present we will assume it is $1.50, but in a month it is expected to have fallen to $1.30. As the pound is weakening and therefore US dollars (the currency of payment) are strengthening, the UK businessman will *lead* and pay his debt at a rate of $1.50, with a sterling equivalent of £667. If he delays payment for a month the rate will be $1.30, with a sterling equivalent of £769. It is clearly in his interests to settle the debt as quickly as possible. Conversely, it will pay him not to chase the $1 000 due to him, i.e. he will *lag*. If the payment is received when the rate is $1.50, his bank account will be credited with £667; if his American customer can be persuaded to delay payment until the rate is $1.30, he will receive £769. By getting his leads and lags correct this UK businessman has 'saved' himself £204.

(Note: In the above example, for simplicity, buying and selling rates have been ignored.)

It should be stressed that such speculation should not be regarded as normal business practice: as has already been stated, a businessman's role is to make a trading profit and the risk of reduced profit resulting from exchange rate fluctuations should, wherever possible, be removed by the use of forward contracts.

To summarise:

Lead: pay in strong currencies
receive in weak currencies

Lag: receive in strong currencies
pay in weak currencies

Questions:

Will a businessperson lead or lag under the following circumstances? (Answers on page 45).

1. A UK businessperson has to pay US dollars, which are weakening.   He/she will .....

2. A US businessperson has to pay sterling, which is weakening.   He/she will .....

3. A UK businessperson is to receive Swiss francs, which are strengthening.   He/she will .....

4. A UK businessperson has to pay French francs, which are strengthening.   He/she will .....

5. An Italian businessperson has to pay in sterling, which is strengthening.   He/she will .....

6. A French businessperson has to pay in sterling, which is weakening.   He/she will .....

❑ Examination hints

- The examination often requires knowledge of methods of avoiding exchange risks, perhaps as a *part* of a question.

- It is essential to know the definition of a currency option, and to be able to explain its benefits to a customer.

- The use of currency accounts is becoming more prevalent for exporters and importers, and has featured in quite a number of questions.

- More specialist questions are set from time-to-time on such topics as the European Monetary System, and ECUs.

Know Your .... Avoidance of Exchange Risks

1.   List the methods by which an exporter can avoid an exchange risk, other than by taking out a forward contract.

2.   What are leads and lags?

3.   A UK importer has to make payment in foreign currency and suspects that the currency in which payment is to be made will depreciate against sterling within the next few days. What advice would you give?

4.   A UK exporter is due to receive a currency payment within the next few days and it is expected that sterling will weaken in terms of the foreign currency. What advice would you give?

5.   What are ECUs and SDRs? When are they likely to be used?

6.   Define a currency option.

7.   Distinguish between an American and a European option.

8.   Who are the two parties to a currency option?

9.   Distinguish between a 'put' and a 'call' option.

10.   Who are the providers of currency options?

11.   Explain how an importer can use currency deposits to avoid an exchange risk.

Past Examination Questions

Note: Answers to asterisked questions are given, in outline form, in Appendix C.

2.1*   Mr Scrooge, one of your wealthy customers, calls to see you to discuss the cost of financing a housing loan which he took out with your bank some five years ago. The outstanding balance is somewhere in the region of £200,000, and Mr Scrooge is complaining about the sterling mortgage interest rate which is $14^{3}/_{8}$%.

Mr Scrooge wants to know if he can switch his borrowing into a currency mortgage in Deutsche Marks or Swiss Francs based upon the interest rates given below. You understand that Mr Scrooge is resident in the UK and does not wish to set up residence in either Switzerland or Germany.

The current interest rates quoted by a foreign exchange dealer are as follows:

	Deutsche Marks	Swiss Francs
6 months	$8^{9}/_{16}$%	$8^{7}/_{8}$%
1 year	$8^{9}/_{16}$%	$8^{5}/_{8}$%

Exchange rates are as follows:
Deutsche Marks/£

Spot	2.7213	2.7320
6 months	2.6383	2.6525
1 year	2.5748	2.5900

Swiss Francs/£

Spot	2.4809	2.4914
6 months	2.4079	2.424
1 year	2.3489	2.3654

Mr Scrooge, being a very careful man, also indicates that, although he wants to reduce the cost of borrowing, he would not wish to do so if the risks to him were excessive.

REQUIRED:
In brief note form:

(a)   Explain whether you believe that it is in your customer's interests to switch his mortgage from sterling into either of the other two currencies.   *[9]*

(b)   Demonstrate arithmetically the advantages, or disadvantages, if your customer wishes to switch into foreign currency and also have some protection. For the purposes of this calculation, use the one year interest rates and currency rates quoted above in respect of both currencies.   *[9]*

(c)   Indicate whether your answer would be different (and, if so, how) if the customer received a regular income in either Deutsche Marks or Swiss Francs. Show how your customer might obtain protection.   *[2]*
[Total marks for question - 20]
(question 7, October 1990)

2.2*   Veterinary Sciences Plc manufacture, and also merchant, many veterinary pharmaceutical products both in the UK and overseas. In overseas countries where they are unable to establish an enterprise to manufacture under their own brand name, they have sold the rights to manufacture under licencing agreements. They are now expanding their activities in the EU by similar means and are at present discussing a project with a Spanish manufacturer which will mean that, for the first time, Veterinary Sciences Plc will manufacture a 'foreign' product under licence in the UK.

Mr Bull, the Finance Director, calls to see you to discuss any implications which the company should consider. Past experience, and your files, show that the company has been less than forward looking when it has been involved in foreign exchange exposure: any licence fees it has received have been settled in a variety of currencies, and the funds, upon receipt by the company, have been sold for sterling. However, a few sterling cheques/payments are received by Veterinary Sciences Plc from the London offices of the remitters' banks.

Mr Bull has now discovered that his company will have to pay the Spanish company for the licence in foreign currency and has decided to cover this foreign exchange exposure. He asks you to explain the courses of action now open to him.

REQUIRED:

(a)   Your suggestions to Mr Bull which would cover this new exposure as well as redirecting the company's existing exposure on lines which offer some control by your customer.   *[9]*

(b)   Define and explain the methods you have suggested in (a) and indicate any risks which Veterinary Sciences Plc should consider.   *[11]*

[Total marks for question—20]
(question 3, amended, October 1991)

2.3*   *Scenario*
Euro Multinational Co Ltd: see page 268

Question
(a)   Euro Multinational's finance director, Mr Money, telephones to say that he is pleased to read of the dollar's weakness.

Mr Money notes that the market reacted favourably to the growth in UK business confidence. He asks what other factors might affect the sterling/dollar rate.

REQUIRED:

(i)   Why should Mr Money be pleased at the dollar's weakness?   *[2]*

(ii)   Name the main factors that affect exchange rates and explain how they might affect the sterling/US$ exchange rate.   *[8]*

(iii)   Would your answer in (ii) above be different if you were asked to give the factors that affect the sterling/D-Mark rate?
Give reasons for your answer.   *[4]*

(b)   Euro Multinational is considering a contract to on-sell goods to a UK buyer, Regional Distribution plc, and payment is expected seven working days after delivery to the UK buyer.

Mr Money asks whether he could invoice Regional Distribution in US$ to avoid exchange risk.

REQUIRED:

(i)   What banking arrangements could Euro Multinational make with your bank to ensure that there would be no exchange risk if it invoiced Regional Distribution in US$?   *[3]*

(ii)   What procedures should Regional Distribution follow to pay Euro Multinational in US$?
          [3]
[Total marks for question—20]
(question 2, Spring 1993)

❏ Lesson 2: answers to questions

Answers to questions on page 40   (currency options)

1.   (a)   USD 100 000 at 1.5750   =   £63 492.06 DR
            Cost of premium 2.5% of £63 492   =   £1 587.30 DR
            Cost to customer   £65 079.36 DR

     (b)   USD 100 000 at 1.5425   =   £64 829.82 DR
            Cost of premium on currency option   =   £1 587.30 DR
            Cost to customer   £66 417.12 DR

2.   (a)   Fixed forward contract: USD 1.4750 less 1.35 c.pm = 1.4615
            USD 500 000 at 1.4615   = £342 114.26 CR

            Option forward contract at USD 1.4750
            USD 500 000 at 1.4750   = £338 983.05 CR

     (b)   USD 500 000 at 1.4525   = £344 234.07 CR
            Cost of premium 2.5% of £344 234   =   £8 605.85 DR
            Net credit to customer   £335 628.22 CR

            Bank to buy USD 500 000 at spot rate of 1.4880   = £336 021.50 CR
            Cost of premium on currency option   =   £8 605.85 DR
            Net credit to customer   = £327 415.65 CR

            The former course would be better.
            A currency option is useful where currency proceeds are not certain to be received and a
            customer wishes to 'hedge' the currency risk.

Answers to questions on page 41   (leads and lags)

1. lag   2. lag   3. lag   4. lead   5. lead   6. lag

Lesson Three
Methods of Payment in International Trade

This lesson is concerned firstly with the methods of securing payment between exporters and importers, secondly with methods of settlement, and thirdly with the way in which banks handle international settlements between themselves.

❑ Securing Payment

The terms and method of payment in international trade are agreed between the exporter and importer in their contract. The terms required by the seller will depend very much on previous experience, if any, of the particular market, on knowledge of the customer, on the latter's financial standing, and the degree of competition between other sellers for the business. Because of the extra risks involved in international trade, the exporter will be even more concerned about the degree of security in the payment, the speed of its transmission and the costs involved in receiving it.

The main methods of obtaining payment in increasing order of security from the exporter's viewpoint are:

• open account
• bills of exchange and documents for collection
• payment under a letter of credit
• payment in advance

The order is reversed for importers who will prefer open account trade, and dislike payment in advance.

We shall briefly consider each of these now, although letters of credit and collections are dealt with more fully in later lessons.

Open account

Where an exporter is dealing with a first-class overseas buyer, goods are often despatched on an open account basis: this means that the exporter simply sends the documents of title for each shipment direct to the buyer and requests settlement by a certain date. This is similar to the way in which credit sales are made between businesses within the same country: provided their credit is considered satisfactory, goods are supplied and a regular statement of account sent out, payment being made by cheque. The only differences in international trade are that the distances involved are greater and the documentation is more involved; also it is more difficult to chase up any bad payers.

Very often the open account basis of international trade is forced on exporters because of short sea journeys which do not give time to process documents so as to enable more secure methods of payment to be used. The development of the waybill (see page 100), which does not constitute a document of title, has assisted the expansion of open account trade by enabling goods to be shipped to a named consignee. The disadvantage for the exporter of open account trading is that control is lost of the goods and the title to them. Therefore it is advisable to establish the business integrity of overseas customers by obtaining a banker's opinion. Importers, however, much prefer open account trade because it allows them to receive and inspect the goods (and perhaps even sell them) before making settlement.

Bills of exchange and documents for collection

This method involves an exporter in shipping the goods to the overseas buyer and then sending a bill of exchange and documents for collection through a bank. The exporter will hand to the bank the documents, often including the document of title to the goods (e.g. the bill of lading), and give instructions as to the terms under which the documents may be released to the buyer. A bill of exchange drawn by the exporter on the buyer and payable either at sight or for a term will accompany the documents of title.

The exporter's bank forwards the bill of exchange and documents to a convenient correspondent bank in the buyer's country. The documents will be released to the buyer either against 'documents against payment' (D/P) or 'documents against acceptance' (D/A) of the bill according to the exporter's instructions. When the bill is paid, the proceeds of the collection are remitted back to the exporter's bank. Thus the exporter is able to retain a measure of control over the goods as it is known that the documents of title will only be released by the overseas bank in accordance with the instructions given.

From the point of view of the importer, collections are usually acceptable when open account terms cannot be agreed. Where the collection allows the importer to take the shipping documents after acceptance of a term bill of exchange, a measure of credit is afforded to the importer. This will give sufficient time to sell the goods and perhaps collect the proceeds before having to settle the bill of exchange.

While collections mainly apply in international trade, they can also be used in domestic trade within a country.

Note: This is only a brief summary of the collections procedures - Lesson 9 deals more fully with the topic.

Letters of credit

Letters of credit are more fully discussed in lessons 7 and 8 but it is appropriate here to make a brief mention of them. In simple terms a letter of credit is issued by the buyer's bank at the request of its customer. It is a guarantee of payment by that bank and details of the letter are advised to the exporter through a bank in his/her own country. It is then for the exporter to present the appropriate documents - as required by the letter of credit - to this advising bank. If the documents are in order, the exporter will either receive cash immediately from the advising bank by having a sight bill of exchange paid, or a bill of exchange will be accepted or negotiated. The documents, meanwhile, are sent by the advising bank to the bank which opened the credit so that the buyer may obtain the goods when they arrive in his/her country.

An importer will not view a letter of credit with the same enthusiasm as an exporter, although there are some advantages (see pages 158/9). It is the importer who has to ask his/her bank to open the credit. As such, the credit adds to the importer's total finance facilities with the bank. Also, there is little provision for the importer to take delivery of the goods before payment has to be made - usually the exporter receives settlement in full upon presentation of the correct shipping documents at a specified bank in his/her own country.

Letters of credit can also be used for domestic trade.

There are various types of letters of credit:
• confirmed or unconfirmed
• revocable or irrevocable

These will be looked at in detail in lesson 7. However, an exporter will prefer a confirmed irrevocable letter of credit, then an irrevocable letter of credit (unconfirmed), then - as a last resort - a revocable letter of credit. The importer will prefer these in reverse order.

Note: Again, this is only a very brief summary of the letter of credit system - there are several different forms of credit, each with implications for bankers, exporters and importers - see Lessons 7 and 8.

Payment in advance

This is undoubtedly the safest way to receive payment for exports but, from an importer's point of view, it is the least acceptable. Buyers are seldom prepared to pay for goods in full in advance of shipment, other than for small consignments, e.g. spare parts. Under this method the buyer is extending credit to the supplier and relies on the integrity of the exporter to deliver the goods, in a satisfactory condition on the agreed date. It is more common to find that the buyer is prepared to pay a cash deposit in advance, the balance being settled by one of the other three methods.

❏ Countertrade

While most import and export transactions will involve a settlement of money between buyer and seller, a growing amount of business is handled by means of *countertrade*.

What is countertrade?

Countertrade is a 'different' way of selling goods abroad and is a type of barter. A number of countries nowadays do not have the cash or credit facilities to pay for imports and so, for those wishing to supply goods to such countries, countertrade has become the only means of arranging deals. Countertrade may be defined as:

export sales to a particular market that are made conditional upon undertakings to accept imports from that market.

Forms of countertrade

Countertrade takes a variety of forms, which include the following:

* *Barter*
  The direct exchange of one lot of goods for another, with no cash changing hands.

* *Counterpurchase*
  A popular form of countertrade, a UK exporter will enter into two contracts:
  (i)   to sell goods to a country for cash, and
  (ii) to use this cash to purchase goods (counterpurchase goods) from the same country (a penalty may be imposed if the purchase is not made within a set time).

* *Compensation trade or buyback*
  This takes the form of a UK exporter selling capital plant and equipment. The goods subsequently manufactured by that plant are accepted in repayment of the purchase cost.

* *Linked purchases*
  Here a UK exporter agrees to sell his goods to a country for cash and, at the same time, a UK importer, under a separate contract, agrees to buy other goods of the same value from the same country for cash.

* *Offset*
  A condition of exporting some products, especially those using advanced technology, to some countries is that the exporter incorporates into his final products specified materials, components or sub-assemblies manufactured in the importing country.

* *Evidence accounts*
  The UK exporter and overseas importer agree that sales from the UK shall be matched, over time, in certain ratio by sales to the UK from that country. An evidence account is kept of all transactions and settlement of the balance is made in cash at agreed intervals.

Problems of countertrade for the exporter

Main problems are:

- Under counterpurchase, penalty payments may have to be made if counterpurchase goods are not taken within a set time.

- The exporter may be required to take goods which are unsaleable or in which he/she has no experience of selling; a countertrade specialist may have to be used to dispose of the unwanted goods.

- The costs of arranging the counterpurchase, including selling costs incurred, may reduce or eliminate the profit on the sale of the principal goods.

- Estimating the likely discount in the counterpurchase goods when they come to be sold: this may vary from 2%-3% for high-grade minerals and commodities, up to 40%-50% for low-quality manufactured goods and machinery. Wherever possible, the exporter must allow a sufficient margin or premium in the selling price to cover such costs.

Bank assistance to the countertrade exporter

Most major banks have countertrade sections which are actively pursuing this type of business. Banks are able to assist their exporter customers involved in countertrade in the following ways:

- by providing finance (see lesson 12 - ECGD*-backed buyer credit facilities) to the overseas buyer to enable UK exports to be paid for

   * Export Credits Guarantee Department - see lessons 10 and 12

- by providing bonds or guarantees to cover penalties payable if the UK exporter does not take the counterpurchase goods

- by advising exporters on the problems of countertrade, including advice on the 'premium' which should be added to the export price to offset the sale costs of the counterpurchase goods

- by using computer techniques to match potential exporters and importers from amongst their wide

Summary

Undoubtedly, with an increasing number of countries facing liquidity crises, countertrade is a solution to a problem. It permits an exporter to make a sale that would, otherwise, be lost, and allows an overseas buyer to obtain the goods needed. However, the buying country usually overpays - the premium - to compensate for the problems the exporter faces in disposing of the counterpurchase goods.

❏ Methods of Payment through the Banking System

There are four means of payment between importer and exporter used in international trade:

- buyer's cheque;
- bank draft;
- mail transfer or SWIFT transfer;
- telegraphic/cable transfer or priority SWIFT transfer.

Buyer's cheque

Unlike inland trade, a cheque is not usually a satisfactory method of paying an overseas supplier. There are three particular problems in using cheques. The first is that to send a cheque to a supplier may contravene the exchange control regulations of the buyer's country, so that there could be a delay in the seller receiving payment while the necessary authorisation is obtained. The second problem is that the exporter receiving a cheque from an overseas customer will have to ask the bank to collect it. This will involve the exporter in collection charges (unless the customer can be persuaded to pay these) and there will inevitably be a delay before the proceeds are received. The third problem is that, when the cheque is presented to the foreign bank on which it is drawn, it may not be paid.

For lower value cheques, banks will sometimes negotiate (i.e. buy) them. With negotiation, banks send off the cheques in bulk to a main correspondent bank - or a subsidiary bank - which then puts them through the local clearing system. Thus the cheques could be returned unpaid after several weeks.

'Locked box' system of collecting cheques
An exporter receiving a large number of small payments by cheque from overseas customers may well use a 'locked box' system to speed the collection of payments. Using this system customers are instructed to post their payment to a numbered post office box. The exporter's bank is authorised to collect this post, open the mail and put cheques received into the clearing system. This system cuts down on delays and, for exporters, is of particular benefit where there are a large number of customers mainly in one or two countries. (The locked box system can also be used for collection of domestic cheques and, again, has the benefit of saving time.)

Bank draft

A bank draft is a cheque drawn in a foreign currency by the international department of the buyer's bank, normally on one of its correspondent bank accounts in the exporter's country. A customer requesting a draft has his/her account debited in the home currency and is handed the draft to send direct to the beneficiary, who is able to obtain payment through his/her own bank. As the draft is generally drawn on a bank in his/her own country, the exporter should suffer very little delay in obtaining payment.

The disadvantage of a bank draft is that the customer, having obtained the draft from the bank, must attend to mailing it to the beneficiary. Thus it can be a slower method than a mail or telegraphic transfer. It suffers too, in that it could be lost, stolen or destroyed, and banks are generally reluctant to stop their own drafts because, in the eyes of the public, a bank draft is a guarantee of payment.

Drafts used in paying overseas debts are normally made out in a foreign currency. If required, they can be made out in the home currency and drawn on the issuing bank's head office.

'Mail' transfer

The importer of goods may ask the bank to use this method of transfer to make payment to a supplier abroad. The bank will send instructions by SWIFT message (airmail is used infrequently nowadays), to an appropriate overseas *correspondent bank,* asking it to credit the exporter or his bank with the proceeds. The importer's bank account is debited in his/her own currency while the beneficiary - the exporter - receives the amount due in his/her own currency. All charges are normally debited to the sender's account but can, if required, be deducted from the amount received by the beneficiary.

'Telegraphic/cable' transfer

This method is identical to the mail transfer except that the instructions are sent by priority SWIFT message (telex/cable is used infrequently nowadays). Consequently the cost is higher, but it is a speedier method.

SWIFT

Some 2600 banks from about sixty countries take part in an international communications network to speed up the transfer of international payments and other messages between themselves. This network is called *SWIFT* (the Society for Worldwide Interbank Financial Telecommunications) and uses the computer systems of participating banks. Thus when an importer wishes to make an international payment by mail transfer, his/her bank, if a participant in SWIFT, will, if their correspondent is also a member, send an international money transfer (IMT) by means of a 'SWIFT message'. Transfers and messages previously sent by telegraph or cable become 'priority SWIFT messages', and are referred to as express international money transfers (EIMT).

As a safeguard, whenever funds are sent by priority SWIFT message or telegraphic transfer, a form of coding is included which is checked by the recipient bank to prove the authenticity of the instruction. Similarly with mail transfers and bank drafts (see below), a bank receiving instructions will check the signatures of officials of the remitting bank.

Note: Naturally the methods of making international payments mentioned here are not solely for the use of importers wishing to pay their overseas suppliers. They can equally be used for all other purposes, e.g. anything from settling for purchases made by private individuals, to sending a birthday present to your great-aunt in Australia. The way in which the banks settle between themselves for these is considered below.

Developments in electronic cross-border payments systems

The European Commission has set the goal of ensuring that "payments move across national boundaries as quickly ... as within a single country." To meet this objective the last year or two has seen rapid developments in electronic cross-border payments systems.

Bank groupings

As well as international payments systems which use the SWIFT system, a number of banks have linked to develop their own electronic systems for cross-border payments. Examples are:
- 'Eurogiro' – owned by European Postbank/Giro organisations (including the UK's Girobank) but which also includes the Japanese Postbank
- 'TIPA-Net' – linking the Co-operative Bank in the UK with banks in France, Germany, Italy, Belgium and Canada with further countries to be added soon
- 'IBOS' (Inter-Bank On-Line System) – linking The Royal Bank of Scotland in the UK with banks in Spain, Portugal and France
- 'Relay' – linking National Westminster Bank in the UK with banks in Europe and North America

The aim of these bank groupings is to provide faster payments at lower cost. Further developments will include a system whereby the payer, who is a customer of the bank, can originate international payments from a computer linked to the bank's computer system.

International bank clearings

There are moves to link the banks' Automated Clearing Houses in Europe to ease the system of making payments. This will enable cheques, direct debits and credits to be processed more easily.

❑ International Payments between Banks

All international trading transactions (with the exception of countertrade transactions) require a payment to be made between importer and exporter. It will help to understand the transfer of funds if it is realised that, whenever there is a payment for a debt or a gift, a foreign exchange deal takes place somewhere. For example, if you, as a UK bank customer, wish to pay a debt in US dollars, you must request your bank to sell you US dollars in exchange for sterling: thus a foreign exchange deal takes place. Similarly, if you send an amount of sterling to a beneficiary in Australia, the beneficiary must ask the bank to sell Australian dollars in exchange for sterling - hence a foreign exchange deal.

The transfer of funds from one person in one country to another person abroad is made possible because all the major banks have their *correspondent banks* in countries overseas with whom they maintain accounts designated in the local currency of the country. Similarly the correspondent banks maintain accounts here, designated in the currency of this country. These accounts are known as *nostro* and *vostro* accounts - the Latin words for 'our' and 'your' respectively - and this is precisely what is meant by these accounts.

Nostro accounts (our account with you)

From the point of view of a UK bank, its nostro accounts are those currency accounts which are maintained in its name in the books of banks overseas. For example, if Midland Bank has an account maintained in US dollars with the Bank of America, San Francisco, then this is a nostro account for Midland Bank.

Vostro accounts (your account with us)

Again, from the point of view of a UK bank, its vostro accounts are those sterling accounts in the names of overseas banks that are maintained with it. For example, if Bank of America maintains a sterling account with Midland Bank, London, then this is a vostro account for Midland Bank.

Notice that, like most things in finance of international trade, nostro and vostro accounts can be looked at *the other way round*. Consider the accounts mentioned above from the point of view of Bank of America: its nostro account is its sterling balance maintained with Midland Bank, London; while its vostro account is the dollar account maintained with it in the name of Midland Bank.

The method of transferring funds is simple but we must be careful to distinguish between payments made in the home currency and those made in a foreign currency. We will consider an example of each.

Payment in the home currency

A customer of a UK bank wishes to remit sterling to an overseas beneficiary in, for example, Toronto, Canada. The procedure is as follows:

- the customer completes a bank application form stating the beneficiary and the method of remittance to be used – SWIFT transfer (including mail or telegraphic transfers), or bank draft
- the bank selects an appropriate Toronto correspondent bank and then debits its UK customer with the amount and credits the (sterling) vostro account of the correspondent bank
- the remittance* is then made and the beneficiary receives, or his bank account is credited with, the Canadian dollar equivalent of the sterling amount at the rates ruling on the day of receipt by the bank in Canada
- to complete the book-keeping, the Toronto bank debits, with the sterling amount, a record account it maintains in its books which 'mirrors' its sterling account in London

If the beneficiary in Canada had operated a foreign currency account designated in sterling, then clearly this could have been credited with the sterling amount, rather than converting it into Canadian dollars. In other respects the transactions would have been the same.

The funds represented by the balances of customer's foreign currency accounts are normally held on the *nostro* accounts of the bank. Thus, in practice, a foreign currency account maintained by a customer with his bank's international department is not normally represented by a separate bank account overseas. However, nowadays, there is nothing to prevent a UK customer - private or corporate - from opening a bank account abroad designated in a foreign currency. The ability to do this for bank customers of other countries will vary from country to country depending on the exchange control regulations in force.

> * If the remittance is made by SWIFT transfer (including mail or telegraphic transfers), the payment instructions will be sent from the UK bank to the correspondent bank. If the remittance is made by means of a bank draft, the UK bank will make out a draft drawn either on its own head office or on the correspondent bank (depending on whether the payment is to be made in sterling or a foreign currency – see below – respectively) and hand this to the customer who will mail it to the beneficiary. When this is received, the beneficiary will either ask his/her own bank to obtain payment (sterling or foreign currency drafts), or will go to the correspondent bank on which it is drawn for payment (foreign currency drafts).

Payments in a foreign currency

A customer of a UK bank wishes to remit a foreign currency, e.g. US dollars, to a beneficiary in New York. The procedure is as follows:

- the customer completes the bank application form, as above
- the bank debits its customer with the sterling equivalent of the dollars or, if the customer operates a foreign currency account designated in dollars, debits that account

- the UK bank credits the dollar amount to the account in its books which mirrors the dollar account maintained with its New York correspondent

- the remittance (see also * above) is then made and the New York bank debits the UK bank's nostro account (to the New York bank this is a vostro account) and credits the beneficiary with the dollar amount

It is important that you should know the method of operation of nostro and vostro accounts because they are, as already mentioned, going to be used for almost all international payments. The concept of the *mirror account* often causes problems to students because it always has an exactly opposite balance to that of the appropriate nostro account, i.e. if the nostro account of a UK bank held in America has a *credit* balance of USD 10 000, then the mirror - or record - account maintained in the UK will have an equal but opposite *debit* balance of USD 10 000. A record account also records the balance of the nostro account designated in the home currency.

We will now consider a few transactions and pass them through the accounts of the home bank and the overseas bank.

Example 1

Midland Bank, London, maintains an account designated in sterling on behalf of the Bank of America, San Francisco. The balance of this account is currently £20 000 and the rate of exchange is £1 = USD 2.
Note: to Midland Bank this account is a vostro account.

(a) A customer of Midland Bank wishes to remit £1 000 to a supplier, in San Francisco by mail transfer.

> **Action:** **Midland Bank**
> 1. Debit customer with £1 000
> 2. Credit vostro account in name of Bank of America with £1 000
>
> **Bank of America**
> 1. Debit mirror account with £1 000
> 2. Credit customer with USD 2 000

(b) A customer of Bank of America wishes to remit £250 to a supplier in London by mail transfer.

> **Action:** **Bank of America**
> 1. Debit customer with USD 500
> 2. Credit mirror account with £250
>
> **Midland Bank**
> 1. Debit vostro account in name of Bank of America with £250
> 2. Credit customer with £250

In terms of ledgers, the entries will appear as follows:

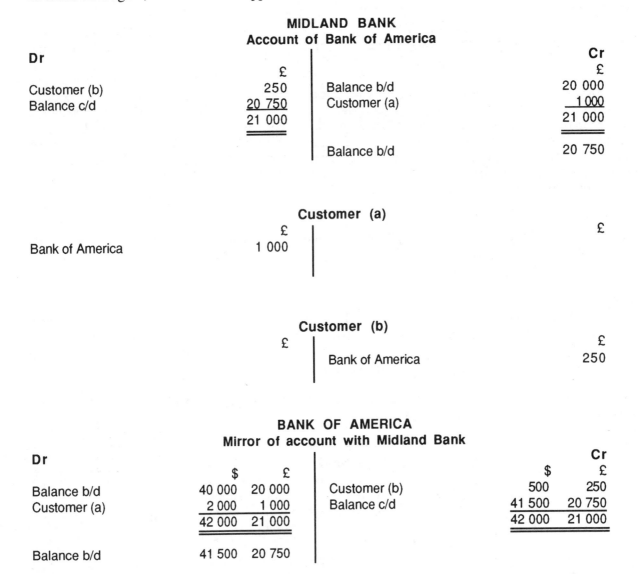

MIDLAND BANK
Account of Bank of America

Dr	£		Cr £
Customer (b)	250	Balance b/d	20 000
Balance c/d	20 750	Customer (a)	1 000
	21 000		21 000
		Balance b/d	20 750

Customer (a)

	£		£
Bank of America	1 000		

Customer (b)

	£		£
		Bank of America	250

BANK OF AMERICA
Mirror of account with Midland Bank

Dr	$	£		Cr $	£
Balance b/d	40 000	20 000	Customer (b)	500	250
Customer (a)	2 000	1 000	Balance c/d	41 500	20 750
	42 000	21 000		42 000	21 000
Balance b/d	41 500	20 750			

Example 2

Midland Bank, London, maintains a US dollar account with Bank of America, San Francisco (to Midland Bank this is a nostro account, while to Bank of America it is a vostro account). The balance of this account is currently USD 10 000 and the rate of exchange is £1 = $2.

(a) A customer of Midland Bank wishes to remit USD 1 000 to a supplier in San Francisco by mail transfer.

> **Action:** **Midland Bank**
> 1. Debit customer with £500
> 2. Credit mirror account with USD 1 000
>
> **Bank of America**
> 1. Debit Midland Bank's nostro account with USD 1 000
> 2. Credit customer with USD 1 000

(b)   A customer of Bank of America wishes to remit USD 2 000 to a supplier in London by mail transfer.

Action: Bank of America
1.   Debit customer with USD 2 000
2.   Credit Midland Bank's nostro account with USD 2 000

Midland Bank
1.   Debit mirror account with USD 2 000
2.   Credit customer with £1 000

Now try working out the ledger entries for yourself.

Answer   (excluding entries on customers' accounts):

BANK OF AMERICA
Account of Midland Bank

Dr			Cr
	$		$
Customer (a)	1 000	Balance b/d	10 000
Balance c/d	11 000	Customer (b)	2 000
	12 000		12 000
		Balance b/d	11 000

MIDLAND BANK
Mirror of account with Bank of America

Dr.				Cr.	
	£	$		£	$
Balance b/d	5 000	10 000	Customer (a)	500	1 000
Customer (b)	1 000	2 000	Balance c/d	5 500	11 000
	6 000	12 000		6 000	12 000
Balance b/d	5 500	11 000			

By now, you should understand how mirror accounts operate! Do not imagine that a bank will allow a balance to build up in its overseas currency (nostro) account. Its dealers will buy currency from the market and sell currency to the market (at market selling and buying rates respectively) in order to keep the balance as low as possible. To achieve this it is more profitable for a bank to 'match' buy and sell transactions for its own customers rather than to have to buy currency from the market or to sell currency to the market at market rates.

As explained in lesson 1, a bank rarely leaves itself overbought ('long') or oversold ('short') in its foreign exchange dealings. However, sometimes, dealers do 'run a position', i.e. leave themselves overbought or oversold, for a few days in the hope that rates will move in their favour, thus enabling them to make a dealing profit. This is a form of speculation and banks operating on the London foreign exchange market are strictly controlled in this respect by the Bank of England.

Control of nostro accounts

The problem for the foreign exchange department of a bank is that transactions are continually taking place and it is difficult to keep track of them unless a good system is in operation. Such a system will incorporate the following points:

- A bank will often have more than one nostro account for major trading currencies such as the US dollar and it is more efficient to move currency amounts from one account to another to meet current payments than to buy currency in the market (at market selling rates) to meet payments on one account.

- *Value dating* of transactions passed through the nostro account to indicate the expected date when the funds are likely to be available for use or paid out of the account abroad.

- Reconciliation of the foreign exchange dealer's position sheets with the mirror account record.

- Checking and reconciling bank statements received from the overseas bank, showing the balance and transactions that have taken place on the nostro account.

- Investigation of any discrepancies or irregularities.

It is likely that, with fluctuating exchange rates, a dealing profit or loss will be made between the sterling balance recorded on the mirror account and the balance of the nostro account.

An important point

A further problem in payment between banks occurs when a transfer has to be made between a buyer and seller in two different countries but the currency to be transferred is that of a *third country*. For example, an examination question might say:

> " Describe the various methods by which a remittance of 10 000 Swiss francs
> might be made by an importer in London to his supplier in France."

In answering this question the one thing we cannot do is to change the currency of France to Swiss francs! The transfer between banks must therefore take place in a country which uses Swiss francs, i.e. Switzerland. The payment may be made in one of the following ways:

- mail transfer;
- telegraphic transfer;
- bank draft.

In the case of the first two the procedure is for the UK bank to instruct its Swiss correspondent bank to make a transfer to the French beneficiary, by debit to the UK bank's Swiss franc nostro account. The Swiss bank can, depending on the requirements of the beneficiary, either credit his own Swiss franc account (if he has one) or instruct their French correspondent bank to make a remittance to him of the French franc equivalent, by crediting the French bank's Swiss franc nostro account. The book-keeping entries are:

UK bank	{ DR. Customer { CR. Mirror a/c *[which reflects nostro a/c in Switzerland]*
Switzerland	{ DR. UK bank's nostro a/c { CR. French bank's nostro a/c
France	{ DR. Mirror a/c *[which reflects nostro a/c in Switzerland]* { CR. Customer

Thus, the UK customer is sold Swiss francs for sterling, whereas the French bank will buy Swiss francs from its customer in exchange for French francs.

Where the transfer is to be made by bank draft the UK bank would hand their customer a draft for 10 000 Swiss francs drawn on its nostro account with the Swiss correspondent. The customer would send this to the beneficiary in France. She would then either have to negotiate the cheque through her own bank in France and obtain the French francs equivalent of 10 000 Swiss francs or she could credit the draft to a Swiss franc account if she maintained one in her own name. In either case, reimbursement would be as above with the Swiss bank debiting the Swiss franc account of the UK bank (its nostro account) and crediting the Swiss franc account of either the French bank or the beneficiary. The same transactions will take place as listed above; however, the order will be different because the draft is sent direct to the beneficiary in France. The claim on the UK bank's nostro account in Switzerland will then be made as the French bank collects the proceeds of the cheque for its customer.

Paying the money to the beneficiary

Once an international payment has been received by a correspondent bank it is then necessary for that bank to make payment to the beneficiary. At its most simple, the beneficiary may have an account with the correspondent bank, in which case the beneficiary's account can be credited. However, if the beneficiary does not bank with the correspondent bank, then the payment must be put through the domestic banking system for the credit of the beneficiary's account. In the UK, inwards payments are made by means of:

- CHAPS (Clearing House Automated Payments System)
- bank drafts
- bank giro credits

CHAPS

This method can be used when payments are £1,000 or more. It offers a same-day electronic payment system to the bank account of the beneficiary. The funds are guaranteed as being cleared and so can be used immediately by the beneficiary.

Bank drafts

This is a bank payment drawn on the head office of the bank – effectively a 'bank cheque'. It is sent by the correspondent bank to the beneficiary. The disadvantage is that, while it is certain to be paid if issued by a reputable bank, the beneficiary will not be able to draw against it until it is cleared, and will not receive interest on the funds until after the three-day clearing cycle.

Bank giro credits

Here the correspondent bank puts a payment through the banking system to the bank account of the beneficiary. The advantage is that the beneficiary receives cleared funds. It will take between one and three days (depending on which banks are involved) for the payment to reach the beneficiary's account.

❑ Money 'laundering'

Money laundering is the collection and remittance of funds for illegal purposes

In dealing with the transfer of money – on both an international and a domestic level – banks have to be on the lookout for money 'laundering'. This is the process by which criminals 'launder' the proceeds of crime by passing them through a number of bank accounts in order to conceal the original source. In the UK money laundering is an offence and three recent Acts of Parliament contain reference to money laundering:

- the Drug Trafficking Offences Act, 1986
- the Prevention of Terrorism Act, 1989
- the Criminal Justice Act, 1993

The last-named Act extends the law beyond drug trafficking and terrorism to cover the general possession and use of proceeds of any serious crime such as robbery, fraud, blackmail, etc. It is a criminal offence to undertake transactions if you know or suspect that you may be handling funds derived from drug trafficking, terrorism or serious crime. In the cases of drug trafficking and terrorism, it is an offence to fail to report the knowledge or suspicion that money laundering is taking place. Thus each bank has established a central point to which staff should report their suspicions, eg a fraud office. It is the responsibility of the bank's fraud office to pass the information to the Financial Intelligence Unit of the National Criminal Intelligence Service.

With international payments it is important to watch out for:

- large round-sum transfers (eg £10,000, £100,000, etc) to beneficiaries abroad, especially where the remitter has only recently opened an account
- electronic transfers being made by relatively new customers
- the routeing of trade and payments through an intermediate country, eg to try and avoid United Nations sanctions against countries
- 'message passing' on behalf of a customer, where the bank's name could be used to give legitimacy to an illegal transaction
- the use of fraudulent shipping documents
- fraudulent documentary credits purporting to be issued by UK banks

While each of these could be innocent transactions, the bank must be sure that money laundering is not taking place. The best way of preventing money laundering is to ensure that the bank's internal systems are followed, particularly when opening accounts (eg taking up references), and when taking instructions from customers (eg following the customer's mandate and authentication of authorised signatures).

❏ Examination hints

- Be able to explain to an exporter or importer the advantages and disadvantages of each of the methods of payment (documentary credits, and collections will be dealt with in more detail in later lessons).

- Note the growing use of countertrade and, in particular, the ways in which banks can assist customers in this growing area of international trade.

- Learn the different methods of making payments abroad, together with the advantages and disadvantages of each.

- Be up-to-date with developments in electronic cross-border payments systems.

- Learn the definitions of nostro and vostro accounts (remember to state from which bank's viewpoint you are describing them).

- Know the book-keeping entries involved in international payments, especially transactions involving three countries.

- Be aware of the characteristics of money laundering and the reporting procedures to be followed.

Know Your .... Methods of Payment in International Trade

1. What are the advantages and disadvantages to an exporter of open account trade?

2. Define 'nostro' accounts.

3. Define 'vostro' accounts.

4. Distinguish between a nostro account and a mirror account.

5. Using the SWIFT system cable transfers and mail transfers are known as .... and .... respectively.

6. Why are personal cheques unsuitable as a method of payment in international trade?

7. What are the disadvantages of a bank draft as a method of payment in international trade?

8. Outline the procedures for the remittance of £1 000 from the UK to a beneficiary in America by mail transfer.

9. Outline the procedures for the remittance of USD 5 000 from the UK to a beneficiary in America by mail transfer.

10. What is countertrade? Explain the main forms which this type of trade may take.

Past Examination Questions

3.1 Nye-Eve Ltd is a company which has recently been established to import goods from overseas. One of the directors calls to see you to discuss the way in which you can arrange to remit funds overseas in respect of the company's imports. He asks you to explain the methods by which payments can be made overseas and you are given to understand that payments will be effected both in sterling and in foreign currency. The customer indicates that he had thought originally that all the company had to do was to send one of the company's own 'domestic' cheques overseas in settlement of any accounts which were received.

REQUIRED:
Brief notes on:

the various methods by which UK banks remit funds abroad on behalf of their customers;   *[4]*

the procedures, including the accounting procedures, to be adopted in respect of the methods listed in (a).   *[16]*

Note: *Assume for the purposes of your answer in (b) above that an account relationship exists between your bank and any overseas bank involved.*

[Total marks for question - 20]
(question 8, September 1987)

3.2*   A. Payne, the senior partner of your customers, Orkward and Meen, calls to see you to discuss export business. During the course of your discussions you discover he is trying to ascertain the methods of payment which are available to an exporter or importer and the advantages and disadvantages of these methods of payment for each of the parties.

REQUIRED:

(a)   A list of the various methods of payment which you would discuss with Mr. Payne.   *[6]*

(b)   Brief notes showing *both* the risks and the advantages to Orkward and Meen when they enter into an agreement to accept   (i) *the safest* and   (ii) *the least safe method of settlement/payment discussed in (a) above.*   *[4]*

(c)   From your list in (a) above, state a compromise method of payment which may be regarded as satisfactory by both exporter and importer.   *[1]*

(d)   List the risks which both exporter and importer will have to consider in accepting this compromise.   *[9]*

[Total marks for question - 20]
(question 8, May 1988)

3.3   *Scenario*

UK Auto Mart Ltd

UK Auto Mart Ltd is a medium-sized corporate; it imports car components and spares on a worldwide basis. From humble beginnings, it has grown into a major wholesaler and distributor to the motor trade and also has a network of retail outlets in the UK.

The directors are very experienced and capable and are well-regarded by your bank. The financial affairs are run prudently and there have been no problems in obtaining credit control sanction for facilities.

The company has to date been trading on very favourable terms but the purchasing director, Mr A Daily, advises you that contracts are at present being negotiated with existing suppliers and less attractive terms are being offered.

Question

In view of the vast range of components, it is not possible for UK Auto Mart Ltd to stock every line.

Instead, they have arrangements with a relatively small number of suppliers in the EC to provide hundreds of shipments of components on a "just in time" basis by air or road. Clean payments are required on receipt of goods.

The company has tended to settle by cheque in sterling or foreign currency, using the cheque book on their sterling account. The suppliers have been complaining about the time and cost in clearing these cheques.

UK Auto Mart are keen to keep their suppliers happy and Mr Daily writes to ask about ways of overcoming this problem.

REQUIRED:

(a)   List the alternative methods of payment which will provide cleared funds more quickly.   *[4]*

(b)   Outline developments that have been taking place in Europe to streamline international payments.   *[10*

(c)   Explain the potential benefits of these new services.   *[6]*

[Total marks for question - 20]
(question 3, Autumn 1993)

Author's note: the EC is now usually referred to as the EU (European Union).

Multiple-Choice Questions: Set 2

Read each question carefully. Choose the *one* answer you think is correct.
Answers are given on page 318.

1.   The currency denominator of the European Monetary System is the:

     A   SWIFT
     B   LIFFE
     C   ECU
     D   SDR

2.   The buyer and seller of a currency option are, respectively,:

     A   holder; writer
     B   putter; writer
     C   writer; holder
     D   holder; intermediary

3.   A currency option which can be exercised at any time up to the expiry date is known as:

     A   a forward option contract
     B   a European option
     C   a put option
     D   an American option

4.   A UK businessman is to make payment for imports from two different countries. Country A's currency is strengthening against sterling, while that of country B is weakening. Respectively, the businessman should:

     A   lag; lead
     B   lead; lead
     C   lead; lag
     D   lag; lag

5.   A bank customer wishes to send some money abroad urgently. Which method would be used?

     A   International Money Transfer
     B   bank draft, sent by air mail
     C   Express International Money Transfer
     D   personal cheque, sent by air mail

6.   There are four main methods of securing payment in international trade. These are:
          (i) payment under documentary credit,
          (ii) open account,
          (iii) collection, i.e. documents against payment or acceptance of a bill of exchange
          (iv) payment in advance.

     From an exporter's point of view, the order of preference is:

     A   (iv), (ii), (iii), (i)
     B   (iv), (iii), (i), (ii)
     C   (iv), (i), (iii), (ii)
     D   (ii), (iv), (i), (iii)

7.   International payments and other messages are often sent through an international computer network called:

    A   SITPRO
    B   SWIFT
    C   ECGD
    D   EIMT

8.   National Barllands Bank, London, has a US dollar account with Bank of America; at the same time it maintains a sterling account for a Swiss bank, Credit Suisse. Respectively, to National Barllands, these accounts are:

    A   vostro; nostro
    B   mirror; vostro
    C   nostro; mirror
    D   nostro; vostro

9.   Your bank has to remit, on behalf of one of your customers, sterling to a beneficiary in German. Which book-keeping transactions are correct?

A	debit customer; credit vostro	(UK bank)
	debit mirror; credit beneficiary	(German bank)
B	debit customer; credit mirror	(UK bank)
	debit vostro; credit beneficiary	(German bank)
C	debit customer; credit nostro	(UK bank)
	debit mirror; credit beneficiary	(German bank)
D	debit customer; credit vostro	(UK bank)
	debit nostro; credit beneficiary	(German bank)

10.   If the above transaction had been the remittance of an amount of Deutschemarks, which would have been correct?

    A
    B
    C
    D

Lesson Four
Travel Facilities

Giving advice about travel facilities to customers going abroad is a topic which will affect every branch bank at some time or another. Bank staff must be able to give the advantages and disadvantages of each facility and be able to provide facilities appropriate to the customer's needs. An obvious example of this is if the customer is touring America: it would not be very sensible to make arrangements for him/her to be able to draw cash only from a bank in New York!

When advising on travel facilities for bank customers, you should give thought to a number of points which include:

• Sterling or foreign currency?
If only one country is being visited then it would be better to arrange travel facilities in the currency of that country. Such facilities are easier to use and there is no need to spend time seeking out a bank to convert sterling bank notes or travellers' cheques.

• Exchange risk
With all travel facilities there is an exchange risk somewhere. In practice, exchange rate fluctuations during the period of a holiday should not be too dramatic so as to have a major effect on holiday spending money. Nevertheless, over a number of years rates have altered quite considerably.

• Ease of replacement
If travel facilities are lost or stolen the effect varies from a major crisis to some inconvenience. When advising on travel facilities one should always bear in mind how easy they are to replace, and all travellers should be aware of their bank's emergency cash facilities (see pages 65-66).

Travellers may obtain their cash requirements abroad by use of one or several of the following:

Short-term travel facilities, e.g. day trip to Calais:
• notes of the traveller's own country
• foreign currency notes

Medium-term travel facilities, e.g. holiday/business trip for up to three weeks:
• sterling or home currency travellers' cheques
• foreign currency travellers' cheques
• use of a credit card
• use of a cheque card

Longer-term travel facilities, e.g. visit lasting weeks or months:
• cheque encashments by prior arrangement
• remittances to various points
• bank draft payable at a named correspondent bank

Facility for all travellers:
• emergency cash

❏ Notes of the traveller's own country

It is always advisable to take some notes of one's own currency. This is useful at the beginning of a holiday on planes and ships and, particularly in the UK, cross-channel ferries. On the way home it is a good idea to have some of the home currency readily available to take care of taxis, airport coaches and perhaps payments to customs. However, as the main method of taking travel facilities, it is not to be recommended.

Advantages
- no need to organise travel facilities

Disadvantages
- danger of loss
- may be bulky to carry
- many countries impose restrictions on the amount of the home currency that can be taken out
- there may be difficulties of exchanging into the local currency (particularly outside banking hours)
- a poor rate of exchange might be obtained
- adverse exchange rate fluctuations may reduce the amount of foreign currency into which it may be converted

❏ Foreign currency notes

Most people going abroad will wish to take some money already changed into the currencies of the country (or countries) they are to visit. This makes good sense because the tourist will then have a quantity of currency until a travellers' cheque, etc. can be changed. Some people will wish to take all of their money abroad in this way. When foreign currency is supplied in this way the amount is converted into sterling at the current exchange rate and this amount will be debited to the customer's bank account or payment can be made in cash. A service charge is usually made for the provision of foreign currency.

Advantages
- the risk of fluctuating exchange rates is eliminated once the currency has been obtained
- convenient - no need to waste time during the holiday in obtaining local currency by means of other travel facilities

Disadvantages
- danger of loss
- may be bulky to carry
- many countries impose restrictions on the import (and export) of local and other currencies
- after the holiday foreign coins cannot normally be exchanged into the home currency - therefore they need to be spent before leaving the country
- not all bank branches hold stocks of foreign currency so an order has to be placed beforehand
- when the traveller returns home, any unused notes will normally be converted back into local currency - during the period of the holiday, exchange rates may have fluctuated adversely

Note: There is no reason why a traveller should not take notes in an 'internationally-accepted' currency such as US dollars, Swiss francs, Deutschemarks, even though these countries are not being visited. Similar disadvantages will apply including the risk of exchange rate fluctuations, but the advantage is that they will be accepted in most countries and are ideal for the traveller visiting several countries in quick succession.

❏ Sterling travellers' cheques

A lot of people going abroad use travellers' cheques as a simple, convenient way of protecting their money against loss or theft. They can be cashed at most banks throughout the world or used to pay for holiday expenses in shops, hotels and restaurants, etc. A small charge is usually made for the provision of travellers' cheques and, when they are cashed abroad, a further small commission charge is usually made.

When travellers' cheques are bought they are signed in one place by the traveller. When abroad and wishing to encash one, the bank cashier, hotel clerk or shop assistant will ask for the cheque to be signed again in his or her presence. By comparing the second signature with the first he or she will know that the traveller is the proper owner of the cheque. The face value of the cheque will then either be changed into the local currency or accepted for goods at the appropriate exchange rate for the day.

Advantages
- a refund service is generally available if they are lost or stolen
- travellers' cheques may be purchased by both customers and non-customers
- they are available in a range of denominations and therefore may be less bulky than taking bank notes
- encashable at many places other than banks

Disadvantages
- risk of fluctuating exchange rates
- travellers' cheques issued by a less well-known bank are not always readily encashable abroad, especially in shops, hotels, etc

Note: Settlement between the banks for travellers' cheques encashed will be effected through the nostro and vostro account system, depending on whether they are designated in sterling or a foreign currency. For example, sterling travellers' cheques cashed by a French bank will be settled through the vostro (sterling) account maintained in London by that bank.

❏ Foreign currency travellers' cheques

In the UK travellers' cheques are available denominated in US dollars and in a number of other currencies, including ECUs (European Currency Units) - the common currency of the European Community. Purchase and encashment procedures are as for sterling travellers' cheques. It is essential for customers travelling to USA and Canada to take travellers' cheques denominated in US and Canadian dollars respectively. This is because a number of banks in America find cashing non-dollar travellers' cheques unprofitable.

Advantages
- as for sterling travellers' cheques
- the exchange risk is eliminated - provided they are in the currency of the country being visited
- travellers' cheques denominated in ECUs can be encashed easily in most European countries

Disadvantages
- unless issued by large well-known banks, etc. there may be problems of encashment, particularly in shops, hotels, etc
- upon return home, the traveller will normally wish to convert any unused foreign currency travellers' cheques back into the home currency - while away, the exchange rates may have fluctuated adversely

❏ Use of a credit card

Issuers of credit cards in the UK are usually members of international bank card systems and their cards can be used at all outlets of these systems. The two largest international card systems are the VISA system and the Interbank Card Association, which uses the 'ACCESS', 'Master Card' and 'Eurocard' symbols.

Credit cards can be used in the normal way for the purchase of goods and services abroad, subject to the holder's credit card limit. The amount of such purchases are converted into sterling (generally at the rate of exchange prevailing when received in the UK), and will appear on the monthly statement in the normal way.

Credit cards can also be used to obtain cash advances abroad of up to £350 in local currency (subject to local regulations which may restrict the amount) in any one day are available to cardholders (provided, of course, that they have sufficient credit available). Identification, such as a passport, may be requested, and the advances can be obtained at most banks displaying the appropriate international bank card sign. There is usually a handling charge for the service and any cash advanced in this way will appear on the monthly statement as usual. Interest will be charged in the normal way on the cash advance, i.e. on a daily basis on the amount of the advance outstanding.

Advantages
- avoids carrying too much cash or bulky travellers' cheques
- cash can be drawn from banks as and when required
- goods and services can be paid for at retail outlets
- useful 'back-up' if travellers' cheques or currency are lost or stolen

Disadvantages
- danger of loss of credit card
- use restricted to credit card limit
- possible exchange risk between encashment/payment in currency and conversion into sterling/home currency

Cash can also be obtained, with a credit card, from a number of Automated Teller Machines (ATMs) throughout Europe.

❏ Use of a cheque card

Most banks in Europe are members of the Eurocheque scheme and many readers will be familiar with the red and blue 'EC' symbol displayed in banks. The scheme permits the encashment of personal cheques at participating banks and allows for the payment of goods and services by cheque in retail outlets, both abroad, and also in the home country. In Britain most bank customers are offered the Eurocheque service, with its distinctive uniform Eurocheque, and supporting cheque card - both being common to all participating banks (except for the name of the bank).

The procedure is as follows:

- the traveller draws his or her cheque in the currency of the European (and Mediterranean) country being visited

- the normal cheque card precautions apply, i.e. signed in the presence of bank cashier or payee, validity of cheque card, comparison of signatures, and cheque book and cheque card in order

- if everything is in order, the card number is written by the cashier or payee on the reverse of the cheque and cash or goods are handed over

- the cheque book and cheque card are returned to the customer, while the cheque that has been cashed or used in payment will be remitted to the drawer's bank

• the cheque will be converted into sterling (generally at the rate of exchange prevailing when presented in the UK) and debited to the drawer's account, even though it may bear technical irregularities or the customer does not have sufficient funds in the account to meet it

Cheques can be written in the currency of any European and Mediterranean country where they are being used (up to a maximum of the equivalent of £100, at present, for UK bank customers). Also there is no limit to the number of cheques that may be used for any one transactions.

In the UK retailers and others can accept, subject to certain limitations, uniform Eurocheques up to £200 from visitors to the UK. The usual cheque card precautions apply, and the payee is requested to present the cheque to his bank on the next working day, whenever possible. Retailers' accounts are credited when the cheques are paid into their bank. The cheques themselves are paid to the debit of central sterling accounts held by member banks in the UK. There is no recourse to the retailer if they are unpaid, provided they have been accepted within the limitations and under the conditions of the Eurocheque scheme.

Advantages
• avoids carrying too much cash or bulky travellers' cheques
• cash can be drawn from banks as and when required
• goods and services can be paid for at retail outlets
• cheques are drawn in the currency of the country being visited: no problems of 'poor' exchange rates

Disadvantages
• danger of loss of bank card and cheque book
• a limited number of cheques in each cheque book
• possible exchange risk between encashment/payment in currency and conversion of cheque into sterling/home currency

The Eurocheque card can also be used at a number of Automated Teller Machines (ATMs) throughout Europe.

❏ Cheque encashments by prior arrangement

This travel facility, often known as an *open credit,* is a simple way of arranging money abroad for a customer who is going to be in one place for some time. It operates in a similar way to the open credit facility within a country. The customer tells his own branch bank where he is going and when he will be there. They arrange with the customer an agreed correspondent bank in the overseas town or city which will cash his cheques up to a certain amount. A specimen of the customer's signature is sent to the overseas bank. When he wishes to use the facility the customer will cash his own sterling cheques in the normal way at the overseas bank and will receive the equivalent amount in local currency less charges. The overseas bank will present the cheque to the home bank and claim re-imbursement.

Note: In some countries, open credit facilities are difficult to establish and, on occasions, travellers have had great difficulty in obtaining cash through this facility.

Advantages
• no risk of loss while travelling because funds are drawn in the foreign centre
• avoids carrying too much cash or travellers' cheque
• cash can be drawn as and when required

Disadvantages
• encashment facilities restricted to a named bank and branch
• drawings are usually made in sterling, therefore there is an exchange risk

❏ Remittances to various points

Using this method funds are transferred through the banking channels, using the SWIFT system (or by making mail/telegraphic transfers), to a bank near where the customer is to stay. The facility is available in either sterling or foreign currency and the money will await collection by the traveller who, subject to identification, will be paid.

Advantages
* no risk of loss while travelling
* if the currency of the overseas country is sent, the exchange risk will be eliminated

Disadvantages
* encashment facilities restricted to one bank
* if sterling is remitted, there is a risk of exchange rate fluctuations
* higher cost of 'telegraphic' transfer
* mail transfer takes longer

Note: The difference between speeds of making the remittance should be pointed out to a customer. While priority SWIFT (or telegraphic transfers) is much quicker (the funds will be available in most major centres in two or three business days) it is more costly. If a SWIFT message (or mail transfer) is used, it will be cheaper but sufficient time should be allowed for the facility to be made available (seven days should be ample time for major overseas centres, but extra time would be needed for more remote areas).

❏ Bank draft payable at a named correspondent bank

This is similar to an open credit facility except that a bank draft, rather than the beneficiary's personal cheque, is used to obtain cash. Such a facility is commonly used by a company that wishes to make funds available to an overseas representative. Under such circumstances the beneficiary may well not be a customer of the home bank. Arrangements can be made at the home bank for the beneficiary to obtain cash by means of drafts at one specified bank branch. The drafts, which may be in either sterling or foreign currency, will be drawn by the home bank and sent to the overseas bank for payment to the beneficiary against his signature, a specimen of which will have been sent to it by the opening bank. (It would, of course, be possible for a person working abroad for any length of time to operate a bank account in the foreign centre, which could then be 'fed' with remittances from home - see below).

Advantages
* no risk of loss in transit
* if drafts are drawn in the currency of the overseas country there will be no exchange risk

Disadvantages
* facilities restricted to one (occasionally more) bank branch
* withdrawal amounts limited to the amount of the facility
* if drafts are drawn in sterling, there is an exchange risk

❏ Emergency cash

Any person going abroad should be aware of the availability of his or her bank's emergency cash facilities. Provided the funds are in the customer's account most banks are prepared, in an emergency, to transfer funds by telegraphic transfer. The procedure is for the traveller to cable or telephone either the bank branch where the account is held or the international department of the bank giving the following details:

- full name (possibly including the address where the customer is staying)
- the address of the branch of the bank where the account is maintained (if not cabling the branch direct)
- the amount required (there may be a maximum amount that the bank will cable out)
- the name and address of the nearest large bank, where the customer requires the money

Normally the required funds will be available at the named bank within one business day. It should be stressed that this service should only be used in emergencies: it is costly, with two cable charges involved and also bank charges.

A person not having a bank account would need to cable a relative or friend and ask them to take some money into a bank and request it to be sent by telegraphic transfer to the overseas centre.

❑ Travel insurance

When providing travel facilities to a customer, most banks will take the opportunity to try and sell travel insurance. Such insurance policies, for a relatively small premium, cover the following:

- personal accident, i.e. death, loss of limbs or eyes, or permanent total disablement

- medical and other expenses, including additional hotel and repatriation costs

- hospital benefits

- baggage and personal money, including replacement of necessities when baggage is lost in transit for more than 12 hours

- personal liability, i.e. indemnity for liability at law for injury or damage to third parties or their property

- travel delay, for more than 12 hours

- cancellation and curtailment of the journey or holiday, unavoidably caused through illness, etc. of the traveller or close relative

- failure of public transport

The money amount of cover for each risk varies.

❑ Expatriate employees

Besides travel facilities for holidaymakers and business travellers, banks are also able to provide services for customers who go to work abroad. Such services fall into two main categories:

- establishment of overseas banking facilities
- looking after the customer's UK interests

Overseas banking facilities
If the customer is likely to be abroad for a short period, perhaps only a few months, an open credit facility (see above) will be an appropriate encashment facility. Where the stay is to be longer than six months, it would be advisable to open a local bank account overseas. The UK bank can arrange to open an account either with an overseas branch or subsidiary of the bank, or with a correspondent bank. A reference and a specimen of the customer's signature (duly certified as being genuine) should

be sent to the chosen bank branch, and the customer should be given a letter of introduction addressed to the bank. If the customer continues to be paid in sterling in the UK, it will be necessary to transfer some part of the salary each month to the overseas bank account. The amount, and method of remittance, can probably be agreed before the customer leaves the UK.

Customer's UK interests

A number of points need to be considered, and the UK bank can assist with:

- *taxation*, making arrangements for UK tax matters to be handled
- *investments*, appraising investments and advising on changes
- *property*, advising on selling or letting a UK property
- *insurance*, selecting appropriate policies
- *current account and deposit account*, advising on the use of gross interest or 'offshore' (usually Channel Islands or Isle of Man) bank accounts, in order to take advantage of tax concessions
- *safe custody*, looking after documents and valuables

Some banks have established specialist advisory services for expatriates. The main point to remember is that the customer will still have expenses in the UK, e.g. mortgage, insurance, etc. which will have to continue to be paid from the UK bank account.

❏ Company services

Travel facilities offered to companies with staff who travel abroad include the use of company credit cards. Here, the card is in the name of the company, but is signed by the member of staff. Thus business expenses incurred abroad (and in the UK) are charged to the company's credit or charge card account.

Some companies also hold stocks of blank travellers' cheques. These are ready for issue to staff travelling abroad and would be signed before leaving the UK.

A company might also need an overseas bank account, if it was involved in, say, a building project abroad, or was establishing a subsidiary abroad. Such a bank account can be opened in the same way as for individuals. However, if borrowing is contemplated on the account, the UK bank would, most probably, have to provide a guarantee to the overseas bank.

If medium and long-term borrowing is required through the bank, a Eurocurrency loan (see pages 251-2) can be arranged.

❏ Examination hints

- Travel facilities questions always take the form of business or group travel.

- Do not use the 'splatter' technique of mentioning every travel facility you can think if; instead, the facilities suggested must meet the needs of the customer.

- List the travel facilities you recommend in a preferred order - starting with the best. Give reasons for your choices and, for most questions, state the advantages and disadvantages of each. Ensure that customers know the bank's emergency cash facilities.

- Some travel questions go further than the needs of travellers and may go on to include the needs of staff working abroad.

- Often travel facilities form only part of a question (it is often linked to methods of settlement), so you should have a good knowledge of other topics.

Know Your .... Travel Facilities

1.   What points need to be considered when selecting travel facilities for a customer?

2.   State two advantages of sterling travellers' cheques for use abroad.

3.   State two disadvantages of sterling travellers' cheques for use abroad.

4.   There are certain advantages in taking travellers' cheques designated in the currency of the country to be visited. What are they? What are the disadvantages?

5.   A customer of your bank is to visit the USA shortly. What travel facilities would you advise, and why?

6.   Describe the facilities available to UK bank customers who wish to use personal cheques in Europe.

7.   Would you advise a bank customer going abroad on a business trip to take sterling or foreign currency bank notes with her? Briefly give your reasons.

8.   A customer is going to work abroad in Geneva for a year. During this time his salary will still be paid into his account with you. How would you solve his cash requirements while he is abroad?

9.   What bank services are available to customers who go to work abroad?

10.   What emergency cash facilities do banks offer to their customers who are abroad?

Past Examination Questions

4.1*   Mr. Ring Culture, who is a plant breeder and a customer of your bank, calls to see you some two weeks before his departure on a two months' working holiday to California. He asks you the following questions:

(a)   Will you please cash his cheque for £1 000 to give him initial spending money in the USA?   [3]

(b)   Can he order sterling travellers cheques for his forthcoming visit?   [3]

(c)   Will you please remit to California the sterling equivalent of 2 000 US dollars to pay for his hotel accommodation during his stay in California? You understand that these funds should be paid at least 10 days before his arrival in California.   [8]

(d)   As he has the bank's telephone number in the event of emergency, will the bank be able to remit funds urgently to him, if requested?   [6]

REQUIRED:
The replies, in brief, with reasons, that you would give to Mr. Culture. Include any further suggestions you consider appropriate.

[Total marks for question - 20]
(question 7, September 1987)

4.2   Arthur Rose, a director of Hybrid Plants Ltd which is a customer of good standing, calls to see you to discuss a business trip he is making to France, Germany and Switzerland in the near future.

The company arranges for parties of keen gardeners to visit well known sites around the world, and Mr Rose's forthcoming trip is designed to visit a number of gardens with a view to creating a new tour for gardening club members.

He asks you to recommend travel facilities which would be appropriate to his needs. He understands that problems have been encountered by people visiting the Continent, particularly for payment of motorway tolls.

You also discuss the methods by which funds can be remitted to the three countries in settlement of tour expenses which will be incurred if the company's plans are successful and future tours are organised.

Subsequently, during Mr Rose's visit abroad, you receive a telephone call from him, asking you to send 50,000 Swiss Francs to Switzerland from the company's account, to settle pre-payments for future tours.

REQUIRED:

(a)   A description of the travel facilities that you would recommend to Mr Rose for *his* visit to the three countries, giving reasons for your answers.

(b)   Your suggestion for the travel facility, other than local currency, which would enable Mr Rose to pay motorway tolls during his visit.

(c)   *A brief description* of a system by which you could arrange to remit funds to the three countries for future tours. *Indicate briefly* the accounting procedures which would be used when effecting payments on behalf of the company.

(d)   A brief description of the method by which you would remit the sum of 50,000 Swiss francs, following Mr Rose's telephone call. Include any safeguards which would be necessary to protect the interests of the bank and your customer.

[Total marks for question - 20]
(question 7, May 1988)

4.3   Your customer, Mr B Sprout, is a civil servant working for the UK Government. He has been sent to Brussels on attachment to the European Commission to work for the next six months. During his stay in Brussels, his salary will be paid by the UK Government in sterling in the UK. Shortly before leaving for Brussels, he asks you the various methods by which he could obtain funds while in Brussels to cover his day-to-day living expenses.

REQUIRED:

(a) A brief note of the suggestions you would make to Mr Sprout which would be appropriate to his needs.

[10]

(b) A brief description of the relative advantages and disadvantages of the methods discussed under (a) above.

[7]

(c) The means by which you could arrange to remit funds to Mr Sprout in Brussels in the event of an emergency arising.

[3]
[Total marks for question - 20]
(question 8, October 1989)

[5]

4.4   Runway Renovators Ltd is one of your important customers and has been awarded a contract to repair and extend the airport runways in Singapore. The company has also been awarded a contract to maintain the airport facilities over the next 10 years.   [2]

One of the directors, Mr Highflyer, calls to see you to discuss the setting up of an arrangement to provide their expatriate engineers with initial cash during their first few days in Singapore, and another arrangement whereby monthly expenses for their engineers can be provided other than by establishing a local bank account.

Further, in order to service the maintenance contract, Runway Renovators intends to establish a small company on a joint venture basis with local Singapore contractors.   [8]

REQUIRED:

(a) Suggestions which would help the expatriate engineers initially during their first few days in Singapore.   [4]

(b) Methods by which monthly expenses of, say, £20,000 incurred by the expatriate engineers can be serviced from the United Kingdom.   [7]

(c) Methods by which *working capital* for the joint venture might be provided until the joint venture company can become self-sufficient and self-financing in Singapore.   [3]

(d) Any methods of raising the initial supply of bank medium-term finance for the joint venture.   [6]

Note: Ignore the initial supply of CAPITAL for the joint venture company.

[Total marks for question - 20]
(question 8, October 1988)

4.5*   As the Manager of the city centre branch of your bank, you call to see one of your retail customers who sells clothing and souvenir giftware, principally to overseas tourists, from a shop situated in the middle of a world-famous cathedral city. The proprietor of the retail outlet, Mr T Shirt, asks you to discuss with him the various ways in which he might speed the clearance of cheques tendered in payment for goods by overseas visitors.

Your discussions reveal that the visitors, principally from the USA and the EU, frequently pay for goods by means of personal cheques expressed in foreign currency. Although Mr Shirt is not happy about accepting these cheques, he has no alternative if he wishes to maintain his volume of sales, as a refusal would probably lose the custom. These cheques are sent to the drawee's bank on a collection basis. You are also told that it takes between 30 to 40 days before the proceeds are received and credited to the company's account. Mr Shirt finds his accounting difficult because he is not quite sure what the value of the cheques will be when payment is eventually received.

REQUIRED:
Describe in brief note form:

(a) your suggestion(s) which might speed up the clearance time for cheques and improve Mr Shirt's cashflow position. Indicate if there are any implications for your customer in your suggestion(s).

[11]

(b) your suggestions which might enable Mr Shirt to ascertain approximately the sterling value of the cheques he receives. Indicate any implications for your customer in your suggestion(s).   *[5]*

(c) any alternative suggestion(s) which might help your customer with his payment/cash flow problems.   *[4]*

[Total marks for question - 20]
(question 3, October 1990)

4.6   Mr Rich, a wealthy and influential customer, makes an appointment to see you to discuss funding his son's education in Switzerland. You understand that the son, Ernest Lee Rich, is to be given a small allowance but the bulk of the education costs (fees, board, etc) is to be remitted, at regular intervals, direct to the educational foundation in Basle. You note from your records that the father receives regular dividends from various Swiss corporations and these are always received by means of inward payments or cheques drawn on, and payable by, London banks, the proceeds being expressed in sterling.

REQUIRED:

(a) A list of the points you would wish to discuss with Mr Rich:

(i)   to enable him to take advantage of the dividends, or other benefits of foreign currency, and to protect him from any risk(s) involved;   *[6]*

(ii)   to pay his son's living allowance (pocket money, etc);   *[4]*

(iii)   to satisfy the requirements of the educational foundation.   *[4]*

(b) Indicate the accounting procedures involved in your suggestions above.   *[6]*

[Total marks for question - 20]
(question 6, October 1991)

4.7   El Grappo Ltd imports a range of wines from many countries of the world. It also arranges tours for amateur wine enthusiasts. You receive a visit from the proprietor, Mr Claret, who wishes to discuss three matters with you:

(i)   He will be organising a large party to tour Australia and New Zealand in the near future. He is particularly anxious to know when, and how, the exchange risk can be covered.

(ii)   One of his staff, Mr Cork, is to be attached to a famous chateau in France for one year.

(iii)   Mr Claret has been successful in obtaining supplies of good quality wine which will be bottled for him by growers in Alsace and shipped by them at the appropriate time to the UK as his house wine.

REQUIRED, in brief note form:

(a) What should Mr Claret and his party take to Australia and New Zealand to cover their day-to-day expenses and why?

[5]

(b) How should remittances be made to Australia and New Zealand to pay advance hotel and tour bookings?

[3]

(c) What are your recommendations to Mr Claret to provide day-to-day and out-of-pocket expenses for Mr Cork during his attachment to the chateau in France? Explain how your recommendations would be carried out.

[6]

(d) What methods can Mr Claret use to calculate the sterling cost of the house wine which is to be shipped to the UK in about six months' time? Are there any disadvantages in any, or all, of your suggestions?

[6]

[Total marks for question - 20]

(question 7, May 1992)

Lesson Five
Selling Abroad

For a trading nation such as the UK - a small industrialised country with a large population and limited natural resources - international trade is especially important. Few countries anywhere in the world could survive for long nowadays without importing goods and, as a result, exporting other goods to pay for them. Even if a country could survive without international trade, it would suffer a much reduced standard of living.

Many businesses - especially smaller firms - are tempted to ignore world markets and to concentrate on selling at home: sooner or later, however, an enquiry will be received from abroad and the firm will have to consider the implications of exporting its goods. A firm receiving an overseas enquiry for the first time will probably go to its bank to seek advice. Whenever a business trades abroad its bank is usually involved at some stage: handling the documentation, making or receiving payments, granting advances - perhaps at concessionary rates of interest - or giving advice. Lesson 14 discusses more fully the services provided by the banks for their exporter (and importer) customers. This lesson is concerned with the ways in which exporters can enter foreign markets.

❏ Why export?

The main reason for deciding to export is that new markets for a company's products will be opened, so making the business less vulnerable to fluctuations in the home market: this leads to a more stable manufacturing base which provides the right environment for growth, increased profits and good employment prospects. Additional markets should lead to increased sales, which will lead to lower production costs so making the products more competitive in all markets.

Inevitably a potential exporter must spend time finding out information about potential markets and in particular the following points:

- demand for the firm's products in particular countries
- rival products in these countries
- names of potential overseas buyers and agents
- the political and economic situation in potential markets
- details of import restrictions, tariffs and exchange control regulations in potential markets

In addition the potential exporter must consider if the product will have to be modified in any way to meet the legal requirements of certain countries or to satisfy local tastes. Thought must be given as to how the product is to be packaged and presented to overseas buyers. Publicity material must be prepared, and the need for an advertising campaign, using appropriate media, must be investigated.

A lot of information is available on these and other topics from a bank and assistance is also available from Government agencies.

❏ Department of Trade and Industry (DTI)

The Department of Trade and Industry, together with the Foreign and Commonwealth Office, provides a wide range of services to UK exporters. These services, which are integrated under the name *Overseas Trade Services*, are provided through the British Overseas Trade Board (BOTB) which is supervised by the DTI.

BOTB's responsibilities to industry and commerce are to provide encouragement and support in overseas trade with the aid of appropriate governmental and non-governmental organisations at home and overseas; to provide information, advice and help to the exporter; to organise collective trade promotions; and to stimulate export promotion publicity. In addition to providing direct help to exporters the Board has several responsibilities to the government: it advises on strategy for overseas trade; directs and develops export promotion services on behalf of the DTI; contributes to the exchange of views between government, industry and commerce in the field of overseas trade; and searches for solutions to trade problems.

Financial Assistance

BOTB offers two major financial contribution schemes:
* the Overseas Projects Fund (OPF)
* the Export Marketing Research Scheme

The *Overseas Projects Fund* is designed to encourage firms to put greater effort into the pursuit of major, complex and difficult project contracts outside the European Union. The fund can, subject to prior agreement, contribute up to fifty per cent of the pre-contractual expenses of companies pursuing such contracts but, to qualify, the project must offer a minimum UK content of £10 million in goods and services, with the main emphasis being on the goods element. The fund can also make contributions towards pre-contractual expenses for consultancy and project management contracts which provide a net return of £1 million or more to the balance of payments. Contributions are repayable if the contract is won. The Fund is administered by the *Projects and Export Policy Division* of the Department of Trade and Industry. This Division, which operates under the general guidance of BOTB provides a single focus for co-ordinating the Government support for industry in pursuing capital projects overseas and for advising on export policy questions generally.

The *Export Marketing Research Scheme* is a scheme designed to help and encourage UK firms to undertake marketing research outside the European Union as an essential part of their export effort. The scheme provides a free professional overseas marketing research advisory service, with financial support for export marketing research. The support varies according to the organisation: individual companies may receive up to half of the cost of research up to a maximum contribution of £20 000; groups of unconnected businesses participating in joint research may receive up to fifty per cent of the cost (limit of £30 000); and trade associations may receive up to three-quarters (limit of £40 000).

Export Promotions

The *Overseas Promotions Support* branch administers the Outward and Inward Missions Schemes. The *Outward Missions Scheme* encourages British exporters to visit overseas markets to assess prospects, or to reinforce their overseas marketing effort - some financial assistance is available. Assistance is also available under the *Inward Missions Scheme,* where groups of companies in a particular industry wish to bring to the UK overseas businesspeople and others who may place orders for British goods.

The Overseas Promotions Support branch also administers:

* The *Store Promotion Scheme*, which can organise a promotion on a 'UK theme' in a big retail outlet overseas. When there is a specifically UK flavour to the event, BOTB can often provide support in staging such a promotion.

* The *Promotion of Trade Fairs Services*, which helps exporters to exhibit their goods at specialised trade fairs. (When these events are outside Western Europe the BOTB assists with a contribution towards exhibitors' travel costs.)

* The *Overseas Seminar Scheme*, which arranges seminars to increase overseas awareness of UK goods and services. Costs in staging such events can be shared by the exporter and BOTB.

- The *New Products from Britain Scheme*, which helps to publicise new products abroad in technical and business magazines, and newspapers in selected markets.

Informative Assistance

Besides financial assistance the BOTB assists exporters in the provision of information.

There are a number of separate *Market Branches* which advise on conditions in specific overseas markets, and are the focus for briefing exporters on current conditions, tariffs, regulations, business customs, personalities, market prospects, competitors' activities and the climate for investment. Market branches include Europe, Japan, North America, Middle East, etc.

Other sources of information available to exporters through the BOTB are:

- *Export Market Information Centre*, which has a world-wide collection of overseas trade statistics and commercial directories
- *Export Intelligence Service,* which provides daily information to subscribers on specific export opportunities (this service is operated for BOTB by a private sector company)
- *Export Representative Service*, which is able to provide names of overseas representatives who would be interested in handling specific UK products
- *Overseas Status Report Service,* which provides information about the interests and capabilities of specific overseas companies, covering the scope of their activity, after-sales servicing facilities, technical know-how, etc. (these reports are *not* assessments of financial standing)
- *World Aid Section,* which advises exporters about opportunities for the provision of goods and services under the aid programmes administered by the international lending agencies
- *Export Publications*, which provides a wide range of publications on overseas markets in the form of individual country profiles (notes on a country's markets, trade, population, etc.), sector reports (market research on key areas), and other publications

❏ Business Links

A network of *Business Links* – or 'one-stop shops' – has been set up throughout the UK on the initiative of the DTI. They seek to bring business support services together under one roof: this will save businesses seeking advice from having to 'shop around' the various agencies involved in providing assistance.

A number of export consultants are used by Business Links to work with companies in order to help them develop an export strategy and to make it succeed. There are further plans for Business Links to develop a package of promotional services for exporters, training and support for exporters, and to encourage and help more companies to become exporters.

❏ British Standards Institution

Its *Technical Help to Exporters (THE)* service, run for the British Overseas Trade Board, collects information about technical standards and regulations in countries. An exporter will need to know a particular country's technical standards and whether a product meets them or can be modified to do so.

❏ Simpler Trade Procedures Board (SITPRO)

SITPRO is wholly funded by BOTB, through an annual grant, but acts independently within its agreed terms of reference. (SITPRO is discussed more fully on page 93).

❏ Chambers of Commerce, Trade Associations, Export Clubs

In the UK, Chambers of Commerce and trade associations also receive information about opportunities for selling goods abroad and provide a service to their members who wish to export, and often organise trade missions abroad. There are also *export clubs* in the UK. These are informal associations, usually formed on a regional basis by a number of local manufacturers, often with representatives of local shipping and forwarding agents, banks and insurance companies, etc. They are a method of pooling the export experiences of member firms so that advice can be made available on overseas markets and export procedure. In some cases practical help may be given by selling through a marketing group or by organising trade missions and exhibitions overseas.

❏ Entering Overseas Markets

Having carried out the necessary research and decided to enter the export business, there are a number of different methods of selling the firm's products abroad. These methods can take the form of direct representation or indirect representation.

Direct representation

A company with a considerable volume of export sales in a limited range of markets may choose to make a direct investment in manufacturing or distribution. Service to customers, both before and after sale, will be improved and such representation may be entered into either as a joint venture with a local concern or by establishing a subsidiary company.

It is more likely that, certainly in the early years of the development of export markets, the product and the volume of sales will not justify the costs of direct representation.

Indirect representation

Export houses: Export merchants and export agents/manager (see also lesson 12)
These are suitable methods where an exporter has little or no experience of selling in overseas markets and where he wishes to avoid the inevitable complications of the export trade. Export houses can offer a variety of services including the following:

- As an export merchant, they will buy goods in one country and export them in their own right, i.e. they act as principals. Thus, for the manufacturer, the sale is similar to a domestic sale.

- As an export agent/manager they will act as an agent of the exporter by promoting his product abroad. The manufacturer will usually receive cash on shipment, credit being extended to the overseas buyer by the export agent.

Often export houses will attend to the necessary clerical work, handling, packing, shipping, insurances, and deal with formalities abroad. Naturally the more services that are used by a manufacturer, the higher will be the cost. Most export houses specialise in particular markets or goods, or in certain types of products for specific markets. In the UK, details of export merchants and export agents can be obtained from the British Export Houses Association.

Export houses: Confirming houses (see also lesson 12)
Some export houses are also confirming (or indent) houses. These act as buying agents for overseas importers. They receive orders (or indents) from foreign importers who require particular types of goods. The confirming house finds a manufacturer who can supply the goods, and passes the order to them, adding their confirmation to the order, i.e. assuming responsibility for the debt. The goods are received from the manufacturer, and the confirming house settles with him and arranges to ship and insure the goods. The advantages to a manufacturer are that he has a firm order and is assured of payment when the goods are despatched. Thus the manufacturer is able to export his goods without the necessity of involving himself in the complexities of export documentation, etc. and, if problems arise in manufacturing or packaging, etc., the confirming house is close at hand to give advice.

Foreign buying houses
In the UK, certain large overseas retail store groups - particularly from America and Canada - maintain permanent buying houses through whom they buy the bulk of their British goods. The buyers of other store groups make regular visits to Britain. (Information about both of these selling opportunities is available through the BOTB's Export Intelligence Service). This method of selling represents a ready and simple means of exporting for a manufacturer who does not have the volume of export business to set up his own overseas selling organisation.

Agents

A method which can be adopted is to appoint an agent to act as the exporter's representative abroad. The agent appointed may have an office in the exporter's country, with its main organisation in overseas countries, or a firm of overseas agents operating entirely abroad. An agent will usually be paid on a commission basis and sometimes the appointment will be on a 'del credere' basis where, in addition to securing orders, the agent will also assume responsibility for bad debts in return for increased increased commission. Great care is needed in appointing agents as they will be entirely responsible for promoting the exporter's business within the allocated area. The BOTB can assist firms to find agents and it is always advisable to make a status enquiry before making the apointment.

Note that for the UK exporter of goods (not services) appointing an agent within the European Union, the *Commercial Agent Directive* of 1986 applies:

- the exporter has to keep the agent informed of any unexpected fall in business
- the agent can claim compensation for losses suffered within one year of the termination of the agency agreement (even if the proper legal procedures were followed to terminate)

Import houses overseas

Such concerns import goods and sell them in their own country. A manufacturer selling goods to an overseas import house will normally have to undertake shipment and documentation, but the marketing is taken out of his hands.

❏ The Single European Market

The European Union (EU) of which Britain is a member, has instituted a programme of measures for the completion of the European internal market. This presents a number of business opportunities (a market with more than 320m people) and threats (there will be more competition in the home market from other European businesses). The following are the main changes which either have taken, or will shortly take place:

Physical barriers

- control of goods at internal frontiers abolished
- harmonisation of public health standards
- for individuals, the removal of immigration and passport controls

Technical barriers

- technical barriers to trade within the EU removed
- free movement of goods, capital, services and workers
- transport services within the EU freed from restrictions
- agreement on common industrial standards
- public purchasing opened up so that public bodies will buy on the basis of fair competition, not national identity
- common protection for intellectual property, eg trademarks and patents

Fiscal barriers

- approximation of indirect taxation, eg VAT and excise duties
- restrictions on financial services, eg banking, insurance, investment, removed

European Economic Area (EEA)

In January 1994, the European Economic Area was established, as the world's largest free-trade zone. the EEA is a single market comprising:

- the twelve countries of the EU

five members of the European Free Trade Association (EFTA): Austria, Finland, Iceland, Norway, Sweden (these countries – except for Iceland – are expected to join the EU before too long)

The EEA widens the scope of the European internal market: it gives Britons and British companies access to a market of 370 million people without trade barriers or restrictions in freedom of movement.

European Union support for exporters

The European Union operates an export promotion programme which aims to increase the exports of EU firms to countries outside of the Union, Promotional activities include support for EU stands in pavilions at international trade fairs, investment and technical conferences, market studies, and trade missions. In order to be included, activities have to appeal to industry across several EU countries.

❏ Terms of the Contract

When exporters are arranging to sell goods to a customer overseas the terms of the contract between them must be agreed. Contracts will always specify the following:

* *Goods*
  A full description of the items to be supplied including the quality and quantity.

* *Method of payment*
  These have already been considered briefly in lesson 3, and constitute the agreement as to the means of payment between exporter and overseas buyer. From the exporter's viewpoint, payment in advance is to be preferred, with open account trade being least sought after; the importer, however, will see things differently. If neither of these methods is acceptable, the solution will be either documentary credit or a collection: both of these will be considered in detail in later lessons.

* *Insurance and terms of trade*
  In the contract the buyer and seller must agree who is to meet the various freight and insurance charges (including stating the risks to be covered). Terms of trade and export documentation will be looked at in the next lesson.

❏ Examination hints

* Recent questions have taken on a marketing approach, particularly in selling to European Union countries.

* Often methods of selling abroad are included as a part of another question and, in the past, have been linked to questions on bank services, and forward exchange contracts.

* Ensure that you know the difference between export merchants, export agents, and confirming houses.

Know Your .... Selling Abroad

1. Why should a company with a healthy home market consider exporting?

2. What marketing questions need to be answered before a firm can start to sell its goods abroad?

3. What financial assistance is available through British Overseas Trade Board?

4. What non-financial information is available from BOTB?

5. How does 'Technical Help to Exporters' assist UK manufacturers wishing to sell abroad?

6. How can an export club help UK exporters?

7. What functions are performed by an export merchant?

8. What does a confirming house do?

9. What is a 'del credere' agent?

10. List the main points that will be covered in a contract between exporter and importer.

Past Examination Questions

The contents of this lesson often feature as part of another question, usually linked to general bank services (see lesson 14).

5.1   Welsh Crafts is a small company, based in Wales, which produces high quality hand-made items that are very popular amongst people of Welsh descent.

The company has a successful home market in the UK but, as a result of great enthusiasm shown by overseas visitors to Wales, Mrs Leek, the proprietress, now wishes to develop markets in the USA, Australia and New Zerland.

You call to see Mrs Leek to discuss ways in which your bank can assist.

REQUIRED:
Brief notes indicating the basic considerations which you would bring to your customer's attention, the ways in which you could assist in finding outlets and the method(s) of payment you would suggest.

(question 7, Spring 1987)

5.2*   Uniform Products Ltd manufacture antique types of military uniforms for sale to the general public. Hitherto, they have only sold in the UK but have recently embarked upon an export campaign. They have successfully obtained provisional orders from several large department stores based in the USA. The method of payment has yet to be decided.

You called to see the Managing Director, Mr Hussar, to discuss any problems. Further enquiry discloses that the department stores will be placing the orders through US buying houses based in London which will be purchasing the goods on an EXW basis. Payment will be effected in sterling.

Mr Hussar proudly informs you that he has successfully opened a 'second front' for exports to the USA. These other sales will be made through the medium of three 'main agents' who have long and well established reputations in the southern states of the USA. The three main agents involved are based in Atlanta, Houston and Miami. These agents have agreed to act for Uniform Products in the USA. The terms of shipment will be DDP and payment will be effected in US dollars.

Mr Hussar asks you to explain to him the various methods of obtaining payment and any risks which he must consider if he confirms and accepts the orders to supply goods through the two schemes described above.

REQUIRED in brief note form:

(a) State the only practical method(s) of payment available to your customer for the two proposed schemes. Your answer should also outline the responsibilities of the parties and explain any other points which your customer must consider when entering into these transactions. *[9]*

(b) Any other major risk which the company must consider when entering into an agreement to see through the 'main agents' in the USA. Your answer should include definitions of the methods by which such a risk might be reduced. *[11]*

[Total marks for question - 20]

(question 7, May 1991)

Author's note: *terms of trade, e.g. EXW, DDP, will be explained in the next lesson.*

5.3 *Scenario*

SPECIAL OPTICS LTD

Your UK customer, Special Optics Ltd, has a turnover of between £1-2m achieved with a skilled workforce of six people. the company produces quality products for which there is a good demand from leading industrial companies in the UK.

Few large companies around the world compete in this market because of the specialist expertise and equipment needed.

Up until now, Special Optics has received occasional export orders from:

1. one-off approaches from other UK companies for goods to be on-sold abroad;
2. overseas companies visiting Special Optic's stand at leading industrial exhibitions in the UK;
3. responses from abroad to news reports on new products covered in UK trade magazines.

Export orders have tended to be expressed in sterling in the £5-50,000 range and Special Optics has required either payment in advance or, more usually, irrevocable documentary credits (some of which have been confirmed) payable at sight.

When appropriate, Special Optics has employed an export management company to raise the necessary documentation to present under the documentary credit.

The managing director of Special Optics, Mr I Glass, is looking for a significant increase in exports.

Question

Following a trade promotion activity, Special Optics Ltd has achieved an early breakthrough in France. It has identified a distributor in Paris through whom it could export, rather than exporting direct to a number of buyers throughout France.

In view of the extent of the potential market, it will be necessary for Mr Glass to make regular visits to Paris, staying overnight.

It has been suggested that Special Optics should operate a collection account with a French bank in Paris to which export proceeds could be paid.

REQUIRED:

(a) What would be the main advantages and disadvantages to Special Optics of employing a distributor rather than exporting direct to buyers?   *[8]*

(b) Describe specific travel services offered by UK banks that would assist Mr Glass during his trips to Paris.   *[6]*

List and explain the advantages and disadvantages if Special Optics opens a collection account as suggested.   *[6]*

[Total marks for question - 20]

(question 8, Spring 1993)

5.4   *Scenario*

TELECOM EXPORTS LTD: see page 21

Question

Telecom Exports has been active in its existing markets for a number of years. However, as yet, it has not been successful in breaking into Eastern Europe.

Telecom Exports is shortly to launch a new product and its parent company wants to use this as a springboard to develop new markets.

Mrs Daws is to conduct desk research before the Group devises a market strategy. She is to see an export adviser from the DTI (Dept of Trade and Industry) shortly and asks for your help in drawing up a list of questions to ask and points to raise.

REQUIRED:

(a) Name and describe appropriate trade promotion services offered by the DTI that Mrs Daws should be considering.   *[10]*

(b) In view of the Group's inexperience in Eastern Europe, briefly explain in what ways they might develop new business in this market area.   *[10]*

[Total marks for question - 20]

(question 7, Autumn 1993)

Lesson Six
Incoterms; Commercial and Financial Documents

This lesson is concerned with *Incoterms* – an internationally accepted set of terms for trade transactions – and with the types of commercial and financial documents in use.

❏ Incoterms

The International Chamber of Commerce publishes an internationally accepted standardised set of terms, called *Incoterms*, for trade transactions. These detail the responsibilities of all parties to a transaction and are uniformly interpreted by courts in exactly the same way throughout the world.

In order to be bound by a particular Incoterm, buyers and sellers should incorporate words in the commercial contract such as 'subject to Incoterms 1990', and then specify the relevant term. (1990 was the date of the latest revision of the terms.) Sellers should also refer to the relevant Incoterm in price lists, quotations and invoices.

There are four groups of terms, known as Group E, F, C and D:

Group E
The seller makes the goods available to the buyer at the seller's own premises:

EXW   Ex Works

Group F
The seller delivers the goods to a carrier appointed by the buyer:

FCA   Free Carrier
FAS   Free Alongside Ship
FOB   Free on Board

Group C
The seller has to contract and pay for carriage, but is not responsible for loss or damage to the goods after shipment and despatch:

CFR   Cost and Freight
CIF   Cost, Insurance and Freight
CPT   Carriage Paid To
CIP   Carriage and Insurance Paid To

Group D
The seller has to bear all costs and risks needed to bring the goods to the country of destination:

DAF   Delivered At Frontier
DES   Delivered Ex Ship
DEQ   Delivered Ex Quay
DDU   Delivered Duty Unpaid

Summary of Incoterms

(handwritten margin notes: Exporter / Importer)

INCOTERM	MODE OF TRANSPORT	MAIN RESPONSIBILITIES OF SELLER	MAIN RESPONSIBILITIES OF BUYER
EXW (Ex Works ... named place)	Any	• Make the goods available at his/her premises (ie works, factory, warehouse, etc) to the buyer. • Goods appropriately packed for the mode of transport arranged by the buyer. • Provide the buyer with an invoice, or equivalent electronic† message.	• Take delivery of the goods at the seller's premises. • Bear all costs and risks from the seller's premises (it is advisable for the buyer to insure the goods from the seller's premises).

Note: EXW represents the minimum obligation for the seller. If the seller arranges export formalities, then the FCA term (see below) should be used.

INCOTERM	MODE OF TRANSPORT	MAIN RESPONSIBILITIES OF SELLER	MAIN RESPONSIBILITIES OF BUYER
FCA (Free Carrier ... named place)	Any	• Deliver the goods to the carrier named by the buyer at the named place or point. • The goods must be cleared for export (if appropriate), ie any export licence must be obtained and export customs formalities must be completed. • Pay the costs of customs formalities, together with export duties and taxes. • Provide the buyer with an invoice, or equivalent electronic message. • Provide the buyer with proof of delivery to the carrier (eg dock receipt), or transport document (eg bill of lading or waybill), or equivalent electronic† message.	• Give the seller notice of the name of the carrier. • Accept delivery of the goods at the named point. • Arrange and pay for contract of carriage from the named place. • Bear all risks of loss of or damage to the goods from the time they have been delivered to the carrier (it is advisable for the buyer to insure the goods from the named point). • Obtain any import licence and pay duties and taxes.

† *Incoterms 1990 makes provision for documentation to be replaced by Electronic Data Interchange (EDI) messages.*

INCOTERM	MODE OF TRANSPORT	MAIN RESPONSIBILITIES OF SELLER	MAIN RESPONSIBILITIES OF BUYER
FAS (Free Alongside Ship ... named port of shipment)	Sea or inland waterway	• Deliver the goods alongside the vessel at the named port of shipment (named by the buyer). • Provide the buyer with an invoice, or equivalent electronic message. • Provide the buyer with proof of delivery (eg dock receipt), transport document (eg bill of lading or waybill), or equivalent electronic message. • Give notice of delivery to the buyer.	• Arrange and pay for contract of carriage from the named port of shipment. • Arrange and pay insurance charges from port of shipment. • Give notice to the seller of the vessel name, loading place and required delivery time. • Obtain any export and import licences and pay duties and taxes. • Accept delivery of goods at named port of shipment. • Bear all risks of loss of or damage to the goods from the time they have been delivered alongside the ship at the named port of shipment.

Note: When the buyer is not able to carry out export formalities, FCA or FOB (see below) terms should be used.

INCOTERM	MODE OF TRANSPORT	MAIN RESPONSIBILITIES OF SELLER	MAIN RESPONSIBILITIES OF BUYER
FOB (Free On Board ... named port of shipment)	Sea or inland waterway	• Deliver the goods on board the vessel at the named port of shipment (the seller's obligations to deliver cease when the goods pass over the ship's rail). • Pay port loading costs (if not included in carriage charge). • Obtain any export licence and carry out necessary export customs formalities. Pay costs of customs formalities, duties and taxes. • Provide the buyer with an invoice, or equivalent electronic message. • Provide the buyer with proof of delivery. • Give notice of delivery to the buyer.	• Arrange and pay for contract of carriage from the named port of shipment. • Arrange and pay insurance charges from port of shipment. • Give notice to the seller of the vessel name, loading place and required delivery time. • Bear all risks of loss of or damage to the goods once they have passed over the ship's rail at the named port of shipment. • Obtain any import licence and pay duties and taxes.

Note: This term is similar to FCA except that:
— with FCA the seller's obligations are completed when the goods are delivered to the carrier at a named place, eg seller's premises, carrier's premises, railway terminal, container yard, etc.
— with FOB the seller's obligations are completed when the goods pass over the ship's rail at the named port of shipment.

For roll-on/roll-off or container traffic, where the ship's rail serves no practical purpose, it is more appropriate to use the FCA term.

INCOTERM	MODE OF TRANSPORT	MAIN RESPONSIBILITIES OF SELLER	MAIN RESPONSIBILITIES OF BUYER
CFR (Cost and Freight ... named port of destination)	Sea or inland waterway	• Arrange and pay for contract of carriage to the named port of destination. • Deliver the goods on board the vessel at the port of shipment. • Obtain any export licence and carry out necessary export customs formalities. Pay costs of customs formalities, duties and taxes. • Pay loading costs, and unloading costs to the extent that they are included in the carriage charge. • Provide the buyer with an appropriate transport document (eg bill of lading or waybill) for the port of destination.	• Arrange and pay insurance charges from port of shipment. • Accept delivery of the goods at the named port of destination. • Bear all risks of loss of or damage to the goods once they have passed over the ship's rail at the named port of shipment. • Pay unloading costs (if not included in carriage charge). • Obtain any import licence and pay duties and taxes.

Note: For roll-on/roll-off or container traffic, where the ship's rail serves no practical purpose, it is more appropriate to use the CPT term (see later).

INCOTERM	MODE OF TRANSPORT	MAIN RESPONSIBILITIES OF SELLER	MAIN RESPONSIBILITIES OF BUYER
CIF (Cost, Insurance and Freight ... named port of destination)	Sea or inland waterway	• Arrange and pay for contract of carriage to the named port of destination. • Deliver the goods on board the vessel at the port of shipment. • Obtain any export licence and carry out necessary export customs formalities. Pay costs of customs formalities, duties and taxes. • Arrange and pay insurance charges during the carriage. • Pay loading costs, and unloading costs to the extent that they are included in the carriage charge. • Provide the buyer with an appropriate transport document for the port of destination. • Provide the buyer with an invoice, or equivalent electronic message. • Provide the buyer with the insurance policy or other evidence of insurance cover.	• Accept delivery at the named port of destination. • Bear all risks of loss of or damage to the goods once they have passed over the ship's rail at the named port of shipment (insurance cover is arranged by the seller, but the buyer makes any claim). • Pay unloading costs (if not included in carriage charge). • Obtain any import licence and pay duties and taxes.

Note: For roll-on/roll-off or container traffic, where the ship's rail serves no practical purpose, it is more appropriate to use the CIP term (see later).

INCOTERM	MODE OF TRANSPORT	MAIN RESPONSIBILITIES OF SELLER	MAIN RESPONSIBILITIES OF BUYER
CPT (Carriage Paid To ... named place of destination)	Any	• Arrange and pay for contract of carriage to the named place of destination. • Deliver the goods to the carrier (or first carrier, if more than one is to be used for the journey). • Obtain any export licence and carry out necessary export customs formalities. Pay costs of customs formalities, duties and taxes. • Provide the buyer with an invoice, or equivalent electronic message. • Provide the buyer with an appropriate transport document.	• Arrange and pay insurance charges from delivery of the goods to the carrier (or first carrier). • Accept delivery of the goods at the named place of destination. • Bear all risks of loss of or damage to the goods once they have been delivered to the carrier (or first carrier). • Obtain any import licence and pay duties and taxes.

Note: The CPT term is similar to CFR, but it covers all modes of transport.

INCOTERM	MODE OF TRANSPORT	MAIN RESPONSIBILITIES OF SELLER	MAIN RESPONSIBILITIES OF BUYER
CIP (Carriage and Insurance Paid to ... named place of destination)	Any	• Arrange and pay for contract of carriage to the named place of destination. • Deliver the goods to the carrier (or first carrier, if more than one is to be used for the journey). • Obtain any export licence and carry out necessary export customs formalities. Pay costs of customs formalities, duties and taxes. • Arrange and pay insurance charges during the carriage. • Provide the buyer with an invoice, or equivalent electronic message. • Provide the buyer with an appropriate transport document. • Provide the buyer with the insurance policy or other evidence of insurance cover.	• Accept delivery at the named place of destination. • Bear all risks of loss of or damage to the goods from the time they have been delivered to the carrier (or first carrier) – insurance cover is arranged by the seller, but the buyer makes any claim. • Obtain any import licence and pay duties and taxes.

Note: The CIP term is similar to CIF, but it covers all modes of transport.

INCOTERM	MODE OF TRANSPORT	MAIN RESPONSIBILITIES OF SELLER	MAIN RESPONSIBILITIES OF BUYER
DAF (Delivered At Frontier ... named place)	Any, but primarily for use by rail or road	• Arrange and pay for contract of carriage to the named place. • Obtain any export licence and carry out necessary export customs formalities. Pay costs of customs formalities, duties and taxes. • Provide the buyer with an invoice, or equivalent electronic message. • Provide the buyer with an appropriate transport document or other evidence of delivery at the named place at the frontier. • At the buyer's request and expense, provide a through document of transport from a point of dispatch to final destination. • Bear all risks of loss of or damage to the goods until they have been delivered at the named place at the frontier.	• Take delivery of the goods at the named place at the frontier. (The buyer pays for any further carriage.) • Bear all risks of loss of or damage to the goods from the time they have been delivered at the named place at the frontier. • Obtain any import licence and pay duties and taxes.

Note: The seller's obligations are fulfilled when the goods are made available at the named frontier, but before the customs border of the adjoining country. The frontier named could be the country of export, so it is vital that the frontier point and place is named in the term.

INCOTERM	MODE OF TRANSPORT	MAIN RESPONSIBILITIES OF SELLER	MAIN RESPONSIBILITIES OF BUYER
DES (Delivered Ex Ship ... named port of destination)	Sea or inland waterway	• Deliver the goods on board the vessel at the named port of destination. • Arrange and pay for contract of carriage to the named port of destination. • Obtain any export licence and carry out necessary export customs formalities. Pay costs of customs formalities, duties and taxes. • Bear all risks of loss of or damage to the goods until they have been delivered on board the vessel at the named port of destination. • Provide the buyer with an invoice or equivalent electronic message. • Provide the buyer with a delivery order or transport document to enable the buyer to take delivery of the goods.	• Take delivery of the goods from on board the ship at the named port of destination. • Bear all risks of loss of or damage to the goods from the named port of destination. • Pay unloading costs at the port of destination. • Obtain any import licence and pay duties and taxes.

Note: In theory there is no need for the seller to insure the goods on their voyage, although it would be unwise not to do so. The seller is responsible for all risks until delivery at the named port of destination.

INCOTERM	MODE OF TRANSPORT	MAIN RESPONSIBILITIES OF SELLER	MAIN RESPONSIBILITIES OF BUYER
DEQ (Delivered Ex Quay, duty paid, ... named port of destination)	Sea or inland waterway	• Deliver the goods on the quay or wharf at the named port of destination. • Obtain any export and import licences and carry out necessary export and import customs formalities. Pay costs of customs formalities, duties and taxes. • Bear all the risks of loss of or damage to the goods until they have been delivered to the quay at the named port of destination. • Arrange and pay for contract of carriage to the named port of destination. • Pay unloading costs at the port of destination. • Provide the buyer with an invoice, or equivalent electronic message. • Provide the buyer with a delivery order or transport document to enable the buyer to take the goods and remove them from the quay.	• Take delivery of the goods from the named port of destination. • Render every assistance to the seller in obtaining any import licence or other official import authorisation. • Bear all risks of loss of or damage to the goods from the time they are placed at his/her disposal on the quay at the named port of destination.

Notes: • *This term should not be used if the seller cannot obtain the import licence.*
• *In theory there is no need for the seller to insure the goods on their voyage, although it would be unwise not to do so.*
• *The term can be amended to exclude various taxes, eg 'DEQ duty unpaid', 'DEQ VAT unpaid'.*

INCOTERM	MODE OF TRANSPORT	MAIN RESPONSIBILITIES OF SELLER	MAIN RESPONSIBILITIES OF BUYER
DDU (Delivered Duty Unpaid ... named place of destination)	Any	• Deliver the goods at the named place in the country of importation. • Bear all the costs and risks of loss of or damage to the goods in bringing the goods to the named place of destination, except for import duties, taxes, or other charges (the seller is not responsible for import licences, customs formalities, duties and taxes). • Provide the buyer with an invoice or equivalent electronic message. • Provide the buyer with a delivery order or transport document to enable the buyer to take delivery of the goods.	• Take delivery of the goods at the named place of destination. • Obtain any import licence and carry out necessary import customs formalities. Pay costs of import customs formalities, duties and taxes. • Bear all risks from the time the goods have been delivered at the named place of destination.

Note: The term can be amended to include some of the import costs, eg 'DDU, VAT paid'.

Exporter

Importer

INCOTERM	MODE OF TRANSPORT	MAIN RESPONSIBILITIES OF SELLER	MAIN RESPONSIBILITIES OF BUYER
DDP (Delivered Duty Paid ... named place of destination)	Any	• Deliver the goods at the named place in the country of importation. • Bear all the costs and risks of loss of or damage to the goods in bringing the goods to the named place of destination (including import licence, customs formalities, duties and taxes). • Provide the buyer with an invoice, or equivalent electronic message. • Provide the buyer with a delivery order or transport document to enable the buyer to take delivery of the goods.	• Take delivery of the goods from the named place of destination. • Bear all risks from the time the goods have been delivered at the named place of destination.

Notes:
• DDP represents the maximum obligation of the seller.
• The seller is responsible for all costs involved in delivering the goods to the named place of destination.
• The term can be amended to exclude some of the seller's obligations, eg 'DDP, VAT unpaid'.

Notes:

- It is important with trade terms to state the named place or port to which the term applies. Thus a UK importer should specify terms such as 'CIF Southampton' rather than 'CIF UK port': with the latter, the exporter has complied with the terms when the goods are on board a vessel bound for any UK port.

- Incoterms permits the use of the electronic transmission of documents by means of Electronic Data Interchange (EDI). The use of EDI needs the agreement of seller and buyer to communicate electronically in this way.

- The word 'Incoterms' must be included for Incoterms 1990 to apply: for example, 'Incoterm CIF' is an Incoterm; 'CIF' is a trade term.

❏ Documents of International Trade

Documents are important in international trade because they control the movement of goods; in some cases they are the legal title to the goods. It is important that the correct documents should be in the right place at the right time and, in order to speed delivery of the goods and subsequent payment, that they should all be correctly completed. A seemingly minor descrepancy in documentation will almost certainly lead to a delay in the exporter receiving his payment.

Efforts have been, and are currently being made to introduce, on a national and an international level, a method of standardising and simplifying export documentation and procedures. In the UK the Simpler Trade Procedures Board (SITPRO) was set up to 'guide, stimulate and assist the rationalisation of international trade procedures and the documentation and information flows associated with them'. SITPRO is independent of government but is funded by the BOTB through an annual grant.

SITPRO is probably best known for the UK's aligned series of export documents. The documents are produced by typing all the common information on a 'master document' (see fig. 6.1) and then only the relevant information is transferred, using overlays and masks, thus eliminating much repetitive typing and checking. The required documents can also be produced by means of 'exportsets' - self-carbonated paper formsets which contain the documents; by typing once, the various documents will be completed. Another method of producing the documents is to use a computer software program developed by SITPRO and called 'SPEX': this prints the documents to a laser or bubble jet printer, and can also be used to prepare collection orders (see Lesson 9).

A recent development is the electronic transmission of documents by means of Electronic Data Interchange (EDI). EDI gives quicker, cheaper and more secure communication than with paper forms. This technique replaces paper documents with standard electronic messages. The development of EDI is recognised by Incoterms 1990 which allows for documents to be substituted by electronic messages.

❏ Commercial documents and financial documents

In international trade a distinctions is made between *commercial documents* and *financial documents*.

Commercial documents deal with the goods being exported rather than the means of payment. The three main commercial documents for any international trade transaction are:

- invoice
- transport document, e.g. bill of lading, or air waybill
- insurance certificate or policy.

There are many other commercial documents, including a certificate of origin, an inspection certificate.

Financial documents are the means of obtaining payment and include bills of exchange, promissory notes, cheques, etc.

We will now describe the information to be found on the more important documents of international trade and list the documents that are required when a contract specifies one of the more common trade terms mentioned previously.

● SITPRO 1992

MASTER DOCUMENT

Exporter VAT no. 237 4581 12	**Invoice no.** 1234		**Customs reference/status**
Rowcester Engineering Co Ltd	**Invoice date** 1 Aug. 19-1	**Carrier's bkg. no.**	**Exporter's reference** 1234/1
Deansway House			
ROWCESTER			
RW1 5TQ	**Buyer's reference** Contract 7541		**Forwarders reference**
United Kingdom			

U N I C

Consignee VAT no.	**Buyer** VAT no.
TO ORDER	Far Eastern Traders (HK) Ltd
Far Eastern Traders (HK) Ltd	Hong Kong
KOWLOON	
Hong Kong	

Freight forwarder VAT no.	**Country of despatch** GB	**Carrier** International Shipping	**Country of destination code** HK
	Country of origin EU - United Kingdom	**Country of final destination** Hong Kong	

Other UK transport details	**Terms of delivery and payment** CIF Hong Kong
	Payment at sight against presentation of documents through British International Bank

Vessel/flight no. and date SEAFARER II	**Port/airport of loading** Southampton		
Port/airport of discharge Hong Kong	**Place of delivery** Hong Kong	**Insured value** GBP £11,000	**EUR 1 or C.of O remarks**

Shipping marks: container number	Number and kind of packages: description of goods *	Item No.	Commodity code 85.01		
Far Eastern	One case containing:		**Quantity 2**	**Gross weight (Kg)** 900	**Cube (m3)** 1.5m^3
Hong Kong	One Rowcester Moulding		**Procedure**	**Net weight (kg)** 850	**Value (£)**
1234/No.1	Machine, Mk 2. Serial No. 12345				
			Summary declaration/previous document		

* DANGEROUS GOODS: Refer to IMDG, ADR, IATA, CIM and UK regulations as appropriate and specify: proper shipping name, hazard class, UN no., flashpoint deg C.

LIMIT OF SAD BOX31 ►

			Commodity code		
			Quantity 2	**Gross weight (Kg)**	**Cube (m3)**
			Procedure	**Net weight (kg)**	**Value (£)**
			Summary declaration/previous document		

			Commodity code		
			Quantity 2	**Gross weight (Kg)**	**Cube (m3)**
			Procedure	**Net weight (kg)**	**Value (£)**
			Summary declaration/previous document		

Identification of warehouse	FREE DISPOSAL	**Invoice total (state currency)** GBP £10,000.00	
		Total gross wt (kg) 900	**Total cube (m3)** 1.5m^3

Freight payable at Southampton	**Signatory's company and telephone number** Rowcester Engineering 0905 8081
Number of bills of lading 3 Original 4 Copy	**Name of signatory** J. B. LONG. Export clerk
	Place and date ROWCESTER 1 Aug. 19-1
	Signature J.B.Long

Fig. 6.1: SITPRO Master Document

❏ Invoices

There are several different types of invoice, the main ones being a *pro-forma invoice,* a *commercial invoice* and a *consular invoice.*

Pro-forma invoice

This is a type of quotation given by a seller to a potential buyer. It takes the form of a commercial invoice (see below), but the words 'pro-forma' are clearly stated as an invitation for the buyer to place a definite order. A pro-forma invoice is often required so that the potential buyer can obtain an import licence into his country, or the necessary permission to make payment of foreign exchange out of his country. Pro-forma invoices are also used where payment in advance is required by an exporter. When a definite order is placed, or payment is made, a commercial invoice will be prepared with exactly the same details.

Commercial invoice (see Fig. 6.2)

This is prepared by the seller of the goods and contains the following details:

- name and address of the seller
- name and address of the buyer
- date of the invoice
- a description of the goods together with the price
- details of the way in which the goods are packed - for instance whether they are in cases, crates or drums - and shipping or other marks stamped or written on the packing
- the terms of sale (CIF, CFR, FOB and so forth); the charges for insurance and freight, if applicable, will also be detailed on the invoice
- if applicable, details of import/export licences
- the total amount payable
- exporter's signature

The details of the invoice should link up with the contract of sale and, if a documentary letter of credit has been opened, the invoice should correspond strictly with its terms. Several copies of the seller's commercial invoice are normally required for the use of the buyer, customs and the importation authorities abroad.

Consular invoice

Some importing countries require a consular invoice - which is a specially printed invoice issued in the exporter's country by the consulate of the importing country. This invoice confirms the details of the shipment and may be used by a country in an attempt to prevent 'dumping' of foreign-made goods at low prices; it may also form the basis of the calculation of import duty.

Another type of invoice is a *legalised invoice* which is required by some countries - particularly those in the Middle East. Here the commercial invoice must be legalised by the country's embassy or consulate in the seller's country, for which a fee may be charged, before the goods will be allowed into the country.

❏ Bills of lading (see Fig. 6.3)

Where goods are transported by ship, the marine bill of lading is one of the most important documents. Depending on the terms of the contract, either the exporter or the overseas importer will arrange with a shipping company for the carriage of the goods. The bill of lading is issued by the shipping company as a receipt for the goods and forms the evidence of a contract of carriage. It is especially important because signed copies of the bill of lading are 'negotiable' and are the document of title to the goods,

Seller (name, address, VAT reg. no.)   237 4581 12

Rowcester Engineering Co Ltd
Deansway House
ROWCESTER   RW1 5TQ
United Kingdom

INVOICE RECHNUNG FACTURE FACTURA ناتــــورة

U N I C

Invoice number	
1234	
Invoice date (tax point)	Seller's reference
1 Aug. 19-1	1234/1
Buyer's reference	Other reference
Contract 7541	

© SITPRO
1992

Consignee VAT no	Buyer (if not consignee) VAT no
TO ORDER Far Eastern Traders (HK) Ltd KOWLOON Hong Kong	Far Eastern Traders (HK) Ltd Hong Kong

Country of origin of goods	Country of destination
EU - United Kingdom	Hong Kong

Terms of delivery and payment

CIF Hong Kong

Payment at sight against presentation of
documents through British International Bank

Vessel/flight no. and date	Port/airport of loading
SEAFARER II	Southampton
Port/airport of discharge	Place of delivery
Hong Kong	Hong Kong

Shipping marks: container number	No. and kind of packages: description of goods	Commodity code	Total gross wt (Kg)	Total cube (m3)
Far Eastern Hong Kong 1234/No.1	One case containing: One Rowcester Moulding Machine, Mk 2. Serial No. 12345	85.01	900	1.5m^3
			Total net wt(Kg) 850	

Item/packages	Gross/net/cube	Description	Quantity	Unit price	Amount
1 case	900/850/1.5	Rowcester Moulding Machine Mk 2. Serial No. 12345	1	–	10,000

Invoice total
GBP £10,000.00

Name of signatory
J. B. LONG, Export Clerk

Place and date of issue
ROWCESTER   1 Aug. 19-1

Signature
J. B. Long

It is hereby certified that this invoice shows the actual price of the goods described, that
no other invoice has been or will be issued, and that all particulars are true and correct.

v5

Fig. 6.2: A commercial invoice

subject to the payment of any freight charges due. However, although bills of lading are often described as 'negotiable', and can be endorsed to transfer goods from one person to another, they do not have the same attributes as a negotiable instrument, such as a cheque or a bill of exchange. A bill of lading is *quasi-negotiable,* and is more akin to a cheque which is crossed 'not negotiable', in that the endorsee does not obtain a better title than that of the endorser. Thus, as a bill of lading is not a fully negotiable instrument, it follows that if a person who transfers it has no title or a defective title to the goods, the person to whom it is transferred obtains no better title than that of the transferor.

The following details are normally to be found on a bill of lading:

- name of the shipping company
- name of the shipper (usually the exporter)
- name of the consignee, or order (see below)
- name of the notify party (i.e. the person to be notified on arrival of the shipment, usually the buyer)
- name of the carrying vessel
- port of loading and discharge
- description of the goods, together with identification marks and numbers
- whether the freight charge has been paid or is payable at destination
- date the goods were received for shipment and if they have been loaded on board the carrying vessel
- terms of the contract of carriage
- number of signed (or original) bills of lading
- signature of the ship's master or his agent

Bills of lading are usually consigned to order - this enables the exporter, by endorsement, to transfer ownership of the goods. They are issued in sets, several copies of which may be signed by the ship's master or his agent: as each one is quasi-negotiable, any one of these original bills gives title to the goods. It is therefore important for a bank handling bills of lading to ensure that it is in possession of a full set. A bill of lading may be either *received for shipment* or *on board* (sometimes known as *shipped*). The former merely confirm that the shipping company has the goods in its custody, but they have not yet been placed on board the carrying vessel. An on board bill of lading indicates that the goods have been loaded. A received for shipment bill may be converted into an on board bill by a suitable annotation of the shipping company. Bills of lading are normally *clean* in that they do not bear any clause declaring a defective condition of the goods or packaging; a *claused* bill may say, for example, 'drums leading' or 'cases damaged'.

There are several types of bills of lading, notably short form bills, liner bills, charter party bills and container bills.

Short form bill of lading

This does not contain full details of the contract of carriage. Instead it uses a standard clause to incorporate the conditions of carriage, and generally refers to a 'master document' which details all the clauses of the contract. Thus the complex 'small print' is removed from the reverse of the document.

Through bill of lading or Combined Transport bill of lading

This is issued where the journey will involve two or more carriers, using different forms of transport, for the goods to reach their final destination. The issuer of the bill accepts liability for the whole journey. Such a bill covers the complete journey. It will usually show a port of loading and discharge, and will also indicate the place at which the goods were taken in charge, and where they will be delivered - normally an inland port. A *transhipment bill* will be used where goods have to be transhipped from one vessel to another at a named transhipment port.

Liner bill

As the name suggests, this is issued for ships operating to a strict timetable with a berth reserved at the port of destination. From the exporter's point of view this means that his goods should arrive in the buyer's country by a set date, rather than relying on a slower ship which may call at a variety of ports on route to the final destination.

Bill of Lading for Combined Transport shipment or Port to Port shipment

Shipper		
Rowcester Engineering Co Ltd Deansway House ROWCESTER RW1 5TQ United Kingdom	B/L No. 123456 Booking Ref.: Shipper's Ref.:	

Consigned to the order of
Far Eastern Traders (HK) Ltd
KOWLOON
Hong Kong

International Shipping

**The Docks
Southampton**

Notify Party/Address (It is agreed that no responsibility shall attach to the Carrier or his Agents for failure to notify of the arrival of the goods (see clause 20 on reverse))

Far Eastern Traders (HK) Ltd
Hong Kong

Place of Receipt (Applicable only when this document is used as a Combined Transport Bill of Lading)

Vessel and Voy. No.

Place of Delivery (Applicable only when this document is used as a Combined Transport Bill of Lading)

SEAFARER II

Port of Loading
Southampton

Port of Discharge
Hong Kong

Marks and Nos; Container Nos;	Number and kind of Packages; description of Goods	Gross Weight (kg)	Measurement (cbm)
Far Eastern Hong Kong 1234/No.1	One case containing: One Rowcester Moulding Machine, Mk 2. Serial No. 12345	900	$1.5m^3$

On board
date 2 Aug. 19-1
pp International Shipping
A. Short
authorised signatory

Freight paid
date 2 Aug. 19-1
pp International Shipping
A. Short
authorised signatory

Above particulars as declared by Shipper, but not acknowledged by the Carrier (see clause 11)

*Total No. of Containers/Packages received by the Carrier

Movement

Freight and Charges (indicate whether prepaid or collect):

Origin Inland Haulage Charge	prepaid
Origin Terminal Handling/LCL Service Charge ...	prepaid
Ocean Freight	prepaid
Destination Terminal Handling/LCL Service Charge ...	prepaid
Destination Inland Haulage Charge	collect

ICS
CT B/L
April 78

Received by the Carrier from the Shipper in apparent good order and condition (unless otherwise noted herein) the total number or quantity of Containers or other packages or units indicated in the box opposite entitled "*Total No. of Containers/Packages received by the Carrier" for Carriage subject to all the terms and conditions hereof (INCLUDING THE TERMS AND CONDITIONS ON THE REVERSE HEREOF AND THE TERMS AND CONDITIONS OF THE CARRIER'S APPLICABLE TARIFF) from the Place of Receipt or the Port of Loading, whichever is applicable, to the Port of Discharge or the Place of Delivery, whichever is applicable. Before the Carrier arranges delivery of the Goods one original Bill of Lading, duly endorsed, must be surrendered by the Merchant to the Carrier at the Port of Discharge or at some other location acceptable to the Carrier. In accepting this Bill of Lading the Merchant expressly accepts and agrees to all its terms and conditions whether printed, stamped or written, or otherwise incorporated, notwithstanding the non-signing of this Bill of Lading by the Merchant.

Place and Date of Issue
Southampton   1 Aug. 19-1

Number of Original Bills of Lading
Three (3)

IN WITNESS of the contract herein contained the number of originals stated opposite has been issued, one of which being accomplished the other(s) to be void.

For the Carrier:

James Orelin

As Agent(s) only.

P&OCL B/L1 10/91

024687

Fig. 6.3: A bill of lading

Charter-party bill

This is issued when a vessel is chartered by a hirer and there is surplus space available for extra cargo. An exporter using this 'spare' space to ship his goods makes a contract of carriage with the hirer of the vessel, and not with the ship owner. Therefore such a contract is subject to the terms of the contract of hire. Bills of lading issued for his goods will state 'subject to charter party'. Such bills of lading will normally be rejected by banks handling documentary credits in accordance with the terms of 'Uniform Customs and Practice for Documentary Credits' (see lesson 7).

Container bill of lading

The widespread use of containers in international trade means that shipping companies issue bills of lading which simply describe the goods as a container. These could cause problems because the goods are invariably not described on the bill of lading; however, such bills are generally accepted by banks handling documentary credits. Container bills of lading may be issued to cover goods from port-to-port or from an inland point of departure to an inland point of destination. Included in the context of containers are palletised cargoes, and those contained on 'LASH' barges which are loaded onto larger vessels without disturbing the cargo.

The traditional negotiable marine bill of lading has several advantages. Of particular note is the fact that it is a quasi-negotiable document of title and, until it has been endorsed in favour of the buyer, and is in his hands, the goods cannot normally be removed from the port of discharge. Thus it is useful as a controlling document, particularly where documents are not released to the buyer by the banking system until the goods have been paid for.

Points for consideration by a bank

When a bank handles a bill of lading, it will need to consider various points:

- Is the type of bill of lading acceptable for the purposes of the bank?

- Does the bank hold the full set of signed (i.e. negotiable) bills of lading?

- Are any alterations confirmed by the shipping company or its agents?

- If it is issued to 'order', is it endorsed in blank by the shipper?

- Does the payment of freight link up with the terms of the contract, i.e. if a CIF contract, the bill of lading will be marked 'freight paid'.

- Do the goods described on the bill of lading link in with the other documentation?

- Is it a 'clean' bill of lading?

- If the bank is involved with a documentary credit, is the bill of lading dated not later than the latest shipment date specified in the credit?

- Are the goods loaded 'on board' the named vessel or does the bill of lading state 'received for shipment'?

- Are the goods loaded on deck?

Sea Waybill

A disadvantage of the bill of lading is that it often has to pass through many hands from the time it is handed to the exporter as a receipt for the goods, to the time the buyer presents it at the port of destination in order to collect the goods. Delays may set in and, if the goods arrive at the destination before the bill is received by the buyer, they will have to be stored, causing extra costs and additional risks to be incurred. The increasing use of short-sea journeys and open account trading has led to decreasing use of this traditional bill of lading; in its place has been developed a non-negotiable transport document - a *waybill*. This provides for delivery of the goods to a named consignee without production of the transport document.

In the UK, SITPRO has assisted the Chamber of Shipping in developing a *non-negotiable standard sea waybill* for exports. It has the following features:

- as a waybill, it is non-negotiable and the goods will be delivered to the named consignee without production of the document

- it is in a common form and therefore is not pre-printed with the name of the shipping company, but can be used by any carrier after completion of the appropriate details

- it is in a short form, i.e. does not give full details of the conditions of carriage, but uses a standard clause referring to the conditions of carriage of the carrier who has issued it

❏ Insurance documents (see Fig. 6.4)

Goods for export should always be covered by adequate insurance from the time they leave the factory to the time the buyer takes delivery. The terms of the contract between buyer and seller will establish who is responsible for arranging and paying for insurance at the different stages of transportation. The insurance documents will contain the following details:

- name of the insurer

- name of the insured

- where applicable, the endorsement of the insured so that the right to claim under the policy may be transferred (for instance, the exporter might take out a policy but it could be the importer who makes any claim)

- a description of the risks covered and the sum insured

- a description of the goods

- the place where claims are payable

The insurance documents consist of either the insurance policy itself or, more likely, a certificate of insurance. Regular exporters will take out an overall (open cover or floating) marine policy - commonly a Lloyd's MAR (Marine) Policy, plus a number of Institute Cargo Clauses (ICC) - and will issue certificates of insurance to cover an individual shipment. The insurance certificate contains the same details as the policy, except that there is an abbreviated version of the provisions of the policy.

The risks covered by the insurance should agree with those called for by the buyer in the contract. When a documentary credit has been opened (see lesson four) the insurance documents must be as detailed in the credit and unless otherwise specified, should show that cover is effective from the date of shipment or despatch. The insurance documents must be expressed in the same currency as the credit and the minimum amount for which insurance must be effected is the CIF value of the goods plus ten per cent. The risks covered should be as stated in the credit.

Exporter	**CERTIFICATE OF INSURANCE**	

Exporter Rowcester Engineering Co Ltd Deansway House Rowcester RW1 5TQ United Kingdom	Ins. Cert. No. 113417	Exporters Ref: 1234/1
	Code No. 66/KK/ 10234	Agents Ref:

This is to certify that

Rowcester Engineering Co Ltd

have been issued with an Open Policy and this certificate conveys all rights of the policy (for the purpose of collecting any loss or claim) as fully as if the property were covered by a special policy direct to the holder of this certificate but if the destination of the goods is outside of the United Kingdom this certificate may require to be stamped within a given period in order to comply with the laws of the country of destination. Notwithstanding the description of the voyage stated herein, provided the goods are at the risk of the Assured this insurance shall attach from the time of leaving the warehouse, premises or place of storage in the interior.

Norwich Union Fire Insurance Society Ltd.

Maritime Insurance Company Ltd. ✓

NORWICH HOUSE, WATER STREET,
LIVERPOOL L2 8UP.

Vessel SEAFARER II	Port of Loading Southampton	Insured Value (State Currency)
Port of Discharge Hong Kong	Final Destination Hong Kong	GBP £11 000 so valued

Marks, Nos. / Container No.	No. and Kind of Packages	Description of Goods
Far Eastern Hong Kong 1234/No.1	One case containing: One Rowcester Moulding Machine, Mk 2. Serial No.12345	

SPECIMEN

PROCEDURE IN THE EVENT OF LOSS OR DAMAGE FOR WHICH UNDERWRITERS MAY BE LIABLE

LIABILITY OF CARRIERS, BAILEES OR OTHER THIRD PARTIES

It is the duty of the Assured and their Agents, in all cases, to take such measures as may be reasonable for the purpose of averting or minimising a loss and to ensure that all rights against Carriers, Bailees or other third parties are properly preserved and exercised. In particular, the Assured or their Agents are required —

1. To claim immediately on the Carriers, Port Authorities or other Bailees for any missing packages

2. In no circumstances except under written protest, to give clean receipts where goods are in doubtful condition

When delivery is made by Container, to ensure that the Container and its seals are examined immediately by their responsible official

3. If the Container is delivered damaged or with seals broken or missing or with seals other than as stated in the shipping documents, to clause the delivery receipt accordingly and retain all defective or irregular seals for subsequent identification

4. To apply immediately for survey by Carriers' or other Bailees' Representatives if any loss or damage be apparent and claim on the Carriers or other Bailees for any actual loss or damage found at such survey

5. To give notice in writing to the Carriers or other Bailees within three days of delivery if the loss or damage was not apparent at the time of taking delivery

NOTE - The Consignees or their Agents are recommended to make themselves familiar with the Regulations of the port Authorities at the port of discharge

SURVEY AND CLAIM SETTLEMENT

In the event of loss or damage which may involve a claim under this insurance, immediate notice of such loss or damage should be given to and a Survey Report obtained from the Office or Agent nominated herein.

In the event of any claim arising under this insurance, request for settlement should be made to the Office or Agent nominated herein.

DOCUMENTATION OF CLAIMS

To enable claims to be dealt with promptly, the Assured or their Agents are advised to submit all available supporting documents without delay, including when applicable —

1. Original policy or certificate of insurance

2. Original or copy shipping invoices, together with shipping specification and/or weight notes

3. Original Bill of Lading and/or other contract of carriage

4. Survey report or other documentary evidence to show the extent of the loss or damage

5. Landing account and weight notes at final destination

6. Correspondence exchanged with the Carriers and other Parties regarding their liability for the loss or damage

CONDITIONS

Subject to Institute Cargo Clauses (A) as over   Subject to Institute Replacement Clause (as applicable)

Notwithstanding anything to the contrary contained herein this insurance covers War and Strikes Risks in accordance with the Institute War Clauses (Cargo) dated 1.1.82 and Institute Strikes Clauses (Cargo) dated 1.1.82 which are deemed to be attached to and to form part of this certificate.

SURVEY CLAUSE

In the event of loss or damage which may give rise to a claim under this certificate, notice must be given immediately to the undernoted agent/s so that he/they may appoint a Surveyor if he/they so desire.

Agents at ...... HONG KONG ...... are ...... HK Insurance Ltd ......
...... Gloucester Tower, Hong Kong ......

CLAIMS

In the event of a claim arising under this Certificate it is agreed that it shall be settled in accordance with English law and Custom and shall be so settled in

Liverpool or at ...... HONG KONG ......

by ...... as above ......

G. W. Urmson
Liverpool Marine Underwriter

This Certificate is not valid unless Countersigned

For, Rowcester Engineering Co Ltd	
Dated	1 Aug. 19-1
Signed	*J. B. Long* Export Clerk

The original certificate must be produced when claim is made and must be surrendered on payment.

Fig. 6.4: An insurance certificate

There are three main Institute Cargo Clauses, (A), (B) and (C). These give varying degrees of cover against basic cargo risks; the fullest cover is provided by (A), the least by (C). Which of the three is required will depend upon the voyage, destination and the nature of the goods involved.

They all include the 'transit' clause which states that, in general terms, cover begins when the goods leave the premises of the sender and it ends when they reach the premises of consignee. Under certain circumstances the cover will cease, e.g. if the goods take longer than sixty days from leaving the ship to reaching their destination, cover ceases at the end of that time.

To consider each of these clauses in more detail:

Institute Cargo Clauses (A)
This insurance covers 'all risks' of loss or of damage, including:
- marine perils - covering accidental loss or damage cuased by stranding, sinking, collision, heavy weather or sea water
- damage or loss caused in loading, transhipment or discharge
- fire - including smoke damage
- theft (excluding pilferage)

An all risks policy provides cover against total loss, partial loss and contributions to general average (see below).

The following risks are specifically excluded (although cover is often available on payment of an additional premium):
- strikes, riots, terrorism and civil commotions
- war, capture and seizure
- pilferage

Note: In marine insurance the word *'average'* means partial loss or damage; the words *'particular average'* mean a partial loss caused by a peril insured against and which is not a general average loss.

A *general average* loss occurs when property is voluntarily sacrificed or extraordinary expenses are incurred in time of peril to save the rest of the goods on the shipping vessel at that time. Thus general average provides that any losses resulting from such a deliberate act, e.g. hosing down the cargo to put out a fire, should be shared amongst all parties in proportion to their interests. Therefore if, by putting out the fire, some goods were damaged and other destroyed, the owner of undamaged goods must contribute to the loss of others because the deliberate act of damage was carried out in his interests.

Institute Cargo Clauses (B)
This insurance covers total or partial losses or damage accidently caused by marine perils; it also covers general average (see above). However, it does not cover theft, although this could be added to build up the cover.

Institute Cargo Clauses (C)
This covers more limited risks, but does include cover for total losses and general average (see above).

Institute Cargo Clauses (Air)
These insure goods sent by air on an 'all risks' basis.

Points for consideration by a bank
When a bank is handling insurance documents it will need to consider various points:

- Nature of the document: policy, certificate or cover note; is it appropriate for the bank's purpose? If a documentary credit (see lessons 7 and 8) is involved, Article 34 of Uniform Customs and Practice for Documentary Credits says that cover notes issued by brokers will not be accepted, unless specifically authorised by the credit.

- Insurance document should be signed by the insurer.

- Name of the person in whose name it is issued, and if the rights under the policy are assigned to either bank or buyer by endorsement.

- Insured value should be at least the CIF/CIP amount (usually ten per cent over this value).

- Currency of the insurance document - with a documentary credit, unless otherwise specified, Uniform Customs and Practice require it to be expressed in the same currency as the credit.

- Risks covered - they should be as required by the bank or as stated in the letter of credit.

- Insurance document should be effective, at the latest, from the date of shipment or despatch (Uniform Customs and Practice).

- Place where the claims are payable.

- Duration of the insurance - is it appropriate for the transaction?

- Details given on the insurance document should link up with the other shipping documents as regards description of the goods, marks and numbers, voyage, etc.

- Where the bill of lading indicates that the goods are loaded on deck, the insurance document should give cover against the risks of jettison and being washed overboard.

❏ Other documents

Certificate of origin (see Fig. 6.5)
This confirms that the goods come from a particular country. In the UK certain Chambers of Commerce are authorised by the Department of Trade and Industry to make declarations of origin.

Air waybill (see Fig. 6.6)
When goods are sent by air this takes the place of a bill of lading or sea waybill. Like all waybills it is not a document of title to the goods, being an acknowledgement of goods received for despatch. As we have seen earlier, the goods will be delivered to the named consignee without surrender of the document of movement.

Consignment note
An international consignment note, known as a CMR, is used when goods are sent by road. CMR stands for *Contrat de Transport International de Marchandises par Route*. Upon delivery, the consignee signs the note – the driver is thus able to prove that delivery was made. This document is non-negotiable, and is not a document of title.

Rail Consignment note
An RCN is used in the same way as a CMR, except that it is used when goods are sent by rail.

Blacklist certificate
This document is often required by the importer's country. It usually states that:
- the goods or any part of them do not originate from a particular country
- the ship is not scheduled to call at any ports in that particular country and will not be entering their waters during the voyage or, for aircraft, that the plane will not land at an airport in that particular country nor enter its airspace
- none of the parties concerned in the transaction is on a blacklist for the type of goods involved

As can be seen from the above, a blacklist certificate is required for political reasons to ensure that goods being imported to a country do not come from certain countries for reasons of politics, religion, or war.

There is no standard format for a blacklist certificate and it can be issued by the exporter and/or the shipper on ordinary headed notepaper.

1 Consignor	No. 9871234	ORIGINAL
Rowcester Engineering Co Ltd Deansway House ROWCESTER RW1 5TQ United Kingdom		

2 Consignee	**EUROPEAN UNION**
Far Eastern Traders (HK) Ltd KOWLOON Hong Kong	**CERTIFICATE OF ORIGIN**
	3 Country of Origin European Union – United Kingdom

4 Transport details (Optional)	5 Remarks
SEAFARER II: Southampton to Hong Kong	

6 Item number: marks, numbers, number and kind of packages; description of goods	7 Quantity
Far Eastern One case containing Hong Kong One Rowcester Moulding Machine. Mk 2. 1234/No.1 Serial No. 12345	900 kg

8 THE UNDERSIGNED AUTHORITY CERTIFIES THAT THE GOODS DESCRIBED ABOVE ORIGINATE IN THE COUNTRY SHOWN IN BOX 3

The Rowcester and District Chamber of Commerce

Place and date of issue, name, signature and stamp of competent authority

M. Lloyd

Rowcester   1 August   19-1

Fig. 6.5: A certificate of origin

	CSR/ECI

Shipper's Name and Address	Shipper's Account Number A/123456	Not Negotiable **Air Waybill**	**ABC Airline** Gatwick Airport United Kingdom

Rowcester Engineering Co Ltd
Deansway House
ROWCESTER RW1 5TQ
United Kingdom

Copies 1, 2 and 3 of this Air Waybill are originals and have the same validity

Consignee's Name and Address	Consignee's Account Number B/567890

Far Eastern Traders (HK) Ltd
KOWLOON
Hong Kong

It is agreed that the goods described herein are accepted in apparent good order and condition (except as noted) for carriage SUBJECT TO THE CONDITIONS OF CONTRACT ON THE REVERSE HEREOF. THE SHIPPER'S ATTENTION IS DRAWN TO THE NOTICE CONCERNING CARRIER'S LIMITATION OF LIABILITY. Shipper may increase such limitation of liability by declaring a higher value for carriage and paying a supplemental charge if required.

ISSUING CARRIER MAINTAINS CARGO ACCIDENT LIABILITY INSURANCE

Issuing Carrier's Agent

XYZ Forwarding Ltd   Gatwick

Accounting Information

Agent's IATA Code LGW7923	Account No. 1234567

Airport of departure (Addr. of First Carrier) and Requested Routing
London Gatwick

To	By First Carrier	Routing and Destination	to	by	to	by	Currency	CHGS Code	WT/VAL		Other		Declrd Val for Carrg.	Declrd Val for Customs
	ABC1022						GBP		PPD	COLL	PPD	COLL	£455	£455

Airport of Destination	Flight/Date	For Carrier Use Only	Flight/Date
Hong Kong			

Handling Information

1 package   Far Eastern
                   Hong Kong   No.1

No. of Pieces RCP	Gross Weight	kg lb	Rate Class / Commodity Item No.	Chargeable Weight	Rate / Charge	Total	Nature and Quantity of Goods (incl. Dimensions or Volume)
1	50	k	N	50	£2	£100	Spare parts for Rowcester Moulding Machine, Mk 2 $0.5m^3$
1	50					£100	

Prepaid	Weight charge	Collect	Other Charges

Valuation Charge

Tax

Total Other Charges Due Agent

Shipper certifies that the particulars on the face hereof are correct and that insofar as any part of the consignment contains dangerous goods. such part is properly described by name and is in proper condition for carriage by air according to the applicable Dangerous Goods Regulations.

Total Other Charges Due Carrier

J. B. Long

Signature of Shipper or his agent

Total prepaid	Total collect

Currency conversion rates	cc charges in dest. currency

7 October 19-1   Gatwick

Executed on (date)   at (place)

A. B. Leviot

Signature of Issuing Carrier or its agent

For Carrier's Use only at Destination	Charges at Destination	Total Collect Charges

Original 3 - (For Shipper)

Fig. 6.6: A specimen air waybill

Freight Forwarder's Receipt

Many exporters use the services of a freight forwarder – firms which specialise in export documentation and procedures. They are able to advise and arrange transport, prepare some of the necessary documents, and arrange insurance cover. They are of particular benefit to smaller exporters and, in particular, are able to offer a 'groupage service' where the goods of several exporters can be combined together, thus resulting in lower freight and other charges.

A freight forwarder's receipt is issued upon receipt of the goods. (Note that, when dealing with documentary letters of credit – see Lesson 7 – freight forwarders' receipts are not normally acceptable under Uniform Customs and Practice for Documentary Credits).

Inspection/analysis/phytosanitary certificate

This is given by an independent party who has inspected the goods, usually at the request of the buyer or the authorities in his country. The quality or quantity of the goods being exported may thus be checked.

Packing/weight list

This details the goods that have been packed and may also list the weight of individual items, together with a total weight.

❏ European Union Documentation

The principle of trade between countries of the European Union (of which Britain is a member) is that goods should be free to circulate in and through all member countries without payment of duties at each border. Goods will either originate in the EU or are in free circulation within the Union (i.e. they have been imported from outside the EU, but duties, etc. have been paid).

Since January 1993 the sale of goods by a seller in one EU member country to a buyer in another member country will, at its simplest, require only an invoice. The invoice can be sent separately from the goods, which are likely to be accompanied by a shipping note. There are VAT implications (see below) for buyers and sellers within the EU. In addition, businesses that carry out a large amount of trade with the EU (turnover of between £120 000 and £140 000 per annum) will be required to submit monthly statistics of transactions carried out.

Value Added Tax and intra-EU trade

The next few years will see an increased harmonisation of Value Added Tax (VAT) within the EU: the long-term aim is to have the same VAT rates in each member country. VAT is charged by the supplier on all trade within the EU. Buyers, registered for VAT, are able to recover VAT in their own country on their VAT returns. This is known as the *origin principle*, with VAT due in the country of the supplier. It requires that suppliers quote the buyer's VAT number on invoices.

TIR carnets

Most readers will have seen the 'TIR' (transport international routier) letters on lorries or containers. This system is designed to ease the international road transport of goods in customs-approved vehicles or containers. The system applies for journeys between countries which are members of the Customs Convention - most of Europe, USSR, USA and parts of Asia. However, journeys wholly within the EU – where the goods are in free circulation – do not use the system. Under the TIR system, the procedure is for the vehicle or container to be sealed by the Customs in the country of departure. During the journey there is a minimum of formality at borders. No duty is payable on the goods in intermediate countries.

❑ Bills of exchange (see Fig. 6.7)

The definition of a bill of exchange is:

> *an unconditional order in writing addressed by one person to another, signed by the person giving it, requiring the person to whom it is addressed to pay on demand, or at a fixed or determinable future time, a sum certain in money to or to the order of a specified person or bearer.*
> *(Bills of Exchange Act, 1882)*

In international trading the bill of exchange is widely used as a method of giving or receiving a period of credit while, at the same time, clearly establishing a legal undertaking to pay a sum of money. In particular it solves the problem of the buyer of goods not wishing to pay for them until he has had the opportunity to receive them and make sales; on the other hand, the exporter may not wish to relinquish his control over the goods until he has either obtained payment or a legal undertaking that payment will be made at a 'fixed or determinable future time'.

You will probably know from your legal studies that an exporter will draw up the bill and is therefore known as the *drawer*. He will send the bill to the person on whom it is drawn and who has to make payment, known as the *drawee,* who will normally be the buyer of the goods. The bill may be sent direct to the buyer or through the banking system. A bill may either be a *term bill* (drawn for a certain term) or it may be a *sight bill* (payable at sight). Term bills are also known as 'tenor' or 'usance' bills. In the case of a term bill, it must be sent to the drawee for *acceptance* (i.e. acceptance of his liability), which is carried out by him signing his name on the bill and agreeing to pay the bill at maturity. Alternatively, a bank in the exporter's country may be authorised to accept bills on the drawee's behalf.

On the due date the bill will be presented for payment by the holder who, of course, may no longer be the drawer, if he has *discounted* the bill.

Liability of the parties to a bill of exchange

A bank is often the holder of a bill of exchange particularly where finance has been provided to an exporter by discounting or negotiating the bill (see lesson 12). A holder, especially a holder in due course, is the person in the strongest position to enforce the bill. Such a holder can sue on the bill in his own name and his title will not be affected by the defects in title of earlier holders of the bill (although this does not apply where there has been prior forgery).

The various parties to a bill are liable as follows:

- ### The acceptor
  Primary liability on a bill of exchange rests with the drawee once he has accepted the bill, i.e. he becomes the *acceptor*. When a bill is dishonoured either by non-acceptance or non-payment, other parties to the bill become liable on it.

- ### The drawer
  The drawer is primarily liable on the bill until it is accepted (if a term bill) and the drawer is also liable to pay the holder if the bill is dishonoured. Furthermore, the drawer must compensate any endorser who has had to pay on the bill because of dishonour, provided that proper notice of dishonour was given.

- ### The endorser
  An endorser is liable to pay the holder if the bill is dishonoured, or to compensate any subsequent endorser who has had to pay on the bill, because of dishonour, provided that proper notice of dishonour was given. He then has the right to claim against any previous endorser (including the payee) and against the drawer.

It follows from the above that, when a bank discounts or negotiates a bill of exchange on behalf of a customer, it invariably has a right of recourse against the customer in the event of non-acceptance or non-payment.

Note: It is not appropriate in a study manual on Trade Finance to go into details of acceptance, endorsement, discharge and dishonour of bills of exchange. A reader who wishes to look into these points is advised to study a specialised commercial or banking law book.

```
1 Aug. 19-1                                                  £10 000

At sight of this first of exchange pay to our order the sum of
sterling pounds ten thousand only for value received.


To: Far Eastern Traders (HK) Ltd     For and on behalf of
      Kowloon                        ROWCESTER ENGINEERING CO LTD
      Hong Kong
                                     R.O.W. Cester
                                     Director
```

Fig. 6.7: A bill of exchange

It is not unusual, where goods are being exported, to find that there are two bills of exchange covering the same shipment of goods and for exactly the same amount. This allows the exporter, or his bank where they are handling the documentation, to send *two* sets of documents to the buyer by different posts. Thus if the first set of documents is lost, then hopefully the second set of documents, posted at a later date, will get through to the buyer. As far as the instrument of payment - the bill of exchange - is concerned, one will read 'pay this first bill of exchange, second of the same tenor and date unpaid', while the other will read 'pay this second bill of exchange, first of the same tenor and date unpaid'.

Bills may be drawn either in sterling or in a foreign currency:

• **Drawn in sterling**
For a bill drawn in sterling and collected by a bank, the UK exporter will receive the face value of the bill less foreign stamp duty (if applicable), and collection charges.

• **Drawn in foreign currency**
If his bank collects a bill of exchange drawn in a foreign currency, the exporter will receive the sterling equivalent (calculated at the rate of exchange on the date that proceeds are received) less foreign stamp duty (if applicable) and collection charges. (This assumes that the customer is not operating a foreign currency account designated in the currency of the bill and requires the bill amount to be placed to that account.)

❏ Promissory note

This is defined as:

> *an unconditional promise in writing made by one person to another signed by the maker, engaging to pay, on demand or at a fixed or determinable future time, a sum certain in money, to, or to the order of, a specified person or to bearer.*
> *(Bills of Exchange Act, 1882)*

Thus, while a promissory note is not a bill of exchange, it can be used for a similar purpose, namely that of settling indebtedness. Instead of being drawn by the person expecting to be paid (as is a bill of exchange), they are made out by the person who owes the money (the maker), in favour of the beneficiary (the payee). A promissory note is *inchoate* (incomplete) until delivery has been made to the payee or bearer.

When a note is due for payment it is presented to the maker for payment by the holder, who may be the payee or someone to whom the note has been negotiated.

❏ Summary

The more important commercial documents found of international trade are:

- an invoice
- a transport document
- an insurance document

Financial documents include bills of exchange, promissory notes, cheques, etc.

In international trade, banks are often involved in handling documents for collection (see lesson 9) or under the terms of a letter of credit (see lessons 7 and 8). It is therefore important to know for which documents the exporter is responsible.

- In a CIF contract the exporter is responsible for providing invoices, the insurance policy or certificate, and a full set of 'on board' bills of lading (or waybills) marked 'freight paid'. (Under a DDP contract, the exporter will have to produce through bills of lading and insurance documents covering the goods to delivery at the buyer's warehouse.)

- With a CFR contract the exporter is required to produce invoices and a full set of 'on board' bills of lading (or waybills) marked 'freight paid'. Insurance is the responsibility of the buyer.

- For an FOB contract the documents required from the exporter are the invoices and a full set of 'on board' bills of lading (or waybills) stating that the freight is payable at the destination, the freight charge being the responsibility of the buyer. Again, insurance is the responsibility of the buyer.

- Where the contract is FAS, the exporter will produce invoices and a receipt from the port of departure indicating that he has delivered the goods. Freight and insurance are the responsibility of the buyer.

The responsibilities for documentation under other terms are listed on pages 85-93.

❏ Examination hints

- A popular and relatively straightforward topic.

- Know the main terms of trade and be able to explain to a customer, who may be either an exporter or an importer, which party is responsible for the freight and insurance costs.

- Be aware of the three main commercial documents, i.e. invoice, transport document and insurance document.

- Understand the different types of bills of lading, and the difference between a bill of lading and a waybill (and particularly the circumstances in which the latter would be used).

Know Your .... Incoterms; Commercial and Financial Documents

1. An exporter sells on CFR terms. Is he/she responsible for:
    (i)   insurance?
    (ii) freight charges?

2. A UK importer is buying goods from abroad on terms which state:
    "CIF: UK port".
    What particular problems might these terms pose for the importer?

3. A UK exporter sells on CIF terms. What are the basic documents covering the shipment?

4. Who issues a certificate of origin in the UK?

5. Complete the following sentences:
    " The bill of lading is a r............ for the goods and evidence of the c............... of c.............. It is also a d................... of t................... enabling the exporter to transfer ownership or possession of the goods".

6. How does a sea waybill differ from a bill of lading?

7. What is a short-form bill of lading?

8. What is a charter party bill of lading?

9. When goods are sent by air the airline will issue an ....
    This is not a .... of ....

10. State six particulars to be found on a commercial invoice.

11. How does a consular invoice differ from a commercial invoice?

12. Why do some bills of exchange state "pay this first of exchange (second of the same tenor and date unpaid)"?

13. What costs will be incurred by an exporter selling on FOB terms?

14. What do the letters SITPRO stand for? What is the main objective of this organisation?

15. State six particulars to be found on a bill of lading.

16. Distinguish between a 'clean' and a 'claused' bill of lading.

17. What is a through bill of lading?

18. What does the term 'DDP' mean?

19. What is a blacklist certificate?

20. What are 'Incoterms'? How can buyers and sellers ensure that 'Incoterms 1990' apply?

Past Examination Questions

Note: See also past questions at the end of other lessons.

6.1*   Much Wallop Ltd sells wine, spirits and beers at many retail outlets including its own licensed stores. It is always seeking new sources of supply, and the bank's intelligence unit has provided the name of a European suplier of German and Austrian beers.

You understand that the new supplier will quote prices per container load in Deutsche marks, and the terms of shipment will be CFR Felixstowe.

You are asked to discuss the situation with one of the company's directors, Mr Halfpinta. Your discussions will cover the meaning of the shipping terms mentioned, including the responsibilities of the parties, and the relative advantages and disadvantages of paying for supplies in sterling, or in foreign currency.

REQUIRED:
Notes covering the points you would make to Mr Halfpinta in connection with:

(a)   the meaning of the term 'CFR Felixstowe', and the responsibilities of the parties involved;
[7]

(b)   the advantages/disadvantages to the company if they are able to pay for the goods in sterling;   [3]

(c)   the advantages/disadvantages if they are forced to pay for the goods in Deutsche marks;
[4]

(d)   the means by which any disadvantages mentioned in (c) might be overcome.   [6]

[Total marks for question - 20]
(question 6 [amended], May 1989)

6.2   As Manager of a local branch of your bank, you are asked to take part in a panel of experts at a joint meeting of the local Chamber of Commerce and the local Export Association. During the course of the evening, a number of questions are asked from the floor including the following two questions from a local manufacturer:

(1)   'The single European Market after 1992 should mean that I can sell my goods as readily in Frankfurt or in Amsterdam as I can in the UK. Why therefore should I busy myself learning about export documentation which will no longer apply?'

(2)   'Furthermore, I have often been asked to quote on terms which I do not understand, such as CFR, CIP and DDP. Surely these terms will not be required in the future?'

REQUIRED:

(a)   In brief form, indicate the reply you would give to the two questions asked by the manufacturer.   [7]

(b)   Explain fully the shipping terms mentioned above, indicating the responsibilities for both buyer and seller. Refer to any international publications or rules which might apply regardless of the parties involved.   [13]

[Total marks for question - 20]
(question 8 [amended], October 1990)

6.3*   Seaside Supliers Ltd import a range of products sold to the tourist industry, particularly in the UK. Mr Niknak, a recently appointed director, calls to see you to discuss the renewal of the company's banking facilities. During the course of your conversation he mentions that he has recently been asked to buy goods from overseas on terms which are completely new to him. You are asked to explain the meaning of some of these terms including the responsibilities of the parties in respect of carriage and insurance.

REQUIRED, in brief note form, your answers to the following:

(a)   What international standards might apply to these terms?   [1]

(b)   Explain the following terms, showing who is responsible for carriage and insurance and when the risks are transferred to the buyer:
(i)   FOB Manila;
(ii)   CFR Southampton;
(iii) CIF Southampton.   [14]

(c)   Will the terms in (b) above apply if goods are transported by roll-on/roll-off or container transport. If not, what other terms will apply?   [4]

(d)   If goods are to be transported from Turkey by road/rail through a nominated carrier, which term(s) would be appropriate?   [1]

[Total marks for question - 20]
(question 5, May 1991)

Multiple-Choice Questions: Set 3

Read each question carefully. Choose the *one* answer you think is correct.
Answers are given on page 318.

1.   A customer is going on a two-month touring holiday to France next week. She is concerned that, whilst she is abroad, sterling may depreciate against the French franc and asks you which of the following travel facilities will eliminate the exchange rate risk:

    A   immediate purchase of sterling travellers' cheques
    B   immediate purchase of French franc travellers' cheques
    C   Eurocheque facility - she will draw cheques in French francs whilst on holiday
    D   the use of her credit card whilst on holiday.

2.   A customer of your bank is on holiday in Spain and has, unfortunately, had his wallet, containing travellers' cheques and credit card, stolen. He needs money immediately and has just telephoned your branch. How will the money be sent?

    A   a priority SWIFT message (EIMT)
    B   a bank draft
    C   a new credit card
    D   a stock of travellers' cheques sent in the next post

3.   Which one of the following organizations helps exporters to reduce the administrative cost of preparing documents?

    A   THE
    B   SITPRO
    C   BOTB
    D   SWIFT

4.   An export house receives an order from a customer abroad, passes it to an appropriate UK manufacturer, and takes responsibility for payment. This export house is acting as:

    A   an agent
    B   a foreign buying house
    C   an export merchant
    D   a confirming house

5.   The export term CIF means:

    A   carriage, insurance and freight
    B   cost, insurance and freight
    C   cost including freight
    D   charges, insurance and freight

6.   An exporter customer sells goods abroad on FOB and on CIF terms. Respectively, who is responsible for the freight charges in each?

    A   importer; exporter
    B   importer; importer
    C   exporter; importer
    D   exporter; exporter

7.   Under FOB terms the bill of lading would state:

        A   goods loaded on board, freight paid
        B   goods loaded on board, freight payable at destination
        C   goods received for shipment, freight paid
        D   goods received for shipment, freight payable at destination

8.   What is the name of the document that an exporter receives from the shipping company when goods have been placed on board the ship?

        A   invoice
        B   bill of lading
        C   certificate of origin
        D   bill of exchange

9.   Which is the odd-one out?

        A   air waybill
        B   bill of lading
        C   carrier's receipt
        D   bill of exchange

10.   Which one of the following is *not* a commercial document?

        A   blacklist certificate
        B   insurance document
        C   certificate of origin
        D   bill of exchange

Lesson Seven
Documentary Letters of Credit: 1

Documentary letters of credit (often called documentary credits, or letters of credit) have already been mentioned briefly and it has been seen that, after payment in advance, they represent the safest and fastest way of obtaining payment for exports. The reason for this is because the exporter can personally retain control of the documents of title to the goods until the moment of payment or acceptance of his bill of exchange. Documentary credits can also be used as a method of payment in domestic trade: in this case they will be usually marked 'inland'.

❑ Definition

The definition of documentary credits is given in the International Chamber of Commerce Publication No. 500 entitled *Uniform Customs and Practice for Documentary Credits* (see page 122), Article 2, as:

> ... any arrangement, however named or described, whereby a bank (the "Issuing Bank"), acting at the request and on the instructions of a customer (the "Applicant") or on its own behalf,
>
> i. is to make payment to or to the order of a third party (the "Beneficiary"), or is to accept and pay bills of exchange (Draft(s)) drawn by the Beneficiary, or
>
> ii. authorises another bank to effect such payment, or accept and pay such bills of exchange (Draft(s)), or
>
> iii. authorises another bank to negotiate,
>
> against stipulated document(s), provided that the terms and conditions of the Credit are complied with.

In short, a documentary credit is an instrument by which a bank undertakes to pay a seller against stipulated documents for his goods providing the seller complies with the conditions laid down in the credit.

❑ Parties to a credit

The parties to a credit are:
- *the applicant* (usually the buyer), who arranges to open the credit in accordance with the terms of the commercial contract
- *the beneficiary* (usually the seller), in whose favour the credit is issued
- *the issuing bank,* which commits itself in accordance with the applicant's instructions
- *the advising bank,* which is usually located in the same country as the beneficiary and is usually the issuing bank's correspondent

❏ **Method of operation**

Where the terms of the contract call for payment under a credit, the buyer (applicant) applies to his/her bank (the issuing bank) to open a credit in favour of the exporter (the beneficiary). Before issuing a credit the bank must make certain of its customer's creditworthiness; if this is satisfactory, the credit is despatched by the issuing bank – by airmail, telex, or SWIFT – to an agent bank in the exporter's country. The credit is then advised to the exporter by the agent bank (advising bank). Under the terms of the credit, the issuing bank undertakes that the seller will be paid for the goods providing he/she complies with certain stated conditions: these will call for the presentation of certain documents, such as invoice, bills of lading and insurance documents (depending on the responsibility of the exporter) covering the quantity and quality of goods agreed in the contract between the exporter and his overseas buyer. Provided that the documents presented to the advising bank agree exactly with the requirements of the credit, the exporter receives the payment due in exchange for the documents. The advising bank sends the documents to the issuing bank by air mail; upon receipt, they may be handed to the buyer, who then awaits the arrival of the carrying vessel. When the ship docks, the buyer presents the bills of lading to the representatives of the shipping company and, in discharge of the shipping company's responsibilities under the contract of carriage, receives the goods. Payment for the goods by the buyer to the issuing bank is a matter of arrangement between them and is of no concern to the exporter. The settlement between the banks for the amount paid by the issuing bank is carried out through their agency (nostro and vostro) accounts, depending on the currency of payment.

Note: There are risks in documentary credits: forged letters of credit are not unknown. Also, because credits deal in documents and not in goods, the exporter will be paid provided he complies with the terms and conditions of the credit even though the crates supposedly containing the goods have been packed with rubbish or perhaps sub-standard goods. There are two ways around this problem: the first is for a status enquiry to be taken up on the exporter, and/or, secondly for the buyer to require a certificate of inspection to be obtained from an independent third party as one of the required documents.

❏ **An example transaction**

An example of a simplified transaction will show the sequence of events, and should be studied in conjunction with Fig. 7.1:

- ABC Engineering Ltd. of London have entered into a CIF contract with XYZ Import Co. Ltd. of New Zealand to supply certain specialised machinery. The contract stipulates that payment is to be made under the terms of a documentary letter of credit, the required documents being:

  1. commercial invoice in triplicate

  2. certificate of origin issued by a Chamber of Commerce

  3. a full set of clean, on-board marine bills of lading made out to order and endorsed in blank, marked 'freight paid' and 'notify XYZ Import Co. Ltd.'

  4. insurance policy or certificate in duplicate covering marine and war risks to the buyer's warehouse for invoice value of the goods, plus ten per cent

- The machinery is manufactured by ABC Ltd.

- Meanwhile, XYZ Co. Ltd. have asked their bank, the North and South Bank, to open a credit in favour of ABC Ltd. As their customers are creditworthy, the bank instructs its correspondent bank in London, National Barrlands, to advise a credit in favour of ABC Ltd. for the invoice value (which will include insurance and freight charges).

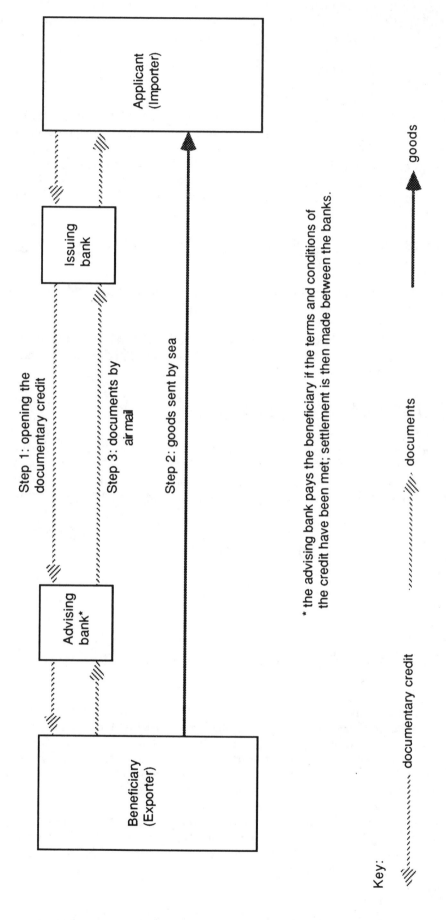

Fig. 7.1:   The use of a documentary letter of credit

- Insurance and shipping details for the journey are arranged by ABC Ltd.; the machinery is delivered to the docks and the freight charges are paid. Once the goods are loaded on board the carrying vessel, the shipping company issues a set of on-board bills of lading marked 'freight paid'.

- ABC Ltd must ensure that the details on all documents comply with the terms of the contract and the requirements of the credit.

- ABC Ltd. now presents the documents at the branch of National Barllands bank specified in the credit and, provided they agree exactly with the requirements of the credit, receives payment.

- Meanwhile the goods are on their way to New Zealand by sea and the London bank sends the documents to the North and South Bank by air mail (perhaps making up the documents into two sets, either one enabling the goods to be collected upon arrival in New Zealand), and sending them at different times.

- The documents are received by the North and South Bank which releases them to their customers XYZ Ltd.

- When the ship arrives, upon presentation of a signed copy of the bill of lading to the representative of the shipping company, the goods may be taken away.

- The banks involved effect book-keeping transactions between themselves to settle the transaction and, at the North and South bank, the account of XYZ Ltd. is debited with the amount involved.

❑ Sight and acceptance credits

In the above example the credit was at *sight,* i.e. payment was made on demand. It could have been an *acceptance credit;* this would have meant that the bill drawn by ABC Ltd. would have had to be drawn for a stipulated tenor, perhaps 30, 60 or 90 days. The credit would have specified on whom the bill had to be drawn - the applicant, the issuing bank or the confirming bank (see below).

❑ Revocable and irrevocable credits

Documentary credits are of two types:
- revocable
- irrevocable

If the credit does not indicate whether it is revocable or irrevocable, it is deemed to be irrevocable (Article 6 of *Uniform Customs and Practice*).

A *revocable credit* gives no undertaking (guarantee) to the exporter that payment will actually be made or a bill of exchange accepted because it may be cancelled or amended at any time without prior notice to the beneficiary. Not surprisingly, because of this, they are seldom used. However, under *Uniform Customs and Practice,* the issuing bank must honour payments, acceptances and negotiations made by the advising bank which comply with the terms and conditions of the credit (and with any amendments) prior to receipt by it of notice of amendment or of cancellation.

An *irrevocable credit* does not suffer from the disadvantage of a revocable credit and, as a consequence, is widely used. Under such a credit, the issuing bank gives its irrevocable undertaking (guarantee) that, provided the terms and conditions of the credit are complied with, payment, acceptance or negotiation will be made. Such a credit can only be amended or cancelled with the consent of all parties.

An irrevocable credit may be *confirmed or unconfirmed.* When it is *confirmed* the issuing bank authorises or requests the advising bank to add its own undertaking to that of the issuing bank. An *unconfirmed* credit still carries the issuing bank's irrevocable undertaking but the advising bank does not add its own, merely advising the beneficiary of the terms and conditions of the credit. Naturally, from an exporter's point of view, the best payment method under a credit is by means of a confirmed, irrevocable documentary letter of credit, because it contains the irrevocable undertaking of two banks, one of which is in his/her own country (usually), and the terms of the credit cannot be altered without his/her knowledge; provided the exporter complies with all the terms, he/she knows that either payment will be made or the bill of exchange will be accepted.

Notes:
- It is often thought that an exporter will automatically receive payment under a sight documentary credit as soon as he has presented the correct documents. This is not necessarily so: if the advising bank (which, by now, is known as the negotiating bank because it is negotiating the documents) does not itself have immediate access to reimbursement, then payment will not be immediately available. The undertaking to pay is given by the issuing bank and a negotiating bank may not wish to settle with the exporter until it has received reimbursement. It may consider that for various reasons, e.g. political or economic, reimbursement will not be forthcoming from the issuing bank.These comments do not apply where the credit is confirmed and the documents are presented at the confirming bank - a sight credit would then be payable immediately. If the exporter does not bank with the confirming bank and does not, himself, wish to present the documents to the confirming bank, he can ask his own bank to do this for him.

- First-class banks are not prepared to advise or confirm letters of credit issued by banks which are considered to be financially unsound.

❏ Details to be found on a documentary credit

Fig. 7.2 shows a confirmed irrevocable letter of credit. The following details are numbered for reference:

❶   The type of credit (revocable or irrevocable).

❷   The name and address of the beneficiary (the exporter).

❸   The name and the address of the applicant (the importer).

❹   The amount of the credit in sterling (or could be in foreign currency).

❺   The name of the party on whom the drafts (bills of exchange) are to be drawn and whether they are to be at sight or tenor*.

❻   The terms of the contract and shipment – in this case CIF Toronto.

❼   Precise instructions as to the documents against which payment is to be made.

❽   A brief description of the goods covered by the credit.

❾   Shipping details, including whether partshipments and/or transhipments are allowed; also the latest date for shipment and the names of the ports of shipment and discharge.

❿   Whether the credit is available for one or several part shipments.

⓫   The expiry date of the credit.

Most credits will state that they are subject to *Uniform Customs and Practice for Documentary Credits (1993 Revision) International Chamber of Commerce Publication No. 500.*

*Note: Where it is an acceptance credit calling for tenor or term bills of exchange, such bills might, depending on the details stated in the credit, be drawn on the applicant, the issuing bank or the advising bank. When it is drawn on the applicant or the issuing bank, the advising bank will usually negotiate the bill. When it is drawn on the advising bank it will be accepted by that bank: the bill can

BARCLAYS BANK PLC
MANCHESTER INTERNATIONAL SERVICES BRANCH
THIRD FLOOR, 51 MOSLEY STREET, MANCHESTER M60 2BU. UK.
PHONE: 061 228 3322 TELEX: 667565 ANSWERBK: BARMAN G

BENEFICIARY:
NATHAN AND COLES LIMITED
NATHAN ROAD
LONDON SE11 8JB
UNITED KINGDOM

ADVICE OF
IRREVOCABLE DOCUMENTARY CREDIT
NUMBER: TODC 603921
DATED 20TH JUNE 1994
DATE OF EXPIRY: 31ST AUGUST 1994
PLACE OF EXPIRY: UNITED KINGDOM
AMOUNT: UP TO GBP 160,000.00
UP TO ONE HUNDRED SIXTY THOUSAND
AND 00/100'S POUNDS STERLING
OUR ADVICE NUMBER: MRDC708447

OPENING BANK:
BARCLAYS BANK OF CANADA
PO BOX 377
COMMERCE COURT POSTAL STATION
TORONTO, ONTARIO
CANADA

APPLICANT:
MURRAY CORPORATION LIMITED
1052 CAUSEWAY BOULEVARD
TORONTO

30TH JUNE 1994

DEAR SIR(S)

THIS LETTER OF CREDIT IS AVAILABLE WITH BARCLAYS BANK PLC: BY PAYMENT AGAINST PRESENTATION OF THE DOCUMENTS DETAILED HEREIN AND OF YOUR DRAFTS AT SIGHT DRAWN ON BARCLAYS BANK PLC, MANCHESTER FOR 100 PER CENT OF INVOICE VALUE.

DOCUMENTS REQUIRED:-

1 - COMMERCIAL INVOICE IN QUADRUPLICATE
2 - INSURANCE POLICY/CERTIFICATE IN DUPLICATE COVERING MARINE AND WAR RISKS FOR 110 PER CENT OF THE INVOICE VALUE
3 - FULL SET OF CLEAN ON BOARD BLANK ENDORSED PORT TO PORT BILLS OF LADING MARKED NOTFIY MURRAY CORPORATION LIMITED, 1052 CAUSEWAY BOULEVARD, TORONTO, ONTARIO.

COVERING THE FOLLOWING GOODS:-

16 - PRINTING MACHINES NATHAN AND COLES MODEL CAXTON EXCELSIOR 1470
COST, INSURANCE & FREIGHT TORONTO
PARTIAL SHIPMENTS: NOT ALLOWED
TRANSHIPMENTS: ALLOWED
SHIPMENT FROM: UK PORT
NO LATER THAN: 15TH AUGUST 1994
FOR TRANSPORTATION TO: TORONTO

DOCUMENTS MUST BE PRESENTED AT PLACE OF EXPIRATION WITHIN 15 DAYS OF ISSUE DATE OF TRANSPORT DOCUMENT AND WITHIN THE L/C VALIDITY.

DOCUMENTS ARE TO BE ACCOMPANIED BY YOUR DRAFTS DRAWN ON BARCLAYS BANK PLC AT SIGHT MARKED 'DRAWN UNDER IRREVOCABLE LETTER OF CREDIT NO TODC 603921 OF BARCLAYS BANK OF CANADA AND QUOTING OUR REFERENCE NUMBER MRDC708447.

IMPORTANT: PLEASE CAREFULLY CHECK THE DETAILS OF THIS CREDIT AS IT IS ESSENTIAL THAT DOCUMENTS TENDERED CONFORM IN EVERY RESPECT WITH THE CREDIT TERMS. IF YOU ARE UNABLE TO COMPLY, PLEASE COMMUNICATE WITH YOUR BUYERS PROMPTLY IN ORDER THAT THEY MAY ARRANGE A SUITABLE AMENDMENT WITHOUT DELAY. IF DOCUMENTS ARE PRESENTED WHICH DIFFER FROM THE CREDIT TERMS, WE RESERVE THE RIGHT TO MAKE AN ADDITIONAL CHARGE.

WE ADD OUR CONFIRMATION TO THIS CREDIT AND UNDERTAKE THAT DRAFT(S) AND DOCUMENTS DRAWN UNDER AND IN STRICT CONFORMITY WITH THE TERMS THEREOF WILL BE HONOURED ON PRESENTATION.

THIS CREDIT IS SUBJECT TO THE UNIFORM CUSTOMS AND PRACTICE FOR DOCUMENTARY CREDITS (1993 REVISION), ICC PUBLICATION NUMBER 500.

YOURS FAITHFULLY

SPECIMEN

SPECIMEN

....
AUTHORISED SIGNATURE

....
AUTHORISED SIGNATURE

Member of IMRO
Registered in London, England, Reg. No 1026167. Reg. Office: 54 Lombard Street, London EC3P 3AH

Fig. 7.2: Specimen letter of credit

then either be held by the drawer until maturity, or discounted, thus receiving the proceeds, less discount, quickly. As the bill has been accepted by a bank it has the advantage of being readily discountable at a fine rate of discount. (Negotiation and discounting are considered more fully in lesson 12).

❑ Uniform Customs and Practice for Documentary Credits

This is a standardised code of practice issued by the International Chamber of Commerce (ICC). It assists banks, exporters and importers throughout the world in the interpretation of terms used in documentary credit work, so that the maximum degree of uniformity is achieved.

The current set of Uniform Customs and Practice is ICC publication number 500 – hence it is commonly known as 'UCP 500' – and is the 1993 revision which became effective from 1 January 1994. The revisions were made in order to:

*   address new developments in the transport industry
*   address new technological applications, such as the teletransmission credits
*   improve the functions of UCP, for example, by reducing the number of rejections caused by discrepancies in documents
*   bring UCP into line with *Incoterms 1990*

The layout of UCP 500 (which runs to 49 'articles') is as follows:

A	General Provisions and Definitions	Articles 1-5
B	Form and Notification of Credits	Articles 6-12
C	Liabilities and Responsibilities	Articles 13-19
D	Documents	Articles 20-38
E	Miscellaneous Provisions	Articles 39-47
F	Transferable Credit	Article 48
G	Assignment of Proceeds	Article 49

Note that when a credit is issued subject to UCP 500:
*   if the terms of the credit conflict with UCP, then the terms of the credit apply
*   if a country's laws conflict with UCP, then the laws apply

The text of the 1993 revision now follows: it should be studied carefully:

UNIFORM CUSTOMS AND PRACTICE FOR DOCUMENTARY CREDITS (1993 REVISION)

The International Chamber of Commerce Publication No. 500

A.   GENERAL PROVISIONS AND DEFINITIONS

Article 1
Application of UCP

The Uniform Customs and Practice for Documentary Credits, 1993 Revision, ICC Publication No 500, shall apply to all Documentary Credits (including to the extent to which they may be applicable, Standby Letter(s) of Credit) where they are incorporated into the text of the Credit. They are binding on all parties thereto, unless otherwise expressly stipulated in the Credit.

Article 2
Meaning of Credit

For the purposes of these Articles, the expressions "Documentary Credit(s)" and "Standby Letter(s) of Credit" (hereinafter referred to as "Credit(s)"), mean any arrangement, however named or described, whereby a bank (the "Issuing Bank") acting at the request and on the instructions of a customer (the "Applicant") or on its own behalf,

i.   is to make a payment to or to the order of a third party (the "Beneficiary"), or is to accept and pay bills of exchange (Draft(s)) drawn by the Beneficiary,

or

ii.   authorises another bank to effect such payment, or to accept and pay such bills of exchange (Draft(s)),

or

iii.   authorises another bank to negotiate,

against stipulated document(s), provided that the terms and conditions of the Credit are complied with.

For the purposes of these Articles, branches of a bank in different countries are considered another bank.

Article 3
Credits v. Contracts

(a)   Credits, by their nature, are separate transactions from the sales or other contract(s) on which they may be based and banks are in no way concerned with or bound by such contract(s), even if any reference whatsoever to such contract(s) is included in the Credit. Consequently, the undertaking of a bank to pay, accept and pay Draft(s) or negotiate and/or to fulfil any other obligation under the Credit, is not subject to claims or defences by the Applicant resulting from his relationships with the Issuing Bank or the Beneficiary.

(b)   A Beneficiary can in no case avail himself of the contractual relationships existing between the banks or between the Applicant and the Issuing Bank.

Article 4
Documents v. Goods/Services/Performances

In Credit operations all parties concerned deal with documents, and not with goods, services and/or other performances to which the documents may relate.

Article 5
Instructions to Issue/Amend Credits

(a)   Instructions for the issuance of a Credit, the Credit itself, instructions for an amendment thereto, and the amendment itself, must be complete and precise.

In order to guard against confusion and misunderstanding, banks should discourage any attempt:

i.   to include excessive detail in the Credit or in any amendment thereto;

ii.   to give instructions to issue, advise or confirm a Credit by reference to a Credit previously issued (similar Credit) where such previous Credit has been subject to accepted amendment(s), and/or unaccepted amendment(s).

(b)   All instructions for the issuance of a Credit and the Credit itself and, where applicable, all instructions for an amendment thereto and the amendment itself, must state precisely the document(s) against which payment, acceptance or negotiation is to be made.

B.   FORM AND NOTIFICATION OF CREDITS

Article 6
Revocable v. Irrevocable Credits

(a)   A Credit may be either

    i.   revocable,

        or

    ii.   irrevocable.

(b)   The Credit, therefore, should clearly indicate whether it is revocable or irrevocable.

(c)   In the absence of such indication the Credit shall be deemed to be irrevocable.

Article 7
Advising Bank's Liability

(a)   A Credit may be advised to a Beneficiary through another bank (the "Advising Bank") without engagement on the part of the Advising Bank, but that bank, if it elects to advise the Credit, shall take reasonable care to check the apparent authenticity of the Credit which it advises. If the bank elects not to advise the Credit, it must so inform the Issuing Bank without delay.

(b)   If the Advising Bank cannot establish such apparent authenticity it must inform, without delay, the bank from which the instructions appear to have been received that it has been unable to establish the authenticity of the Credit and if it elects nonetheless to advise the Credit it must inform the Beneficiary that it has not been able to establish the authenticity of the Credit.

Article 8
Revocation of a Credit

(a)   A revocable Credit may be amended or cancelled by the Issuing Bank at any moment and without prior notice to the Beneficiary.

(b)   However, the Issuing Bank must:

    i.   reimburse another bank with which a revocable Credit has been made available for sight payment, acceptance or negotiation – for any payment, acceptance or negotiation made by such bank – prior to receipt by it of notice of amendment or cancellation, against documents which appear on their face to be in compliance with the terms and conditions of the Credit;

    ii.   reimburse another bank with which a revocable Credit has been made available for deferred payment, if such a bank has, prior to receipt by it of notice of amendment or cancellation, taken up documents which appear on their face to be in compliance with the terms and conditions of the Credit.

Article 9
Liability of Issuing and Confirming Banks

(a)   An irrevocable Credit constitutes a definite undertaking of the Issuing Bank, provided that the stipulated documents are presented to the Nominated Bank or to the Issuing Bank and that the terms and conditions of the Credit are complied with:

    i.   if the Credit provides for sight payment – to pay at sight;

    ii.   if the Credit provides for deferred payment – to pay on the maturity date(s) determinable in accordance with the stipulations of the Credit;

    iii. if the Credit provides for acceptance:

        a.   by the Issuing Bank – to accept Draft(s) drawn by the Beneficiary on the Issuing Bank and pay them at maturity,

            or

b.   by another drawee bank – to accept and pay at maturity Draft(s) drawn by the Beneficiary on the Issuing Bank in the event the drawee bank stipulated in the Credit does not accept Draft(s) drawn on it, or to pay Draft(s) accepted but not paid by such drawee bank at maturity;

iv.   if the Credit provides for negotiation – to pay without recourse to drawers and/or bona fide holders, Draft(s) drawn by the Beneficiary and/or document(s) presented under the Credit. A Credit should not be issued available by Draft(s) on the Applicant. If the Credit nevertheless calls for Draft(s) on the Applicant, banks will consider such Draft(s) as an additional document(s).

(b)   A confirmation of an irrevocable Credit by another bank (the "Confirming Bank") upon the authorisation or request of the Issuing Bank, constitutes a definite undertaking of the Confirming Bank, in addition to that of the Issuing Bank, provided that the stipulated documents are presented to the Confirming Bank or to any other Nominated Bank and that the terms and conditions of the Credit are complied with:

i.   if the Credit provides for sight payment – to pay at sight;

ii.   if the Credit provides for deferred payment – to pay on the maturity date(s) determinable in accordance with the stipulations of the Credit;

iii.   if the Credit provides for acceptance:

a.   by the Confirming Bank – to accept Draft(s) drawn by the Beneficiary on the Confirming Bank and pay them at maturity,

or

b.   by another drawee bank – to accept and pay at maturity Draft(s) drawn by the Beneficiary on the confirming Bank, in the event the drawee bank stipulated in the Credit does not accept Draft(s) drawn on it, or to pay Draft(s) accepted but not paid by such drawee bank at maturity;

iv.   if the Credit provides for negotiation – to negotiate without recourse to drawers and/or bona fide holders, Draft(s) drawn by the Beneficiary and/or document(s) presented under the Credit. A Credit should not be issued available by Draft(s) on the Applicant. If the Credit nevertheless calls for Draft(s) on the Applicant, banks will consider such Draft(s) as an additional document(s).

(c)   i.   If another bank is authorised or requested by the Issuing Bank to add its confirmation to a Credit but is not prepared to do so, it must so inform the Issuing Bank without delay.

ii.   Unless the Issuing Bank specifies otherwise in its authorisation or request to add confirmation, the Advising Bank may advise the Credit to the Beneficiary without adding its confirmation.

(d)   i.   Except as otherwise provided by Article 48, an irrevocable Credit can neither be amended nor cancelled without the agreement of the Issuing Bank, the Confirming Bank, if any, and the Beneficiary.

ii.   The Issuing Bank shall be irrevocably bound by an amendment(s) issued by it from the time of the issuance of such amendment(s). A Confirming Bank may extend its confirmation to an amendment and shall be irrevocably bound as of the time of its advice of the amendment. A Confirming Bank may, however, choose to advise an amendment to the Beneficiary without extending its confirmation and if so, must inform the Issuing Bank and the Beneficiary without delay.

iii.   The terms of the original Credit (or a Credit incorporating previously accepted amendment(s)) will remain in force for the Beneficiary until the Beneficiary communicates his acceptance of the amendment to the bank that advised such amendment. The Beneficiary should give notification of acceptance or rejection of amendment(s). If the Beneficiary fails to give such notification, the tender of documents to the Nominated Bank or Issuing Bank, that conform to the Credit and to not yet accepted amendment(s), will be deemed to be notification of acceptance by the Beneficiary of such amendment(s) and as of that moment the Credit will be amended.

iv.   Partial acceptance of amendments contained in one and the same advice of amendment is not allowed and consequently will not be given any effect.

Article 10
Types of Credit

(a)   All credits must clearly indicate whether they are available by sight payment, by deferred payment, by acceptance or by negotiation.

(b) i. Unless the Credit stipulates that it is available only with the Issuing Bank, all Credits must nominate the bank (the "Nominated bank") which is authorised to pay, to incur a deferred payment undertaking, to accept Draft(s) or to negotiate. In a freely negotiable Credit, any bank is a Nominated Bank.

Presentation of documents must be made to the Issuing Bank or the Confirming Bank, if any, or any other Nominated Bank.

ii. Negotiation means the giving of value for Draft(s) and/or document(s) by the bank authorised to negotiate. Mere examination of the documents without giving of value does not constitute a negotiation.

(c) Unless the Nominated Bank is the Confirming Bank, nomination by the Issuing Bank does not constitute any undertaking by the Nominated Bank to pay, to incur a deferred payment undertaking, to accept Draft(s), or to negotiate. Except where expressly agreed to by the Nominated Bank and so communicated to the Beneficiary, the Nominated Bank's receipt of and/or examination and/or forwarding of the documents does not make that bank liable to pay, to incur a deferred payment undertaking, to accept Draft(s), or to negotiate.

(d) By nominating another bank, or by allowing for negotiation by any bank, or by authorising or requesting another bank to add its confirmation, the Issuing Bank authorises such bank to pay, accept Draft(s) or negotiate as the case may be, against documents which appear on their face to be in compliance with the terms and conditions of the Credit and undertakes to reimburse such bank in accordance with the provisions of these Articles.

Article 11
Teletransmitted and Pre-Advised Credits

(a) i. When an Issuing Bank instructs an Advising Bank by an authenticated teletransmission to advise a Credit or an amendment to a Credit, the teletransmission will be deemed to be the operative Credit instrument or the operative amendment, and no mail confirmation should be sent. Should a mail confirmation nevertheless be sent, it will have no effect and the Advising Bank will have no obligation to check such mail confirmation against the operative Credit instrument or the operative amendment received by teletransmission.

ii. If the teletransmission states "full details to follow" (or words of similar effect) or states that the mail confirmation is to be the operative Credit instrument or the operative amendment, then the teletransmission will not be deemed to be the operative Credit instrument or the operative amendment. The Issuing Bank must forward the operative Credit instrument or the operative amendment to such Advising Bank without delay.

(b) If a bank uses the services of an Advising Bank to have the Credit advised to the Beneficiary, it must also use the services of the same bank for advising an amendment(s).

(c) A preliminary advice of the issuance or amendment of an irrevocable Credit (pre-advice), shall only be given by an Issuing Bank if such bank is prepared to issue the operative Credit instrument or the operative amendment thereto. Unless otherwise stated in such preliminary advice by the Issuing Bank, an Issuing Bank having given such pre-advice shall be irrevocably committed to issue or amend the Credit, in terms not inconsistent with the pre-advice, without delay.

Article 12
Incomplete or Unclear Instructions

If incomplete or unclear instructions are received to advise, confirm or amend a Credit, the bank requested to act on such instructions may give preliminary notification to the Beneficiary for information only and without responsibility. This preliminary notification should state clearly that the notification is provided for information only and without the responsibility of the Advising Bank. In any event, the Advising Bank must inform the Issuing Bank of the action taken and request it to provide the necessary information.

The Issuing Bank must provide the necessary information without delay. The Credit will be advised, confirmed or amended, only when complete and clear instructions have been received and if the Advising Bank is then prepared to act on the instructions.

C.   **LIABILITIES AND RESPONSIBILITIES**

Article 13
Standard for Examination of Documents

(a)   Banks must examine all documents stipulated in the Credit with reasonable care, to ascertain whether or not they appear, on their face, to be in compliance with the terms and conditions of the Credit. Compliance of the stipulated documents on their face with the terms and conditions of the Credit, shall be determined by international standard banking practice as reflected in these Articles. Documents which appear on their face to be inconsistent with one another will be considered as not appearing on their face to be in compliance with the terms and conditions of the Credit.

Documents not stipulated in the Credit will not be examined by banks. If they receive such documents, they shall return them to the presenter or pass them on without responsibility.

(b)   The Issuing Bank, the Confirming Bank, if any, or a Nominated Bank acting on their behalf, shall each have a reasonable time, not to exceed seven banking days following the day of receipt of the documents, to examine the documents and determine whether to take up or refuse the documents and to inform the party from which it received the documents accordingly.

(c)   If a Credit contains conditions without stating the document(s) to be presented in compliance therewith, banks will deem such conditions as not stated and will disregard them.

Article 14
Discrepant Documents and Notice

(a)   When the Issuing Bank authorises another bank to pay, incur a deferred payment undertaking, accept Draft(s), or negotiate against documents which appear on their face to be in compliance with the terms and conditions of the Credit, the Issuing Bank and the Confirming Bank, if any, are bound:

   i.   to reimburse the Nominated Bank which has paid, incurred a deferred payment undertaking, accepted Draft(s), or negotiated.
   ii.   to take up the documents.

(b)   Upon receipt of the documents the Issuing Bank and/or Confirming Bank, if any, or a Nominated Bank acting on their behalf, must determine on the basis of the documents alone whether or not they appear on their face to be in compliance with the terms and conditions of the Credit. If the documents appear on their face not to be in compliance with the terms and conditions of the Credit, such banks may refuse to take up the documents.

(c)   If the Issuing Bank determines that the documents appear on their face not to be in compliance with the terms and conditions of the Credit, it may in its sole judgment approach the Applicant for a waiver of the discrepancy(ies). This does not, however, extend the period mentioned in sub-Article 13(b).

(d)   i.   If the Issuing Bank and/or Confirming Bank, if any, or a Nominated Bank acting on their behalf, decides to refuse the documents, it must give notice to that effect by telecommunication or, if that is not possible, by other expeditious means, without delay but no later than the close of the seventh banking day following the day of receipt of the documents. Such notice shall be given to the bank from which it received the documents, or to the Beneficiary, if it received the documents directly from him.

   ii.   Such notice must state all discrepancies in respect of which the bank refuses the documents and must also state whether it is holding the documents at the disposal of, or is returning them to, the presenter.

   iii.   The Issuing Bank and/or Confirming Bank, if any, shall then be entitled to claim from the remitting bank refund, with interest, of any reimbursement which has been made to that bank.

(e)   If the Issuing Bank and/or Confirming Bank, if any, fails to act in accordance with the provisions of this Article and/or fails to hold the documents at the disposal of, or return them to the presenter, the Issuing Bank and/or Confirming Bank, if any, shall be precluded from claiming that the documents are not in compliance with the terms and conditions of the Credit.

(f)   If the remitting bank draws the attention of the Issuing Bank and/or Confirming Bank, if any, to any discrepancy(ies) in the document(s) or advises such banks that it has paid, incurred a deferred payment undertaking, accepted Draft(s) or negotiated under reserve or against an indemnity in respect of such discrepancy(ies), the Issuing Bank and/or Confirming Bank, if any, shall not be thereby relieved from any of their obligations under any provision of this Article. Such reserve or indemnity concerns only the relations between the remitting bank and the party towards whom the reserve was made, or from whom, or on whose behalf, the indemnity was obtained.

Article 15
Disclaimer on Effectiveness of Documents

Banks assume no liability or responsibility for the form, sufficiency, accuracy, genuineness, falsification or legal effect of any document(s), or for the general and/or particular conditions stipulated in the document(s) or superimposed thereon; nor do they assume any liability or responsibility for the description, quantity, weight, quality, condition, packing, delivery, value or existence of the goods represented by any document(s), or for the good faith or acts and/or omissions, solvency, performance or standing of the consignors, the carriers, the forwarders, the consignees or the insurers of the goods, or any other person whomsoever.

Article 16
Disclaimer on the Transmission of Messages

Banks assume no liability or responsibility for the consequences arising out of delay and/or loss in transit of any message(s), letter(s) or document(s), or for delay, mutilation or other error(s) arising in the transmission of any telecommunication. Banks assume no liability or responsibility for errors in translation and/or interpretation of technical terms, and reserve the right to transmit Credit terms without translating them.

Article 17
Force Majeure

Banks assume no liability or responsibility for the consequences arising out of the interruption of their business by Acts of God, riots, civil commotions, insurrections, wars or any other causes beyond their control, or by any strikes or lockouts. Unless specifically authorised, banks will not, upon resumption of their business, pay, incur a deferred payment undertaking, accept Draft(s) or negotiate under Credits which expired during such interruption of their business.

Article 18
Disclaimer for Acts of an Instructed Party

(a)   Banks utilizing the services of another bank or other banks for the purpose of giving effect to the instructions of the Applicant do so for the account and at the risk of such Applicant.

(b)   Banks assume no liability or responsibility should the instructions they transmit not be carried out, even if they have themselves taken the initiative in the choice of such other bank(s).

(c)   i.   A party instructing another party to perform services is liable for any charges, including commissions, fees, costs or expenses incurred by the instructed party in connection with its instructions.

ii.   Where a Credit stipulates that such charges are for the account of a party other than the instructing party, and charges cannot be collected, the instructing party remains ultimately liable for the payment thereof.

(d)   The Applicant shall be bound by and liable to indemnify the banks against all obligations and responsibilities imposed by foreign laws and usages.

Article 19
Bank-to-Bank Reimbursement Arrangements

(a)   If an Issuing Bank intends that the reimbursement to which a paying, accepting or negotiating bank is entitled, shall be obtained by such bank (the "Claiming Bank"), claiming on another party (the "Reimbursing Bank"), it shall provide such Reimbursing Bank in good time with the proper instructions or authorisation to honour such reimbursement claims.

(b)   Issuing Banks shall not require a Claiming Bank to supply a certificate of compliance with the terms and conditions of the Credit to the Reimbursing Bank.

(c)   An Issuing Bank shall not be relieved from any of its obligations to provide reimbursement if and when reimbursement is not received by the Claiming Bank from the Reimbursing Bank.

(d)   The Issuing Bank shall be responsible to the Claiming Bank for any loss of interest if reimbursement is not provided by the Reimbursing Bank on first demand, or as otherwise specified in the Credit, or mutually agreed, as the case may be.

(e)   The Reimbursing Bank's charges should be for the account of the Issuing Bank. However, in cases where the charges are for the account of another party, it is the responsibility of the Issuing Bank to so indicate in the original Credit and in the reimbursement authorisation. In cases where the Reimbursing Bank's charges are for the account of another party they shall be collected from the Claiming Bank when the Credit is drawn under. In cases where the Credit is not drawn under, the Reimbursing Bank's charges remain the obligation of the Issuing Bank.

D.   DOCUMENTS

Article 20
Ambiguity as to the Issuers of Documents

(a)   Terms such as "first class", "well known", "qualified", "independent", "official", "competent", "local" and the like, shall not be used to describe the issuers of any document(s) to be presented under a Credit. If such terms are incorporated in the Credit, banks will accept the relative document(s) as presented, provided that it appears on its face to be in compliance with the other terms and conditions of the Credit and not to have been issued by the Beneficiary.

(b)   Unless otherwise stipulated in the Credit, banks will also accept as an original document(s), a document(s) produced or appearing to have been produced:

i.   by reprographic, automated or computerized systems;

ii.   as carbon copies;

provided that it is marked as original and, where necessary, appears to be signed.

A document may be signed by handwriting, by facsimile signature, by perforated signature, by stamp, by symbol, or by any other mechanical or electronic method of authentication.

(c)   i.   Unless otherwise stipulated in the Credit, banks will accept as a copy(ies), a document(s) either labelled copy or not marked as an original – a copy(ies) need not be signed.

ii.   Credits that require multiple document(s) such as "duplicate", "two fold", "two copies" and the like, will be satisfied by the presentation of one original and the remaining number in copies except where the document itself indicates otherwise.

(d)   Unless otherwise stipulated in the Credit, a condition under a Credit calling for a document to be authenticated, validated, legalised, visaed, certified or indicating a similar requirement, will be satisfied by any signature, mark, stamp or label on such document that on its face appears to satisfy the above condition.

Article 21
Unspecified Issuers or Contents of Documents

When documents other than transport documents, insurance documents and commercial invoices are called for, the Credit should stipulate by whom such documents are to be issued and their wording or data content. If the Credit does not so stipulate, banks will accept such documents as presented, provided that their data content is not inconsistent with any other stipulated document presented.

Article 22
Issuance Date of Documents v Credit Date

Unless otherwise stipulated in the Credit, banks will accept a document bearing a date of issuance prior to that of the Credit, subject to such document being presented within the time limits set out in the Credit and in these Articles.

Article 23
Marine/Ocean Bill of Lading

(a)   If a Credit calls for a bill of lading covering a port-to-port shipment, banks will, unless otherwise stipulated in the Credit, accept a document, however named, which:

i.   appears on its face to indicate the name of the carrier and to have been signed or otherwise authenticated by:

- the carrier or a named agent for or on behalf of the carrier, or

- the master or a named agent for or on behalf of the master.

Any signature or authentication of the carrier or master must be identified as carrier or master, as the case may be. An agent signing or authenticating for the carrier or master must also indicate the name and the capacity of the party, i.e. carrier or master, on whose behalf that agent is acting,

and

ii.   indicates that the goods have been loaded on board, or shipped on a named vessel.

Loading on board or shipment on a named vessel may be indicated by pre-printed wording on the bill of lading that the goods have been loaded on board a named vessel or shipped on a named vessel, in which case the date of issuance of the bill of lading will be deemed to be the date of loading on board and the date of shipment.

In all other cases loading on board a named vessel must be evidenced by a notation on the bill of lading which gives the date on which the goods have been loaded on board, in which case the date of the on board notation will be deemed to be the date of shipment.

If the bill of lading contains the indication "intended vessel", or similar qualification in relation to the vessel, loading on board a named vessel must be evidenced by an on board notation on the bill of lading which, in addition to the date on which the goods have been loaded on board, also includes the name of the vessel on which the goods have been loaded, even if they have been loaded on the vessel named as the "intended vessel".

If the bill of lading indicates a place of receipt or taking in charge different from the port of loading, the on board notation must also include the port of loading stipulated in the Credit and the name of the vessel on which the goods have been loaded, even if they have been loaded on the vessel named in the bill of lading. This provision also applies whenever loading on board the vessel is indicated by pre-printed wording on the bill of lading,

and

iii.   indicates the port of loading and the port of discharge stipulated in the Credit, notwithstanding that it:

a.   indicates a place of taking in charge different from the port of loading, and/or a place of final destination different from the port of discharge,

and/or

b.   contains the indication "intended" or similar qualification in relation to the port of loading and/or port of discharge, as long as the document also states the ports of loading and/or discharge stipulated in the Credit,

and

iv.   consists of a sole original bill of lading or, if issued in more than one original, the full set as so issued,

and

v.   appears to contain all of the terms and conditions of carriage, or some of such terms and conditions by reference to a source or document other than the bill of lading (short form/blank back bill of lading); banks will not examine the contents of such terms and conditions,

and

vi.   contains no indication that it is subject to a charter party and/or no indication that the carrying vessel is propelled by sail only,

and

vii.   in all other respects meets the stipulations of the Credit.

(b) For the purpose of this Article, transhipment means unloading and reloading from one vessel to another vessel during the course of ocean carriage from the port of loading to the port of discharge stipulated in the Credit.

(c) Unless transhipment is prohibited by the terms of the Credit, banks will accept a bill of lading which indicates that the goods will be transhipped, provided that the entire ocean carriage is covered by one and the same bill of lading.

(d) Even if the Credit prohibits transhipment, banks will accept a bill of lading which:

   i. indicates that transhipment will take place as long as the relevant cargo is shipped in Container(s), Trailer(s) and/or "LASH" barge(s) as evidenced by the bill of lading, provided that the entire ocean carriage is covered by one and the same bill of lading,

   and/or

   ii. incorporates clauses stating that the carrier reserves the right to tranship.

Article 24
Non-Negotiable Sea Waybill

(a) If a Credit calls for a non-negotiable sea waybill covering a port-to-port shipment, banks will, unless otherwise stipulated in the Credit, accept a document, however named, which:

   i. appears on its face to indicate the name of the carrier and to have been signed or otherwise authenticated by:

   – the carrier or a named agent for or on behalf of the carrier, or

   – the master or a named agent for or on behalf of the master.

   Any signature or authentication of the carrier or master must be identified as carrier or master, as the case may be. An agent signing or authenticating for the carrier or master must also indicate the name and the capacity of the party, i.e. carrier or master, on whose behalf that agent is acting,

   and

   ii. indicates that the goods have been loaded on board, or shipped on a named vessel.

   Loading on board or shipment on a named vessel may be indicated by pre-printed wording on the non-negotiable sea waybill that the goods have been loaded on board a named vessel or shipped on a named vessel, in which case the date of issuance of the non-negotiable sea waybill will be deemed to be the date of loading on board and the date of shipment.

   In all other cases loading on board a named vessel must be evidenced by a notation on the non-negotiable sea waybill which gives the date on which the goods have been loaded on board, in which case the date of the on board notation will be deemed to be the date of shipment.

   If the non-negotiable sea waybill contains the indication "intended vessel", or similar qualification in relation to the vessel, loading on board a named vessel must be evidenced by an on board notation on the non-negotiable sea waybill which, in addition to the date on which the goods have been loaded on board, includes the name of the vessel on which the goods have been loaded, even if they have been loaded on the vessel named as the "intended vessel".

   If the non-negotiable sea waybill indicates a place of receipt or taking in charge different from the port of loading, the on board notation must also include the port of loading stipulated in the Credit and the name of the vessel on which the goods have been loaded, even if they have been loaded on a vessel named in the non-negotiable sea waybill. This provision also applies whenever loading on board the vessel is indicated by pre-printed wording on the non-negotiable sea waybill,

   and

   iii. indicates the port of loading and the port of discharge stipulated in the Credit, notwithstanding that it:

a. indicates a place of taking in charge different from the port of loading, and/or a place of final destination different from the port of discharge,

and/or

b. contains the indication "intended" or similar qualification in relation to the port of loading and/or port of discharge, as long as the document also states the ports of loading and/or discharge stipulated in the Credit,

and

iv. consists of a sole original non-negotiable sea waybill, or if issued in more than one original, the full set as so issued,

and

v. appears to contain all of the terms and conditions of carriage, or some of such terms and conditions by reference to a source or document other than the non-negotiable sea waybill (short form/blank back non-negotiable sea waybill); banks will not examine the contents of such terms and conditions,

and

vi. contains no indication that it is subject to a charter party and/or no indication that the carrying vessel is propelled by sail only,

and

vii. in all other respects meets the stipulations of the Credit.

(b) For the purpose of this Article, transhipment means unloading and reloading from one vessel to another vessel during the course of ocean carriage from the port of loading to the port of discharge stipulated in the Credit.

(c) Unless transhipment is prohibited by the terms of the Credit, banks will accept a non-negotiable sea waybill which indicates that the goods will be transhipped, provided that the entire ocean carriage is covered by one and the same non-negotiable sea waybill.

(d) Even if the Credit prohibits transhipment, banks will accept a non-negotiable sea waybill which:

i. indicates that transhipment will take place as long as the relevant cargo is shipped in Container(s), Trailer(s) and/or "LASH" barge(s) as evidenced by the non-negotiable sea waybill, provided that the entire ocean carriage is covered by one and the same non-negotiable sea waybill,

and/or

ii. incorporates clauses stating that the carrier reserves the right to tranship.

Article 25
Charter Party Bill of Lading

(a) If a Credit calls for or permits a charter party bill of lading, banks will, unless otherwise stipulated in the Credit, accept a document, however named, which:

i. contains any indication that it is subject to a charter party,

and

ii. appears on its face to have been signed or otherwise authenticated by:

– the master or a named agent for or on behalf of the master, or

– the owner or a named agent for or on behalf of the owner.

Any signature or authentication of the master or owner must be identified as master or owner as the case may be. An agent signing or authenticating for the master or owner must also indicate the name and the capacity of the party, i.e. master or owner, on whose behalf that agent is acting,

and

iii.   does or does not indicate the name of the carrier,

and

iv.   indicates that the goods have been loaded on board or shipped on a named vessel.

Loading on board or shipment on a named vessel may be indicated by pre-printed wording on the bill of lading that the goods have been loaded on board a named vessel or shipped on a named vessel, in which case the date of issuance of the bill of lading will be deemed to be the date of loading on board and the date of shipment.

In all other cases loading on board a named vessel must be evidenced by a notation on the bill of lading which gives the date on which the goods have been loaded on board, in which case the date of the on board notation will be deemed to be the date of shipment,

and

v.   indicates the port of loading and the port of discharge stipulated in the Credit,

and

vi.   consists of a sole original bill of lading or, if issued in more than one original, the full set as so issued,

and

vii.   contains no indication that the carrying vessel is propelled by sail only,

and

viii.   in all other respects meets the stipulations of the Credit.

(b)   Even if the Credit requires the presentation of a charter party contract in connection with a charter party bill of lading, banks will not examine such charter party contract, but will pass it on without responsibility on their part.

Article 26
Multimodal Transport Document

(a)   If a Credit calls for a transport document covering at least two different modes of transport (multimodal transport), banks will, unless otherwise stipulated in the Credit, accept a document, however named, which:

i.   appears on its face to indicate the name of the carrier or multimodal transport operator and to have been signed or otherwise authenticated by:

– the carrier or multimodal transport operator or a named agent for or on behalf of the carrier or multimodal transport operator, or

– the master or a named agent for or on behalf of the master.

Any signature or authentication of the carrier, multimodal transport operator or master must be identified as carrier, multimodal transport operator or master, as the case may be. An agent signing or authenticating for the carrier, multimodal transport operator or master must also indicate the name and the capacity of the party, i.e. carrier, multimodal transport operator or master, on whose behalf that agent is acting,

and

ii.   indicates that the goods have been dispatched, taken in charge or loaded on board.

Dispatch, taking in charge or loading on board may be indicated by wording to that effect on the multimodal transport document and the date of issuance will be deemed to be the date of dispatch, taking in charge or loading on board and the date of shipment. However, if the document indicates, by stamp or otherwise, a date of dispatch, taking in charge or loading on board, such date will be deemed to be the date of shipment,

and

iii.   a.   indicates the place of taking in charge stipulated in the Credit which may be different from the port, airport or place of loading, and the place of final designation stipulated in the Credit which may be different from the port, airport or place of discharge,

and/or

b.   contains the indication "intended" or similar qualification in relation to the vessel and/or port of loading and/or port of discharge,

and

iv.   consists of a sole original multimodal transport document or, if issued in more than one original, the full set as so issued,

and

v.   appears to contain all of the terms and conditions of carriage, or some of such terms and conditions by reference to a source or document other than the multimodal transport document (short form/blank back multimodal transport document); banks will not examine the contents of such terms and conditions,

and

vi.   contains no indication that it is subject to a charter party and/or no indication that the carrying vessel is propelled by sail only,

and

vii.   in all other respects meets the stipulations of the Credit.

(b)   Even if the Credit prohibits transhipment, banks will accept a multimodal transport document which indicates that transhipment will or may take place, provided that the entire carriage is covered by one and the same multimodal transport document.

Article 27
Air Transport Document

(a)   If a Credit calls for an air transport document, banks will, unless otherwise stipulated in the Credit, accept a document, however named, which:

i.   appears on its face to indicate the name of the carrier and to have been signed or otherwise authenticated by:

–   the carrier, or

–   a named agent for or on behalf of the carrier.

Any signature or authentication of the carrier must be identified as carrier. An agent signing or authenticating for the carrier must also indicate the name and the capacity of the party, i.e. carrier, on whose behalf that agent is acting,

and

ii.   indicates that the goods have been accepted for carriage,

and

iii.   where the Credit calls for an actual date of dispatch, indicates a specific notation of such date, the date of dispatch so indicated on the air transport document will be deemed to be the date of shipment.

For the purpose of this Article, the information appearing in the box on the air transport document (marked "For Carrier Use Only" or similar expression) relative to the flight number and date will not be considered as a specific notation of such date of dispatch.

In all other cases, the date of issuance of the air transport document will be deemed to be the date of shipment,

and

iv.   indicates the airport of departure and the airport of destination stipulated in the Credit,

and

v.   appears to be the original for consignor/shipper even if the Credit stipulates a full set or originals, or similar expressions,

and

vi.   appears to contain all of the terms and conditions of carriage, or some of such terms and conditions, by reference to a source or document other than the air transport document; banks will not examine the contents of such terms and conditions,

and

vii.   in all other respects meets the stipulations of the Credit.

(b)   For the purpose of this Article, transhipment means unloading and reloading from one aircraft to another aircraft during the course of carriage from the airport of departure to the airport of destination stipulated in the Credit.

(c)   Even if the Credit prohibits transhipment, banks will accept an air transport document which indicates that transhipment will or may take place, provided that the entire carriage is covered by one and the same air transport document.

Article 28
Road, Rail or Inland Waterway Transport Documents

(a)   If a Credit calls for a road, rail, or inland waterway transport document, banks will, unless otherwise stipulated in the Credit, accept a document of the type called for, however named, which:

i.   appears on its face to indicate the name of the carrier and to have been signed or otherwise authenticated by the carrier or a named agent for or on behalf of the carrier and/or to bear a reception stamp or other indication of receipt by the carrier or a named agent for or on behalf of the carrier.

Any signature, authentication, reception stamp or other indication of receipt of the carrier, must be identified on its face as that of the carrier. An agent signing or authenticating for the carrier, must also indicate the name and the capacity of the party, i.e. carrier, on whose behalf that agent is acting,

and

ii.   indicates that the goods have been received for shipment, dispatch or carriage or wording to this effect. The date of issuance will be deemed to be the date of shipment unless the transport document contains a reception stamp, in which case the date of the reception stamp will be deemed to be the date of shipment,

and

iii.   indicates the place of shipment and the place of destination stipulated in the Credit,

and

iv.   in all other respects meets the stipulations of the Credit.

(b)   In the absence of any indication on the transport document as to the numbers issued, banks will accept the transport document(s) presented as constituting a full set. Banks will accept as original(s) the transport document(s) whether marked as original(s) or not.

(c)   For the purpose of this Article, transhipment means unloading and reloading from one means of conveyance to another means of conveyance, in different modes of transport, during the course of carriage from the place of shipment to the place of destination stipulated in the Credit.

(d)   Even if the Credit prohibits transhipment, banks will accept a road, rail, or inland waterway transport document which indicates that transhipment will or may take place, provided that the entire carriage is covered by one and the same transport document and within the same mode of transport.

Article 29
Courier and Post Receipts

(a) If a Credit calls for a post receipt or certificate of posting, banks will, unless otherwise stipulated in the Credit, accept a post receipt or certificate of posting which:

    i. appears on its face to have been stamped or otherwise authenticated and dated in the place from which the Credit stipulates the goods are to be shipped or dispatched and such date will be deemed to be the date of shipment or dispatch,

    and

    ii. in all other respects meets the stipulations of the Credit.

(b) If a Credit calls for a document issued by a courier or expedited delivery service evidencing receipt of the goods for delivery, banks will, unless otherwise stipulated in the Credit, accept a document, however named, which:

    i. appears on its face to indicate the name of the courier/service, and to have been stamped, signed or otherwise authenticated by such named courier/service (unless the Credit specifically calls for a document issued by a named Courier/Service, banks will accept a document issued by any Courier/Service),

    and

    ii. indicates a date of pick-up or of receipt or wording to this effect, such date being deemed to be the date of shipment or dispatch,

    and

    iii. in all other respects meets the stipulations of the Credit.

Article 30
Transport Documents Issued by Freight Forwarders

Unless otherwise authorised in the Credit, banks will only accept a transport document issued by a freight forwarder if it appears on its face to indicate:

i. the name of the freight forwarder as a carrier or multimodal transport operator and to have been signed or otherwise authenticated by the freight forwarder as carrier or multimodal transport operator,

    or

ii. the name of the carrier or multimodal transport operator and to have been signed or otherwise authenticated by the freight forwarder as a named agent for or on behalf of the carrier or multimodel transport operator.

Article 31
"On Deck", "Shipper's Load and Count", Name of consignor

Unless otherwise stipulated in the Credit, banks will accept a transport document which:

i. does not indicate, in the case of carriage by sea or by more than one means of conveyance including carriage by sea, that the goods are or will be loaded on deck. Nevertheless, banks will accept a transport document which contains a provision that the goods may be carried on deck, provided that it does not specifically state that they are or will be loaded on deck,

    and/or

ii. bears a clause on the face thereof such as "shipper's load and count" or "said by shipper to contain" or words of similar effect,

    and/or

iii. indicates as the consignor of the goods a party other than the Beneficiary of the Credit.

Article 32
Clean Transport Documents

(a) A clean transport document is one which bears no clause or notation which expressly declares a defective condition of the goods and/or the packaging.

(b)   Banks will not accept transport documents bearing such clauses or notations unless the Credit expressly stipulates the clauses or notations which may be accepted.

(c)   Banks will regard a requirement in a Credit for a transport document to bear the clause "clean on board" as complied with if such transport document meets the requirements of this Article and of Articles 23, 24, 25, 26, 27, 28 or 30.

Article 33
Freight Payable/Prepaid Transport Documents

(a)   Unless otherwise stipulated in the Credit, or inconsistent with any of the documents presented under the Credit, banks will accept transport documents stating that freight or transportation charges (hereafter referred to as "freight") have still to be paid.

(b)   If a Credit stipulates that the transport document has to indicate that freight has been paid or prepaid, banks will accept a transport document on which words clearly indicating payment or prepayment of freight appear by stamp or otherwise, or on which payment or prepayment of freight is indicated by other means. If the Credit requires courier charges to be paid or prepaid banks will also accept a transport document issued by a courier or expedited delivery service evidencing that courier charges are for the account of a party other than the consignee.

(c)   The words "freight prepayable" or "freight to be prepaid" or words of similar effect, if appearing on transport documents, will not be accepted as constituting evidence of the payment of freight.

(d)   Banks will accept transport documents bearing reference by stamp or otherwise to costs additional to the freight, such as costs of, or disbursements incurred in connection with, loading, unloading or similar operations, unless the conditions of the Credit specifically prohibit such reference.

Article 34
Insurance Documents

(a)   Insurance documents must appear on their face to be issued and signed by insurance companies or underwriters or their agents.

(b)   If the insurance document indicates that it has been issued in more than one original, all the originals must be presented unless otherwise authorised in the Credit.

(c)   Cover notes issued by brokers will not be accepted, unless specifically authorised in the Credit.

(d)   Unless otherwise stipulated in the Credit, banks will accept an insurance certificate or a declaration under an open cover pre-signed by insurance companies or underwriters or their agents. If a Credit specifically calls for an insurance certificate or a declaration under an open cover, banks will accept, in lieu thereof, an insurance policy.

(e)   Unless otherwise stipulated in the Credit, or unless it appears from the insurance document that the cover is effective at the latest from the date of loading on board or dispatch or taking in charge of the goods, banks will not accept an insurance document which bears a date of issuance later than the date of loading on board or dispatch or taking in charge as indicated in such transport document.

(f)   i.   Unless otherwise stipulated in the Credit, the insurance document must be expressed in the same currency as the Credit.

         ii.   Unless otherwise stipulated in the Credit, the minimum amount for which the insurance document must indicate the insurance cover to have been effected is the CIF (cost, insurance and freight (... "named port of destination")) or CIP (carriage and insurance paid to (... "named place of destination")) value of the goods, as the case may be, plus 10%, but only when the CIF or CIP value can be determined from the documents on their face. Otherwise, banks will accept as such minimum amount 110% of the amount for which payment, acceptance or negotiation is requested under the Credit, or 110% of the gross amount of the invoice, whichever is the greater.

Article 35

Type of Insurance Cover

(a)   Credits should stipulate the type of insurance required and, if any, the additional risks which are to be covered. Imprecise terms such as "usual risks" or "customary risks" shall not be used; if they are used, banks will accept insurance documents as presented, without responsibility for any risks not being covered.

(b)   Failing specific stipulations in the Credit, banks will accept insurance documents as presented, without responsibility for any risks not being covered.

(c)   Unless otherwise stipulated in the Credit, banks will accept an insurance document which indicates that the cover is subject to a franchise or an excess (deductible).

Article 36

All Risks Insurance Cover

Where a Credit stipulates "insurance against all risks", banks will accept an insurance document which contains any "all risks" notation or clause, whether or not bearing the heading "all risks", even if the insurance document indicates that certain risks are excluded, without responsibility for any risk(s) not being covered.

Article 37

Commercial Invoices

(a)   Unless otherwise stipulated in the Credit, commercial invoices:

    i.   must appear on their face to be issued by the Beneficiary named in the Credit (except as provided in Article 48),

    and

    ii.   must be made out in the name of the Applicant (except as provided in sub-Article 48(h)),

    and

    iii.   need not be signed.

(b)   Unless otherwise stipulated in the Credit, banks may refuse commercial invoices issued for amounts in excess of the amount permitted by the Credit. Nevertheless, if a bank authorised to pay, incur a deferred payment undertaking, accept Draft(s), or negotiate under a Credit accepts such invoices, its decision will be binding upon all parties, provided that such bank has not paid, incurred a deferred payment undertaking, accepted Draft(s) or negotiated for an amount in excess of that permitted by the Credit.

(c)   The description of the goods in the commercial invoice must correspond with the description in the Credit. In all other documents, the goods may be described in general terms not inconsistent with the description of the goods in the Credit.

Article 38

Other Documents

If a Credit calls for an attestation or certification of weight in the case of transport other than by sea, banks will accept a weight stamp or declaration of weight which appears to have been superimposed on the transport document by the carrier or his agent unless the Credit specifically stipulates that the attestation or certification of weight must be by means of a separate document.

E.   MISCELLANEOUS PROVISIONS

Article 39

Allowances in Credit Amount, Quantity and Unit Price

(a)   The words "about", "approximately", "circa" or similar expressions used in connection with the amount of the Credit or the quantity or the unit price stated in the Credit are to be construed as allowing a difference not to exceed 10% more or 10% less than the amount or the quantity or the unit price to which they refer.

(b)   Unless a Credit stipulates that the quantity of the goods specified must not be exceeded or reduced, a tolerance of 5% more or 5% less will be permissible, always provided that the amount of the drawings does not exceed the amount of the Credit. This tolerance does not apply when the Credit stipulates the quantity in terms of a stated number of packing units or individual items.

(c)   Unless a Credit which prohibits partial shipments stipulates otherwise, or unless sub-Article (b) above is applicable, a tolerance of 5% less in the amount of the drawing will be permissible, provided that if the Credit stipulates the quantity of the goods, such quantity of goods is shipped in full, and if the Credit stipulates a unit price, such price is not reduced. This provision does not apply when expressions referred to in sub-Article (a) above are used in the Credit.

Article 40
Partial Shipments/Drawings
(a)   Partial drawings and/or shipments are allowed, unless the Credit stipulates otherwise.

(b)   Transport documents which appear on their face to indicate that shipment has been made on the same means of conveyance and for the same journey, provided they indicate the same destination, will not be regarded as covering partial shipments, even if the transport documents indicate different dates of shipment and/or different ports of loading, places of taking in charge, or dispatch.

(c)   Shipments made by post or by courier will not be regarded as partial shipments if the post receipts or certificates of posting or courier's receipts or dispatch notes appear to have been stamped, signed or otherwise authenticated in the place from which the Credit stipulates the goods are to be dispatched, and on the same date.

Article 41
Instalment Shipments/Drawings
If drawings and/or shipments by instalments within given periods are stipulated in the Credit and any instalment is not drawn and/or shipped within the period allowed for that instalment, the Credit ceases to be available for that and any subsequent instalments, unless otherwise stipulated in the Credit.

Article 42
Expiry Date and Place for Presentation of Documents
(a)   All Credits must stipulate an expiry date and a place for presentation of documents for payment, acceptance, or with the exception of freely negotiable Credits, a place for presentation of documents for negotiation. An expiry date stipulated for payment, acceptance or negotiation will be construed to express an expiry date for presentation of documents.

(b)   Except as provided in sub-Article 44(a), documents must be presented on or before such expiry date.

(c)   If an Issuing Bank states that the Credit is to be available "for one month", "for six months", or the like, but does not specify the date from which the time is to run, the date of issuance of the Credit by the Issuing Bank will be deemed to be the first day from which such time is to run. Banks should discourage indication of the expiry date of the Credit in this manner.

Article 43
Limitation on the Expiry Date
(a)   In addition to stipulating an expiry date for presentation of documents, every Credit which calls for a transport document(s) should also stipulate a specified period of time after the date of shipment during which presentation must be made in compliance with the terms and conditions of the Credit. If no such period of time is stipulated, banks will not accept documents presented to them later than 21 days after the date of shipment. In any event, documents must be presented not later than the expiry date of the Credit.

(b)   In cases in which sub-Article 40(b) applies, the date of shipment will be considered to be the latest shipment date on any of the transport documents presented.

Article 44
Extension of Expiry Date

(a)   If the expiry date of the Credit and/or the last day of the period of time for presentation of documents stipulated by the Credit or applicable by virtue of Article 43 falls on a day on which the bank to which presentation has to be made is closed for reasons other than those referred to in Article 17, the stipulated expiry date and/or the last day of the period of time after the date of shipment for presentation of documents, as the case may be, shall be extended to the first following day on which such bank is open.

(b)   The latest date for shipment shall not be extended by reason of the extension of the expiry date and/or the period of time after the date of shipment for presentation of documents in accordance with sub-Article (a) above. If no such latest date for shipment is stipulated in the Credit or amendments thereto, banks will not accept transport documents indicating a date of shipment later than the expiry date stipulated in the Credit or amendments thereto.

(c)   The bank to which presentation is made on such first following business day must provide a statement that the documents were presented within the time limits extended in accordance with sub-Article 44(a) of the Uniform Customs and Practice for Documentary Credits, 1993 Revision, ICC Publication No. 500.

Article 45
House of Presentation

Banks are under no obligation to accept presentation of documents outside their banking hours.

Article 46
General Expressions as to Dates for Shipment

(a)   Unless otherwise stipulated in the Credit, the expression "shipment" used in stipulating an earliest and/or a latest date for shipment will be understood to include expressions such as, "loading on board", "dispatch", "accepted for carriage", "date of post receipt", "date of pick-up", and the like, and in the case of a Credit calling for a multimodal transport document the expression "taking in charge".

(b)   Expressions such as "prompt", "immediately", "as soon as possible", and the like should not be used. If they are used banks will disregard them.

(c)   If the expression "on or about" or similar expressions are used, banks will interpret them as a stipulation that shipment is to be made during the period from five days before to five days after the specified date, both end days included.

Article 47
Date Terminology for Periods of Shipment

(a)   The words "to", "until", "till", "from" and words of similar import applying to any date or period in the Credit referring to shipment will be understood to include the date mentioned.

(b)   The word "after" will be understood to exclude the date mentioned.

(c)   The terms "first half", "second half" of a month shall be construed respectively as the 1st to the 15th, and the 16th to the last day of such month, all dates inclusive.

(d)   The terms "beginning", "middle" or "end" of a month shall be construed respectively as the 1st to the 10th, the 11th to the 20th, and the 21st to the last day of such month, all dates inclusive.

F.   TRANSFERABLE CREDIT

Article 48
Transferable Credit

(a)   A transferable Credit is a Credit under which the Beneficiary (First Beneficiary) may request the bank authorised to pay, incur a deferred payment undertaking, accept or negotiate (the "Transferring Bank"), or in the case of a freely negotiable Credit, the bank specifically authorised in the Credit as a Transferring Bank, to make the Credit available in whole or in part to one or more other Beneficiary(ies) (Second Beneficiary(ies)).

(b)   A Credit can be transferred only if it is expressly designated as "transferable" by the Issuing Bank. Terms such as "divisible", "fractionable", "assignable", and "transmissible" do not render the Credit transferable. If such terms are used they shall be disregarded.

(c)   The Transferring Bank shall be under no obligation to effect such transfer except to the extent and in the manner expressly consented to by such bank.

(d)   At the time of making a request for transfer and prior to transfer of the Credit, the First Beneficiary must irrevocably instruct the Transferring Bank whether or not he retains the right to refuse to allow the Transferring Bank to advise amendments to the Second Beneficiary(ies). If the Transferring Bank consents to the transfer under these conditions, it must, at the time of transfer, advise the Second Beneficiary(ies) of the First Beneficiary's instructions regarding amendments.

(e)   If a Credit is transferred to more than one Second Beneficiary(ies), refusal of an amendment by one or more Second Beneficiary(ies) does not invalidate the acceptance(s) by the other Second Beneficiary(ies) with respect to whom the Credit will be amended accordingly. With respect to the Second Beneficiary(ies) who rejected the amendment, the Credit will remain unamended.

(f)   Transferring Bank charges in respect of transfers including commisisons, fees, costs or expenses are payable by the First Beneficiary, unless otherwise agreed. If the Transferring bank agrees to transfer the Credit it shall be under no obligation to effect the transfer until such charges are paid.

(g)   Unless otherwise stated in the Credit, a transferable Credit can be transferred once only. Consequently, the Credit cannot be transferred at the request of the Second Beneficiary to any subsequent Third Beneficiary. For the purpose of this Article, a retransfer to the First Beneficiary does not constitute a prohibited transfer.

Fractions of a transferable Credit (not exceeding in the aggregate the amount of the Credit) can be transferred separately, provided partial shipments/drawings are not prohibited, and the aggregate of such transfers will be considered as constituting only one transfer of the Credit.

(h)   The Credit can be transferred only on the terms and conditions specified in the original Credit, with the exception of:
- the amount of the Credit,
- any unit price stated therein,
- the expiry date,
- the last date for presentation of documents in accordance with Article 43,
- the period for shipment,

any or all of which may be reduced or curtailed.

The percentage for which insurance cover must be effected may be increased in such a way as to provide the amount of cover stipulated in the original Credit, or these Articles.

In addition, the name of the First Beneficiary can be substituted for that of the Applicant, but if the name of the Applicant is specifically required by the original Credit to appear in any document(s) other than the invoice, such requirement must be fulfilled.

(i)   The First Beneficiary has the right to substitute his own invoice(s) (and Draft(s)) for those of the Second Beneficiary(ies), for amounts not in excess of the original amount stipulated in the Credit and for the original unit prices if stipulated in the Credit, and upon such substitution of invoice(s) (and Draft(s)) the First Beneficiary can draw under the Credit for the difference, if any, between his invoice(s) and the Second Beneficiary's (ies') invoice(s).

When a Credit has been transferred and the First Beneficiary is to supply his own invoice(s) (and Draft(s)) in exchange for the Second Beneficiary"s(ies') invoice(s) (and Draft(s)) but fails to do so on first demand, the Transferring Bank has the right to deliver to the Issuing Bank the documents received under the transferred Credit, including the Second Beneficiary's(ies') invoice(s) (and Draft(s)) without further responsibility to the First Beneficiary.

(j)   The First Beneficiary may request that payment or negotiation be effected to the Second Beneficiary(ies) at the place to which the Credit has been transferred up to and including the expiry date of the Credit, unless the original Credit expressly states that it may not be made available for payment or negotiation at a place other than that stipulated in the Credit. This is without prejudice to the First Beneficiary's right to substitute subsequently his own invoice(s) (and Draft(s)) for those of the Second Beneficiary(ies) and to claim any difference due to him.

G.   ASSIGNMENT OF PROCEEDS

Article 49
Assignment of Proceeds
The fact that a Credit is not stated to be transferable shall not affect the Beneficiary's right to assign any proceeds to which he may be, or may become, entitled under such Credit, in accordance with the provisions of the applicable law. This Article relates only to the assignment of proceeds and not to the assignment of the right to perform under the Credit itself.

ICC Uniform Customs and Practice for Documentary Credits – 1993 Revision
ICC Publication 500 – ISBN 92.842.1155.7
Published in its official English version by the International Chamber of Commerce, Paris
Copyright © 1993 – International Chamber of Commerce (ICC)
Available from: ICC Publishing SA, 38 Cours Albert 1er, 75008 Paris, France
And from: ICC United Kingdom, 14/15 Belgrave Square, London SW1X 8PS

❏ Documents and *Uniform Customs and Practice*

Documents have already been fully discussed in lesson 6 but it is appropriate here to summarise the requirements of *Uniform Customs and Practice* with regard to the main documents, i.e. bills of lading/transport documents, insurance documents and commercial invoices. Note the following general points about documents:

- Banks must examine documents with reasonable care to ensure that they appear to be in order and in accordance with the terms and conditions of the credit. Where there are inconsistencies, they will be considered as not being in accordance with the terms and conditions of the credit (Article 13).

- Documents not stipulated in the credit will not be examined by banks: any such non-stipulated documents will either be returned to the presenter or passed on without responsibility (Article 13).

- Banks have a reasonable time – not exceeding seven banking days following the day of receipt of the documents – in order to determine whether to take up or refuse the documents (Article 13).

- Banks assume no liability for the genuineness of documents (Article 15).

- Unless otherwise stipulated in the credit, banks will accept as originals documents produced or appearing to have been produced by photocopier, computer, and carbon copies, provided that they are marked as originals and, where necessary, appear to be signed. Note that a signature can be by means of handwriting, facsimile signature, perforated signature, stamp, symbol or other means of authentication (Article 20).

Marine/Ocean Bill of Lading (Article 23)

The following bills of lading will be accepted unless otherwise stipulated in the credit:

- a bill of lading that indicates a place of taking in charge different from the port of loading, and/or a place of final destination different from the port of discharge

- a short form bill of lading

- a bill of lading which indicates that the goods will be transhipped (provided that the entire ocean carriage is covered by one and the same bill of lading)

Note that even if a credit prohibits transhipment, banks will accept a bill of lading which indicates that transhipment will take place – provided that the goods are shipped in containers, trailers and/or LASH barges, and that the entire ocean carriage is covered by one and the same document. Banks will also accept clauses stating that the carrier reserves the right to tranship.

The following bills of lading will not be accepted unless specifically authorised in the credit:

- a charter party bill of lading (see also Article 25)

- a bill of lading covering shipment by a vessel propelled by sail only

- a bill of lading which contains the indication "intended vessel", unless the bill is marked 'on board' and includes the date of loading and the name of the vessel (even if it is the same name as the "intended vessel")

To be acceptable under *Uniform Customs and Practice*, bills of lading should be 'clean' (Article 32) and 'on board'. If a credit calls for 'on board' bills of lading, a 'received for shipment' bill is not acceptable; an 'on board' notation, which also gives the date of loading, is acceptable. A full set of bills of lading is required; if only one original bill is issued, then that is acceptable.

Unless otherwise stated in the credit, banks will refuse 'foul' or 'claused' bills of lading (Article 32), and also those that indicate the goods are loaded on deck (Article 31).

Other transport documents (Articles 24-30)

Uniform Customs and Practice includes Articles on:

- Non-Negotiable Sea Waybill (Article 24)
  – similar provisions as for the Marine/Ocean Bill of Lading
- Charter Party Bill of Lading (Article 25)
- Multimodal Transport Document (Article 26)
  – acceptable, unless otherwise stipulated in the credit, where a credit calls for a transport document covering at least two different modes of transport
- Air Transport Document (Article 27)
- Road, Rail or Inland Waterway Transport Documents (Article 28)
- Courier and Post Receipts (Article 29)
- Transport Documents issued by Freight Forwarders (Article 30)

Insurance Documents (Articles 24-36)

- The insurance document must be issued and signed by insurance companies or underwriters or their agents.
- Unless specifically authorised by the credit, cover notes will not be accepted.
- The insurance documents must establish that cover is effective, at the latest, from the date of loading on board/dispatch/taking in charge as indicated on the transport document.
- The insurance document must be expressed in the same currency as the credit.
- The amount covered must be at least CIF or CIP value plus 10% (where CIF or CIP value cannot be determined, banks will accept cover for a minimum amount of 110% of the credit or 110% of the invoice, whichever is the greater).
- Credits should stipulate the type of insurance required and, if any, the additional risks which are to be covered. (Where a credit stipulates "insurance against all risks", banks will accept an insurance document containing the words "all risks" even if it then says that certain risks are excluded).

Commercial Invoices (Article 37)

- The description of the goods in the invoice must correspond with the description of the goods in the credit. (In all other documents, the goods can be described in general terms).
- Unless otherwise stipulated in the credit, banks may refuse commercial invoices issued for amounts in excess of the amount permitted by the credit.
- The invoice must appear to have been issued by the beneficiary named in the credit (except for transferable credits – see Lesson 8), and must be made out in the name of the applicant.
- Invoices need not be signed.

Other points

- Allowances in Credit Amount, Quantity and Unit Price (Article 39)
  - The words 'about', 'approximately', 'circa' or similar expression are construed as allowing a difference not exceeding 10% or 10% less in the credit amount, quantity, or unit price.
  - Unless the credit stipulates that the quantity of the goods specified must not be exceeded or reduced, a tolerance of 5% either way is permissible, provided that the amount of the drawings does not exceed the amount of the credit. This tolerance does not apply when the credit stipulates a certain number of packing units or individual items.
- Limitation on the Expiry Date (Article 43)
  - Unless otherwise stipulated, banks will not accept documents presented later than 21 days after the date of shiping.
  - In any event, documents must be presented not later than the expiry date of the credit.

❏ **Examination hints**

• Documentary credits have featured in all papers in recent years and, so, are an important topic: watch for the phrase 'secure methods of payment' in a question - this hints at the use of documentary credits.

• You need to be able to explain to a customer what a documentary credit is, and to explain its advantages and disadvantages to either exporter or importer.

• The examiner sometimes asks for a comparison between a documentary credit and a collection.

• From time-to-time questions have been asked about the commercial documents that are acceptable under UCP. On a similar theme the problem of discrepancies in documents and how a bank is to handle them should be known (see also pages 157-8).

Know Your .... Documentary Credits: 1

1.   Define a documentary credit.

2.   Distinguish between a revocable and an irrevocable letter of credit.

3.   What is a confirmed letter of credit?

4.   "In credit operations all parties concerned deal with .... and not with ...."

5.   Define a clean transport document.

6.   Bills of Lading for a particular credit are marked "Received for shipment". Is this acceptable under *Uniform Customs and Practice?*

7.   Are any of the following documents specifically rejected under *Uniform Customs and Practice* if nothing to the contrary is written into the credit?
     Insurance policy
     Insurance certificate
     Insurance cover note

8.   A credit calls for "1,000 tons of coal".
     Would you accept invoices for   a) 1,075 tons?   b) 1,025 tons?

9.   Would your answer to 8 have been different had the credit stipulated "about 1,000 tons"?

10. Under *Uniform Customs and Practice,* what are the requirements of a commercial invoice which must correspond to the terms of the credit unless specified in the credit to the contrary?

11. Is a letter of credit bound by the sales contract in any way?

12. A credit is stated to expire on 10 December 1995. As this is a Sunday, on what date will it in fact expire?

13. What types of bills of lading are usually *acceptable* under *Uniform Customs and Practice?*

14. What types of bills of lading are usually *unacceptable* under *Uniform Customs and Practice?*

15. State the features of insurance documents required by *Uniform Customs and Practice.*

Past Examination Questions

7.1   Rainwear Ltd imports a range of garments from the Far East which are unobtainable elsewhere. Mr Mackintosh, Financial Director, calls to see you to discuss payments for these imports which have always been by irrevocable letters of credit. He knows from bitter experience that, if the exporter presents the documents strictly in accordance with the terms of the letter of credit, the exporter receives immediate payment from the bank authorised to pay under the credit, even if totally unsatisfactory goods are shipped. He asks you to explain the advantages of a documentary letter of credit to an importer, and at the same time to explain how he can obtain the highest degree of protection.

REQUIRED:

(a)   A list of the disadvantages of a letter of credit from an importer's point of view.   *[7]*

(b)   An explanation of the advantages of a letter of credit to Mr Mackintosh's company.   *[7]*

(c)   An explanation as to how some of the disadvantages in (a) might be removed, and how Rainwear Ltd could obtain the required degree of protection.   *[6]*

[Total marks for question - 20]
(question 6, May 1988)

7.2   Mementos Ltd, a UK sterling-based company and one of your customers, imports consumer items from many parts of the world. The company is highly profitable but control of its borrowing from the bank does cause you some concern. Recently the company has signed a contract to purchase a range of consumer items to be sold to the tourist industry in the UK. The goods have to be paid for in US dollars and the suppliers require a secure method of payment on a 'sight' basis. Your customer is seeking a period of credit of approximately 90 days. You are asked to suggest an appropriate banking instrument which should be acceptable to both Mementos Ltd and its suppliers.

REQUIRED:

(a)   Brief notes describing the appropriate banking instrument to be arranged through your office which should be acceptable to both buyer and seller.   *[11]*

(b)   A list of the documents you would expect to see if the goods are to be imported on a CIF UK port basis, including a brief description of the essential elements of each of the documents listed.

[9]
[Total marks for question - 20]
(question 5, October 1989)

7.3   Mr Spark, the financial director of one of your company customers, Flash Ltd, calls to see you in a state of excitement. He tells you that the company has successfully negotiated a contract to obtain from Taiwan supplies of raw materials covering the next year's order book, at very advantageous prices. The contract price, which covers the full cost of the goods and all charges for delivery to the company's premises in the UK, was signed in April. The goods are to be despatched during the last quarter of the year and payment is to be effected by means of an irrevocable letter of credit expressed in US dollars. Further enquiries and discussions with Mr Spark and his colleagues at Flash Ltd have established that few of the implications of signing such a contract have been considered by them.

REQUIRED:
Brief notes describing:

(a)   the risks which Flash Ltd has incurred when agreeing to the terms of the commercial contract; *and*

[6]

(b)   the methods by which, with your agreement, Flash Ltd could reduce those risks.   *[14]*

[Total marks for question - 20]
(question 6, October 1989)

7.4   Granite Chips Ltd is an importer of fine quality facing stones from many overseas countries. Its Managing Director, Mr Stoneface, calls to see you (as the company's sole banker) to discuss potential imports from Rome, Italy. Prior to your meeting you examined the latest management accounts and noted that the customer's banking facilities were fully utilised. You may be willing to extend the facilities a little further.

During the course of the discussions, Mr Stoneface advises you that he can obtain some 60 days credit providing the Italians receive secure methods of payment and these are in Italian lire. He will be purchasing the goods on an 'FCA Rome' basis, whereas goods have normally been imported on a CIF or CIP basis. Mr Stoneface believes that, as Granite Chips Ltd will be receiving some 60 days credit, this should not affect its banking facilities.

REQUIRED:

(a)   What undertaking will the bank have to give and what would be its obligations if it supports the customer?   [5]

(b)   What are the risks the bank incurs in issuing such an undertaking?   [5]

(c)   What considerations must the customer bear in mind in connection with this transaction?   [5]

(d)   Describe the banking instruments and other services you would suggest to Mr Stoneface which will overcome some of the risks mentioned in (b) and (c)   [5]

[Total marks for question - 20]
(question 4 [amended], May 1990)

7.5*   Tintinnabulum Ltd produce handbells. Recent innovations include the introduction of computer controlled machinery in the company's foundry and manufacturing processes. They have ascertained that they can buy equipment more cheaply from the Federal Republic of Germany than from the UK, but the suppliers have suggested that payment should be made in advance in Deutsche Marks. However, Tintinnabulum are not happy with this suggested method of payment.

At the request of Mr Clapper, the Financial Director, you call to see him to discuss methods by which alternative arrangements can be made to pay for the goods. He informs you that Tintinnabulum Ltd is prepared to make arrangements to offer some form of undertaking to the suppliers, subject to Tintinnabulum being satisfied as to the quality and reliability of the equipment and also being able to establish with a fair degree of certainty the cost of the equipment in sterling terms.

REQUIRED:

Brief notes covering the following:

(a)   An explanation of an alternative payment method which might be acceptable to the buyers as well as the suppliers.   [6]

(b)   Your suggestion(s) to Mr Clapper as to how his company could calculate the total cost in sterling terms of this transaction with a reasonable degree of certainty.   [6]

(c)   If your suggestion(s) under (b) is accepted, indicate the responsibilities of the parties involved, showing your customer's contractual position in relation to the foreign exchange commitment.

[8]
[Total marks for question - 20]
(question 6, May 1990)

7.6*   Toolcraft Ltd manufacture machine tools but are finding that competition, particularly from the Far East, is causing a drop in their order book. They have therefore tried to overcome some of their difficulties by seeking a franchise to market and sell, worldwide, items manufactured in Taiwan, while still using their own product name. At Toolcraft's request, you have established in favour of the Taiwanese supplier a number of 90 day letters of credit, but a dispute has now arisen between your customer and the supplier because you have refused to honour the documents presented to you through a Taiwanese bank. Your customer agreed that the bank should be fully protected, that all the insurance documents called for must be available for the bank's protection and that the rest of the documents have to be acceptable to you, as well as your customer. The credits are subject to UCP no 500.

The letters of credit called for, among other things:

- Drafts expressed in US Dollars, drawn at ninety days sight, on yourselves for the full invoice value.
- Invoices showing full CIP value.
- Insurance policy/certificate in a transferable form, in the same currency as the credit, for 110% of the CIP price including Institute A Clauses, War Clauses and SRCC*, showing claims payable in the UK.
- Full set of clean 'On Board' shipping company's bills of lading showing goods consigned to Toolcraft Ltd, covering the journey through to the container depot in Bradford, UK, and indicating that the freight has been paid.
- Partial shipments/drawings are NOT allowed.

The latest set of documents included the following:

(i)   drafts drawn at sight on your customer for a net invoice value;

(ii)   only one invoice was presented showing a deduction of 5%;

(iii)   the insurance certificate presented is in the name of your customer, is for the sterling gross invoice value, and shows that the 'normal/usual' risks have been covered;

(iv)   four sets of 2/3 'Received for Shipment' bills of lading presented, showing goods consigned to the order of the shipper in Kaohsiung, Taiwan, all dated on different dates, showing the name of the vessel 'Eastern Rose', marked 'freight prepayable'. They show the destination as 'Bradford container depot'.

(v)   an indemnity from the negotiating bank covering 'Any and ALL discrepancies'.

Toolcraft ask you to explain why the bank is unhappy with this latest set of documents and wish to know what is the solution to the problem.

REQUIRED:

(a)   The explanation you would give to your customer, commencing specifically on points (i) to (v) above.   [12]

(b)   Indicate, briefly, the solution(s) to the point(s)/problem(s) you have covered in (a).   [8]
[Total marks for question - 20]
(question 4, amended, May 1991)

(* *author's note:* SRCC = Strikes Riots and Civil Commotions)

7.7*   Stoneface Plc quarry, manufacture and sell wholesale facing stones made out of natural stone to the construction and building industries. They have recently become aware of a range of granite stones available from Eastern Europe.

Mr Millstone, the company's senior director, calls to see you to discuss payment terms which might be appropriate if the company decides to use this source of supply. Among the topics you discuss are the currency of the transaction, the shipment terms and the method of payment. You learn that the suppliers wish to be assured that they will be paid in Deutschemarks (DEM) immediately upon despatch of the goods. They will provide the goods suitably crated at a carrier's depot.

As Stoneface Plc has not dealt with overseas suppliers before, Mr Millstone does not wish to enter into a commercial contract without some security that the goods ordered will be despatched to their finishing yard in reasonable condition. He is also seeking a credit period of ninety days, which will enable the company to finish and deliver the finished product before payment.

Your discussions also reveal that Mr Millstone is of the opinion that the supplier will arrange for shipment and will be fully responsible for the goods until they are delivered into the company's premises, excluding the payment of any duty or VAT. He states that he expects you, as his banker, to protect his company's interests at all times, even if this may be to the detriment of the supplier.

REQUIRED, in brief note form, your explanation of the following:

(a)   What is the first step your customer should take in considering dealing with this new supplier?   *[1]*

(b)   What are the risks, if any, in agreeing to pay the suppliers in DEM? How would it be possible to reduce any risk(s)?   *[2]*

(c)   What method of payment would you suggest which will satisfy the needs of both supplier and buyer? Are there any international rules which apply to this method?   *[4]*

(d)   What are the implied terms of shipment and are these satisfactory to both parties? What are the responsibilities of the respective parties?   *[8]*

(e)   Depending on what you have stated in answer to (c) and (d), what documentation would you expect to see in this case?   *[3]*

(f)   In agreeing to the above terms in accordance with UK and internationally agreed procedures, to whom is the bank responsible?   *[2]*

[Total marks for question - 20]
(question 6, May 1991)

7.8*   *Scenario*

Telecom Exports Ltd: see page 21

Question

Telecom Exports has received an irrevocable letter of credit for £1,500 from the Middle East. It expires at your bank's counters and has the following terms:

1.   10% against a performance bond – payment at sight;

2.   80% against shipping documents on despatch of goods – payment 90 days after date of shipment;

3.   10% against an acceptance certificate after installation and training – payment at sight.

Mrs Daws contacts you to discuss the operation of this letter of credit.

REQUIRED:

(a)   Describe the risks that you should point out to Mrs Daws if Telecom Exports goes ahead with this contract.   *[8]*

(b)   What banking facilities may be organised by Telecom Exports on receipt of the letter of credit?   *[8]*

(c)   Later, on presentation of shipping documents, your bank identifies the following discrepancies:
    (i)   incorrect description of goods on the invoices;
    (ii)   one original bill of lading not presented to the bank;
    (iii)   late shipment by one day.

What is the effect of these discrepancies and what action might Telecom Exports be able to take?   *[6]*

[Total marks for question - 20]
(question 5, Autumn 1993)

Lesson Eight
Documentary Letters of Credit: 2

This second lesson on documentary credits looks at the different types of credits that may be used in certain circumstances. It then goes on to consider the position of the banks involved in documentary credits, i.e. issuing, advising and confirming banks. Following this are listed the common discrepancies which may occur when handling credits; finally the lesson looks at the advantages and disadvantages of documentary credits to exporters and importers.

❑ Other types of credit

There are a number of special types of credit that may be used in certain circumstances. Three types are mentioned in *Uniform Customs and Practice;* these are:
• standby credits
• deferred credits
• transferable credits

Other types of credits include:
• back-to-back credits
• revolving credits
• reinstatement credits
• red-clause credits

❑ Standby credits

As their name suggests, standby credits act as a 'back-up' to other trade facilities. They are often issued to support open account trade so that, if the buyer should fail to settle the amount owing in the normal way, the seller will look to settlement under a standby letter of credit of which he is the beneficiary. Where an exporter is using collections, a standby credit could be opened by the buyer to add support to the collection in respect of unpaid bills of exchange. In both these circumstances, the standby letter of credit gives 'back-up' to other facilities. The bank issuing such a credit gives its undertaking that, if certain circumstances arise, then a claim can be made under the standby credit. For example, under open account trade, the beneficiary might submit an invoice, accompanied by a declaration that payment has not been received by any other means. Similarly, a credit opened to cover unpaid bills of exchange might pay out to the beneficiary upon presentation of a declaration that the bill is unpaid, accompanied by the bill itself. Standby credits are usually irrevocable.

A standby credit used in conjunction with collections or open account trade is preferable, from both issuing bank and importer's viewpoint, to a full letter of credit. For example, take a commercial contract which specifies that £120,000 of goods are to be supplied in a year, at the rate of £10,000 per month. It is far preferable for the importer to arrange this on a collection basis with a standby letter of credit for, say, £20,000 (covering two months' purchases), than a letter of credit for £120,000. Both the importer (applicant for the credit) and the issuing bank will have reduced their liabilities to £20,000, instead of £120,000.

Standby credits are also used where banks are requested to issue a guarantee on behalf of one of their customers (see lesson 11) but are unable to do so because of local laws in the beneficiary's country. A letter of credit, where *Uniform Customs and Practice* are followed in both applicant's and beneficiary's country, is usually an acceptable alternative. It provides for payment to the beneficiary only if certain circumstances arise, and against the production of certain documentary evidence.

❏ Deferred credits

Most letters of credit require the production of specified shipping documents and then, if a period of credit is being given by the beneficiary, a term bill of exchange will be accepted on behalf of the applicant. In many countries, but not in Britain, bills of exchange attract stamp duty at high rates (e.g. Italy), and so a deferred credit aims to retain a measure of credit given by the beneficiary and, at the same time, avoid stamp duty costs. Therefore it works in almost the same way as a 'normal' letter of credit, except that there is no bill of exchange. Once the required documents have been submitted by the beneficiary to the advising or confirming bank, payment will be made at some future determinable date, e.g. 90 days after shipment, but without the use of bills of exchange. A disadvantage to the beneficiary is that he could have used an accepted bill of exchange to obtain immediate finance without waiting for the bill to mature - nevertheless, the high costs of stamp duty are avoided.

❏ Transferable credits

Article 48 of *Uniform Customs and Practice* defines a transferable credit as

> *a Credit under which the Beneficiary (First Beneficiary) may request the bank authorised to pay, incur a deferred payment undertaking, accept or negotiate (the "Transferring Bank"), or in the case of a freely negotiable Credit, the bank specifically authorised in the Credit as a Transferring Bank, to make the Credit available in whole or in part to one or more other Beneficiary(ies) (Second Beneficiary(ies)).*

Such a credit is likely to be used where a middleman operates between the buyer and seller of the goods, i.e. a buyer requests him to supply certain goods and he then seeks out a seller of such goods. Naturally his profit will be the difference between the price at which he buys and that at which he sells, less his expenses. A transferable credit suits such a middleman very well, particularly because it relieves him of the problem of financing the purchase of the goods, and no limit will be marked up against him by his own bank.

As indicated above the credit from the buyer of the goods allows the beneficiary – the middleman – to request the advising, confirming or negotiating bank to transfer some or all of the credit to one or more second beneficiaries (see Fig. 8.1). Note that, before a credit can be transferred, it must be expressly designated as 'transferable'. It can only be transferred once but, under certain circumstances (see Article 48), fractions can be transferred separately. A credit can be transferred to a second beneficiary in the same country, or in another country, unless the credit states otherwise.

The method of operation is that, having found a buyer and a supplier for the goods, the middleman requests settlement from the buyer by means of a transferable letter of credit. As soon as he is told by the advising bank that a credit has been opened in his favour, the middleman requests that the credit is transferred in favour of the supplier of the goods but, of course, for a lower amount. The supplier, who is now the second beneficiary obtains or manufactures the goods and ships them, either direct to the ultimate buyer or, if the middleman does not wish to divulge his name, to an agent or third party. The supplier of the goods presents his documents as required to the advising bank, and obtains payment of his invoice price. The first beneficiary will then be called upon to substitute his own invoices for those of the second beneficiary and, when he does so, will receive the difference, being his profit. The advising bank is now in possession of the necessary documents as called for by the applicant of the credit. These are then sent by air mail to the issuing bank in the normal way. If for any reason the first beneficiary fails to supply his own invoices, the bank involved may send to the issuing bank the documents it has received, including the second beneficiary's invoices, without further responsibility to the first beneficiary.

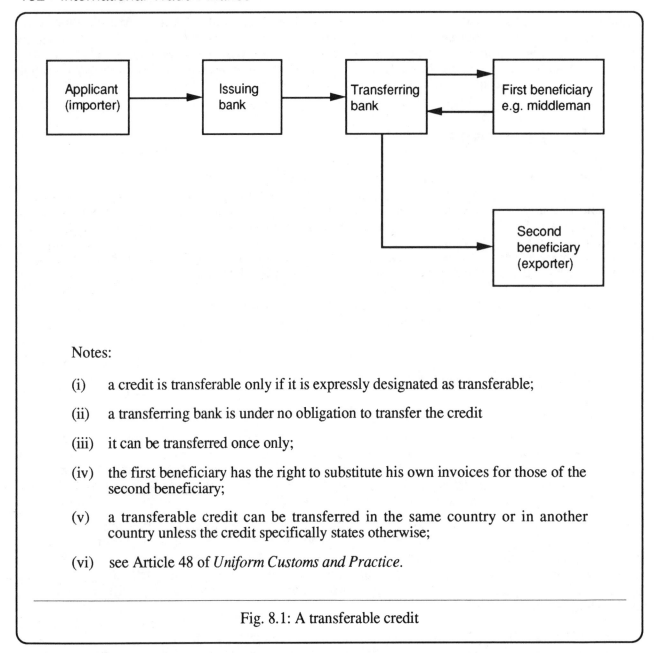

Notes:

(i)   a credit is transferable only if it is expressly designated as transferable;

(ii) a transferring bank is under no obligation to transfer the credit

(iii) it can be transferred once only;

(iv) the first beneficiary has the right to substitute his own invoices for those of the second beneficiary;

(v)   a transferable credit can be transferred in the same country or in another country unless the credit specifically states otherwise;

(vi) see Article 48 of *Uniform Customs and Practice*.

Fig. 8.1: A transferable credit

Note that a credit can be transferred only on the terms and conditions specified in the original credit, except that:

• the amount of the credit and any unit prices stated may be reduced (this gives the middleman his profit element);

• the expiry date of the credit and the latest shipment date may be reduced;

• the last date for presentation of documents;

• the name of the first beneficiary can normally be substituted for that of the applicant for the credit;

• the middleman can stipulate the percentage for which insurance cover must be effected. (This allows a transferable credit to be used where the shipping terms are CIF, or similar. The middleman can stipulate to the second beneficiary the insurance cover that he needs in order to meet the needs of the applicant of the credit.)

Although, as we have seen earlier, a credit may be transferred once only, fractions of the credit can be transferred separately (the total of such transfers being considered as only one transfer). Such separate transfers permit a middleman to obtain goods for an overseas buyer from a number of different suppliers. i.e. a 'shopping basket' operation. However, for such a buying operation to take place, the original credit will have to allow part shipments as each second beneficiary will need to produce the required shipping documents before being entitled to payment. If part shipment is not allowed there can only be one second beneficiary.

Article 48 of *Uniform Customs and Practice* deals fully with transferable credits and should be read carefully.

From the point of view of a bank making a transfer to a beneficiary under a transferable letter of credit, the bank will ensure that it is transferred on the same terms and conditions as the original with the exception of the points listed above, i.e. amount of credit, unit prices, period of validity, latest shipment date, and substitution of name of first beneficiary for that of the applicant for the credit. By doing this the bank will not need to record any contingent liability for their undertaking under the letter of credit since they are entitled to submit the original documents presented for the lesser amount to the opening bank, and obtain reimbursement for the value paid away.

Neutral names: It should be noted that it is usual for documents to be called for under 'neutral' names to protect all parties; this is in the interests of both buyer and seller who agree, when setting up a transferable credit, that neutral names should be used in respect of shipment, inspection documents, etc. Neutral names are also used for back-to-back credits (see below).

❏ Back-to-back credits

Such credits are where a second credit to a second beneficiary is opened on the strength of a first credit in favour of a first beneficiary. Like transferable credits, this type of credit is of particular assistance to middlemen or merchants who are seeking a means of financing a trading transaction; however, in practice, these credits are rare, because of the risks to the middleman's bank.

To follow an example transaction (see Fig. 8.2):

- A London middleman has received an order to supply specialist aircraft spares to a company in the Middle East. Settlement is to be by means of an irrevocable credit.

- The middleman finds a supplier of the parts in America, but the exporter insists on an irrevocable credit.

- As soon as the first credit has been opened in the middleman's favour from the Middle East, he can ask his bank to open a second credit in favour of the American supplier. (Note here that the middleman's bank has a *quasi-security,* in that provided their customer produces the correct documents he will receive payment. They may have been perfectly prepared to open the credit in favour of the American exporter without the security of the first credit but, if their customer is lacking in working capital but is nevertheless worthy of assistance, the first credit will give the bank the assurance they need.)

- The American supplier ships the goods, presents the correct documentation to the bank that has advised the second credit to him, and receives payment.

- The documents are received by the issuing bank on the second credit who will now be financing their customer for the amount drawn under the second credit. They will now call on their middleman customer to substitute his invoices (at increased prices) in place of those of the American supplier.

- When the middleman has produced his invoices, the documents can then be presented at the bank which has advised the first credit.

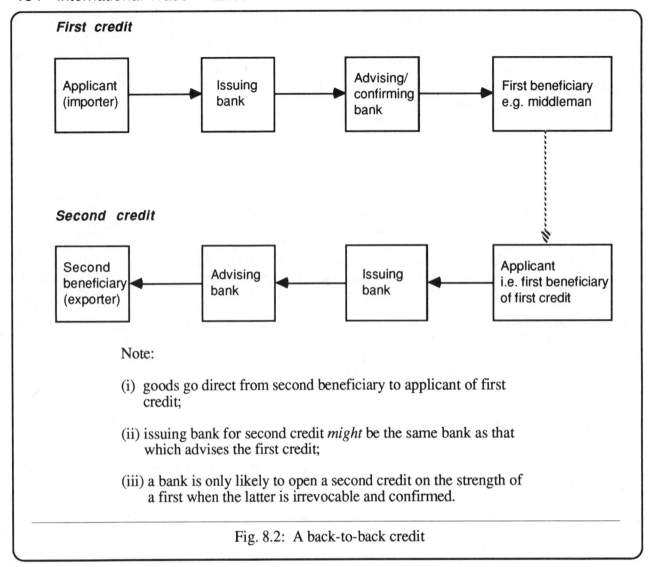

First credit

Applicant (importer) → Issuing bank → Advising/confirming bank → First beneficiary e.g. middleman

Second credit

Second beneficiary (exporter) ← Advising bank ← Issuing bank ← Applicant i.e. first beneficiary of first credit

Note:

(i) goods go direct from second beneficiary to applicant of first credit;

(ii) issuing bank for second credit *might* be the same bank as that which advises the first credit;

(iii) a bank is only likely to open a second credit on the strength of a first when the latter is irrevocable and confirmed.

Fig. 8.2: A back-to-back credit

It should be noted that, when back-to-back credits are used, there are *two* credits. The second is separate from the first, being issued on the strength of the first. It would be prudent for the bank issuing the second credit to retain control of the documents presented under their credit and to attend to presentation of the documents under the first credit themselves. When opening a second credit on the strength of the first, the issuing bank will bear in mind the requirements of the first. Therefore the second should be issued, as with a transferable credit, for a smaller amount with the period of validity and latest shipment date being reduced. This last point gives the issuing bank of the second credit sufficient time to examine documents and to arrange for substitution of invoices.

With back-to-back credits, since the advising bank has issued its own credit against the security of the inward credit, it will need to record a contingent liability in respect of the credit it has opened. The bank will be liable to pay if documents are presented in order, and so the bank needs to reflect a contingent liability to reflect this. Therefore, with a back-to-back credit a customer's limit or credit facilities would be affected, whereas, with a transferable letter of credit, they would not be affected.

❏ Assignment of a credit

As an alternative to transferable credits and back-to-back credits, the benefits under a letter of credit can be assigned to the ultimate supplier of the goods. Assignment of a credit offers another way of providing pre-shipment finance to a middleman. Once a credit has been opened by the buyer of the goods in the middleman's favour, the middleman requests the advising/confirming bank to assign part of the credit in favour of the ultimate supplier of the goods. This supplier receives a letter from the bank which states that the bank holds the beneficiary's (middleman's) instructions to make payment once goods have been supplied. The disadvantage to the ultimate supplier is that they are not party to the letter of credit and will receive payment only when the middleman has been paid under the terms of the credit: if the credit fails – eg because of incorrect documentation – the ultimate supplier will have difficulty in obtaining payment from the middleman.

❏ Revolving credits

These are used where regular trading takes place between the paries and the credit is automatically renewed after each transaction until a final expiry date is reached. For example, a credit may be established for six months for the sum of £100 000 per month, revolving. When the documents evidencing shipment are presented, payment is made and the credit remains available up to £100 000 in any one month.

The main disadvantage of a revolving credit is that it commits the bank to a considerable financial commitment. For example, £100 000 per month for six months means that the bank is committing facilities of £600 000 to the importer. This is likely to have a detrimental effect on the ability of the importer to obtain further bank facilities for the business.

❏ Reinstatement credits

A reinstatement credit helps to overcome the main disadvantage of a revolving credit. Although the credit is established for a fixed term, eg with an expiry date in six months or twelve months, the commitment of the issuing bank is restricted to one or two months' shipments. This reduces the strain on the importer's bank facilities. The credit bears a clause stating that the issuing bank understands that it will be instructed to reinstate the value of the documents drawn and presented under the credit, but that such undertaking is given without responsibility on the part of the bank. By using such phrasing, the issuing bank has given no specific undertaking that the credit will be reinstated, but the good faith and integrity of the buyer has been demonstrated to the exporter. A reinstatement credit also offers more flexibility to the importers, in that, if they wish to pull out of the commercial contract they could refuse to reinstate the value of documents drawn and presented under the credit.

❏ Red clause credits

A red clause credit enables the beneficiary to draw up to a stated percentage of the credit amount before shipment and before presentation of the documents called for in the credit. It is so called because the clause permitting this was, at one time, always printed in red. It is used particularly in the raw materials trades to provide the necessary pre-shipment finance to enable shippers to buy the materials and prepare them for shipment, e.g. Australian wool, African timber. When the goods have been shipped the exporter presents the documents in the usual way, but will receive the amount of the credit less the amount advanced.

Advances under the credit may be *conditional,* or *unconditional.* Where they are conditional, lending will only be made against presentation of certain documents, such as warehouse warrants. With an unconditional advance, funds will be loaned against the receipt of the beneficiary, which acknowledges the purpose for which the funds have been received. In either case, in the event of default by the beneficiary, the advising bank would look to the issuing bank for reimbursement. In their turn the issuing bank would look to the applicant of the credit, i.e. the importer.

An alternative to a red clause credit is for a credit to be opened which provides for advance payments, often against a bank guarantee issued by the beneficiary's bank. Thus, although the issuing bank and therefore the applicant will be debited almost immediately with the advances, the bank guarantee provides a measure of security.

❏ Bank considerations with regard to documentary credits

We have seen that, in dealing with documentary credits, there are two main banks involved: the issuing bank, and the advising bank (which may also be called upon to confirm a credit).

Issuing Bank

Whenever a bank issues a credit on behalf of a customer it undertakes an obligation. Where the credit is irrevocable we have seen from Article 9 of *Uniform Customs and Practice* that payment or acceptance of bills must be made and that this obligation can only be amended or cancelled with the agreement of all parties. It is essential therefore that a bank asked to issue a credit on behalf of a customer should satisfy itself as to the credit-worthiness of that customer. Such requests must have the same considerations applied to them as if the customer were asking for a loan or overdraft and will, most probably, require the sanction of Head Office. As most importer customers will be requiring the issue of several documentary credits a maximum limit to be outstanding at any one time will usually be established.

The issuing bank can cover itself in a number of ways. It may ask the customer to deposit security - the usual types of bank security being acceptable, e.g. mortgages of property/shares, assignments of life policies, guarantees, floating charges, etc. Alternatively the issuing bank may insist on full or partial cash cover for the amount of the credit, to be placed into a special account to meet drawings under the credit. It is also usual to require the applicant to sign a letter of pledge/hypothecation (often incorporated into the application form for the credit) giving the bank various powers over the documents relating to the shipment and the goods themselves. The letter of pledge/hypothecation will, under certain circumstances, give the bank a power of sale and will allow the bank to charge the customer for warehousing and insuring the goods, as necessary. (Letters of pledge and hypothecation are discussed more fully in lesson 13).

Note that the commercial contract between buyer and seller is of no concern to banks.

Advising Bank

As Article 7 of *Uniform Customs and Practice* states, an advising bank merely gives the beneficiary details of the credit 'without engagement on the part of the advising bank'. Thus there is no liability for payment to the beneficiary on the part of the advising bank and this was why, as explained earlier, an exporter may not receive an immediate payment upon presentation of the correct documentation under a credit which is merely advised. If an advising bank were to pay the beneficiary of an irrevocable credit and then not receive funds from the issuing bank, there are no means of recovering the monies from the beneficiary. However, when handling a credit, an advising bank is required to 'take reasonable care to check the apparent authenticity of the credit which it advises' (Article 7).

Confirming Bank

Article 9 states that where a bank confirms a credit this 'constitutes a definite undertaking of the confirming bank in addition to that of the issuing bank' to pay or accept bills correctly presented under the credit. We have already seen the benefits of a confirmed irrevocable credit to an exporter in that he has the undertaking of payment given by a bank in his own country. Before agreeing to confirm a credit a bank must consider the standing of the issuing bank and the political and economic situation in the country of that bank. If there is likely to be any significant risk the confirming bank should call for full or partial cash cover from the issuing bank, holding this in a separate account pending drawings against the credit. Any unused amount or, if the credit expires before drawings are made, can then be returned to the issuing bank.

❑ Discrepancies in documentation

As should already have been appreciated in this lesson, credits deal in documents and, only if the documents presented to the advising or confirming bank (or through a negotiating bank) are completely in line with the terms and conditions of the credit, can payment be made. The major problem for a bank as pointed out above is that if it pays a beneficiary it cannot recover such monies at a later date. Thus, if there are any errors in the documents not noticed by the advising bank which they should have seen, having paid out against the credit, they cannot recover such amounts. It is very important for the documents tendered under a credit to be studied extremely carefully in order to avoid the problem of *discrepant documents*.

There are a number of discrepancies which might be noticed when studying documentation. Among the more common are the following:

Documentary credit
- Has expired

Bill of Exchange
- Drawn incorrectly or for a sum different from the amount of the credit
- Capacity of signatories not stated if required

Invoice
- Amount exceeds that of the credit
- Amount differs from that of the bill of exchange
- Prices of goods different from those indicated in the credit
- Description of goods differs from that in the credit
- Price basis and shipment terms (FOB, CIF, CFR, etc.) omitted
- Extra charges included are not specified in the credit
- Is not certified, notarised or signed as required by the credit
- Importer's name differs from that mentioned in the credit
- Is not issued by the exporter

Bill of Lading
- Not presented in full set when requested
- Alterations not authenticated by an official of the shipping company or its agent
- Is not 'clean', i.e. carries remarks that the condition and packing of the merchandise is defective
- Is not marked 'on board' when so required
- 'On board' notation not signed or initialled by the carrier or agent
- 'On board' notation not dated
- Is not endorsed by the exporter when drawn to 'order'
- Is not marked 'freight paid' as stipulated in the credit (under CFR, CIF contracts)
- Is made out 'to order' when the credit stipulated 'direct to consignee' (importer) (and vice versa)
- Is dated later than the latest shipping date specified in the credit
- Is not presented within 21 days after date of shipment or such time as specified in the credit
- Includes details of merchandise other than that specified in the credit

Insurance
- Amount of cover is insufficient
- Does not include risks mentioned in the credit
- Is not issued in the currency of the credit
- Is not endorsed by the insured and/or signed by the insurers
- Certificate or policy bear a date later than the date of shipment/dispatch, except where warehouse to warehouse is indicated
- Incorrect description of goods
- Alterations are not authenticated
- Is not in transferable form when required
- Carrying vessel's name not recorded
- Does not cover transhipment when bills of lading indicate it will take place

If some errors are found the problem is then to deal with them. Wherever possible errors should be put right by the beneficiary approaching the person who has issued the document. If errors remain, a way out for the advising/confirming bank is to pay out under the credit only against an indemnity from the beneficiary's bank. When a bank is requested to issue such an indemnity in favour of the advising/confirming bank it will, of course, consider very carefully the credit-worthiness of its customer (the beneficiary) and a counter-indemnity will be taken from the customer. (Whenever indemnities are issued or counter-indemnities are obtained it is important that a bank's internal regulations are strictly followed). It is quite common for the applicant to the credit to require that discrepant documents and bankers' indemnities are *not* acceptable. In this way the buyer is reducing the risk of the wrong goods being supplied.

Where errors in documentation are too great for the advising/confirming bank to be satisfied by the issue of an indemnity, the documents can be sent to the issuing bank on an inspection basis, i.e. the documents are to be delivered to the importer against authority to pay. Alternatively the advising bank might cable (at the beneficiary's expense) the issuing bank for authority to make payment despite discrepancies in documents.

❑ Advantages of a letter of credit

To the exporter

* A letter of credit is generally a very safe method of obtaining payment. Provided the exporter complies with the terms of the credit, payment will either be made in full (subject to the advising bank having access to reimbursement facilities) or a bill of exchange will be accepted or negotiated.

* An irrevocable credit cannot be amended without the exporter's knowledge.

* An irrevocable credit carries a definite undertaking on the part of the issuing bank; there is thus no risk of non-payment in the event of insolvency of the buyer.

* A confirmed irrevocable undertaking, in addition, carries the undertaking of a bank generally in the exporter's country.

* A credit opened in the exporter's favour can often lead to a credit being opened in favour of the supplier (back-to-back credit); alternatively a credit *may* be transferable.

* Finance may be available by means of:
  1. ordinary bank loan/overdraft;
  2. discounting or negotiation of his bills under an acceptance credit.

  See lesson 12 for further details.

* Control of the documents of title does not leave the exporter's hands until payment is received or a bill is accepted.

* Better than collections (see lesson 9) as a means of securing payment.

To the importer

As can be seen from the list of advantages of above, a letter of credit favours the exporter. However, the importer can protect the position by stating the precise documentation required and by specifying a latest shipping date. The importer should consider making a status report on the supplier and, in the case of a large order, call for a performance bond (see lesson 11). Some measure of credit can be obtained from the exporter by insisting on the use of term bills of exchange. The importer could also consider the use of revocable credits, which would be particularly appropriate where the goods are dispatched in part shipments: as soon as the first lot of goods arrive the importer can inspect them and, if they are not up to quality, can cancel the credit, hopefully before other shipments are made.

- The importer knows that payment will only be made by the advising bank when the exact documents specified have been received.

- Once the specified documents, which will usually be the documents of title, are in the hands of the advising bank, then it will only be a matter of time before they are sent to the issuing bank, allowing the importer to collect the goods subject to their safe arrival.

- Finance may be available by means of:
  1. ordinary bank loan/overdraft;
  2. produce loan;
  3. acceptance credit (i.e. the exporter provides the finance for the tenor of the bills)

  See lesson 13 for further details.

- A latest date for shipment can be specified.

❏ Disadvantages of a letter of credit

To the exporter
- Not as safe as payment in advance.

- If the credit is revocable it can be amended or cancelled without the exporter's knowledge.

- If the credit is not confirmed by a bank in the exporter's own country, even if it is irrevocable, payment may not be received immediately if the advising bank does not have access to reimbursement facilities.

- Small discrepancies in documentation may cause delays in obtaining payment.

- A measure of credit under an acceptance credit might have to be allowed.

To the importer
- Has the effort of arranging for the credit to be opened and will have to bear the cost.

- The credit will either form part of the importer's total bank facility, alternatively cash cover may have to be provided.

- Once an irrevocable credit has been opened, it may not be amended or cancelled without the agreement of all parties. Therefore if the importer later finds the same goods at a cheaper price elsewhere, it is not possible to 'get out of' the original credit.

- Payment will still be effected if the documents presented are correct, even if the goods are subsequently found to be sub-standard.

- Late delivery of the goods may occur where the credit does not state a latest shipment date.

❏ Examination hints

- The different types of documentary credits have featured strongly in recent examination papers.

- Transferable credits contrasted with back-to-back credits have been a popular topic, but you should note that a transferable credit is the only solution for a middleman who does not have the financial strength for a second credit to be opened without reliance on the first; as a consequence back-to-back credits are rare because the bank does not wish to become involved in 'hazardous liabilities'.

- Standby credits, a relatively new type, have appeared regularly in recent examination papers.

- Red-clause letters of credit are also popular in the examination, but do remember that not all questions mentioning Australia involve such credits!

Know Your........... Documentary Credits: 2

1.   When may a credit be transferred?

2.   How many times may a credit be transferred?

3.   May a credit be transferred to a beneficiary in another country?

4.   What rights has the first beneficiary under a transferable credit?

5.   What do you understand by a Red Clause Credit?

6.   What is a back-to-back credit?

7.   Briefly describe a revolving credit.

8.   Under what circumstances might a deferred credit be used?

9.   What is a standby letter of credit? When will it be used?

10.   Give two possible advantages and two possible disadvantages of a documentary credit to an exporter.

11.   Give two possible advantages and two possible disadvantages of a documentary credit to an importer.

12.   What options are open to a bank when documents have been tendered incorrectly under a credit?

13.   What is the position if a bank receives unclear instructions about a credit?

Past Examination Questions

8.1 Flotsam and Jetsam Ltd imports a range of consumer items from many overseas countries. The directors have recently asked you to arrange an irrevocable letter of credit in favour of an overseas supplier to cover the company's imports for the next 12 months. Bank facilities are fully utilised and you are reluctant to issue an irrevocable letter of credit covering shipments valued in excess of £50,000 in any one month for the next 12 months. You are, however, prepared to issue an irrevocable letter of credit covering up to 3 months' shipments for a maximum of £150,000 (or the foreign currency equivalent), but you are not prepared to go beyond that limit. Nevertheless, the supplier has insisted that a bank undertaking should be issued in its favour, otherwise the company's source of supply will dry up.

REQUIRED:

(a) Specify the banking instruments which would satisfy the customer's needs utilising irrevocable letters of credit, but which would not extend the bank facilities beyond the limit you are prepared to sanction. *[2]*

(b) Briefly describe how these banking instruments would operate. *[7]*

(c) Make brief notes showing the explanation you would give to the directors describing the advantages and disadvantages to the company, and the beneficiary (its supplier), of each of the methods described in (a) and (b) above. *[11]*

[Total marks for question - 20]
(question 5, October 1988)

8.2 Your customer, Worldwide Traders Ltd, has received an order from a German buyer to supply 1,000 tons of rice at a price agreed at US$100 per ton on a CIF Hamburg basis. The German buyer has agreed to establish an irrevocable letter of credit in favour of Worldwide Traders Ltd. Your customer is able to purchase the rice from Padifields Ltd of Bangkok at a price of US$80 per ton CIF European Port, on condition that a documentary letter of credit can be established in favour of the Thai exporter who will then arrange for the appropriate documents to be presented under that letter of credit.

The Financial Director calls to see you to discuss this deal and asks you to outline the alternative ways of handling the documentary letters of credit. At the same time he asks you to explain any difficulties or points of view which must be considered when formalising these banking instruments.

REQUIRED:

(a) Identify the two types of letters of credit which are appropriate for this transaction. *[2]*

(b) Describe briefly the appropriate shipping documents which would satisfy the needs of all the parties. *[4]*

(c) List under two separate headings the points which will have to be taken into consideration to protect the bank and its customer in respect of *each* of your suggested answers in (a). Mention any appropriate special restrictions contained in the internationally accepted procedures. *[14]*

[Total marks for question - 20]
(question 7, October 1988)

8.3   You have had an initial discussion with the Managing Director of Viking Products Ltd, Mr Odin, regarding importing from Norway. Following your initial visit to Viking Products Ltd, Mr Odin contacts you to discuss the method by which he has been asked to effect payment to his suppliers in Norway. He informs you that initially he will have to arrange a bank undertaking or guarantee covering payments for the imports, and he asks you what instrument you could arrange as a matter of urgency to cover this transaction. He also informs you that, if a satisfactory pattern of trading is established between the two companies, the suppliers in Norway will require a continuing guarantee/undertaking for one year which could be reviewed at the end of that period.

Whilst you are willing to establish some form of appropriate bank undertaking, you are not prepared to grant the company substantial facilities based upon their current balance sheet and the latest management acounts you have seen.

REQUIRED:
In brief note form, state the following:

(a)   the initial bank undertaking that you would recommend should be established to cover the first order;   *[7]*

(b)   the obligations that both the company and the bank will enter into if such an instrument is established;   *[5]*

(c)   a compromise solution which might be established if a satisfactory pattern of trade develops;   *[3]*

(d)   in the event of the supplier still demanding some form of bank undertaking, the instrument you would suggest which might operate in conjunction with the compromise solution suggested in (c).
                                                                                                          [5]
                                                                            [Total marks for question - 20]
                                                                                 (question 5, May 1989)

8.4*   Your customer, New World Computers Ltd, manufactures sophisticated computer equipment which is used for dedicated control processes. Many of the parts used in the equipment are imported from EC countries and are purchased on a one-off customised basis. In other words, they are useless for projects other than those for which they have been specifically purchased.

A large contract for computer equipment in excess of £500,000 is likely to be awarded to New World in the near future by a UK buyer. The Finance and Marketing Directors, Mr Greenlight and Mr Silichip, ask you to discuss with them the various methods of payment they should seek from this UK buyer.

You understand that the UK buyer is prepared to pay up to 15% upon signing the contract and may be prepared to pay for up to half of the total value of the contract when the appropriate parts are received from the EC suppliers, the balance to be paid to New World when the equipment is delivered to the UK buyer.

REQUIRED:

(a)   Details of the financial package which you would suggest that New World Computers Ltd should ask for when completing their negotiations with the ultimate buyer.   *[14]*

(b)   Your suggestions, expressed briefly, indicating alternative(s) to (a) but stating any drawbacks which the customer must bear in mind.   *[6]*
                                                                            [Total marks for question - 20]
                                                                                 (question 7, May 1990)

8.5*   Bric-à-Brac Ltd, a customer of your bank, imports consumer items from the Philippines on an open account basis, and settlement is effected in US dollars. Following a visit to the Far East as part of a trade mission, it has now discovered new sources of supply from Singapore and Malaysia. Bric-à-Brac wishes to purchase the goods on an open account basis, but the supliers have asked for a bank undertaking to cover at least one or two months' supply. The Managing Director of Bric-à-Brac calls to see you to discuss the position and to ascertain if you are able to arrange any other banking instruments which might be of assistance both to his company and to the supplier.

REQUIRED:

(a)   List the banking instruments which you would suggest might be appropriate to your customer's needs, referring to any relevant internationally accepted procedures.   *[8]*

(b)   Detail briefly the implications of the arrangements you have listed in (a) from the point of view of:
(i)   the customer (ie the buyer);   *[6]*
(ii) the bank.   *[6]*

[Total marks for question - 20]
(question 6, October 1990)

8.6*   Surgical Products Ltd is a small manufacturing company with a very small asset base. It has just received its first large export order, with payment at sight on a CIF basis, and has made arrangements with another UK manufacturer to produce some of the order. This manufacturer can supply the goods at a lower price than the CIF export price quoted by Surgical Products Ltd. Your customer does not wish to disclose the name of the manufacturer to the buyer abroad, or vice versa.

REQUIRED:

(a)   Describe briefly any method(s) by which this transaction could be arranged.   *[10]*

(b)   State the specific requirement(s) you would expect to see in any instrument(s) you describe in (a).
[7]

(c)   Indicate whether there are any risks in your suggestion(s) in (a) and (b) and (if appropriate) which method is preferable. Give reasons for your answer.   *[3]*

[Total marks for question - 20]
(question 3, May 1991)

8.7*   *Scenario*
UK Auto Mart Ltd: see page 60
Question
UK Auto Mart Ltd has found a new source of components in the USA. Samples have proved to be very good and the company would be able to secure good prices if it was able to provide irrevocable documentary credits payable at sight.

Mr Daily comes to see you and says that the company has been asked for one letter of credit for £400,000 covering shipments over 6 months.

He has a number of concerns:
1.   issuing such a large letter of credit;
2.   receiving a consistent quality of goods throughout the life of the contract;
3.   experiencing fraud in transit, which he has heard is becoming prevalent in some trades.

REQUIRED:

(a) Your answer to Mr Daily as to whether the letter of credit may be cancelled if the first delivery is not up to the standard of the samples already provided or if the company becomes aware of fraud. *[3]*

(b) Describe ways in which the letter of credit may be worded to cover shipments over a period of 6 months. *[3]*

(c) Name and explain documentary evidence that could be built into the letter of credit to minimise the risk of not receiving goods of the quality required. *[6]*

(d) Outline ways in which the letter of credit requested could be reworded to provide a greater degree of protection to UK Auto Mart Ltd. *[8]*

[Total marks for question - 20]
(question 1, Autumn 1993)

8.8* *Scenario*

Telecom Exports Ltd: see page 21

Question

Telecom Exports has received a large letter of credit payable in US$. In view of the volumes involved, it is to sub-contract some of its manufacturing to another UK company, Moore Lee Electronics Ltd. Moore Lee Electronics would normally be happy to trade on open terms but, for this larger export contract, they wish to share in the benefit of the letter of credit.

Mrs Daws would like to be able to agree but cannot see how this may be achieved.

REQUIRED:

(a) Name and describe methods that Mrs Daws might use so that the benefit of the letter of credit may be made available to Moore Lee Electronics. *[6]*

(b) What would be the risks to Moore Lee Electronics in each type of transaction covered in your answer to (a) above? *[7]*

(c) If Telecom Exports sells on FOB UK Port terms, what implications would this have for each of your suggestions in (a) above? *[3]*

(d) What would be the position for Telecom Exports with each of your suggestions in (a) above, if Moore Lee Electronics wants settlement in sterling? *[4]*

[Total marks for question - 20]
(question 8, Autumn 1993)

8.9 *Scenario*

Nuts about Food Ltd: see page 270

Question

Stage 1

At 4 pm on a Friday afternoon, Colonel Brazil telephones you to say that he has been offered a remarkable deal. He has received an order of US$6,000,000 representing 3 CIF shipments per month (value US$500,000 each shipment) for four months. If he was able to fulfil this order, there was the promise of further large orders.

Shipments would be made to a named developing country against a letter of credit issued from the central bank of that country and confirmed by, and payable at, the counters of a leading bank in Switzerland.

At present your bank is not confirming letters of credit from the developing country in question.

Colonel Brazil enquires about the possibility of your bank issuing a letter of credit in favour of one of his regular suppliers which would be in a position to make shipments on time if Colonel Brazil is able to take action immediately.

Stage 2

The following Tuesday, your bank receives a letter of credit issued by a leading bank in the USA on behalf of the central bank of the developing country. The letter of credit is to be advised by your bank on an inoperative basis pending receipt of the name of a third party who will inspect each shipment.

The first shipment is required urgently, and Colonel Brazil asks you to send a tested telex message advising the company's suppliers that the letter of credit has been received.

Stage 3

An amendment is received from the USA, making the letter of credit both operative and transferable. In view of the urgency, Colonel Brazil sends you a fax on the company's paper giving instructions to transfer the letter of credit to a named supplier in France.

The only change proposed in the transfer is that the value of each shipment is to be US$400,000.

REQUIRED:

(a)   Describe what action you would take in response to the various urgent requests, ie

   (i)   Stage 1 – the issue of a letter of credit.   *[4]*

   (ii)   Stage 2 – the despatch of an urgent telex.   *[4]*

   (iii)   Stage 3 – the transfer of the letter of credit.   *[4]*

   Give reasons for your answers.

(b)   Explain what other changes Colonel Brazil might have considered when requesting the transfer of the letter of credit at Stage 3.   *[8]*

[Total marks for question - 20]
(question 3, Spring 1994)

Multiple-Choice Questions: Set 4

Read each question carefully. Choose the *one* answer you think is correct.
Answers are given on page 318.

1.   A documentary letter of credit is opened at the request of one of your customers. Is the customer:

   A   the exporter
   B   the beneficiary
   C   the importer
   D   the drawer

2.   Which one of the following is *not* a party to a letter of credit?

   A   principal
   B   beneficiary
   C   applicant
   D   issuing bank

3.   Under a documentary letter of credit, which is:

   (i)   the bank in the buyer's country,
   (ii)   the bank in the seller's country?

   A   (i) advising bank;   (ii) issuing bank
   B   (i) issuing bank;   (ii) remitting bank
   C   (i) issuing bank;   (ii) advising bank
   D   (i) advising bank;   (ii) presenting bank

4.   Which type of transport document is usually unacceptable under UCP?

    A   short form bill of lading
    B   charter party bill of lading
    C   container bill of lading
    D   multimodal transport document

5.   The insurance document presented under a particular letter of credit for USD 50 000 is
        (i) a cover note, and (ii) expressed in sterling.
        Are these acceptable under UCP?

    A   (i) No   (ii) No
    B   (i) Yes   (ii) Yes
    C   (i) No   (ii) Yes
    D   (i) Yes   (ii) No

6.   A credit, subject to UCP, calls for "1000 tonnes of coal". Would you accept invoices for
        (i) 1075 tonnes and (ii) 1025 tonnes?

    A   (i) No   (ii) No
    B   (i) Yes   (ii) Yes
    C   (i) No   (ii) Yes
    D   (i) Yes   (ii) No

7.   "In credit operations all parties concerned deal ...."

    A   with goods
    B   with documents
    C   through banks
    D   in transactions which follow the sales contract

8.   A particular credit is described as constituting 'a definite undertaking of the issuing bank'. What
        type of credit is it?

    A   red-clause
    B   confirmed
    C   revocable
    D   irrevocable

9.   Which one of the following credits is referred to specifically in *Uniform Customs and Practice for
        Documentary Credits* ?

    A   red-clause
    B   back-to-back
    C   transferable
    D   revolving

10.   Which type of credit provides for pre-shipment finance?

    A   stand-by
    B   red-clause
    C   back-to-back
    D   transferable

Lesson Nine
Collections

Where it is not possible in the contract between exporter and importer to agree that payment should be made under a documentary letter of credit, an alternative is for the exporter to send the documents on a *collection* basis. Using this method the exporter ships the goods and arranges with his bank for the documents (e.g. bills of lading, invoices and, if appropriate, the insurance policy or certificate), usually together with a bill of exchange, to be dispatched to a suitable overseas correspondent bank. Depending on the instructions received from the exporter and the terms of his contract with the buyer, the documents are only released upon either payment or acceptance of the bill of exchange by the importer (see Fig. 9.1).

Collections can also be used in domestic trade.

For the private customer, collections are used in order to obtain payment for a foreign cheque or bill of exchange.

❏ Documents against payment; documents against acceptance

Documents against payment (often abbreviated to D/P)
If the documents against payment method is used the exporter is able to retain a measure of control over his goods as he knows that the documents of title will not be released by the overseas bank until payment has been made. Cash against documents (CAD) is an equivalent term to D/P.

Documents against acceptance (often abbreviated to D/A)
When documents are released against acceptance of a bill of exchange the exporter loses control of his goods and relies on the credit-worthiness and integrity of his overseas customer to pay on the due date. However, the exporter can partly cover himself against such risks by taking out credit insurance (see lesson 10).

Both these methods have the advantage that the documents, and therefore the title to the goods, remain under the control of the banking system until either the bill is accepted or payment is made. However, if the buyer cannot pay or refuses to accept the bill, the exporter may be involved in considerable time and expense in recovering his goods; with an irrevocable documentary letter of credit, by contrast, the exporter knows that, provided he complies with the terms of the credit, he will receive his payment or have his bill accepted.

Payment for collections will be made between the banks by one of the methods outlined in lesson 3, such as bank drafts, or SWIFT, or mail/telegraphic transfers.

Note that the collection method will sometimes be used where the documents being sent for collection do not represent documents of title, as is the case with, for example, waybills. This use of the collection procedure, which is very close to open account trading, is often used by exporters who wish to have their bill of exchange accepted, using the banking system.

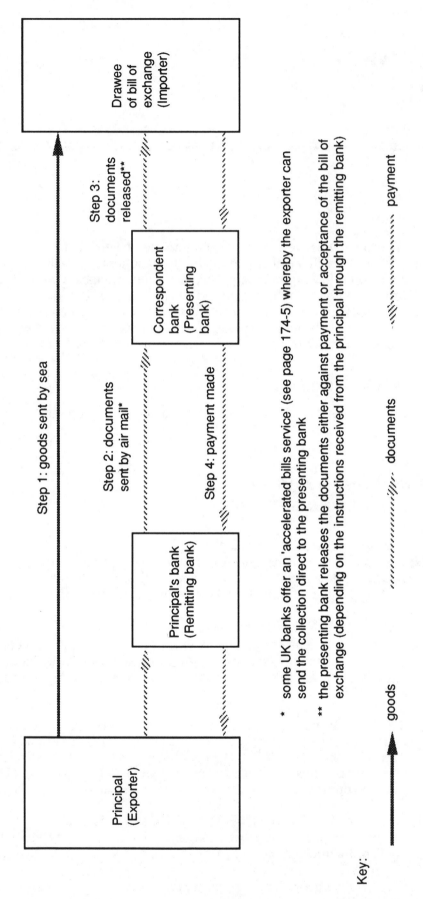

Fig. 9.1: Documents against payment or acceptance of a bill of exchange

❏ *Uniform Rules for Collections*

International rules also apply to collections, known as *Uniform Rules for Collections* (see page 178), and came into force from 1 January 1979.

❏ What is a collection?

Uniform Rules for Collections defines a collection as:

'the handling by banks, on instructions received, of documents .... in order to:

(a) obtain acceptance and/or, as the case may be, payment, or
(b) deliver commercial documents against acceptance and/or, as the case may be, against payment, or
(c) deliver documents on other terms and conditions.'

Note that while the objective of most collections will be to obtain payment or acceptance, this need not necessarily be the case: a collection may be merely to deliver documents to a person overseas.

We should also, at this point, distinguish between outwards and inwards collections. An *outward collection* is where a bank in the home country is remitting documents, relating to an export of goods, to a suitable overseas bank so that payment or acceptance may be obtained from the buyer. An *inward collection* is where a bank in the home country receives documents relating to a shipment of goods which are being imported and is to obtain payment or acceptance from the buyer. Thus a collection is both an outward and an inward collection, depending on the viewpoint from which it is looked.

❏ Documents

Uniform Rules consider documents to be of two types:

* financial documents;
* commercial documents.

Financial documents
These are defined as: 'bills of exchange, promissory notes, cheques, payment receipts or other similar instruments for obtaining the payment of money.'

Commercial documents
These are defined as: 'invoices, shipping documents, documents of title or other similar documents, or any other documents whatsoever, not being financial documents'.

❏ Clean collections and documentary collections

A *clean collection* is the collection of financial documents not accompanied by commercial documents, e.g. the collection of a foreign cheque or bill of exchange, etc. A *documentary collection* is the collection of commercial documents, whether or not they are accompanied by financial documents.

❏ The parties to a collection

• *principal*	the customer entrusting the operation of collection to his bank
• *remitting bank*	the bank to which the principal has entrusted the operation of collection
• *collecting bank*	any bank, other than the remitting bank, involved in processing the collection order
• *presenting bank*	the collecting bank making presentation to the drawee
• *drawee*	the one to whom presentation is to be made according to the collection order

As will be appreciated a collection can relate to documents covering exported goods, in which case the principal will usually be the exporter and the drawee will usually be the buyer, or it can relate to using the banking system to obtain payment for a cheque, etc. which has been received from a person overseas.

❏ A collection order

This contains the 'complete and precise instructions' given by the principal to the remitting bank. All banks involved in the collection are only permitted to act on the instructions given in the collection order, and in accordance with *Uniform Rules for Collections.* Any bank which cannot comply with the instructions contained in a collection order received by it must immediately advise the party from whom it received the order.

Fig. 9.2 shows a collection order used by a major UK bank; fig. 9.3 shows instructions from a principal to the remitting bank. Both of these forms use SITPRO's aligned documentation system.

The principal will give the following instructions:

• *Name of the bank to which the collection should be sent*
This is likely to be the drawee's own bank, but where the drawee has not advised this to the principal, the remitting bank will select a suitable correspondent.

• *The documents comprising the collection*
The order will state the number of each type of commercial document, e.g. two commercial invoices, three bills of lading, etc. Fuller details of the bill of exchange to be collected will be given, such as the date of the bill, tenor (time), amount, drawee and drawer. Brief details of the shipment will usually be given, e.g. 'shipment of plastic gnomes per M.V. Severn Traveller'. As noted previously, documents relating to the shipment might be sent by the remitting bank in two separate posts to avoid the risk of loss.

• *Whether the documents are to be released against payment (D/P) or acceptance (D/A) of the bill of exchange*
Banks must have clear instructions as to whether the documents relating to the shipment should be released against acceptance or payment. From the point of view of the principal, he would obviously prefer them to be released only against payment, whereas the importer would prefer them to be released against acceptance. Nevertheless this is a point which has to be settled between exporter and importer as one of the terms of their contract - the banks handling a collection can only act in accordance with the terms of the collection order. Note that when a collection order does not advise a presenting bank whether documents may be released against payment or acceptance then, under Article 10 of *Uniform Rules for Collections,* the commercial documents will be released only against payment.

© MIDLAND/SITPRO 1989

Midland Bank plc

Drawer/exporter		
	We enclose the undermentioned bill for collection. Please acknowledge receipt quoting our reference and follow the instructions marked X below and any special instructions.	Drawer/exporter ref.
		Midland Bank ref.

Consignee	Drawee (if not consignee)

To (bank)	From **MIDLAND BANK plc**

DOCUMENTS BY FIRST MAILING - ANY BALANCE WILL FOLLOW BY NEXT MAIL

Bill of exchange	Commercial invoice	Certified/consular invoice	Certificate of origin	Insurance policy/certificate	Bill of lading	Parcel post receipt	Air waybill

Combined transport document	Other documents and whereabouts of any missing original bill of lading

RELEASE DOCUMENT AGAINST	ACCEPTANCE	PAYMENT		protest	do not protest
			If unaccepted ——————▶		
If documents are not taken up on arrival of goods *Customs/bonded warehouse if possible Claim expenses from drawee; for our a/c if refused	warehouse goods*	do not warehouse	and advise reason by (confirm case of need notified)	telex/cable	airmail
	insure all risks	do not insure	If unpaid ——————▶	protest	do not protest
Acceptance/payment may be deferred pending arrival of goods	yes	no	and advise reason by (confirm case of need notified)	telex/cable	airmail
Collect all charges from drawee including ours of:	if refused these may be waived	if refused these may not be waived	Advise acceptance and due date by	telex/cable	airmail
Goods and sailing vessel			Remit proceeds by	telex/cable	airmail
In case of need refer to				for assistance only	follow their instructions

SPECIAL INSTRUCTIONS   1.   Represent on arrival of goods if not honoured on first presentation.

PAYMENT INSTRUCTIONS - Please account for proceeds as marked X below.

C Please advise us when definitely paid and then remit the proceeds by authenticated message to the following bank for credit of the account of our London Office requesting them to advise us by authenticated message of the amount credited:

A Remit us first class Bankers' cheque on London in sterling or, if applicable authorise our London Office to debit your account, held in their books, at the same time sending us direct advice. Settlement to be made without loss of exchange to us.

B Credit the account of our London Office under advice to them and to us. Please forward your credit advices only after the item is definitely paid.

Date of bill of exchange	Bill of exchange value/amount of collection
Tenor of bill of exchange	Unless contrary instructions are given above, unaccepted term bills are to be presented for acceptance immediately and, following acceptance, are to be held pending presentation for payment at maturity.
Bill of exchange claused	This collection is subject to the Uniform Rules for Collection (latest version).
	Date

WF500.636

Fig. 9.2: A collection order

® BBA/SITPRO 1976/1981/1987/1992

FOREIGN BILL AND/OR DOCUMENTS FOR COLLECTION

AUTHORISED BY THE BRITISH BANKERS' ASSOCIATION

Drawer/exporter	Drawer's/exporters reference(s) (to be quoted by bank in all correspondence)
Rowcester Engineering Co Ltd Deansway House ROWCESTER RW1 5TQ United Kingdom	1234 1 Aug. 19-1

Consignee	Drawee (if not consignee)
Far Eastern Traders (HK) Ltd KOWLOON Hong Kong	

To (bank)	For bank use only
British International Bank plc High Street ROWCESTER RW1 2BT	

FORWARD DOCUMENTS ENUMERATED BELOW BY AIRMAIL. FOLLOW SPECIAL INSTRUCTIONS AND THOSE MARKED X

Bill of exchange	Commercial invoice	Certified/consular invoice	Certificate of origin	Insurance policy/ certificate	Bill of lading	Parcel post receipt	Air waybill
1	2		1	1	3/3		

Combined transport document	Other documents and whereabouts of any missing original bill of lading

RELEASE DOCUMENTS ON	ACCEPTANCE	PAYMENT X	If unaccepted ➡		Protest	do not protest
If documents are not taken up on arrival of goods	warehouse goods X	do not warehouse	and advise reason by		telex/cable	airmail
	insure against fire	do not insure X	If unpaid ➡		protest	do not protest X
Collect ALL charges			and advise reason by		telex/cable	airmail X
Collect correspondent's charges ONLY		X	Advise acceptance and due date by		telex/cable	airmail
Return accepted bill by airmail			Remit proceeds by		telex/cable X	airmail

In case of need refer to	for guidance	accept their instructions
T. K. Lim & Associates, International Tower, Hong Kong		X

SPECIAL INSTRUCTIONS:

1. Represent on arrival of goods if not honoured on first presentation.

2. Please present through British International Bank, Hong Kong

Date of bill of exchange 1 Aug. 19-1	Bill of exchange value/amount of collection GBP £10,000
Tenor of bill of exchange Sight	
Bill of exchange claused	Please collect the above-mentioned bill and/or documents subject to the Uniform Rules for Collections (1978 Revision), International Chamber of Commerce, Publication No. 322. I/We agree that you shall not be liable for any loss, damage, or delay however caused which is not directly due to the negligence of your own officers or servants.
	Date and signature *J.B. Long* Export Clerk 5 Aug. 19-1

Fig. 9.3: Principal's instructions to the remitting bank handling the collection

Sometimes the goods will be dispatched direct to a bank or consigned to a bank. However, this should only be done with prior agreement on the part of the presenting bank - no bank manager wants to find his banking hall cluttered up with, say, a shipment of plastic gnomes! Nevertheless it is common for smaller items to be sent to an overseas bank by agreement, or consigned in the name of the bank. When this happens the bank is in the position of being able to release the goods, rather than just the documents, to the drawee and will need instructions as to whether this may take place against acceptance or payment.

Note that if the collection order states *release documents against acceptance pour aval*, the bill of exchange must be

- accepted by the drawee, and
- guaranteed for payment at maturity by the drawee's bank

before release of the documents. (The technique of *avalising* bills of exchange and promissory notes is discussed fully in lesson 12 under the heading of 'Forfaiting').

• *Whether acceptance or payment may be deferred pending arrival of the goods*
It is customary in many countries for buyers to defer acceptance or payment until the goods have arrived, and the presenting bank needs to know if this is to be allowed. If no instructions are given on this point the presenting bank must make presentation of the bill without delay.

• *Advice of acceptance*
Where the bill is a tenor (time) bill, principals will instruct that they should be advised of acceptance and also of the date of maturity.

• *Action to be taken by the presenting bank in the event of non-acceptance or non-payment*
Firstly the principal will wish to be advised of non-acceptance or non-payment, and the collection order tells the presenting bank whether such advice is to be given by airmail or cable, together with the reason.

Secondly the order will state whether the bill is to be protested or not. In some countries, if a bill is protested, the reputation of the drawee may be ruined, and it may be considered grounds for petitioning the court for a bankruptcy order. However in Britain, under the Bills of Exchange Act 1882, a presenting bank must protest *foreign* bills which have been dishonoured by non-acceptance and/or non-payment [s.51(2)]; if not protested the drawers and indorsers are discharged. Furthermore, under s.51(4) noting (a preliminary to protest) must take place on the day of dishonour or the next business day - the protest may follow at a later date. A UK bank failing to carry out the correct protest procedures (unless the collection order stated 'do not protest') would not have exercised reasonable care.

• *Case of need*
If the bill is unpaid or not accepted, or other problems arise, the presenting bank may be given the name and address of a 'case of need' by the principal, e.g. his agent in hat country. An indication will be given by the principal as to how far the instructions of this person may be followed and there are usually two levels of assistance: 'for assistance only' or 'follow their instructions without reserve'. This latter instruction means exactly what it says, and it is not unknown for cases of need to dishonestly request the release of documents free of payment.

• *Instructions in the event of documents not being taken up*
The presenting bank will wish to know what to do in the event of the documents not being taken up, i.e. the drawee, for some reason, not wishing to have the goods. This is perhaps the main danger of using a collection as a means of obtaining payment - the goods are shipped in perfect good faith but, if the buyer declines to take the goods, the exporter has the problem of what to do with the goods. The 'case of need' may be able to help here, perhaps by finding an alternative buyer. However, once it is known that the documents are not being taken up, it is essential to do something about the goods quickly. The collection order may instruct that the goods are to be stored and insured; it will give details of the type of storage preferred, e.g. a customs or bonded warehouse, and of the insurance risks to be covered. The costs of such actions are usually claimed from the drawee but, if he refuses to pay them, they will be for the account of the principal.

• *Instructions on interest, charges and expenses*

The presenting bank may be given instructions to collect from the drawee the interest, charges and expenses made by the various banks for their collection services. The collection order will also state whether such costs may or may not be waived if they are refused by the drawee - see also Articles 21 and 22 of *Uniform Rules for Collections* (explained in figs. 9.4 and 9.5). The question of who is to pay the various costs of the collection should be agreed between buyer and seller in their contract.

• *The way in which the proceeds of the collection are to be remitted*

The collection order will tell the collecting bank the method to be adopted in accounting for the proceeds of the collection. This could be by means of mail or telegraphic transfer, or by bank draft. Thus, depending on whether the collection is in the home currency or a foreign currency, the method of transfer between the banks concerned will be as described in lesson 3. However, it should be noted that where the documents are payable in a local currency (i.e. the currency of the country of payment), the presenting bank must only, unless instructed otherwise, release the documents to the drawee if such local currency is immediately available for transfer as specified in the collection order - Article 11.

Note: The Chartered Institute of Bankers' examination often contains questions which ask for the instructions that would be received for either an *inward* or an *outward* collection, presented in the form of a short 'case study',

e.g. 'Your exporter customer, XYZ Ltd., hands you a set of documents for collection on a buyer in Australia ...' etc.

This is *not* the opportunity to list the ten points mentioned above without thought! Certainly they will feature as a large part of the answer but the collection instructions *must fit the circumstances of the case*. For example, if the bill of exchange is payable at sight, it is hardly appropriate to expect the presenting bank to advise you of non-acceptance! Alternatively, if one of the commercial documents handed to you for collection is an air waybill showing the goods dispatched direct to the buyers, the presenting bank will not take too kindly to receiving instructions about storing and insuring the goods in the event of the documents not being taken up!

❑ Accelerated bills service

A variation in the procedure for handling collections is offered by some UK banks as an 'accelerated bills service'. Here the exporter prepares the collection order on their UK bank's paper, using the UK bank's reference numbers. Instead of routeing the collection via the remitting bank, it is sent direct by the exporter to the presenting bank abroad. Details of the transaction are passed to the UK bank – either a copy of the collection order, or the details may be sent electronically. Any subsequent correspondence is handled by the UK bank, and the exporter can check on the progress of the collection with this bank – if the exporter has a computer link with the bank, this can be used to access information. Payment is received by the bank through the international banking system, and passed to the customer's account.

Because the exporter prepares and sends the collection abroad, the advantages of the accelerated bills service for the exporter are:

• a reduction in processing time – this also means that payment should be received more quickly

• a reduction in bank charges

The accelerated bills service is particularly appropriate where exporters deal with particular overseas buyers on a regular basis: the overseas presenting bank can be agreed in advance in conjunction with the UK bank.

Direct collections

It is also possible for exporters to send collections direct to an overseas presenting bank without any involvement of a UK bank. Thus the overseas bank acts as the agent of the UK exporter and remits the proceeds direct to the exporter's bank account.

The advantages of direct collections are that payment should be received faster, and UK bank charges are avoided. The disadvantage is that the exporter has to deal with queries direct with the overseas bank. For the inexperienced exporter it is better to handle collections in the 'traditional' way whereby the UK bank will, as a minimum, check that the documents received appear to be as listed in the collection order.

❏ Liabilities and responsibilities of banks

Banks have a responsibility with regard to the documents of a collection to ensure 'that the documents received appear to be as listed in the collection order'. There is no further obligation to examine the documents, although most banks will give them more than a cursory examination, if only to save their customer from delay in receiving payment. When a bank is making an advance against the collection (see lesson 12) there will be a greater need to examine the documents with care. Where documents are missing, the bank must immediately advise the party from whom they were received, i.e. the principal, the remitting bank, or the collecting bank.

In general, when handling a collection, banks 'will act in good faith and exercise reasonable care'. Presenting banks are required to make presentation for payment or acceptance (as appropriate) 'without delay'. As stated earlier in this lesson, if banks are not given specific instructions, the commercial documents will be released only against payment.

Partial payments in respect of clean collections can be accepted in so far as they are permitted by the law in force in the place of payment. With documentary collections partial payments will only be accepted if allowed by the collection order. However, the documents will only be released when payment in full has been made, subject to the instructions contained in the collection order.

The presenting bank is responsible for making amounts collected (less charges, disbursements, etc.) available without delay to the bank from which the collection order was received. It is also responsible for ensuring that the form of the acceptance of a bill of exchange appears to be complete and correct, but it is not responsible for the genuineness of signatures.

Conflict for a presenting bank

The presenting bank is often placed in a position of conflict because, on the one hand, it must act in accordance with instructions received from the principal and the remitting bank while, on the other hand, the drawee is usually its own customer. Nowhere is this conflict more apparent than when a bank receives a 'Notice of Arrival of Goods' from an airline, with the bank as a notify party. The goods will usually be for a customer of the bank, but it may be several days before the documents of the collection arrive from the overseas bank. The UK bank has an obligation to protect the interest of the overseas customer and bank; however the UK bank must decide what to do with the goods pending receipt of the documentation. The major question is whether the goods should be released to the customer, and under what circumstances. The bank has to be extremely careful and, only if the customer is undoubted can it be prepared to issue a Letter of Release to the airline to make the goods available. In any case, this can only be done against the customer's irrevocable undertaking to make payment of whatever amount is subsequently claimed under the inwards collection.

If there is any doubt about the customer, the full estimated amount of the value of the goods should be debited to the customer's account and placed in a side account before instruction can be issued to release the goods to the customer.

Sometimes a presenting bank will be prepared to release the documents of a collection *on trust* to its customer (the buyer). This can only be done on the strict understanding that the documents are returned to the bank if the buyer does not wish to pay for them or accept the draft. Such action by the presenting bank is entirely its own responsibility and would only be undertaken where the customer is undoubted.

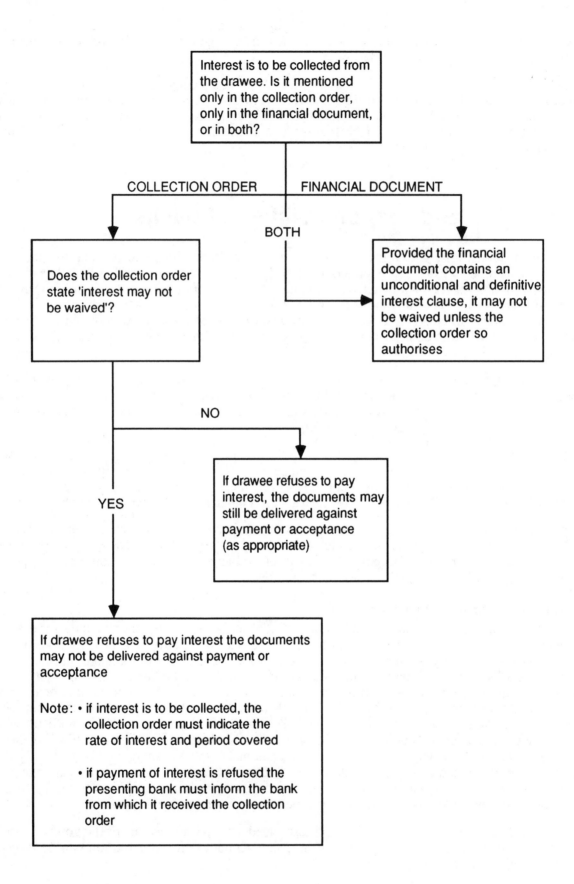

Fig. 9.4: Interest
(see Article 21, *Uniform Rules for Collections*)

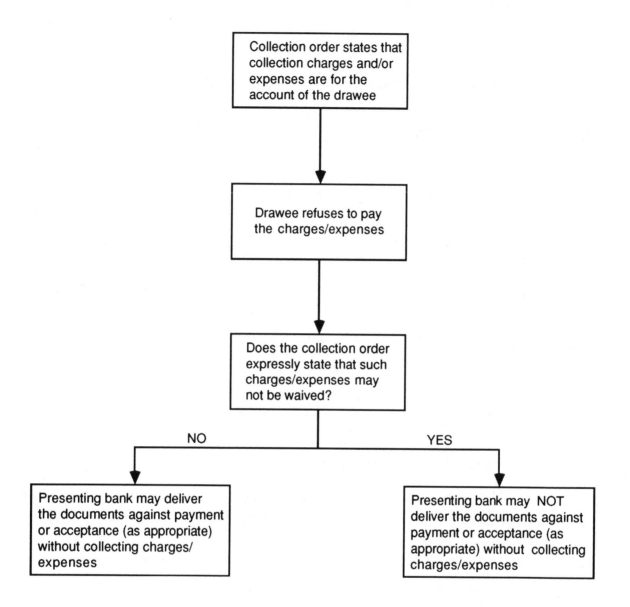

Note: • when payment of charges and/or expenses has been refused, the presenting bank must inform the bank from which it received the collection order

  • when such charges/expenses are waived, they will then be for the account of the principal

  • where the collection order expressly states that such charges shall not be waived, the various banks involved in the collection will not be responsible for any resultant costs or delays

Fig. 9.5: Charges and Expenses
(see Article 22, *Uniform Rules for Collections*)

❏ *Uniform Rules for Collections*

UNIFORM RULES FOR COLLECTIONS

The International Chamber of Commerce Publication No. 322

General Provisions and Definitions

A.   These provisions and definitions and the following articles apply to all collections as defined in (B) below and are binding upon all parties thereto unless otherwise expressly agreed or unless contrary to the provisions of a national, state or local law and/or regulation which cannot be departed from.

B.   For the purpose of such provisions, definitions and articles:

     1.   (i)   'Collection' means the handling by banks, on instructions received, of documents as defined below in (ii), in order to

           (a) obtain acceptance and/or, as the case may be, payment, or

           (b) deliver commercial documents against acceptance and/or, as the case may be, against payment, or

           (c) deliver documents on other terms and conditions.

        (ii)   'Documents' means financial documents and/or commercial documents:

           (a) 'financial documents' means bills of exchange, promissory notes, cheques, payment receipts or other similar instruments used for obtaining the payment of money;

           (b) 'commercial documents' means invoices, shipping documents, documents of title or other similar documents, or any other documents whatsoever, not being financial documents.

        (iii)   'Clean collection' means collection of financial documents not accompanied by commercial documents.

        (iv)   'Documentary collection' means collection of

           (a) financial documents accompanied by commercial documents;

           (b) commercial documents not accompanied by financial documents.

     2.   The 'parties thereto' are:

        (i)   the 'principal' who is the customer entrusting the operation of collection to his bank;

        (ii)   the 'remitting bank' which is the bank to which the principal has entrusted the operation of collection;

        (iii)   the 'collecting bank' which is any bank, other than the remitting bank, involved in processing the collection order;

        (iv)   the 'presenting bank' which is the collecting bank making the presentation to the drawee.

3. The 'drawee' is the one to whom presentation is to be made according to the collection order.

C.   All documents sent for collection must be accompanied by a collection order giving complete and precise instructions. Banks are only permitted to act upon the instructions given in such collection order, and in accordance with these Rules.

If any bank cannot, for any reason, comply with the instructions given in the collection order received by it, it must immediately advise the party from whom it received the collection order.

Liabilities and Responsibilities

Article 1
Banks will act in good faith and exercise reasonable care.

Article 2
Banks must verify that the documents received appear to be as listed in the collection order and must immediately advise the party from whom the collection order was received of any documents missing.

Banks have no further obligation to examine the documents.

Article 3
For the purpose of giving effect to the instructions of the principal, the remitting bank will utilise as the collecting bank:

(i)   the collecting bank nominated by the principal, or, in the absence of such nomination,

(ii)   any bank, of its own or another bank's choice, in the country of payment or acceptance, as the case may be.

The documents and the collection order may be sent to the collecting bank directly or through another bank as intermediary.

Banks utilising the services of other banks for the purpose of giving effect to the instructions of the principal do so for account of and at the risk of the latter.

The principal shall be bound by and liable to indemnify the banks against all obligations and responsibilities imposed by foreign laws or usages.

Article 4
Banks concerned with a collection assume no liability for the consequences arising out of delay and/or loss in transit of any messages, letters or documents, or for delay, mutilation or other errors arising in the transmissions of cables, telegrams, telex, or communication by electronic systems, or for errors in translation or interpretation of technical terms.

Article 5
Banks concerned with a collection assume no liability or responsibility for consequences arising out of the interruption of their business by Acts of God, riots, civil commotions, insurrections, wars, or any other causes beyond their control or by strikes or lockouts.

Article 6
Goods should not be dispatched direct to the address of a bank or consigned to a bank without prior agreement on the part of that bank.

In the event of goods being dispatched direct to the address of a bank or consigned to a bank for delivery to a drawee against payment or acceptance or upon other terms without prior agreement on the part of that bank, the bank has no obligation to take delivery of the goods, which remain at the risk and responsibility of the party dispatching the goods.

Presentation

Article 7
Documents are to be presented to the drawee in the form in which they are received, except that remitting and collecting banks are authorized to affix any necessary stamps, at the expense of the principal unless otherwise instructed, and to make any necessary endorsements or place any rubber stamps or other identifying marks or symbols customary to or required for the collection operation.

Article 8
Collection orders should bear the complete address of the drawee or of the domicile at which presentation is to be made. If the address is incomplete or incorrect, the collecting bank may, without obligation and responsibility on its part, endeavour to ascertain the proper address.

Article 9
In the case of documents payable at sight the presenting bank must make presentation for payment without delay.

In the case of documents payable at a tenor other than sight the presenting bank must, where acceptance is called for, make presentation for acceptance without delay, and where payment is called for, make presentation for payment not later than the appropriate maturity date.

Article 10
In respect of a documentary collection including a bill of exchange payable at a future date, the collection order should state whether the commercial documents are to be released to the drawee against acceptance (D/A) or against payment (D/P).

In the absence of such statement, the commercial documents will be released only against payment.

Payment

Article 11
In the case of documents payable in the currency of the country of payment (local currency), the presenting bank must, unless otherwise instructed in the collection order, only release the documents to the drawee against payment in local currency which is immediately available for disposal in the manner specified in the collection order.

Article 12
In the case of documents payable in a currency other than that of the country of payment (foreign currency), the presenting bank must, unless otherwise instructed in the collection order, only release the documents to the drawee against payment in the relative foreign currency which can immediately be remitted in accordance with the instructions given in the collection order.

Article 13
In respect of clean collections, partial payments may be accepted if and to the extent to which and on the conditions on which partial payments are authorized by the law in force in the place of payment. The documents will only be released to the drawee when full payment thereof has been received.

In respect of documentary collections partial payments will only be accepted if specifically authorized in the collection order. However, unless otherwise instructed, the presenting bank will only release the documents to the drawee after full payment has been received.

In all cases partial payments will only be accepted subject to compliance with the provisions of either Article 11 or Article 12 as appropriate.

Partial payment, if accepted, will be dealt with in accordance with the provisions of Article 14.

Article 14
Amounts collected (less charges and/or disbursements and/or expenses where applicable) must be made available without delay to the bank from which the collection order was received in accordance with the instructions contained in the collection order.

Acceptance

Article 15
The presenting bank is responsible for seeing that the form of the acceptance of a bill of exchange appears to be complete and correct, but is not responsible for the genuineness of any signature or for the authority of any signatory to sign the acceptance.

Promissory Notes, Receipts and Other Similar Instruments

Article 16
The presenting bank is not responsible for the genuineness of any signature or for the authority of any signatory to sign a promissory note, receipt or other similar instrument.

Protest

Article 17
The collection order should give specific instructions regarding protest (or other legal process in lieu thereof), in the event of non-acceptance or non-payment.

In the absence of such specific instructions the banks concerned with the collection have no obligation to have the documents protested (or subjected to other legal process in lieu thereof) for non-payment or non-acceptance.

Any charges and/or expenses incurred by banks in connection with such protest or other legal process will be for the account of the principal.

Case-of-Need   (Principal's Representative) and Protection of Goods

Article 18
If the principal nominated a representative to act as case-of-need in the event of non-acceptance and/or non-payment the collection order should clearly and fully indicate the powers of such case-of-need.

In the absence of such indication banks will not accept any instructions from the case-of-need.

Article 19
Banks have no obligation to take any action in respect of the goods to which a documentary collection relates.

Nevertheless in the case that banks take action for the protection of the goods, whether instructed or not, they assume no liability or responsibility with regard to the fate and/or condition of the goods and/or for any acts and/or omissions on the part of any third parties entrusted with the custody and/or protection of the goods. However, collecting bank(s) must immediately advise the bank from which the collection order was received of any such action taken.

Any charges and/or expenses incurred by banks in connection with any action for the protection of the goods will be for the account of the principal.

Advice of Fate, etc.

Article 20
Collecting banks are to advise fate in accordance with the following rules:

(1)   *Form of advice*   All advices or information from the collecting bank to the bank from which the collection order was received, must bear appropriate detail including, in all cases, the latter bank's reference number of the collection order.

(2)   *Method of advice*   In the absence of specific instructions, the collecting bank must send all advices to the bank from which the collection order was received by quickest mail but, if the collecting bank considers the matter to be urgent, quicker methods such as cable, telegram, telex or communication by electronic systems, etc. may be used at the expense of the principal.

(3)   (a)   *Advice of payment*   The collecting bank must send without delay advice of payment to the bank from which the collection order was received, detailing the amount or amounts collected, charges and/or disbursements and/or expenses deducted, where appropriate, and method of disposal of the funds.

(b)   *Advice of acceptance*   The collecting bank must send without delay advice of acceptance to the bank from which the collection order was received.

(c)   *Advice of non-payment or non-acceptance*   The collecting bank must send without delay advice of non-payment or advice of non-acceptance to the bank from which the collection order was received.

The presenting bank should endeavour to ascertain the reasons for such non-payment or non-acceptance and advise accordingly the bank from which the collection order was received.

On receipt of such advice the remitting bank must, within a reasonable time, give appropriate instructions as to the further handling of the documents. If such instructions are not received by the presenting bank within 90 days from its advice of non-payment or non-acceptance, the documents may be returned to the bank from which the collection order was received.

Interest, Charges, and Expenses

Article 21
If the collection order includes an instruction to collect interest which is not embodied in the accompanying financial document(s), if any, and the drawee refuses to pay such interest, the presenting bank may deliver the documents against payment or acceptance as the case may be without collecting such interest, unless the collection order expressly states that such interest may not be waived. Where such interest is to be collected the collection order must bear an indication of the rate of interest and the period covered. When payment of interest has been refused the presenting bank must inform the bank from which the collection order was received accordingly.

If the documents include a financial document containing an unconditional and definitive interest clause the interest amount is deemed to form part of the amount of the documents to be collected. Accordingly, the interest amount is payable in addition to the principal amount shown in the financial document and may not be waived unless the collection order so authorizes.

Article 22
If the collection order includes an instruction that collection charges and/or expenses are to be for account of the drawee and the drawee refuses to pay them, the presenting bank may deliver the document(s) against payment or acceptance as the case may be without collecting charges and/or expenses unless the collection order expressly states that such charges and/or expenses may not be waived. When payment of collection charges and/or expenses has been refused the presenting bank must inform the bank from which the collection order was received accordingly. Whenever collection charges and/or expenses are so waived they will be for the account of the principal, and may be deducted from the proceeds.

Should a collection order specifically prohibit the waiving of collection charges and/or expenses then neither the remitting nor collecting nor presenting bank shall be responsible for any costs or delays resulting from this prohibition.

Article 23

In all cases where in the express terms of a collection order, or under these Rules, disbursements and/or expenses and/or collection charges are to be borne by the principal, the collecting bank(s) shall be entitled promptly to recover outlays in respect of disbursements and expenses and charges from the bank from which the collection order was received and the remitting bank shall have the right promptly to recover from the principal any amount so paid out by it, together with its own disbursements, expenses and charges, regardless of the fate of the collection.

ICC Uniform Rules for Collections
ICC Publication 322
Published in its official English version by the International Chamber of Commerce, Paris
Copyright © 1978 – International Chamber of Commerce (ICC)
Available from: ICC Publishing SA, 38 Cours Albert 1er, 75008 Paris, France
And from: ICC United Kingdom, 14/15 Belgrave Square, London SW1X 8PS

❏ Advantages of a collection

Although collections, by their very nature, favour the importer there are advantages in their use for exporters also.

To the exporter

- The main benefit for an exporter in using collections as a method of obtaining payment is that there is a degree of protection because the documents are handled by the banking system. Accordingly the presenting bank, acting on behalf of the principal, should be able to seek payment from the drawee in a more effective way than can the exporter from his own country.

- Collections are more secure as a method of payment than open account, and documents against payment is more secure than documents against acceptance.

- Finance may be available by such means as:

  1. ordinary bank loan/overdraft;
  2. advances against collections;
  3. negotiation of bills/documents;
  4. accommodation finance/acceptance house credit;
  5. special 'finance for exports' schemes offered by most banks;
  6. forfaiting.

  See lesson 12 for details of these.

To the importer

- Without doubt a collection is much more convenient and cheaper for an importer than opening a letter of credit: no effort is involved on his part and he is saved the expense of the credit.

- The importer may arrange to defer payment or acceptance until the arrival of the goods (subject to the instructions in the collection order).

- If the collection is documents against acceptance the importer can obtain the goods before payment.

- Finance may be available by such means as:

  1. ordinary bank loan/overdraft;
  2. produce loan;
  3. accommodation finance/acceptance house credit;
  4. documents against acceptance collection.

  See lesson 13 for details.

❏ Disadvantages of a collection

To the exporter

- If the buyer refuses to take up the goods, the exporter will incur additional storage and insurance costs. There will also be the problem of finding an alternative buyer and for reshipping the goods to another destination. (Any loss can be mitigated by taking out credit insurance - see lesson 10).

- Ranks after payment in advance and letters of credit in terms of security of payment.

- The exporter will not be credited with the money until the remitting bank receives payment from the presenting/collecting bank unless, of course, finance has already been obtained against the collection.

- Risk of non-acceptance and non-payment.

To the importer

- With a documents against payment collection there is no opportunity to inspect the goods before payment. In addition payment might have to be made prior to the arrival of the goods.

- Besides a legal action based on goods supplied and not paid for, by accepting a bill of exchange on a documents against acceptance collection, the importer incurs a separate legal liability on the bill of exchange.

- In some countries, if a bill of exchange is protested, this can ruin the reputation of a trader and may be considered grounds for petitioning the court for a bankruptcy order.

❏ Examination hints

- Questions on collections appear regularly in the examination.

- Recent questions have asked for a definition of a collection, and its usefulness to either an exporter or an importer.

- Some questions have asked how various problems would be solved under Uniform Rules: in particular, the problem of the importer customer who does not wish to pay because the goods are sub-standard.

- The instructions on a collection order for a particular shipment of goods could be asked: do not forget to 'tailor' your answer to the particular transaction.

- Be able to compare collections with documentary credits.

- Be aware of banks' responsibilities to the other parties involved in the collection, e.g. where a bill of exchange is unpaid, what happens to the goods? Are they safe? Are they insured? Who should know or give instructions?

Know Your .... Collections

1. Define a collection.

2. What two classes of document are mentioned in *Uniform Rules for Collections?*
   Give *two* examples of each.

3. What is meant by a clean collection?

4. What is meant by a documentary collection?

5. Name the parties to a collection.

6. "All documents sent for collection must be accompanied by a .... giving complete and precise instructions".

7. Briefly outline the "complete and precise instructions" a bank would receive when handling a collection.

8. Are partial payments acceptable in respect of
   • clean collections;
   • documentary collections?

9. Where documents are payable in the currency of the country of payment (local currency), under what circumstances should the documents be released to the drawee?

10. What obligation do banks have to protect the goods to which a collection relates?

11. Who is responsible for a bank's charges and/or expenses in respect of protest, other legal processes, or in connection with the protection of goods.

12. What do *Uniform Rules for Collections* say about the collection of interest?

13. What do *Uniform Rules for Collections* say about collection charges and/or expenses?

14. Give two advantages and two disadvantages of a collection to an exporter.

15. Give two advantages and two disadvantages of a collection to an importer.

Past Examination Questions

9.1   Semiconductors Ltd, your customers, manufacture a whole range of electric switchgear. They have recently agreed to import semiconductors from Taiwan and they have been offered 90 days D/A terms, although interest from the date of acceptance until maturity has to be borne by your customers. Within a few days you receive a set of documents for £100,000 from a Taiwanese bank and are asked to present the bill of exchange for acceptance by your customers. The collection is subject to Uniform Rules for Collections [ICC Publication no 322].

Your customers accept the bill of exchange but at maturity refuse to pay interest from the date of acceptance to the date of maturity.

REQUIRED:

(a)   A brief statement showing all the instructions you, as a collecting banker, would expect to receive, *in this instance,* on the collection order.   *[8]*

(b)   The action you would take upon your customers' refusal to pay interest. Give the reasons for your action.   *[12]*
[Total marks for question - 20]
(question 6, September 1987)

9.2   The directors of Flower Power Ltd, your customer, ask you to visit them regarding a possible contract they are discussing with Dutch purchasers. Your customer has 'bred' a range of plants, and full ownership and rights to the plants are retained by them. However, the actual plants are being grown on their behalf by a UK horticultural factory unit, producing the plants by means of a cloning system. A well known international carrier, who is used to handling produce of this nature, will collect the goods and eliver them to Holland.

Your customer has agreed to pay the growers 70 Dutch cents per plant. the Dutch purchasers have agreed to pay 1.40 Dutch guilders per plant, but have asked for 30 days credit against accepted bills of exchange. You understand that the terms of shipment will be 'ex horticultural unit'. The first series of orders for 10,000 plants a month has been received.

The directors ask you to explain to them the banking method by which the company can claim payments from Holland. They also ask you if there is a simple way in which they can protect themselves against any exchange risks.

REQUIRED:

(a)   A description of the banking method by which you would suggest that claims for payment should be presented to the Dutch purchasers, together with reference to the internationally accepted procedures involved.   *[6]*

(b)   A specific instruction that should be included amongst those given by your customer to the banks involved, which would give further protection to Flower Power Ltd in this particular transaction.   *[3]*

(c)   An explanation of the difference between the terms 30 days D/P and 30 days D/A, indicating whether your customer would obtain any additional protection if D/P terms were used, bearing in mind the method/terms of shipment proposed for this particular transaction   *[7]*

(d)   An explanation of the simple banking arrangement which would enable your customer to obtain protection against the exchange risk.   *[4]*
[Total marks for question - 20]
(question 3, May 1988)

9.3   Angles and Saxons Ltd, a substantial customer of yours, imports a range of farming machinery from Germany.

The invoices are normally expressed in Deutschmarks, and are accompanied by a collection order and a bill of exchange, drawn and payable at 60 days after the date of the invoice. No documents of title are attached to the collection order. The German bank's instructions are to release documents against acceptance, but no protest instructions are given.

You have usually presented the bills of exchange to your customer for acceptance, but the company has not always been meticulous about returning the accepted bills to you. Difficulties have also arisen because your customer often attempts to delay payment of the bills of exchange and owing to the standing of the company you have not wished to apply any pressure with regard to these collections.

You have now received a claim from the remitting bank for your customer's account for one month's interest, which the German suppliers claim is payable because of the failure of your customer to pay the most recent bill of exchange on the specific maturity date.

REQUIRED:
Your comments on:

(a)   your position under current International Chamber of Commerce Rules in connection with the most recent presentation.   *[6]*

(b)   your position under UK banking practice in connection with the presentation of a bill of exchange for acceptance in circumstances similar to those described above.   *[6]*

(c)   the position of your bank and your customer in connection with the claim for interest.   *[4]*

(d)   the specific instruction that could be incorporated in future collection orders and would be acceptable under International Rules and UK law which might encourage your customer to pay the bills promptly at maturity.   *[4]*

[Total marks for question - 20]
(question 5, May 1988)

9.4   Your customer, Snow White Ltd, runs a number of laundrettes. The directors are now discussing with Mr Lee, the London representative of a Hong Kong based manufacturer, Wishy Washy Ltd, a contract to import washing machines from the Far East. The terms that have been quoted are as follows:

(i)   30 days sight D/P; or
(ii)   60 days sight D/A plus interest at 12%, the bank to guarantee the bills of exchange. (*Note*: The interest clause is to be incorporated in the bill of exchange.)

The directors ask you to explain these terms and to indicate any obligations which they and your bank will enter into if the terms are accepted. Snow White Ltd is anxious to agree to Mr Lee's request, as the price of the machines is advantageous to them. You therefore agree to see the directors as a matter of urgency to discuss the proposition.

REQUIRED:
(a)   An explanation of the terms quoted by Wishy Washy Ltd to Snow White Ltd.   *[5]*

(b)   An explanation of the obligations which your customer and your bank will enter into under the terms of both (i) and (ii) above.   *[9]*

(c)   Details of any instructions you would expect to receive if your bank were to act as a collecting bank.
    [6]
[Total marks for question - 20]
(question 4, October 1988)

9.5   A customer of one of your bank's branches, Lumber Ltd, imports timber products from many parts of the world. As Area Manager of the bank, you receive in May a letter of complaint from one of your New York correspondents, alleging that a documentary collection was sent to one of your branches early in December and that settlement has only just been received despite many chasing letters, none of which has been acknowledged by the branch.

Your investigations show the following:

(1)   According to the bills of lading, the goods were despatched on 27 November to your customer as consignee.

(2)   The collection order instructed your branch to release the documents against payment of a sight bill of exchange.

(3)   The collection order stated that in case of dishonour the bill of exchange was to be protested for non-payment.

(4)   The invoices, bills of lading and bills of exchange received with the collection schedule were held by your branch until settlement of the collection, when they were released to the customer. Settlement took place on 15 April.

(5)   The customer was contacted every Friday and refused to pay the collection, stating that the terms of the commercial contract were that Lumber Ltd would pay 15 days after despatch of the goods from a port situated on the eastern seaboard of the USA.

(6)   The bill of exchange was not presented to the customer and was not protested/noted for dishonour.

(7)   The documents were released only upon payment of the full face value of the bill, and settlement was effected on 15 April, as indicated above.

REQUIRED:

(a)   The concise notes you would make as a result of your investigations into this letter of complaint from your correspondents, specifically commenting on the following:

(b)   any mitigating factors you think might be cited in defence of your bank in the circumstances described in the question;   *[3]*

(c)

your bank's responsibility to its customer, Lumber Ltd, and to the supplier of the goods;   *[7]*

the position of your bank/branch in accordance with internationally established procedures and UK banking law and practice, and the conclusion you would reach.   *[10]*

Note: Candidates are NOT required to draft a reply to the letter of complaint but to explain fully and impartially the bank's position.

[Total marks for question - 20]
(question 8, May 1989)

9.6   As manager of a major country branch of Provincial Bank Ltd you are asked to give guidance and assistance to your staff in connection with the four separate problems below which have occurred in respect of inward collections received by your branch, the presenting bank in the UK:

(1)   The buyer of goods offers immediate payment before receipt of the underlying documents, having been advised by you of receipt of a notice of arrival of the goods at a local airport.

(2) You present a bill of exchange (and the underlying documents) in D/A collection to the drawee, a company that banks with a competitor bank. The drawee hands back to you the bill of exchange apparently duly accepted and bearing the 'stamp' of the company. You have no knowledge as to whether the signature on the acceptance is authorised.

(3) The collection order received by your branch simply states that 'interest at 15% per annum is to be collected from the drawees from the date of first presentation until payment of the attached bill of exchange by the drawees'.

(4) You receive a D/A collection with a 30 day bill of exchange and underlying documents showing that goods have been consigned to the drawees at a local airport. You immediately contact the drawees, who advise you: 'The drawees have the right to examine the goods before they agree (or refuse) to accept the bill of exchange.'

REQUIRED:

(a) The guidance you would give your staff in connection with each set of circumstances described in (1) – (4) above.   [16]

(b) Would your answers in (a) be any different if your bank were situated outside the UK? Give reasons in each case.   [4]

[Total marks for question - 20]
(question 4, October 1989)

9.7*   Your branch has recently received two documentary collections drawn on your customer, Flibinite Ltd. The collection order covered 30 day bills of exchange accompanied by various documents. One set of documents included a full set of a shipping company's bills of lading, whereas the other set of documents included a way-bill issued by a shipping company. Among other things, the collection order stated:

(i)   'This is subject to Uniform Rules for collections – publication number 322.'

(ii)   'Release documents against acceptance.'

(iii)   'Protest if unpaid.'

(iv)   'In case of need please refer to our UK agents, Good Samaritans Limited.'

Flibinite Ltd accepted the bills of exchange and the documents were released to them, whilst you retain the bills of exchange in your portfolio until maturity. Upon presentation of the bills of exchange at maturity, your customer refuses to pay the face amount of bills, stating that the goods were not up to standard. However, they advise you that they will be willing to pay 50% of the face amount of the bills. They also inform you that they are expecting another two shipments from the same source.

REQUIRED:
Brief notes on the following:

(a) What is the significance of the statement contained in (i) above?   [4]

(b) What action would you take, giving reasons, in connection with the offer to pay 50%?   [8]

(c) Subsequently, as intimated by the customer, two further inward collections are received on a similar basis and the customer refuses to accept the bills of exchange. Would there be any difference in the position of the seller if you retained both these sets of documents and held them at the seller's disposal, subject to the instructions of the case of need? Give reasons for your answer.   [8]

[Total marks for question - 20]
(question 5, May 1990)

9.8*   Willnotpay Ltd is a long established customer. Mr Hardup, the Managing Director, calls to see you to discuss the settlement of a bill the company has received from a supplier of timber in Norway. The Managing Director produces a copy of a collection order which was apparently sent direct to the customer, Willnotpay Ltd, and not through the banking system. You note that the bill of exchange drawn by the Norwegian supplier, Thor A/S, was payable on a fixed due date and is some 30 days overdue. Attached to the bill of exchange is a Viking Bank A/S collection order which includes the following instructions:

1.   'Documents are to be released against acceptance.'
2.   'Please collect all charges, including our of Norwegian kroner 265.'
3.   'Please protest if unaccepted or unpaid.'
4.   'Remit proceeds by cable transfer/priority SWIFT.'

Mr Hardup authorises you to pay the bill of exchange, and you arrange to remit the amount of the bill, Norwegian kroner 100,000, to the Viking Bank A/S Oslo, one of your correspondents. Mr Hardup informs you that all charges must be borne by the beneficiary. Mr Hardup tells you that he has been advised by Thor A/S that in future they will refuse to forward goods to the company unless they receive some form of undertaking that the company is prepared to pay on the due date. In other words, if the documents are not accepted by the company through the banking system, his source of supply of Norwegian timber will cease.

REQUIRED:
In brief note form, describe the following:

(a)   the method by which you would remit the proceeds of the bill presented for payment through the Viking Bank A/S Oslo.   [4]

(b)   any accounting procedures which would be involved with such a transfer.   [3]

(c)   your explanation to Mr Hardup, outlining the responsibilities of the parties if he accepts documents under a collection order which includes the terms mentioned in 1, 2 and 3 above.   [10]

(d)   your explanation of a banking method by which the company could receive supplies of timber from Thor A/S which would give some form of protection to the suppliers.   [3]

[Total marks for question - 20]
(question 5, October 1990)

9.9   Your branch receives direct through the postal system an inward collection from a correspondent bank in Malaysia. 'CIF' documents are attached to a bill of exchange which is drawn at ninety days sight D/A on one of the major importers in your town, who is not a customer of your bank. The bill of exchange is not claused. The covering collection order, which does not give the full address of the drawee, states the following **and nothing more**:

'1.   Release the documents to the drawee.
2.   Collect all charges including ours of GBP 55.
3.   Collect interest at 14% pa from the date of acceptance until maturity.'

REQUIRED:
(a)   Describe your responsibilities to the remitting bank in respect of the three instructions given above, indicating the source of your answers. Would your answers be different, if you acted solely in accordance with UK banking practice?   [14]

(b)   State what you understand by the term '90 days sight D/A', indicating your responsibility, if any, to the drawer in respect of the acceptance.   [2]

(c)   List the documents you would expect to see attached to the bill of exchange *in this collection,* stating any international 'Rules' which should apply.   [4]

[Total marks for question - 20]
(question 4, October 1991)

9.10 UK Engineering Plc is a merchanting organisation purchasing engineering products from the Far East and selling them to companies based in the EC, including the UK. The company has negotiated advantageous payment terms, in foreign currency, from the Far Eastern suppliers, receiving some 90 days in which to settle bills of exchange presented through your bank on 90 day D/A terms. The purchasers in the EC (including the UK) have in the past paid by means of irrevocable sight letters of credit payable at your counters or the counters of first class UK banks. The goods are despatched direct to the ultimate buyers, the shipping documents showing UK Engineering Plc as shippers.

During the course of discussing the company's progress, your Personal Assistant asks you to explain why you are happy to offer facilities to the company based upon this trade rather than relying on a debenture. He asks you the following specific questions:

(a) What is meant by an irrevocable letter of credit and are there any international rules governing it? [4]

(b) Is this the safest instrument you could rely upon where documents are involved? If not, why not? [2]

(c) What advantages accrue to UK Engineering from the terms of the two payment methods used by the company? [3]

(d) Are there any disadvantages to any of the parties involved in these transactions? If so, what are they? [8]

(e) What other documentation, or operational procedure, are you relying on to give you some security, if not a debenture? [3]

REQUIRED:
The explanation you would give to your Personal Assistant in respect of EACH point listed above.

[Total marks for question - 20]
Note: The marks are shown above for each of your assistant's questions.
(question 7, October 1991)

9.11* *Scenario*
Euro Multinational Co Ltd: see page 268
Question
Arrangements have been made for Euro Multinational Co Ltd to import an urgent supply of goods from a different source.

You have received from a bank abroad a bill of exchange at 120 days' sight with an invoice and a full set of bills of lading. The documents relate to the import of a large supply of components to the value of ECU 700,000 by Euro Multinational.

The foreign bank's instructions are to present the bill on a D/A basis on behalf of their customers, MDI Italiana SRL in Genoa.

This is the first time that Euro Multinational has imported on this basis. The vessel has just arrived and you are asked to telephone Mr Money urgently.

REQUIRED:

(a) Draw up the full wording of the bill of exchange using the information given above. [4]

(b) Provide a full explanation of the term 'D/A' and the procedures involved in the transaction. [6]

(c) Identify and describe the main risks for Euro Multinational in this particular transaction. [6]

(d) Mr Money asks if you can send the documents to him so that he can decide what to do. What is the bank's position and what action should you take? [4]

[Total marks for question - 20]
(question 3, Spring 1993)

Multiple-Choice Questions: Set 5

Read each question carefully. Choose the *one* answer you think is correct.
Answers are given on page 318.

1.   To an exporter, a D/A collection is better than

   A   documents against payment
   B   open account
   C   irrevocable credit
   D   confirmed irrevocable credit

2.   Your customer asks your bank to handle a collection outwards on her behalf. Are you:

   A   the presenting bank
   B   the remitting bank
   C   the issuing bank
   D   the advising bank

3.   Which is the odd one out?

   A   remitting bank
   B   beneficiary
   C   drawee
   D   presenting bank

4.   A clean collection is the collection of

   A   financial documents only
   B   financial documents accompanied by commercial documents
   C   commercial documents only
   D   commercial documents which include a 'clean' bill of lading

5.   Which is the odd one out?

   A   invoice
   B   shipping document
   C   promissory note
   D   insurance certificate

6.   A disadvantage of a D/A collection to an exporter is that

   A   finance is not available
   B   the presenting bank may not follow his instructions
   C   he loses control of his goods when the bill of exchange has been accepted
   D   exchange control regulations may prevent him getting his money out of an overseas country

7.   An advantage of a D/A collection to an importer is that

   A   the presenting bank will look after the importer's interests in the event of a dispute over the quality of the goods
   B   export finance is available
   C   the remitting and collecting banks' charges are for the account of the principal
   D   he can inspect, and sell some or all of, the goods before payment has to be made

8.   Unless the collection order states otherwise, for documentary collections, partial payments:

   A   are permitted
   B   are not permitted
   C   are permitted, subject to the free transfer of funds out of the country of payment
   D   are permitted, less deduction of presenting bank's charges

9.   A particular collection order states that charges are for the account of the drawee. The drawee refuses to pay them. What is the position of the presenting bank?

   A   it may deliver documents, etc. without collecting the charges
   B   it may not deliver documents etc. without collecting the charges
   C   if collection order further states that charges may not be waived, it may still deliver documents, etc. without collecting charges
   D   if collection order further states that charges may not be waived, it may not deliver documents, etc. without collecting charges

10.   Goods relating to a collection are sent direct to the presenting bank. The bank:

   A   must take charge of the goods
   B   has no obligation to take charge of the goods
   C   has a liability under Uniform Rules to warehouse and insure the goods
   D   has a liability to pass the goods to the drawee

Lesson Ten
The Role of Credit Insurance in International Trade Finance

There are two main financial problems for the exporter:
* the risk of non-payment;
* the provision of finance.

The problems of collecting export debts can be troublesome. It is generally not as easy to telephone an overseas customer about non-payment as it is a customer in the UK, it is far less easy to visit a debtor with an overdue account and, if it should come to taking a customer to court for non-payment, the difficulties are very great indeed.

Exports often have to be sold on extended credit and the terms have to match those offered by competitors. Compared with credit transactions in inland trade, which are usually settled within 30 or 60 days, the credit offered to overseas buyers usually needs to be between 90 and 180 days. For large-scale capital projects up to five years' credit, or even longer, may have to be offered.

Solutions to both the main financial problems of the exporter are available:

* credit insurance is available to exporters
    — from NCM Credit Insurance Ltd for credit terms of less than two years
    — from The Export Credits Guarantee Department (ECGD), a government department, for credit terms of two years or more

* the banks offer special finance facilities, usually linked to credit insurance, at preferential interest rates (see lesson 12).

❏ The Credit Insurance Market

The Export Credits Guarantee Department
ECGD is a government department which was formed in 1919. Since 1930 it has assisted exporters of both goods and services by providing a special type of insurance covering two main areas of risk:
* the creditworthiness of overseas buyers
* the economic and political risks arising from events in overseas countries

Until 1991 ECGD insured both short-term (credit terms of less than two years) and long-term (credit terms of two years or more) export business. In 1991, however, the short-term business was sold to NCM Credit Insurance Ltd, a part of the Dutch NCM Group.

ECGD operates on a non-profitmaking (and non-lossmaking) basis. It does not cover those risks dealt with by commercial insurers, such as fire and marine risks.

NCM Credit Insurance Ltd

As noted above, the Dutch NCM Group, the largest private credit insurer in the world bought the short-term business of ECGD in 1991. Export credit insurance is offered through NCM's *International Guarantee* (see below).

In 1992, NCM introduced its *Domestic Policy* (see page 196) which provides credit insurance for sales of goods and services in the domestic market. The risk covered is insolvency.

Other insurers

- *Trade Indemnity,* a company owned by a consortium of leading insurance companies, offers protection against non-payment both in the home and overseas markets. Its main policy is the *Multi-Market Policy.*

- Credit insurers in other European Community countries - e.g. COFACE of France, HERMES in Germany - are able to operate freely in the UK.

❏ The NCM International Guarantee

This policy is designed for exporters who sell on credit terms of up to 180 days, or on cash terms. It is appropriate for companies which:
- have a large number of sales to a variety of markets
- require cover for high value export transactions

NCM is looking for exporters to insure most or all of their export turnover, for a minimum period of twelve months - in this way, a spread of risks between good and bad markets is achieved so enabling premiums for cover to be maintained at reasonable rates.

Risks covered

The risks covered by the NCM International Guarantee can be classified under two broad headings - Buyer Risks and Country Risks. Both types of risks are covered in the same policy.

Buyer Risks
- The insolvency of the buyer
- The buyer's failure to pay within six months after the due date for goods accepted
- The buyer's failure or refusal to accept goods despatched which comply with the contract

Country Risks
- Delays in transferring money from the buyer's country
- Any action of the government of the foreign country which wholly, or partly, prevents performance of the contract
- Political events or economic, legislative or administrative measures occurring outside the UK which prevent or delay transfer of payment
- War, civil war and the like, outside the UK (other than war between the five major powers) preventing performance of the contract
- Cancellation or non renewal of an export licence or the imposition of new restrictions on exports after date of contract
- When NCM agrees that the public buyer (see below) cause of loss applies - the failure or refusal to fulfil any of the terms of the contract

Value of cover

- Insolvency of the buyer, and buyer default: 90% of the loss
- Country risks: 95% of the loss
- Buyer's failure to accept the goods: the exporter bears a first loss of 20% and NCM bears 90% of the balance (ie a maximum of 72% in the event of a total write-off of the goods)

Payment of claims

These are normally payable as follows:

- immediately on proof of the buyer's insolvency
- six months after due date of payment for default on goods accepted
- one month after resale if the original buyer has failed to take up the order
- four months after due date for most other causes of loss

Additional cover

- Public buyers. An additional risk is covered by NCM in the case of public buyers: these include central, regional, provincial and local government buyers. An exporter selling to public buyers will also be covered by NCM against the failure or refusal of the buyer to fulfil any of the terms of the contract.

- Pre-credit risk. Whilst the policy provides an exporter with cover from the *date of dispatch,* an exporter can choose to take out cover, for an additional premium, from the date the contract of sale is made. This pre-credit risk is particularly appropriate for exporters producing specialised goods for a particular buyer - goods which would not easily sell elsewhere if things went wrong.

- Services provided for an overseas customer, such as professional assistance, refits, conversions and repairs.

- Royalties on licensing and franchising agreements.

- Sales made through overseas subsidiaries.

- Goods sold from stock held overseas or after exhibition.

- External trade, i.e. goods manufactured or traded outside the UK.

- Goods invoiced in a range of foreign currencies. Also, where an exporter has used the forward exchange market. NCM can agree that, within limits, claims can take account of any additional losses in meeting the forward exchange commitment.

- Cover for business on goods sold on longer credit terms than 180 days (but less than two years), or which take more than twelve months to manufacture, can be arranged through the addition of the *Extended Risk Endorsement* to the guarantee.

Costs

- An annual premium based on exporter turnover.
- A flat rate premium payable monthly on the value of export business declared.
- For certain overseas markets, where exceptional risks are identified, an additional premium charge is also levied.

Lower premiums will, generally, be paid by the exporter who is able to provide NCM with a wide spread of risks.

❏ The NCM Domestic Policy

This policy covers:
- business carried out within the policyholder's home market
- the risk of insolvency of the buyer
- both goods and services
- from delivery and acceptance of goods (for services, when invoices are rendered)

The policy can also be tailored to meet the requirements for pre-credit risk, so that work-in-progress and contractual commitments are covered. The policy can be linked into finance schemes whereby claims payable can be assigned to a lender.

❏ ECGD Supplier Insurance Policy

We have already seen that, with credit insurance policies for short-term business (i.e. up to two years' credit terms), exporters insure most or all of their export turnover in both good and bad markets. This makes for ease of administration and provides cover at the lowest possible cost. However, transactions involving capital goods or projects on a large scale where credit terms are two years' or more are not suited to this 'comprehensive' treatment and are subject to individual negotiation of credit insurance. Such insurance is offered by ECGD's *Supplier Insurance Policy*; this policy is only available as part of an insurance and finance package under ECGD's *Supplier Credit Financing Facility (see pages 220-1)*.

Causes of loss

The Supplier Insurance Policy may cover the following causes of loss:

Events outside UK

1   Insolvency of the Buyer or Guarantor.

2   The Buyer's or the Guarantor's default or failure to pay within six months of due date for payment.

3   Failure of the buyer or any Guarantor to pay any final judgement or award within six months of the date of the award or judgement.

4   If ECGD agrees the Buyer is a Public Buyer, failure or refusal to perform part of the contract, resulting in prevention of performance of the contract by the Supplier, or failure to pay.

5   A law passed in the buyer's country which discharges the debt if payment is made in a currency other than that of the contract.

6   Prevention of transfer of the contractual payments - political or economic difficulties, or a general moratorium.

7   A measure of any government outside the UK which prevents performance of the contract.

8   Hostilities or natural disasters which prevent performance.

Events within UK

9   Cancellation or non-renewal of a Supplier's export licence.

10   Restrictions introduced after the date of the contract, which prevent performance of the contract.

11   Withdrawal of finance by ECGD in circumstances where ECGD has generally withdrawn cover on the Buyer's country.

Note: Bond Risk cover (see lesson 11) is also available as an optional section of the Supplier Insurance Policy.

Percentage of cover

For the Supplier Insurance Policy the percentage of cover is 90% of the insured amount, with the exporter carrying 10% of the risk.

Links to financing

As stated earlier, the Supplier Insurance Policy is only available as part of a package with ECGD's Supplier Credit Financing Facility (see pages 220-1): the policy is *not* available as a separate free-standing policy. However, an exporter can insure risks under the SIP prior to receipt of finance for the export transaction.

❏ **Other insurance facilities available from ECGD**

Tender to Contract scheme

The Tender to Contract scheme is to help exporters tendering in foreign currency for contracts with a UK content of £5m or more. Cover is available for a range of major currencies, including US dollars, Deutschemarks, Swiss francs, French francs. ECGD will protect the exporter between limits of 1% and 25% of the contract price, against losses arising from exchange rate movements occurring between the *date of tender* and the *date of contract*. (For ERM currencies that are acceptable to ECGD, the limits are between 1% and 13% of the contract price.) If, however, rates have moved in the exporter's favour during this time and the contract is awarded, the exporter pays the amount of the gain to ECGD. Cover can be taken out for tendering periods (i.e. between the date of cover commencing and the award of the contract) of up to nine months.

A *Forward Exchange Supplement* can be combined with the Tender to Contract scheme, or is available as a separate facility. This supplement is for exporters who anticipate problems in arranging forward exchange contracts for large amounts or long-time periods. If the future forward exchange contracts yield less sterling than originally anticipated, ECGD will make up the difference - within the limits mentioned above.

Project Participants' Insolvency Cover

This scheme is designed to protect members of a UK consortium contracting for business overseas. Where such contracts have a value of £20 million or more, cover can be obtained in respect of 90 per cent of losses arising from unavoidable costs, expenses and damages due to the insolvency of a sub-contractor or fellow consortium member. In acceptable cases a UK company can obtain cover in respect of consortia which include non-UK members or sub-contractors.

Overseas Investments Insurance scheme

This provides insurance cover for overseas investments. The scheme is intended to encourage British investment overseas by providing insurance for a period of 3 to 15 years against political risks. Although the scheme is mainly intended for developing countries, virtually all countries are eligible.

The scheme is available to all companies carrying on business in the UK and their overseas subsidiaries. Insurance is available for *new* investments of equity capital in the form of cash, plant or know-how, for loans to overseas enterprises where the mean repayment period is not less than 3 years from the date of disbursement, and for certain guarantees of loans raised outside the UK. Some existing investments may also be eligible for cover.

The UK investor is offered insurance against the following risks:

* *Expropriation.* Cover goes beyond nationalisation, compulsory acquisition or confiscation of assets. It includes indirect forms of expropriation brought about by host government discrimination against the investor or the overseas enterprise.

* *War.* This includes physical damage and operational losses arising from war or revolution.

* *Restrictions on Remittances.* This covers the risk that the investor may not be able to repatriate capital or profits or receive loan repayments in hard currency.

* *Other Specific Political Risks.* Other specific political risks that could have a vital bearing on the viability of an investment may also be considered subject to negotiation.

Note: No insurance is given in respect of the commercial risks of the interest in the investment.

The amount of cover is:

— equity investments: initial investment, plus retained profits up to twice the amount of the initial investment

— loan investments: the principal amount of the loan plus interest

Claims are payable as follows:

- *For expropriation:* twelve months after the onset of the expropriatory action.
- *For war:* on proof of damage to physical assets; or after the overseas enterprise has been out of action for twelve months; if operational, the inability of the overseas enterprise to operate profitably for three successive years.
- *For restrictions on remittances:* after the inability for six consecutive months to repatriate currency. In the case of loan investment, six months must elapse after the due date of the unpaid instalment of capital or interest.
- Compensation and recoveries are shared between the investor and ECGD in the same proportion in which loss is borne.

To take advantage of this insurance, the investor must apply for cover before he has committed himself to the investment.

❏ Interest rates

ECGD is also involved in providing official support to interest rates in order to enable exporters to offer fixed, generally favourable, interest rates to overseas buyers. This scheme is known as the Fixed Rate Export Finance (FREF) scheme. Broadly, this scheme ensures that banks providing funds at fixed rates are reimbursed when the actual cost of funds is greater than the fixed rate.

There are two methods under which interest rates can be fixed under the FREF scheme:

- 'consensus' or 'matrix' rates
- Commercial Interest Reference Rates (CIRRs)

'Consensus' or 'matrix' rates

An international consensus of agreement on export credit has been reached by OECD (Organisation for Economic Co-operation and Development) countries, giving guidelines setting minimum payments by delivery, interest rates and maximum credit periods for officially supported export credits on terms of two years or more. For the purposes of this consensus buying countries are divided into three broad categories - on the basis of their per capita income. Current terms (Summer 1994) are:

	Category I (relatively rich)	Category II (intermediate)	Category III (relatively poor)
Minimum payments by delivery	15%	15%	15%
Minimum interest rates for credits between 2 and 5 years inclusive	not applicable	not applicable	5.95%
Minimum interest rates for credits between 5 - 8½ years	not applicable	not applicable	5.95%
Minimum interest rates for credits between 8½ - 10 years	–	–	5.95%
Maximum credit periods	5 years (exceptionally, 8½ years)	8½ years (10 years for certain countries)	10 years

Interest rates are reviewed every January and July (the latest rates are obtainable from your bank's Export Finance Department.

Commercial Interest Reference Rates (CIRRs)

For exports to Category I and II countries and to the European Union, consensus rates are not applicable. For these countries, a different system of minimum fixed rates applies based on Commercial Interest Reference Rates (CIRRs). Rates are calculated each month for most OECD participants' currencies (so there are CIRRs for all major currencies). CIRRs are calculated in order to reflect what market rates would be for long-term, fixed rate export finance for a first class borrower if such finance were available. CIRRs are revised monthly, but can be held for six months so that an exporter can quote a definite fixed rate to a buyer pending signature of a contract.

Know Your .... Credit Insurance

1.   What are the two main financial problems faced by exporters?

2.   NCM's International Guarantee covers exports sold on credit terms of up to .... days.

3.   State the three buyer risks covered by NCM's International Guarantee.

4.   What percentage of the loss is covered by NCM for the three risks stated above?

5.   Does NCM's International Guarantee cover risks from date of contract or from date of despatch basis?

6.   What additional risk is covered under NCM's International Guarantee when the buyer is a public buyer?

7.   The name of the ECGD policy covering the export of goods on credit terms of two years or more is the ....

8.   What problem is solved by the Tender to Contract scheme?

9.   What type of investor can take out the Overseas Investments Insurance Scheme?

10. State the four risks covered under the Overseas Investments Insurance Scheme.

11. What interest rate support is available to exporters under the Fixed Rate Export Finance scheme?

❏ Past Examination Questions

In recent years there have been few examination questions on this topic alone; however the contents of this lesson often feature as part of another question, usually linked to finance for exporters (see lesson 12) or general bank services (see lesson 14).

10.1   *Scenario*

Special Optics Ltd: see page 83

Question

It has always been the policy of Special Optics Ltd to sell to leading industrial companies. In considering the company's export expansion programme, Mr Glass feels that it will have to look at the mid-corporate market abroad. He would be prepared to trade on an open account basis, which would increase Special Optics's credit risks.

REQUIRED:

Advise Mr Glass:

(a)   Which types of institutions now provide short-term credit insurance cover.   [6]

(b)   The main types of short-term cover available in the credit insurance market.   [4]

(c)   The extent of cover available, including the main risks covered.   [10]

[Total marks for question - 20]

(question 5, Spring 1993)

Multiple-Choice Questions: Set 6

Read each question carefully. Choose the *one* answer you think is correct.
Answers are given on page 318.

1.   NCM's International Guarantee usually covers the export of goods sold on credit terms of up to:

     A   90 days
     B   180 days
     C   2 years
     D   5 years

2.   What percentage of cover is provided by NCM's International Guarantee for insolvency of the buyer?

     A   10%
     B   72%
     C   90%
     D   95%

3.   What percentage of cover is provided by NCM's International Guarantee if the buyer fails to take up goods?

	Exporter (first loss)	NCM (balance)
A	20%	90%
B	20%	72%
C	5%	95%
D	10%	90%

4.   Under NCM's International Guarantee, what percentage of cover is offered for:
     (i) buyer's failure to pay within six months;
     (ii) political risks

A	(i) 95%	(ii) 90%
B	(i) 90%	(ii) 72%
C	(i) 90%	(ii) 95%
D	(i) 90%	(ii) 90%

5.   When are claims for insolvency of the buyer payable under NCM's International Guarantee?

     A   one month after proof of the insolvency
     B   one month after resale of the goods
     C   six months after the due date of payment
     D   immediately on proof of the insolvency

6.   ECGD's Supplier Insurance Policy is available:

     A   as a separate free-standing policy
     B   only as a part of a financing package
     C   to include domestic buyers
     D   to exports involving 'public buyers' only

7.   ECGD's Supplier Insurance Policy covers the export of goods sold on credit terms of:

A   180 days only
B   up to 2 years
C   over 2 years
D   over 5 years

8.   The percentage of cover under ECGD's Supplier Insurance Policy is:

A   10%
B   72%
C   90%
D   95%

9.   ECGD's Tender to Contract Scheme covers:

A   exchange rate movements
B   insolvency of the overseas buyer
C   export of goods to public buyers
D   production-line goods

10.   Which of the following risks is *not* covered by ECGD's Overseas Investments Insurance Scheme?

A   expropriation
B   pre-credit
C   war
D   restrictions on remittances

Lesson Eleven
Bonds and Guarantees

In recent years overseas buyers of capital goods and large projects have increasingly demanded that suppliers and contractors provide them with a bond or guarantee. In the context of export finance, a bond or guarantee is a written instrument issued to an overseas buyer by an acceptable third party (that is, by a surety, normally a bank or insurance company): this instrument guarantees compliance by an exporter or contractor of the obligations, or that the overseas buyer will be indemnified for a stated amount against the failure of the exporter or contractor to fulfil the obligations under the contract.

Note: the terms 'bond' and 'guarantee' are freely interchangeable and, in this context, have no legal distinction.

❏ Parties involved

There will normally be three parties involved in the provision of a bond or guarantee:

- *the exporter, or contractor,* who is to perform the work or supply the goods as detailed in the contract
- *the buyer, or beneficiary,* in whose favour the guarantee is issued
- *the guarantor,* either a bank or surety/insurance company, who is responsible for issuing the guarantee

Note: when a bank is involved in issuing bonds and guarantees, it always takes a counter indemnity from the exporter. This means that, if the bank has to pay out money to an overseas buyer, it then has a claim against its customer, and can debit the customer's account with the amount of the bond call.

❏ Procedures

The way in which a bond or guarantee might be issued is as follows:

- The overseas buyer asks the UK exporter to provide a guarantee in support of work to be undertaken or goods supplied.

- The UK exporter approaches the UK bank requesting a guarantee to be issued in favour of the foreign buyer.

- The UK bank issues the guarantee to the buyer, and takes a counter indemnity from the exporter.

Note: The buyer may insist that the guarantee is issued by a bank in his or her own country. In this case the UK bank will ask a correspondent bank to issue the guarantee. Under these circumstances, the UK bank will be required to counter indemnify the correspondent bank.

❏ Main types of guarantees

The main types of guarantees or bonds which banks are requested to issue on behalf of contractors or suppliers for large overseas projects are:

Bid or tender bond

This is issued in support of a customer's tender, sometimes in lieu of a cash deposit. It is to confirm the genuineness of the tender so that, in the event of the failure of the contractor to enter into any contract granted in accordance with the terms of the tender, a sum (usually between two and five per cent, but sometimes as low as one or as high as ten per cent, of the total tender price) may be claimed by the company or organisation in whose favour it has been issued. This compensates for the additional costs which are likely to be incurred in going through the tendering process again. Tender bonds are usually payable on demand. A specimen tender bond is shown in fig. 11.1 on the next page.

Performance bond

This is given in support of a customer's obligation to fulfil a contractual commitment. When issued by a bank it usually provides for payment to the beneficiary of about ten per cent (but sometimes as low as five or as high as one hundred per cent) of the contract value in the event of the undertaking not being fulfilled. A performance bond is usually issued after the tender guarantee is cancelled, although the tender guarantee may be extended to become a performance bond.

A major problem with performance bonds is that there is usually no provision for the amount of the bond to be reduced as the contract progresses. Therefore the bond is valid until the very moment of handover of the contract on completion. It would be not impossible for an unscrupulous beneficiary to make a call under a performance bond just before the job is completed. To avoid this, the contractor would be advised to insert a clause reducing the liability in accordance with the degree of completeness of the job. A further clause would state that an independent party will, in the event of a bond call, assess the amount of work carried out and this person's decision will be binding on all parties. In a construction contract, the independent party might well be a surveyor.

A specimen performance bond is shown in fig. 11.2 (page 207).

Advance or progress payment bond

This is a variation on a performance bond, whereby it guarantees the refund, in the event of certain terms and conditions not being completed (e.g. if goods are not shipped or a contract complied with), of amounts paid by the purchaser in advance to the contractor; it is therefore issued in favour of the buyer. It can provide for an increase as further amounts are paid to the contractor, or for a reduction as various portions of the contract are fulfilled - usually against the evidence of progress certificates.

An advance payment bond is often used when a commercial transaction requires a down payment on signing the contract. The contractor receives the advance payment only against an advance payment bond issued by his/her bank in favour of the buyer; in the event of default by the contractor the amount of the advance payment would be repaid to the buyer. A requirement for an advance payment bond is often included in a documentary letter of credit. It makes good sense to try to ensure that the advance payment bond does not become operative until the money amount is available to be credited to the contractor's account.

Warranty or retention bond

Most contracts provide for a period during which the contractor or supplier is responsible for the maintenance and effectiveness of the completed project. The bond guarantees financial support to the buyer for the warranty period. It is often issued to obtain the release of funds (often ten per cent of the contract value) on completion of the contract which, under the terms and conditions of the contract, would not otherwise be paid over until the warranty period had expired.

Fig. 11.3 (on page 208) shows how the main bonds and guarantees will be issued at different stages of an overseas contract.

National Westminster Bank PLC ♻

International Trade and Banking Services
Overseas Branch - Bonds and Guarantees Department
National Westminster Tower
25 Old Broad Street, London EC2N 1HQ

Direct Line   071-920
Switchboard 071-920 5555   Telex 885361 NWBLDN G

Your ref

Our ref

Date   March 1992

OUR GUARANTEE (GUARANTEE NUMBER)

We understand that (APPLICANTS NAME) ("the Applicant") (APPLICANTS ADDRESS)
are tendering for the (DESCRIPTION OF GOODS) under your invitation to Tender
(TENDER/CONTRACT NUMBER ETC) and that a Bank Guarantee is required for (AGREED
PERCENTAGE OF CONTRACT) % of the amount of their tender.

We, NATIONAL WESTMINSTER BANK PLC, Overseas Branch, London HEREBY GUARANTEE the
payment to you on demand of up to (AMOUNT IN FIGURES) (say, (AMOUNT IN WORDS))
in the event of your awarding the relative contract to the Applicant and of its
failing to sign the Contract in the terms of its tender, or in the event of the
Applicant withdrawing its tender before Expiry of this guarantee without your
consent.

This guarantee shall come into force on (COMMENCEMENT DATE) being the closing
date for tenders, and will expire at close of banking hours at this office on
(EXPIRY DATE) ("EXPIRY").

Our liability is limited to the sum of (AMOUNT IN FIGURES) and your claim
hereunder must be received in writing at this office before Expiry accompanied
by your signed statement that the Applicant has been awarded the relative
contract and has failed to sign the contract awarded in the terms of its tender
or has withdrawn its tender before Expiry without your consent, and such claim
and statement shall be accepted as conclusive evidence that the amount claimed
is due to you under this guarantee.

Claims and statements as aforesaid must bear the dated confirmation of your
Bankers that the signatories thereon are authorised so to sign.

Upon Expiry this guarantee shall become null and void, whether returned to us
for cancellation or not and any claim or statement received after expiry shall
be ineffective.

This guarantee is personal to yourselves and is not transferable or assignable.

This guarantee shall be governed by and construed in accordance with the Laws of
England and shall be subject to the exclusive jurisdiction of the English
Courts.

                         S P E C I M E N

NWB5006 Rev May 88-2001   Registered Number 929027 England   Registered Office 41 Lothbury, London EC2P 2BP   Member of IMRO

Fig. 11.1: Specimen tender bond

National Westminster Bank PLC ♻

International Trade and Banking Services
Overseas Branch - Bonds and Guarantees Department
National Westminster Tower
25 Old Broad Street, London EC2N 1HQ

Your ref

Our ref

Direct Line   071-920
Switchboard 071-920 5555   Telex 885361 NWBLDN G   Date March 1992

Dear Sirs,

OUR GUARANTEE (GUARANTEE NUMBER)

We understand that you have entered into a Contract (TENDER/CONTRACT NUMBER ETC)
(the Contract) with (APPLICANTS NAME) (the Applicant) (APPLICANTS ADDRESS) for
the (DESCRIPTION OF GOODS) and that under such Contract the Applicant must
provide a Bank Performance Guarantee for an amount of (AMOUNT IN FIGURES) being
(AGREED PERCENTAGE OF CONTRACT) % of the value of the Contract.

We, NATIONAL WESTMINSTER BANK PLC, Overseas Branch, London HEREBY GUARANTEE
payment to you on demand of up to (AMOUNT IN FIGURES) (say, AMOUNT IN WORDS))
in the event of the Applicant failing to fulfil the said Contract, provided that
your claim hereunder is received in writing at this office accompanied by your
signed statement that the Applicant has failed to fulfil the Contract. Such
claim and statement shall be accepted as conclusive evidence that the amount
claimed is due to you under this guarantee.

Claims and statements as aforesaid must bear the dated confirmation of your
Bankers that the signatories thereon are authorised so to sign.

This guarantee shall expire at close of banking hours at this office on (EXPIRY
DATE) ("EXPIRY") and any claim and statement hereunder must be received at this
office before Expiry and after Expiry this guarantee shall become null and void
whether returned to us for cancellation or not and any claim or statement
received after Expiry shall be ineffective.

This guarantee is personal to yourselves and is not transferable or assignable.

This guarantee shall be governed by and construed in accordance with the Laws of
England and shall be subject to the exclusive jurisdiction of the English
Courts.

                    S P E C I M E N

NWB5006 Rev May 88-2001   Registered Number 929027 England   Registered Office 41 Lothbury, London EC2P 2BP   Member of IMRO

Fig. 11.2: Specimen performance bond

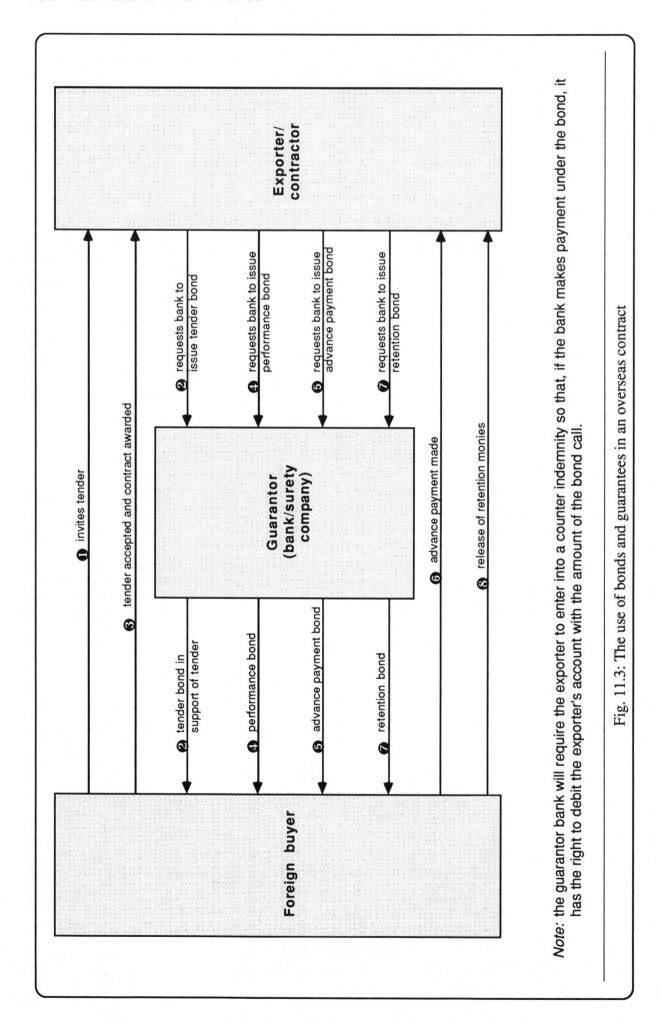

Exporter/contractor

❶ invites tender

❷ requests bank to issue tender bond

❹ requests bank to issue performance bond

❺ requests bank to issue advance payment bond

❼ requests bank to issue retention bond

❸ tender accepted and contract awarded

❻ advance payment made

❽ release of retention monies

Guarantor (bank/surety company)

❷ tender bond in support of tender

❹ performance bond

❺ advance payment bond

❼ retention bond

Foreign buyer

Note: the guarantor bank will require the exporter to enter into a counter indemnity so that, if the bank makes payment under the bond, it has the right to debit the exporter's account with the amount of the bond call.

Fig. 11.3: The use of bonds and guarantees in an overseas contract

❏ Conditional and unconditional guarantees

Any of the guarantees and bonds listed above can be *conditional* or *unconditional*. It is normally the buyer and the laws of his or her country that specify which type of bond has to be supplied by the exporter.

Conditional bonds/guarantees

A conditional bond places an onus upon the buyer to prove default by the exporter; usually an independent arbitrator has to rule that a breach of contract has taken place and makes an arbitration award against the seller. Payment under the bond is generally limited to the extent of the buyer's actual loss, or the amount specified in the bond, whichever is the lower. The amount is payable on demand.

This type of bond gives more protection to the exporter. However, banks will have no wish to become involved in any dispute about contractual obligations, and will require terms in which their obligation to pay is clear.

Unconditional (or on demand) bonds/guarantees

This type of bond can be called for any reason at the sole discretion of the buyer, whether or not the exporter has fulfilled the contractual obligations. Moreover, the payment is not limited to the amount of the buyer's loss, but to the amount of the bond. Such a bond is payable on first demand.

❏ Possible difficulties

Bonds and guarantees present a number of problems to exporters and guarantors. In particular, a number of points should be considered.

Terms of the guarantee

The wording and terms of the guarantee should be checked carefully to ensure that they are consistent with the terms of the contract. The exporter would be well advised to contact the bank that is to issue the guarantee as soon as possible to check whether the bank will be prepared to issue a guarantee in such terms.

Unfair calling

The consequences of unfair calling by the buyer are enormous. Court cases have shown that an exporter cannot prevent the guarantor from making payment under the terms of the bond or guarantee. Under such circumstances the exporter will be required to reimburse the bank under the terms of the counter indemnity. Only if a clear case of proven fraud is established can a claim be avoided. The only other course of action is to sue under the contract but there will be considerable difficulties in establishing and enforcing a claim in the overseas buyer's country.

To some extent, cover against unfair calling is available from credit insurers (see below).

Expiry dates

Often an overseas buyer will request an open-ended guarantee, i.e. one that has no fixed expiry date. From the exporter's, and the guarantor's, viewpoint this is most undesirable as it will be difficult to obtain release from the guarantee commitment.

Extended or pay guarantee

It is quite common for an overseas buyer to insist that a guarantee with a fixed expiry date should be 'extended or paid'. Here the exporter is placed in a difficult position and, really, has little option but to agree to an extension; if he refuses to do this, the overseas buyer will make a demand under the terms of the guarantee. Under such circumstances it would be difficult to claim unfair calling of the bond or guarantee. Thus, even a guarantee with an expiry date, could have to be extended.

Foreign laws

Bonds and guarantees are subject to the local laws and regulations in force in the buyer's country. This makes things difficult for the exporter and guarantor: for example, certain countries do not recognise the expiry date and will hold that the guarantee is still valid for claims made after the expiry date.

However, it is possible to arrange for the issue of a guarantee which is subject to English law and the jurisdiction of the English courts; in such cases the expiry date would apply. Often, though, an exporter is pressurised by competition into accepting a guarantee which is subject to the laws of the buyer's country.

❏ ECGD Bond Risk Cover

ECGD does not itself provide bonds, but Bond Insurance is available as an 'add-on' to the Supplier Insurance Policy (see lesson 10). The types of bonds covered are tender bond, performance bond, advance payment bond, warranty or retention bond. To be covered under the policy, the bonds must be unconditional on demand bonds required under the terms of the contract. The causes of loss are usually the same as those in the Supplier Insurance Policy.

❏ Other bonds and guarantees

Banks (and other providers) are also called upon to issue:

* *Bank facility guarantees*
  Here a bank is issuing a guarantee to another bank that a loan or other facility will be repaid. This is particularly useful when a bank customer wishes to operate in an overseas country by means of a subsidiary company, and that subsidiary requires local banking including loan and other (e.g. letter of credit) facilities.

* *Customs guarantee*
  This is used where an importer wishes to import goods without payment of customs duty. It would be used where goods are going to be exported again shortly, or to enable the temporary import of samples for a trade fair.

* *Bail bond*
  This is issued where either an arrest has taken place, or there is the possibility of arrest under certain circumstances. A bail bond provides a guarantee of the amount of bail. It can be issued for individuals or in connection with ships.

❏ Advantages of guarantees for the exporter

* They enable an exporter or contractor to win overseas contracts. Many overseas buyers insist on bonds or guarantees as part of the terms of the contract.

- Both advance payment and retention bonds improve the exporter or contractor's cash flow by enabling funds to be received earlier than would otherwise have been the case.

- A bank facility guarantee obtains the provision of overseas banking facilities - often at lower rates of interest than if no guarantee was available.

❏ Standby letters of credit

Instead of issuing bonds or guarantees, an alternative is a *standby letter of credit* (see pages 150-1). This is frequently issued where banks are requested to issue a bond on behalf of one of their customers but are unable to do so because local laws in the beneficiary's country do not recognize guarantees (particularly common in the Middle East). In fulfilling a similar role to bonds, standby credits have two advantages:

(i)   they bear a fixed expiry date;
(ii)   they are not subject to local law, but are issued in accordance with Uniform Customs and Practice.

❏ Contingent liabilities

All bonds and guarantees are, from the guarantor bank's viewpoint, contingent liabilities. Therefore the bank will record liability entries in their records for guarantees issued. From the exporter's viewpoint, such guarantees form part of the total liability to the bank, and the issue of guarantees by the bank could seriously impinge on the total credit facilities available.

❏ *Uniform Rules for Contract Guarantees*

In an attempt to avoid misuse of bonds, the International Chamber of Commerce has issued a set of uniform rules entitled *Uniform Rules for Contract Guarantees*. These rules are written with a view to achieving a uniformity of practice between the parties involved, and attempts to find a fair balance between their interests. The rules help to achieve a sense of order, whilst maintaining the commercial purpose of the guarantee.

For the rules to apply, the guarantee must state that it is subject to *Uniform Rules for Contract Guarantees of the International Chamber of Commerce (Publication No. 325)*.

❏ **Examination Hints**

- Bonds and guarantees have been very popular in the examination in recent years.

- You should know the main types of bonds and guarantees issued by banks.

- Note the difference between conditional and unconditional bonds.

- Appreciate the problems of using bonds.

Know Your .... Bonds and Guarantees

1. Who are the parties involved in a bond or guarantee?

2. Why is a counter indemnity taken when a bank issues a bond?

3. A customer of your bank is planning to submit a tender to build a power station in Africa. What types of bonds might the bank be asked to issue now, and in the future?

4. Distinguish between 'conditional' and 'unconditional' bonds.

5. What particular legal points would an exporter consider when an overseas buyer requests a bond?

6. What are the advantages of guarantees for the exporter?

7. Compare the issue of a bond with a standby letter of credit.

Past Examination Questions

11.1*   Ancient Mariners Ltd offers a wide range of services to the shipping world, including the provision of officers and crew on standard ship delivery contracts. These contracts entail the provisioning, crewing and delivery of vessels to the owners or their agents at named ports. The company has a long, satisfactory banking relationship with your branch.

The directors are discussing a potential contract with Neptune Inc of the USA, the new owners of a vessel, to provision, crew, and deliver this vessel to Neptune Inc in Savannah, Georgia, USA.

The terms being considered are:

• 30% payable to Ancient Mariners on signing of the contract;

• 35% payable, at the latest, 10 days after the vessel has sailed for the USA;

• the balance of 35% payable, at the latest, 10 days after delivery of the vessel to Neptune Inc.

Mr David Jones, Managing Director of Ancient Mariners Ltd, calls to see you to discuss this contract. He wishes to ensure that secure methods of payment are used so that, provided the company fulfils the contract terms, payments will be obtained. However, he is aware that Neptune Inc will require some form of undertaking in respect of the 30% advance payment.

REQUIRED:
A brief description of:

(a)   (i)   a banking instrument which could be issued on behalf of Neptune Inc and would give Ancient Mariners Ltd the security it is seeking in respect of all the payments;   [3]

      (ii)   a banking instrument, issued in conjunction with (i) above, which would satisfy the requirements of Neptune Inc in connection with the advance payment.   [3]

(b)   An explanation of how Ancient Mariners Ltd, using these instruments, could claim and obtain access to all the payments mentioned in the question.   [6]

(c)   A brief explanation of the liability which your bank and your customer will enter into under (a) (ii) above, and any conditions which could be included in the instrument to minimise this liability.   [8]

[Total marks for question - 20]
(question 1, Spring 1987)

11.2   The directors of your customer, Naive Ltd, ask you to visit them to discuss a contract to supply capital equipment which the company has been awarded by a buyer in Taiwan. The company has a successful business which has supplied road-making equipment to local authorities in the United Kingdom.

The directors explain to you that this contract, worth in excess of US$1m, will be their first break into the export market. Although the contract has been awarded to them, they have been asked to provide some form of bank undertaking to the buyer. They understand this is in the form of a bond(s). They ask you to explain how your bank can help in connection with this matter and if there is any help from non-banking sources which might be available to them.

REQUIRED:
Your explanation of the way in which your bank can provide support in connection with bonds appropriate to this contract. Your answer should include an explanation of the risks to the customer which would occur if the bank assisted in the provision of the bonds mentioned.

(part of question 2, Autumn 1988)

11.3*   Inshore Waters Ltd is a fishing company specialising in fishing for shrimps, crabs and lobsters. In order to add to its fishing fleet, the company decided to purchase two fishing vessels from a French boat yard. Payment terms are to be by means of a secure method of payment with an advance payment of 30% upon signing the order. Payment is to be effected in French francs. You understand that the vessels will be available for delivery and/or collection at the French boat yard in approximately six months' time from the date of signing the contract.

On 1 October, one of the company's directors, Mr Prawn, called to see you to discuss the position. He was anxious that the company should protect itself as far as possible, yet at the same time provide for the needs of the French boat builder.

Subsequently, you arranged to meet your customer on the following 1 January to complete the formalities, as the suggestions you had made at the meeting dated 1 October had been accepted by both buyer and seller and the contract was signed. You understand that the vessels will be ready for delivery/collection during the month of April.

REQUIRED:

(a)   Describe with brief details:

(i)   the recommendations which you would have made to your customer on 1 October which would provide your customer with as much protection as possible in respect of the secure method of payment.   *[7]*

(ii)   the additional suggestions which you would have made on 1 October that would give security and protection to the buyer.   *[4]*

(b)   any further suggestions which would minimise any other risks which must be borne by your customer.   *[9]*

[Total marks for question - 20]
(question 4, October 1990)

11.4   Internal Construction Plc is a corporate customer of your bank which was successful in maintaining the level of its order book until the down-turn in economic activity had a dramatic effect on its turn-over and cash flow. Although in the past it has had to compete with other UK companies, it is now finding that construction companies based in other EC countries are winning contracts with UK local authorities in preference to Internal Construction. Part of the problem has been a reluctance on the part of the company to tender and/or offer any undertakings in favour of the purchaser of the 'product'.

As a result of a board room shake-out the company has appointed a new Managing Director, Mr Skafold, with a mission to compete energetically both in the UK and overseas. At his invitation you attend part of the next board meeting to outline the ways in which your bank can help him and the company to increase its market share profitably.

REQUIRED in brief note form:

List and describe the methods of support (other than providing finance or advisory services) which your bank could offer in respect of both UK and overseas contracts. Indicate if there are any disadvantages in your suggested methods.   *[16]*

(part of question 8, May 1991)

Lesson Twelve
Finance for Exporters

Several methods of finance are available to exporters; the following are considered in this lesson:

- overdraft or loan
- advances against collections
- negotiation/discount of bills/documents
- accommodation finance/acceptance house credit
- documentary credits
- short-term finance, linked to credit insurance

- ECGD Supplier Credit Facilities
- ECGD-backed buyer credit
- currency borrowing
- factoring, leasing and hire purchase
- forfaiting
- export house finance

For a bank customer who holds a credit insurance policy, the bank may be prepared to offer 'normal' bank facilities, such as an overdraft, advances against collections, or negotiation/discount of bills/documents. The bank may use the policy as security, by means of an assignment of the exporter's interest in the policy to the bank. In addition, most large banks offer special export finance schemes linked to a credit insurance policy held either by customer or bank. Using its Supplier Credit Facilities, for medium-term finance (two years or more), ECGD issues direct guarantees to banks covering export lending. Lending is, from the bank's point of view, absolutely secure under this method; from the exporter's viewpoint such lending is without recourse.

❑ Overdraft or loan

Naturally an exporter can ask for a bank loan or overdraft in the usual way, either unsecured or using any type of acceptable security. A bank will look more favourably on this type of lending if the customer has taken out a credit insurance policy to cover export debtors and acceptable security could be an assignment to the bank of benefits payable under the credit insurance. This method of finance is most likely to be used by traders selling on open account terms or where banks are requested to handle D/A collections.

Such finance could be provided in sterling or in a foreign currency.

❑ Advances against collections

Where a bank is handling collections on behalf of a customer it is usually prepared, subject to normal bank lending considerations, to grant an advance based on an agreed percentage (often 85%) of outstanding collections, pending receipt of the proceeds. Interest charges and other charges are taken at the end of the period so that the full amount of the agreed proportion is advanced to the customer. The bank may specify that the facility is only available for bills drawn on certain regular buyers - in this case the bank would take the precaution of obtaining a banker's opinion as to the reputation and trustworthiness of the buyer. Where advances are made against D/P (documents against payment) collections, the bank's security takes the form of control of the goods and the bank will usually take a letter of pledge/hypothecation (see lesson 13, 'Finance for Importers' - produce loans) over them. However, under a D/A (documents against acceptance) collection, the goods will be delivered to the buyer on his acceptance of the bill so that, instead of the goods, the bank is relying on the creditworthiness of the buyer. In both cases the bank will carefully examine the documents to ensure that the bank will have, if necessary, recourse to the goods and the insurance prior to acceptance/payment of the bill of exchange.

A bank is likely to require an exporter to take out a credit insurance policy, and to assign directly to it any benefits payable under the policy. The bank will retain a right of recourse to its customer in respect of non-acceptance or non-payment of any bill. The potential liability of the customer should be stressed here - even though the advance has been made, the bank has full recourse to the customer for the amount of the bill. Failing this source of repayment, the bank will then look to the goods, under the letter of pledge, to clear the advance.

❏ Negotiation/discount of bills/documents

Banks are usually willing to negotiate (purchase) foreign bills or shipping documents for their exporter customers, up to a total limit. The bank in effect buys the bill or the shipping documents, and credits its customer with the amount while retaining a right of recourse. It is practice for the bank to deduct an estimated amount of interest and other charges from the bill amount which is to be paid over to the customer. Thus a 'net' figure is given to the customer at that stage, and any adjustment is made afterwards. The bank then seeks payment from the overseas buyer by sending the bill, etc. for collection in the normal way. If payment is not forthcoming at the correct time, the bank will debit its customer with the amount, plus interest and collection charges.

Before agreeing to negotiate bills or shipping documents for a customer, normal bank lending considerations will apply. In addition the documents of each collection will be scrutinized to ensure that they are in order and give the bank recourse to the goods and the insurance if necessary. It might also be prudent for the bank to take a banker's opinion on the drawee of the bill prior to negotiation. A letter of pledge/hypothecation will also be taken to hold the goods as security for the bank. As with advances against collections, the customer should realise that the bank has full recourse, as drawer of the bill, in the event of non-acceptance of non-payment. If the customer is unable to pay, then the bank will look to the goods, under the terms of the letter of pledge, to clear the advance.

Negotiations may be effected on the basis of individual items, or a negotiation-line credit may be established with a revolving limit.

Under certain circumstances it is possible for a bank to *discount* bills of exchange instead of negotiating them.

The *first* requirement is that there is a bill of exchange. (It is possible for banks to negotiate shipping documents without a bill being in existence.)

The *second* point is that, to be discounted, a bill must be a term bill and it must have been accepted. Where negotiations are concerned, a bill may be either a sight or a term bill (depending on what has been agreed between buyer and seller) and it will be most unusual for it to have been accepted.

Thirdly the drawee/acceptor needs to be known, i.e. have a good name, in the discount market and the bill should be payable in the same country as that of the discounting bank. This, too, is unlikely to happen with negotiations: the drawee/acceptor is usually the overseas buyer who will not normally be known in the exporter's country, and the bill will usually be payable abroad.

Fourthly, to be effective, the discounting process relies on the existence of a recognised market where bills may be further rediscounted; there is no such market for negotiations.

The idea behind discounting is that the bank or financial institution that has discounted the bill may hold it for a time as an investment, or may rediscount it on the market. With a negotiation the bill is not held for investment purposes but, instead, is sent to the overseas centre for acceptance or payment.

It follows that most bills of exchange tendered under documentary collections will be negotiated rather than discounted. From the point of view of the exporter, both negotiation and discounting provide immediate cash. Discounting of bills features more in acceptance house credits and documentary acceptance credits (see below) as a means of providing finance for the exporter.

❏ Accommodation finance/acceptance house credit

This facility is offered by clearing, merchant, and other banks. The procedure is for the exporter to arrange a credit for a stipulated amount with a revolving limit. The exporter then hands documents and bills for collection to the accepting house or bank, which then accepts a term bill drawn on itself by the exporter for an agreed percentage of the face value of the collections. The exporter now holds an accommodation bill accepted by the accepting house or bank and is able to discount this at a fine rate on the market, thus obtaining finance against the collections. The term of the bill will be for a period slightly longer than the expected date of receipt of the proceeds of the collections, thus providing the bank or accepting house with funds to meet its own accommodation bill. The accepting house or bank will handle the collections and, if any are unpaid, will seek recourse from the exporter.

Fig. 12.1 shows how an acceptance house credit can be used by an exporter.

See also 'Finance for Importers' (lesson 13).

❏ Documentary credits

We saw in lesson 7 that, provided exporters comply with the terms of documentary letters of credit, they will either receive an immediate payment (a sight credit) or may have a bill of exchange accepted. The letter of credit may allow the advising bank to discount such accepted bills. Thus, cash can be received almost immediately and, if the sales contract stipulates that the buyer is to be responsible for such discounting charges, this will be virtually the same as a sight credit.

Note also (from lesson 8) how letters of credit can be used to provide pre-shipment finance – typically a middleman – by means of transferable credits, back-to-back credits, and assignment of a credit.

❏ Short-term finance, linked to credit insurance

Most major banks, as part of their marketing strategy to help exporters, offer products which provide short-term export finance linked to a credit insurance policy (such as NCM's International Guarantee - see lesson 10). Most banks usually offer two schemes:

• *smaller exports scheme* - for an annual export turnover of, typically, less than £1 million

• *finance for exports scheme* - for an annual export turnover of, typically, more than £1 million

The details which follow are an amalgam of various banks' schemes and it would be advisable for you to check the scheme offered by your bank.

Smaller exports scheme
Such schemes are for companies with an annual export turnover of up to £1 million who do not have their own credit insurance policy. The bank will finance up to 100 per cent of the invoice value, less charges, for periods of up to 180 days credit. The schemes are available for trading by means of bills and notes (bills of exchange, and promissory notes), and open account. The finance offered is post shipment, without recourse to the exporter *provided the exporter performs within the terms of the credit insurance and the commercial contract (see note at bottom of page 219)*. The bank takes out its

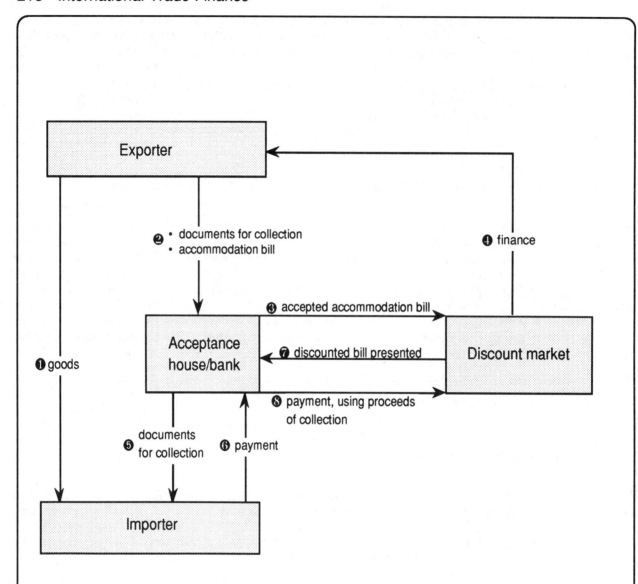

Fig. 12.1: Acceptance house finance for exporters

Notes:
*   If the collection (step 6) is unpaid, the accepting house/bank will seek recourse from the exporter.

*   Payment of the collection (step 6) occurs prior to presentation of the discounted bill (step 7), ie the accommodation bill is drawn for a tenor longer than the expected date of payment for the collection. This gives the acceptance house funds to meet payment of the accommodation bill.

*   The acceptance house will usually take a letter of hypothecation (see lesson 13) from the exporter as security over the goods.

own credit insurance policy (which is managed through a separate policy manager) and covers the customers' exports under this. As credit insurance cover is a maximum of 90 or 95 per cent of the invoice amount, the bank covers the 5 or 10 per cent uncovered portion at its own risk, thus customers obtain up to 100 per cent finance without having to take out their own credit insurance policies.

To set up a facility under the scheme, the bank will consider the eligibility of each applicant. Consideration will be given to the customer's previous trading and export record, and whether the proposed exports fit in with the scheme. If the bank is satisfied, it will offer a facility amount. The exporter is then asked to sign a facility letter and, if possible, to supply details of potential buyers: this enables the bank to make status enquiries and so avoid delays later.

For an export transaction, the scheme works as follows:

- When goods have been shipped, the exporter presents to the bank a lodgement form accompanied by

  either, the bill or note, together with an invoice, evidence of shipment, and a copy of the order from the buyer,

  or, for open account trading, a copy of the invoice sent to the buyer, evidence of shipment, and a copy of the order from the buyer; in addition the invoice must show the terms of payment, and that settlement is to be made direct to the bank.

- If the documents and the buyer's status are in order, the bank will credit the customer's account with up to 100 percent of the invoice amount, less charges and interest. The interest charged is for the credit period allowed to the buyer plus extra days to allow for transmission days.

- The bank's Bill Department remits the bill of exchange/promissory note and/or documents to the buyer's bank for collection.

- Payment is received by Bill Department and an advice is sent to the exporter.

- In the event of non-payment by the buyer, the Bank will seek compensation for a maximum of 90 or 95 per cent under its credit insurance policy, and will cover the balance (if any) itself.

Interest charged under the scheme is often favourable rates, e.g. 1.5% over the bank's base rate. Finance is also available for export orders expressed in major foreign currencies; here the finance is made available in sterling at the forward contract rate ruling on the day of the advance, allowing for the appropriate credit period.

Finance for exports scheme

This scheme is available to customers with a minimum annual export turnover of £1 million, whether or not they hold their own credit insurance policy. The scheme operates in much the same way as for the smaller exports schemes, except that the finance is for up to 90 per cent of the invoice amount - the balance of 10 per cent is paid on maturity of the bill of exchange or promissory note, or upon settlement under open account trade. Credit periods are, generally, for a maximum of 180 days (but could, in some circumstances, be up to 2 years), often at favourable interest rates. For exporters not already holding their own credit insurance policy, subject to their approval by the credit insurer, exporter and the bank become joint policyholders. There is no recourse to the exporter *provided the exporter performs within the terms of the credit insurance policy and the commercial contract (see note below).*

Important note. *Export finance schemes offered by banks are 'with-recourse'. This is because there there is recourse to the exporter where there has been a failure to comply with the commercial contract and/or the credit insurance policy, and where the credit insurance premium has not been paid. However, some major banks have recently reached agreement with insurers to cover the risk of non-compliance with the credit insurance policy and non-payment of the premium. Where such lending is considered to be 'without recourse', the exporter may choose to treat it as off-balance sheet, subject to the views of the auditors.*

❏ ECGD Supplier Credit Financing (SCF) facility

Where export credit is given for between two and five years (and in some cases for longer periods) for goods and services, finance for exporters can be arranged under ECGD's Supplier Credit Financing (SCF) facility. All the major banks participate in the SCF scheme, and each has entered into a Master Guarantee Agreement (MGA) with ECGD – the MGA sets out the terms and conditions under which the banks can offer export finance under the SCF facility.

Finance is provided under the facility against bills of exchange or promissory notes which have been avalised (guaranteed) – see pages 225-8 – by an acceptable third party, eg a bank or financial institution. (Other guarantees of payment, such as a letter of credit, may also be acceptable; under some circumstances, eg undoubted buyers, no guarantee would be required.) The minimum contract value under the facility is £25,000, and exporters can offer buyers credit for up to 85% of the contract price, at a fixed interest rate, with a payment period of between two and five years. Loans can be in sterling or a range of currencies.

Procedures for the SCF facility

- The exporter approaches ECGD via the bank for a preliminary indication of premium and possible terms of cover.

- If the transaction is acceptable to ECGD it will give an indication of premium, interest rate, and conditions of cover. (Interest rates will be at OECD consensus rates – see page 199 – for Category III countries, and at Commercial Interest Reference Rates (CIRRs) for other, including EU, countries - see page 200.) The indication of premium, etc can be held, in most cases, for six months, to enable the exporter to conduct negotiations with the buyer.

- If cover is required, the exporter sends, via the bank, a proposal form to ECGD for SCF. If pre-finance insurance cover under ECGD's Supplier Insurance Policy (SIP) – see page 197 for risks covered – is also required, it must be requested at this stage.

- ECGD send the exporter an Offer of Finance under the SCF, and (if required) an offer of a Supplier Insurance Policy.

- The exporter and bank accept the offer(s) by completing Declaration and Acceptance forms, and paying the premium to ECGD.

- ECGD sends a Certificate of Approval to the bank, with a copy to the exporter. If previously requested, ECGD issues a Supplier Insurance Policy.

- The exporter now performs the export contract and presents documents to the bank comprising:
  - accepted bills of exchange, or promissory notes signed by the buyer - which have been avalised (guaranteed) – see pages 225-8 – by an acceptable third party, eg bank or financial institution
  - evidence that the goods have been delivered, or services performed
  - a warranty confirming that the terms and conditions agreed by the parties have been fulfilled
  - any other documentation required by the bank

Benefits of the SCF facility

- The main benefit of the scheme is that, after finance has been provided by the bank, there is no recourse to the exporter. (For some exporters, ECGD may require the exporter to enter into a recourse obligation - the amount of this would not normally exceed 15% of ECGD's liability.)

- If the buyer defaults, the risk lies with the exporter's bank - who would seek repayment in the first instance from the avalising bank or other guarantor, and ultimately ECGD which provides the bank with a 100% guarantee of payment. (An exporter wishing to cover pre-finance risks can take out insurance under ECGD's Supplier Insurance Policy – see page 197; this insurance is not available as a stand alone policy – it is only available in conjunction with the SCF facility.)

- There is no requirement for exporters to offer all export business for cover under the SCF facility - they can choose which contracts to put forward for cover.

- Bond insurance (see lesson 11) is also available as an add-on to the SCF facility.

Bank-to-bank lending

A variation on the SCF facility is for a UK bank to set up a Loan Contract (for a one-off transaction), or a Line of Credit (for several transactions) with an overseas bank. This would enable finance to be provided to UK exporters of goods and services. The overseas bank would make its own credit arrangements with the buyers.

For such a bank-to-bank arrangement, a bank guarantee could replace the use of bills of exchange or promissory notes as the means of repayment.

❏ ECGD-backed buyer credit

An alternative arrangement to supplier credit is *buyer credit* where finance is usually provided either direct to certain overseas buyers, such as Government organisations or, more usually, to a bank or financial institution, acting on behalf of the overseas customer, in the buyer's country. In essence, ECGD guarantees loans made by UK banks to overseas borrowers. The advantage of this scheme is that a UK exporter enters into what is essentially a contract whereby a cash payment is made upon shipment, the financing being between the overseas buyer and the UK bank. A further advantage is that an exporter can more easily arrange for progress payments at intermediate stages of manufacture. With buyer credit, the actual cost of arranging the finance, namely ECGD premiums and bank charges, are paid by the UK supplier. Only the interest charges on the loan are borne by the overseas buyer.

Buyer credit, which can usually be arranged in sterling or a foreign currency, takes one of two forms:
- Buyer Credit for a single project, or
- Financing a buying programme by means of Lines of Credit.

Buyer Credit

This scheme is available for large single contracts worth £1 million or more (although, in practice, they are for £5 million or more). Finance may be arranged in sterling or foreign currency for between two and five years. The finance provided under this facility is usually limited to 80-85 per cent of the contract price, the buyer being expected to pay the remainder direct to the UK exporter from his own resources. The balance is paid direct to the supplier from a loan made to the buyer by the UK bank. This loan will only be made upon the successful conclusion of a *loan agreement* between the overseas buyer (who will have been approved by ECGD) and the bank. Before the funds are paid to the UK exporter, he will have to produce documentary evidence that the sum claimed is correctly due for payment under the terms of the contract. ECGD will then directly guarantee the bank the amount of the loan and interest, against non-payment for any reason. Fixed preferential interest rates are available on the amount of the loan - through either OECD consensus rates or Commercial Interest Reference Rates (CIRRs).

As mentioned earlier, the exporter has received payment on completion of his side of the contract, with his payment being guaranteed by ECGD. He may also have benefited from stage payments made during the course of manufacture - if permitted, these would have been stated in the loan agreement. There now remains the loan relationship between the overseas buyer and the lending bank, which will be repaid in accordance with the terms of the loan agreement, with ECGD standing as guarantor.

It almost goes without saying that to set up such a credit is a lengthy process and it is necessary for an exporter to approach ECGD at an early stage, and at the same time to make arrangements with a bank with regard to the financing. As soon as possible, the supplier and lender should approach ECGD to discuss the terms of its guarantee, so that the following separate legal agreements can be brought to a conclusion at the same time:

- a *supply contract* between the UK supplier and the overseas buyer, for the supply of plant and equipment and possibly for construction of the project;

- a *premium agreement* between the UK exporter and ECGD, for the exporter to pay the premium and to act in accordance with ECGD's requirements;

- a *guarantee agreement* given by ECGD to the UK financing bank to cover the risk of non-payment of principal or interest;

- a *loan agreement* between the UK financing bank and the overseas borrower to provide finance for the bulk of the payments under the supply contract.

Lines of Credit

ECGD guarantees loans made by UK banks to overseas buyers to purchase a wide range of capital goods and services from various UK suppliers. The finance can usually be made available in either sterling or a foreign currency and fixed preferential interest rates will apply.

There are two types of lines of credit:
- general purpose line of credit
- project lines of credit

With a *general purpose line of credit* contract values down to £15,000 are very often acceptable. Therefore, they can help a UK exporter gain entry to new markets. Usually the loan is made to an overseas bank: the funds can be used to finance unrelated contracts with a variety of buyers. A general purpose line of credit is also suitable where one buyer is purchasing a wide range of unrelated goods from the UK - a 'shopping basket' facility.

Project lines of credit are established for a particular project which requires purchases from a number of UK exporters.

As with buyer credits, 80-85 per cent of the contract value is covered by the credit, the balance being paid on signature and before shipment. Exporters receive cash at the time of shipment and so, for them, the contract is almost the same as a cash transaction. There is no recourse to the exporter. Remaining is the borrowing arrangement between buyer and bank to be agreed as to terms of repayment, etc. Depending on the value of the contract, the repayment period will be two to five years. ECGD will guarantee the loan made to finance the line of credit.

Buyer Credits, Lines of Credit and overseas banks

Buyer credits and lines of credit are increasingly being made available to overseas banks. Here the loan is made by a UK bank to an overseas bank, and ECGD guarantees the loan. The overseas bank then uses the funds to lend money to approved importers in that country to enable them to pay cash on shipment for UK exports. Instead of one single transaction, the sum lent to the overseas bank can be split up by that bank amongst a number of importers. For example, Midland Bank might arrange a line of credit for £10 million to the National Bank of Bahrain. Midland's loan to the Bahrain bank is guaranteed by ECGD although, in practice, there is no likelihood of default. An exporter of capital goods or services to Bahrain, with a buyer seeking long credit terms, would advise the buyer of the facility. The buyer could then approach the National Bank of Bahrain seeking a loan, in order to pay cash on shipment for the goods.

The advantages of making buyer credits available through banks are:

- as the loan is split up by the overseas bank amongst a number of importers, individual contract values can be as low as £15 000;

- the arrangements can be made quickly as ECGD is only concerned with guaranteeing the loan between the banks concerned, rather than with the creditworthiness of individual importers.

If the overseas buyer defaults, the matter is between buyer and the overseas bank. To the UK exporter, the finance is provided to the overseas buyer without recourse to him; preferential rates of interest apply.

Fig. 12.2 summarizes ECGD bank guarantees.

Name of Facility	Supplier Credit Financing	Buyer Credit	Lines of Credit • general purpose • project line
Loan in Name of	Supplier	Buyer, or overseas bank	Buyer, or overseas bank
Interest Rate	Fixed preferential interest rates under OECD consensus rates (Category III countries), or Commercial Interest Reference Rates (CIRRs)		
Amount Advanced	Maximum of 85% of contract value	Generally 80-85% of contract value	Generally 80-85% of contract value
Period of Credit	Between two and five years (sometimes longer)	Between two and five years	Between two and five years

Fig. 12.2: ECGD Bank Guarantees

❏ Currency borrowing

In the UK, exporters are free to borrow available foreign currencies. The benefit of this is that, if an exporter takes a loan in the currency in which the buyer is to make payment, the risk of fluctuating exchange rates will have been eliminated. Any borrowing made in this way would normally be converted into sterling immediately, the foreign currency loan being repaid by the currency proceeds of the export sale. There are risks in such a method of finance: if the buyer defaults the exporter will have to buy currency in the market to repay the loan.

As explained in lesson 1 there is rarely any significant interest differential between selling a currency forward and borrowing currency in the Euro-currency market.

Lesson 14 deals more fully with Eurocurrencies.

❏ **Factoring**

Factoring companies — usually finance companies, some of which are owned by banks — provide a range of services which include:

- providing a sales ledger accounting service;

- giving the exporter 100 per cent credit insurance by taking over the invoices of approved debtors as goods are supplied and by collecting payment (the factoring company may well insure the goods under a credit insurance policy);

- provision of short-term finance by advancing cash immediately for up to 85 per cent of the value of the invoices; the balance being payable on collection or a maximum of 90 days after due date, whichever comes first.

Generally, factoring companies do not purchase trade debts on terms exceeding 120 days, but exceptionally may accept debts for terms of up to 180 days. Factoring is most appropriate for exporters selling on open account terms. When credit insurance is used, finance is non-recourse to the exporter.

The cost of a factor will vary according to which services are used but will usually be between one per cent and three per cent of turnover, depending on the amount of work carried out by the factor. Where cash advances are taken, the rates of interest charged will usually be one or two percentage points higher than those that would be charged on a bank overdraft.

Factoring companies have overseas branches or agents through which arrangements can be made for the collection of payments. Some factoring companies are owned by banks, and others have close links with banks, through which bills and other instruments may be presented for payment, and through which they can obtain status reports on overseas buyers. It is usual for a factoring company giving credit insurance to set a limit for each overseas buyer, allowing the exporter to supply goods up to these limits, and submitting invoices to the factor. Usually the factor will insist on their name being disclosed to the buyer - having bought the debt without recourse, they are better able to collect the debt in their own name, rather than that of the seller - but sometimes 'undisclosed' factoring can be undertaken. As far as finance is concerned, factoring provides an exporter with additional working capital because debtors have been turned into cash. An exporter receiving an immediate cash advance is relieved of the risk of exchange rate fluctuations in respect of foreign currency invoices because they are generally converted into sterling for the exporter's own account at the appropriate rate ruling on the day on which the factor takes over the debt. This then enables prompt payment to be made for purchases to obtain maximum discounts. Factoring, whether it is of export or home debtors, leaves the management of a business free to devote more of its time to important aspects of the business such as selling and manufacturing. However, it should be said that factoring companies are selective of the debts they will factor and, in the case of export debts, with the country of the buyer.

Import factoring is where an exporter uses a factoring company in the country of import. For example, a UK exporter has several buyers in Germany and may well use a German factoring company to collect debts – the exporter would send copies of the invoices direct to the factoring company. The advantages of import factoring are that the German factoring company will be better able to assess buyers' risks and is able to collect the debts faster than would a UK export factoring company. In a similar way, a UK factoring company can offer import factoring services to overseas companies exporting goods to the UK. Within Europe especially, *pan-European finance*, such as import factoring, is likely to develop further as banks and other financial institutions compete for business throughout the countries of the European Union.

Invoice discounting is another service often provided by factoring companies. Here trade debts are sold at a discount to the factoring company, which pays a proportion (normally up to eighty per cent) of the debts. However, this is a simpler service, as the exporter has to collect the debts and remains responsible for bad debts. It has the advantage that the importer continues to settle direct with the seller and, therefore, is usually not aware of the intervention of a factoring company. Finance is generally provided at rates of interest one or two percentage points higher than would be charged on a bank overdraft.

❏ Leasing and instalment finance

These two services are provided by finance companies, some of which are owned by banks.

Leasing

This is a form of finance which, in both the home and export trade, enables a firm to have the use of an asset, such as a machine, without having to make a substantial investment of capital in its acquisition. There are two ways in which leasing can be made available to an overseas buyer:

* by arranging the leasing from the exporter's country direct into the lessee's country (*cross border leasing*); or

* by arranging the leasing in the lessee's country through the international contacts of major leasing companies.

The former method would be better for handling major transactions which will involve much consultation between lessee, seller, and leasing company. Leasing locally is better suited for lower value items involving less complex leasing contracts. There are advantages in 'local' leasing for the lessee in that finance can be obtained for 100 per cent of the delivered cost; also there may be longer payment periods than with other forms of finance. The lessee will not be exposed to any exchange risks, because leasing payments will be made in local currency to a leasing company in the lessee's own country.

The advantage of leasing to an exporter is that payment will be made by the leasing company in full as soon as the equipment has been delivered and installed at the lessee's premises. There will be no recourse to the exporter in the event of default by the lessee.

Leasing, as a means of finance, is medium to long-term and is only suitable for the type of product which can be leased, although nowadays almost any type of fixed asset (machinery, vehicle, office equipment, etc.) comes into this category.

Hire purchase

Hire purchase or instalment finance is an older method of finance than leasing but represents an expanding market for exporters wishing to receive their sale proceeds quickly and, at the same time, give their overseas customer the opportunity to pay for goods by instalments over a period. Like leasing, hire purchase may be organised in two ways:

* by arranging the finance in the exporter's country, sometimes through an overseas branch of the 'home' finance house, or

* by arranging the finance in the hirer's country through international credit clubs (unions) of leading finance houses, which have agreements for introducing credit business to each other.

The advantage for an exporter is that, like leasing, payment will be received in full very quickly on a non-recourse basis. For the overseas customer (hirer), the advantage is that use of the goods (usually machinery, vehicles, other fixed assets and stock) is obtained for a relatively low capital investment (the deposit) and payment for the item is made over a longer period of time than under other credit methods. The disadvantage is that the interest rates charged will be higher than other forms of shorter-term finance and also there may be restrictions on the minimum deposit and maximum repayment period.

❏ Forfaiting

Forfaiting (see fig. 12.3) is the discounting of bank-guaranteed overseas trade bills at a previously agreed rate of discount without recourse to the seller. It provides 100 per cent medium-term non-recourse finance for exporters of capital goods, usually for periods of between three months and

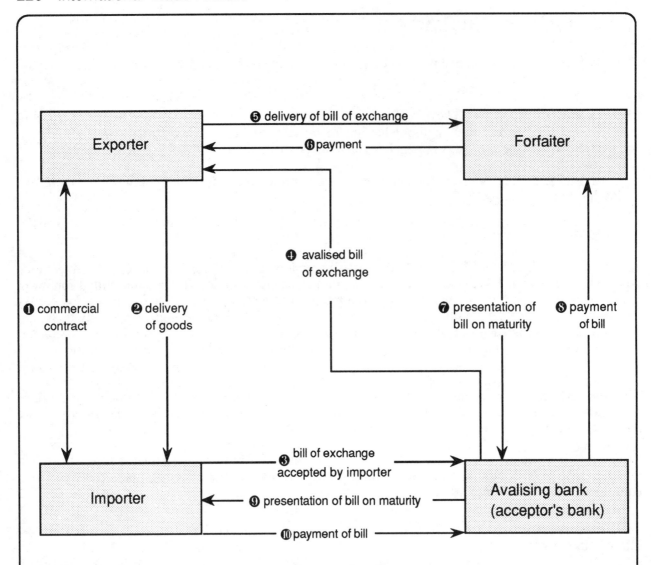

Notes:
* The bill of exchange is avalised by the acceptor's bank (step 4) by endorsement of the bill 'pour aval' and an authorised signature of the bank.

* Payment (step 6) is the face value of the avalised (guaranteed) bill less costs.

* The avalising bank must be a major international bank known to the forfaiter.

* The guarantee – which is usually given by endorsing of the bill or note 'pour aval' – must be unconditional and irrevocable.

* With collections, the drawee's bank may be required to avalise the bill of exchange, so guaranteeing payment at maturity.

Fig. 12.3: Forfaiting

seven years. Under this arrangement, the forfaiter (a bank, finance house or discount house) agrees to buy at a fixed rate of discount, bills of exchange or promissory notes. This fixed rate of discount is often held firm for a certain time, thus enabling the exporter to negotiate the final terms of the contract with the overseas buyer on the basis of known financing costs and credit periods. The buyer is required to accept promissory notes or bills of exchange, guaranteed (endorsed *pour aval* and signed) by his bank. The bills or notes must be unconditional and not dependent upon the exporter's performance, since the forfaiter has no right of recourse against the exporter. Up to 100 per cent finance can be obtained; however, the forfait paper (bills or notes) often represents 80-90 per cent of the value of an export, because 10-20 per cent is usually paid in cash at the time an order is placed for capital goods.

An exporter using forfaiting obtains immediate cash and is relieved of all credit and currency risks. Forfaiting is the equivalent of supplier credit. It is available for up to seven years, principally in four major currencies: US dollars, Deutschemarks, sterling and Swiss Francs, with deals from £500,000. Costs are usually linked to LIBOR plus an appropriate margin to take account of the risk element of the creditor, the country, the term of the bills, and the fixed-rate transaction.

In collections, bills of exchange may be required to be avalised by the drawee's bank; this guarantees payment at maturity (the drawee still accepts the bills in the usual way). The instructions in the collection order will be to *release documents against acceptance pour aval*, and such instructions must be agreed between exporter, importer and the drawee's bank in advance.

Non bank-guaranteed debt can also be forfaited; for example, debt of a major multi-national company with a top credit rating or a government agency would not need to be guaranteed by a bank.

Advantages of forfaiting to an exporter are:

- Debtors are converted into immediate cash in the exporter's books.

- It is non-recourse to the exporter once the forfaiter has bought the bills or notes.

- There are no problems and costs with debt collection and credit control.

- Other credit facilities are still available to the exporter - it is to the avalisor or guarantor that the forfaiter will look.

- Documentation is simple because the finance is provided against bills or notes.

- If the bills or notes are drawn in a foreign currency, the discounted proceeds can be converted immediately at spot rate, thus removing any exchange risks for the exporter.

- The exporter receives immediate liquidity.

- The forfaiter will often hold the fixed rate of discount, perhaps for a fortnight or more and sometimes for up to six months, while the exporter negotiates the final terms of the contract with his buyer.

- A forfaiting facility can usually be established quickly.

- Forfait finance is available for individual export orders — there is no requirement to finance the whole of an exporter's business.

- There is no need for the exporter to take out credit insurance.

Disadvantages of forfaiting to an exporter are:

- In the UK there is no statutory recognition of avalisation of bills of exchange.

- The exporter must draw up the bills of exchange/promissory notes and ensure that they are correctly avalised by the importer's bank.

- The exporter must ensure that the importer can obtain a guarantor acceptable to the forfaiter.

- Financing costs may sometimes be relatively high because the forfaiter assumes all the risks.

Advantages of forfaiting to an importer are:

- Forfait finance is quick and easy to set up.

- As term bills of exchange and promissory notes are used, the buyer obtains credit for the imports.

Disadvantages of forfaiting to an importer are:

- In the UK there is no statutory recognition of avalisation of bills of exchange. (Thus a UK bank would take an indemnity from the importer, allowing the bank to reclaim any monies paid out.)

- The bank guarantee will utilise part of the importer's credit facilities with the avalising bank.

- The importer will have to pay a fee for the guarantee.

- The obligation to pay under the bill of exchange or promissory note is clear and separate from the commercial contract: any dispute about the quality of the goods cannot be used to delay or stop payment.

❏ Export house finance

Export houses (see also lesson 5) can be grouped into the following categories:

- export merchants, who act as principals in their own right;

- export agents/export managers, who act for the exporter;

- confirming houses, who act for the buyer.

Export finance houses, which provide financial services, are also considered.

Export merchants
These organisations buy and sell as principals: they buy goods in one country and export them in their own right. As already noted in lesson 5 they will remove much of the burden of exporting from a manufacturer and will settle their debts in the home currency within the normal period of trade credit. This relieves the manufacturer from having to offer long periods of credit in order to make export sales. Thus, for the manufacturer, the export sale is turned into a domestic sale, with very little credit risks. (Note that an export merchant may well take out credit insurance).

Export agents/export managers
This type of export house provides payment to the manufacturer on evidence of shipment. The export house then gives credit to the overseas buyer in its own name. Thus the manufacturer receives cash at shipment, although he remains in a contractual relationship with the overseas buyer as far as performance of the contract is concerned.

Confirming houses
These act in a similar way to export merchants in that they will provide a manufacturer with a relatively quick settlement of his account. Instead of buying for themselves, they act as agents for foreign buyers but confirm, as principals, orders placed by the foreign buyer. In confirming an order they undertake to pay for the goods on evidence of shipment and, as they will give credit to the overseas buyer, will relieve the manufacturer of credit risks on the transaction. Again, the manufacturer remains in a contractual relationship with the buyer so far as performance of the contract is concerned.

Export finance houses
These are not merchants, but specialists in providing and arranging finance on a non-recourse basis for capital and semi-capital goods. They undertake the financial and administrative burden of arranging

export finance. Suitable credit terms are agreed with the importer, and finance is provided to the manufacturer by the export finance house, usually on a non-recourse basis for 90 per cent or 100 per cent of the amount payable by the buyer over the credit period. There is thus no need for the exporter to take out credit insurance because the transaction is for cash without recourse; however, the export finance house is likely to use credit insurance for the underlying credit which it makes available.

While export finance houses normally provide finance for large items of capital plant and equipment, they may be able to undertake business of a smaller size. With large contracts they can arrange and manage the finance on behalf of a syndicate of banks. The finance may be provided for single transactions, or for a series of orders, as a 'package deal' for a large project, or through a credit line negotiated with a bank in the buyer's country.

They are usually able to provide finance in either the home currency or overseas currencies.

❏ Conclusion

Finance for exporters is a wide topic, and it can be categorized in a number of different ways:

- short-term, medium-term, or long-term
- with recourse, or without recourse (see also note at the bottom of page 219)
- supplier credit, or buyer credit

Figs. 12.4, 12.5 and 12.6 provide a summary of the various financing schemes available.

❏ Examination hints

- In recent past papers, there has always been at least one question on export finance.

- The wording of a question will direct you to appropriate facilities, e.g. *consumer goods* needs short-term finance (up to two years); *capital goods* require medium-term finance 2-5 years); *large projects* need long-term or buyer credits (two to five years - sometimes longer).

- The use of the word 'with recourse' or 'without recourse' will give guidance; this may lead to the banks' 'Finance for Exporters' schemes involving credit insurance (but see note at the bottom of page 219), and to ECGD's Supplier Credit Financing facility and Buyer Credits.

- Reference to 'non-traditional' finance means factoring, invoice discounting, forfaiting, export house finance.

- Reference to finance methods 'common in Europe' most probably refers to forfaiting.

Fig. 12.4: FINANCE FOR EXPORTERS - Short-term finance (up to two years)

Facility	Normal credit period	Minimum/ maximum amounts	Interest rate basis	General comments
WITH RECOURSE				
Overdraft or loan	Up to 12 months renewable	-	Base rate, plus agreed margin	Flexible facility, security often required (e.g. assignment of credit insurance policy). Overdraft/loan could be in sterling or foreign currency.
Advance against Collections	Up to 180 days	-	Base rate, plus agreed margin	Amount advanced often 85 per cent of collection. Revolving facility.
Negotiation/ discount of bills/documents	Up to 180 days	-	Market rate, plus agreed margin	Available for sterling and foreign currency bills.
Acceptance house credit	Up to 180 days	Minimum of £100 000	Discount rate for eligible bank bills	Revolving facility.
Bank smaller exports schemes*	Up to 180 days	Export turnover of up to £1m. p.a.	Favourable rates linked to base rate	Schemes available from major banks. Up to 100 per cent finance, linked to credit insurance.
Bank finance for exports schemes*	Up to 180 days	Minimum export turnover of £1m. p.a.	Favourable rates linked to base rate	Schemes available from major banks, linked to credit insurance. Amount advanced is up to 90 per cent of invoice amount.

* these types of schemes are usually with recourse - see note at bottom of page 219

Facility	Normal credit period	Minimum/ maximum amounts	Interest rate basis	General comments
WITHOUT RECOURSE				
Discount of bills under a letter of credit	Up to 180 days	-	Market rate, plus agreed margin	No recourse to exporter as bills drawn on major bank. Available for sterling and foreign currency bills.
Factoring/invoice discounting	Up to 120 days (may go up to 180 days)	Minimum export turnover of £200 000 p.a.	Base rate plus agreed margin (often more expensive than bank overdraft)	Without recourse when bad debt insurance taken out. Service charges of factoring company will be between one and three per cent of turnover.
Leasing and hire purchase	-	-	-	Immediate payment received from the leasing/hire purchase company.
Export house finance	-	-	-	Immediate payment received from the export house (which may have acted as a confirming house).

Fig. 12.5: FINANCE FOR EXPORTERS - Medium-term Finance (2-5 years)

Facility	Normal credit period	Minimum/ maximum amounts	Interest rate basis	General comments
		WITH RECOURSE		
Bank loan	Up to five years	Often a minimum of £100 000	Base rate, or LIBOR, or Eurocurrency, plus agreed margin.	Flexible facility, usually linked to credit insurance. Capital and/or interest payments might be able to be deferred.
		WITHOUT RECOURSE		
ECGD Supplier Credit Financing facility	2-5 years	£25 000 minimum	Fixed preferential rates: either OECD consensus rates, or Commercial Interest Reference Rates (CIRRs).	Finance is up to 85 per cent of contract value. Finance is usually without recourse once bills accepted or promissory notes signed.
ECGD-backed buyer credit: Buyer Credit	2-5 years	£1m. minimum (usually £5m.+)	Fixed preferential rates: either OECD consensus rates, or Commercial Interest Reference Rates (CIRRs).	Finance provided to buyer, up to 85 per cent of contract value. ECGD Guarantee to lending bank.
ECGD-backed buyer credit: Lines of Credit	2-5 years	£15 000 minimum	Fixed preferential rates: either OECD consensus rates, or Commercial Interest Reference Rates (CIRRs).	Finance provided to buyer, up to 85 per cent of contract value. ECGD Guarantee to lending bank.
Forfaiting	2-5 years (or longer)	£50 000 minimum	Linked to market rates.	Finance is 80-90 per cent of contract value. Available for major currencies.

Fig. 12.6: FINANCE FOR EXPORTERS - Long-term Finance (2-5 years or longer)

Facility	Normal credit period	Minimum/ maximum amounts	Interest rate basis	General comments
		WITH RECOURSE		
Bank loan	Up to ten years	Minimum of £100 000	Base rate, or LIBOR, or Eurocurrency, plus agreed margin.	Only available for large projects (see also medium-term finance)
		WITHOUT RECOURSE		
ECGD Supplier Credit Financing facility	Up to ten years	£25 000 minimum	Fixed preferential rates: either OECD consensus rates, or Commercial Interest Reference Rates (CIRRs).	Only available for large projects (see also medium-term finance)
ECGD-backed buyer credit: Buyer Credit	Up to ten years	£1m. minimum (usually £5m.+)	Fixed preferential rates: either OECD consensus rates, or Commercial Interest Reference Rates (CIRRs).	Only available for large projects (see also medium-term finance)

Know Your .... Finance for Exporters

1.   How can an exporter's credit insurance policy be used as 'security' for bank lending?

2.   Distinguish between a sight credit and an acceptance credit.
        How can an exporter use the latter as a source of finance?

3.   Up to what percentage of the contract price can be financed by the lending bank under ECGD's Supplier Credit Financing facility? Why is this?

4.   What is the benefit to an exporter of ECGD-backed buyer credit?

5.   For what type of transaction is ECGD's Buyer Credit facility appropriate?

6.   What are the two types of lines of credit covered with ECGD-backed buyer credit?

7.   State the three main services provided by factoring companies.

8.   What are the two different ways of providing leasing facilities to an overseas buyer?

9.   Describe the salient features of forfaiting.

10.   In what ways can an export house provide finance to exporters?

Past Examination Questions

12.1   De-Cel Engines Plc manufacture diesel engines and are tendering for a £5m contract with a South American country to supply diesel engines for installation in naval craft. The contract is expressed in US dollars.

For balance sheet purposes De-Cel Engines are anxious to avoid incurring any contingent liabilities and their financial Director, Mr Hoyle, asks for your suggestions which would assist the company:

(i)   to obtain this contract which is being contested by foreign competitors who are quoting prices on or near cash terms, although you understand that some five years credit is being offered;

(ii)   to avoid the problem of showing a large and increasing contingent liability on the company's balance sheet.

You understand that the competitors are based in France and Germany and have the benefit of the support of banks utilising the cheaper fixed interest rates under COFACE and HERMES†.

REQUIRED in brief note form:

A UK bank's financial scheme which would assist the company to overcome the difficulties expressed under (i) and (ii) above, indicating why your suggestion would assist the company to compete against the foreign competitors.

[Total marks for question - 20]
(question 2, May 1988)

† *Author's note:* COFACE and HERMES are, respectively, the French and German equivalents of ECGD.

12.2   Your customer, Artefax Ltd, exports antiques and reproduction furniture to many parts of the world including the USA, Canada, Australia and New Zealand. Export turnover is in excess of £500,000 per annum. It is now negotiating to see its products to Spanish buyers. One of the directors, Mr D W Beetle, recently asked you to see him to discuss the company's export business.

At the meeting you learn that Artefax Ltd usually sells its products through an antiques clearing house based in London. Although goods are despatched by Artefax direct to the ultimate buyers, payment is usually received from the UK clearing house in sterling.

The prospective Spanish deal, however, will require shipment to, and payment direct from, the buyers in spain, and Artefax has been asked to give 30 days' credit from the date of despatch. Mr Beetle tells you that the clearing house usually takes up to 60 days to settle outstanding accounts.   *[4]*

As cashflow considerations are causing both you and Mr Beetle some concern, you wish to discuss Artefax's liquidity position. You are informed that the ultimate buyers in the USA, Canada, Australia and New Zealand are quite willing to settle their accounts direct, and that these companies are regarded as being undoubted and creditworthy. The potantial Spanish buyers, however, are unknown both to you and your customer.

REQUIRED:
Brief details of two schemes which would provide immediate finance for Artefax Ltd and some form of cover against any bad debts, assuming that the company is able to sell direct to the ultimate buyers.

[20]
(question 2, October 1989)

12.3   Euro-Power Plc is a major producer of power-generating equipment, In co-operation with a number of associated companies in the EC, it is negotiating a large capital contract with a South American country. You understand that the managing director, Mr Jenerator, wishes to discuss with you methods of financing the contract which would enable Euro-Power Plc to compete successfully with major competitors based in Japan and the USA.

REQUIRED:
Brief notes on the three schemes, appropriate to this contract, that you would discuss with Mr Jenerator.

(question 3, October 1989)

12.4*   Henri le Blanc, a French national, calls to see you. In view of the coming single market and the fact that EC and Government grants are available, his company Blanc et Blanc SA intends to set up a locally incorporated manufacturing enterprise near your branch to produce bleaching agents.

As the bulk of the products are to be sold overseas on a 90 day bill of exchange basis, your advice is sought concerning the various methods of bank finance which are available in the UK and could assist the needs of this potential customer.

REQUIRED:

Brief details of the various methods by which you would be able to assist this potential customer to finance its exports.   *[20]*
(question 2, May 1990)

12.5*   Frame-Up Ltd manufactures furniture which is sold through retail shops. The furniture is sold in packed-down ready-to-assemble units.

The company has built up a reputation in the UK but it has had little or no experience in overseas markets. As a result of exhibiting at a trade show, it has recently received orders from Scandinavian countries, Holland, Germany and the USA. You understand that the orders were received despite the fact that there is currently a buyer's market in packed-down furniture in these countries.

The Sales Director, Mr Matchwood, calls to see you to discuss the various methods by which his salesmen can accept these orders and expand the company's overseas order book. He has been advised by his Financial Director that he should also discuss the method by which the company can protect its cashflow position, if it accepts overseas orders.

REQUIRED:
Describe TWO appropriate methods of finance which would enable Frame-Up's order book to be expanded and which would also protect the company's cashflow and provide immediate funds/funding.   [20]

(question 2, October 1990)

12.6*   Keepkool Ltd sells, in sterling, a range of refrigeration equipment in many parts of the world. You meet the company's Financial Director, Mr Berg, who requests further facilities, in addition to those already available from you, as the company has just taken out a Short Term Guarantee with ECGD†. He wants to know if you are prepared to increase the current facilities by 100% of the value of the exports, using the ECGD guarantee as your protection.

REQUIRED:
Describe briefly:

(a)   the method by which you could obtain protection using the ECGD guarantee as your security. [3]

(b)   whether you would agree to increase the current facilities by 100% of the value of the exports, assuming that Keepkool Ltd is offering only the ECGD guarantee as additional security.   [4]

(c)   an alternative to (a), using the company's ECGD guarantee, which would provide Mr Berg with what he is seeking. Indicate whether this facility would have an effect on the company's balance sheet or not.   [4]

(d)   any other suggestion you could make which might be of interest to the company so that facilities, either from the bank or another source, could be made available to your custom.   [6]

(e)   whether your answers would differ (and, if so, how) if the company sold in foreign currency instead of sterling.   [3]

[Total marks for question - 20]
(question 2, May 1991)

† *Author's note:* Since this question was set a section of ECGD has been sold by the government to a private credit insurer, NCM. For ECGD Short Term Guarantee please now read NCM International Guarantee.

12.7   Power Jenerators Plc manufactures and installs large power station complexes overseas. It has taken advantage of the 'cheaper' sources of export finance in the past. However, since the UK schemes have recently been changed, you meet the managing director, Mr Engineer, and explore the sources of support and the various methods of providing finance to the suppliers and to the buyers now available.

REQUIRED:
In brief note form, a summary of the relevant features of:

(a)   a scheme available from the UK banks to provide finance direct to the buyers;   [7]

(b)   a scheme available to provide finance to the suppliers;   [7]

(c)   a method available to provide finance to the buyer/supplier using bank undertakings.   [6]

[Total marks for question - 20 marks]
(question 2, May 1992)

12.8* *Scenario*

Special Optics Ltd: see page 83

Question

At a meeting with Special Optics Ltd, Mr Glass advises you that the company has the opportunity to obtain a good-sized contract to provide a series of shipments to a potential new buyer in Hong Kong.

The buyer is a trading house which sells to clients throughout the Far East. The buyer would require credit terms of 60 days after shipment and that invoices be expressed in US$. It is willing to provide irrevocable documentary credits, from one of your bank's correspondent banks, which your bank would be asked to confirm.

This is an important opportunity for Special Optics in this expanding market region, so the first documentary credit needs to be checked thoroughly.

Mr Glass informs you that Special Optics may need to raise finance to complete the transaction under this contract.

REQUIRED:

(a)   Advise Mr Glass of the main details that Special Optics will need to check on receipt of the first documentary credit from Hong Kong.   *[10]*

(b)   Name and explain for him the ways in which documentary credits may be used to raise finance.   *[10]*

[Total marks for question - 20]
(question 4, Spring 1993)

12.9* *Scenario*

Special Optics Ltd: see page 83

Question

Special Optics has the opportunity to quote for a large export order to a major company in Germany.

Mr Glass wishes to consider two ways of obtaining payment which he has heard about recently:

1.   for Special Optics to draw a bill of exchange at 30 days' sight and send the bill directly to the German company's bankers, a leading German bank;

2.   for the German company to send Special Optics a promissory note avalised by the German bank prior to shipment. Mr Glass would ask your bank to collect the proceeds of the promissory note at maturity as an outward bill for collection.

REQUIRED:

(a)   List and explain the advantages and disadvantages to Special Optics of the two options listed above in comparison with its usual requirement of irrevocable documentary credit terms. *[10]*

(b)   How would the procedures to obtain payment after shipment differ in 1 and 2 above?   *[4]*

(c)   Describe the main features of the accelerated bills service provided by some UK banks as an alternative to the two systems mentioned above.   *[6]*

Note: For the purposes of this question, ignore the possibility of stamp duty being payable abroad on either bills of exchange or promissory notes.

[Total marks for question - 20]
(question 6, Spring 1993)

12.10*   *Scenario*

UK Auto Mart Ltd: see page 60

Question

Most of the trading undertaken by UK Auto Mart Ltd over the years has been on an open account basis.

With the worldwide recession, they are finding that a number of their suppliers are no longer willing to grant the 60 days credit terms they require, without more secure payment terms.

Whilst UK Auto Mart do not mind the additional costs in issuing letters of credit, Mr Daily is concerned at:

1.   having to handle shipping documents;

2.   encountering problems because of delays in the movement of this paperwork.

He books an appointment to discuss the possible alternatives.

REQUIRED:

(a)   Name and describe other payment terms that might be arranged by Mr Daily as an alternative to the current open account terms, apart from documentary credits.   *[12]*

(b)   Which of the methods you have described in (a) above would provide secure payment terms?   *[5]*

(c)   Which of the terms you have suggested in (a) above would overcome the problem of handling shipping documents and possible delays in the movement of paperwork?   *[3]*

[Total marks for question - 20]
(question 2, Autumn 1993)

12.11*   *Scenario*

Telecom Exports Ltd: see page 21

Question

Telecom Exports has a contract to provide supplies (components, spares, literature, etc) by air to a company in East Africa which is to service and maintain Telecom Exports' equipment in the region.

This company has been a distributor for Telecom Exports for a number of years and is now taking on the "after sales service".

This is regular business with relatively small invoice values and Telecom Exports has agreed to sell on 30 days sight D/A terms.

Mrs Daws arranges for a meeting with you to talk about the new arrangements.

She says that at present Telecom Exports does not need to finance the credit period granted, as the business is relatively modest.

REQUIRED:

(a)   Outline the extent of the risks in Telecom Exports' trading on this basis, that you should bring up at the meeting.   *[8]*

(b)   Bearing in mind your answer to (a) above, list the steps that may be appropriate if one of the bills is dishonoured. Give reasons for your answer.   *[6]*

(c)   Describe the methods by which the bills might be used to raise finance should the need arise and how these methods differ.   *[6]*

[Total marks for question - 20]
(question 6, Autumn 1993)

12.12   *Scenario*
The scenario concerns the concept of the time-share of apartments. Purchasers of a time-share obtain a fractional ownership of the apartment only. Typically, a purchaser buys the right to use the apartment (normally in a holiday location) for certain weeks each year for a given number of years.

Time's Money PLC
Time's Money PLC is one of your favourite customers, though it is occasionally run on unorthodox lines by its managing director, Mr D Jayson.

The company started as a small family business and has blossomed into a large corporation by acquisition, with a turnover in excess of £250m per annum.

It has combined two areas of business:

1.   Construction of large time-share complexes incorporating entertainment centres and marinas.

2.   The subsequent sale of time-shares of apartments and management of the complexes.

Members of each 'club' pay a lump sum for the use of the apartment for 25 years and an annual subscription for club membership and mooring (of boats) if required.

Such is the demand for apartments that sales are usually well ahead of construction and availability.

Time's Money PLC is the holding company of a group comprising:

(i)   Build in Time Ltd, the group's construction company.

(ii)   Time at Home Ltd, which manages complexes in the UK.

(iii)   Time Abroad Ltd, which manages complexes overseas.

Time's Money PLC owns the land and buildings.

Mr Jayson prides himself on having funded virtually all the expansion from the company's own resources. The company usually has healthy credit balances from sales and subscriptions.

Question
An excited Mr Jayson calls on you without appointment. Time's Money PLC has purchased a former fish market on the south coast of Spain for Spanish Pesetas 5,000m (£25m) payable:
              one-third on signing of the contract;
              one-third on clearance of the site;
              one-third 2 years after completion of the first apartment block.

The company has obtained planning permission to build and manage a complex creating a new resort, Costa del Buoy.

Mr Jayson says that the response to the press release has been 'perfect'.

Building materials would be shipped out from stocks held in the UK and the project should be fully completed in 5 years at a cost of a further £5m for UK costs and Spanish Pesetas 10,000m (£50m) for local costs.

Mr Jayson is flying out to finalise the contract with the land owner and understands that secure payment terms might be required.

In view of the size of the investment, the group will consider ways in which the project might be financed.

REQUIRED:
(a)   What methods could be used to provide secure payment terms over the medium term?   *[6]*

(b)   Briefly explain the main features of the medium-term export finance schemes in which ECGD is involved.   *[14]*
[Total marks for question - 20]
(question 5, Spring 1994)

Multiple-Choice Questions: Set 7

Read each question carefully. choose the *one* answer you think is correct.
Answers are given on page 318.

1.   Which is the chronological sequence for the following?

      (i) Advance payment bond   (ii) Tender bond
      (iii) Warranty bond   (iv) Performance bond

      A   (ii), (i), (iv), (iii)
      B   (ii), (iv), (iii), (i)
      C   (ii), (iv), (i), (iii)
      D   (iv), (ii), (iii), (i)

2.   An alternative to a performance bond is:

      A   ECGD's Tender to Contract scheme
      B   D/A collection
      C   ECGD's Overseas Investments Insurance scheme
      D   standby letter of credit

3.   Which is correct?

      A   a retention bond deals with progress payments
      B   bonds and guarantees are usually subject to the laws of the buyer's country
      C   ECGD issues all types of bonds, except for tender bonds
      D   all bonds are unconditional

4.   'The exporter hands the bank bills for collection; the bank accepts a term bill drawn on itself for an agreed percentage of the collections'. This finance facility is:

      A   an acceptance house credit
      B   an advance against collections
      C   forfaiting
      D   discounting of bills

5.   Credit factoring is:

      A   discounting of bills at a previously agreed rate of discount
      B   finance against debtors
      C   the use of fixed assets, rather than outright purchase
      D   provided by export factors

6.   What is the maximum percentage of the contract price that can be financed by an exporter's bank under ECGD's Supplier Credit Financing facility?

      A   72%
      B   80%
      C   85%
      D   100%

7.   Under which one of the following schemes is finance provided to the buyer?

A   forfaiting
B   factoring
C   ECGD's Supplier Credit Financing facility
D   ECGD's Lines of Credit

8.   'Small exports' and 'finance for exports' schemes provided by major banks offer:

A   finance for up to 180 days credit
B   cheaper finance for exports to the European Union
C   with recourse finance for up to five years credit
D   finance for open account trade only

9.   'Pour aval' together with the signature of a bank on a bill of exchange means:

A   interest is to be charged on the amount of the bill
B   the bank has discounted the bill
C   the bank guarantees payment of the bill
D   the bank certifies the creditworthiness of the acceptor

10.   Forfaiting is:

A   discounting of bills at a previously agreed rate of discount
B   finance against debtors
C   the use of fixed assets, rather than outright purchase
D   provided by confirming houses

Lesson Thirteen
Finance for Importers

Importers can arrange finance in the following ways:

- overdraft or loan
- produce loan
- accommodation finance/acceptance house credit
- documentary acceptance credit
- documents against acceptance collection
- open account trading
- hire purchase and leasing
- forfaiting (avalisation) of bills of exchange
- VAT deferment

❏ Overdraft or loan

Like any other customer of a bank, an importer can arrange a normal loan or overdraft to finance his trade. Such lending will either be secured or unsecured, and the bank manager will apply the usual principles of lending in deciding whether the facility is to be granted and upon what terms. The advantage for both importer and bank is that it is a very flexible form of finance and can be arranged quickly when required.

❏ Produce loan

A produce loan (or merchandise advance) is a loan by a bank to the importer using the goods which the importer has already contracted to purchase as security. The loan is to enable him to pay for the goods and will generally be repaid from the sale proceeds. When making such an advance, a bank should take the following steps:

- *Obtain a pledge from the customer by means of a letter of pledge/hypothecation, embodying a power of sale*
  The letter of hypothecation is an agreement whereby the customer will give a pledge over goods or documents of title as soon as they are to hand. Under a letter of pledge the customer undertakes delivery of the goods as security for his debt. Thus possession passes to the bank, although in practice this is constructive rather than actual possession - the bank will generally warehouse goods in its name. Legal ownership of the goods remains with the customer. A letter of pledge also gives the bank power to sell the goods following an unsuccessful demand for repayment. These two documents are usually combined in a letter of pledge/hypothecation and regular importers will sign a general letter to cover all advances and future lodgements of produce.

- *Take possession of the documents, ensuring that they give the bank control over the goods*
  In particular the bank should ensure that the bills of lading are a full set and are endorsed in blank, and that the marine insurance cover is still valid. In the case of other documents of movement, e.g. sea and air waybills, the goods should be consigned to the order of the bank.

- *Produce loan is made on a separate loan account*
  If there are any discrepancies in documentation, they should be cleared with the customer before making the loan.

- *When the goods arrive they should be cleared to a warehouse*
  The goods should be warehoused in the bank's name. Any duty payable should be paid and either debited to the loan account or to the customer's normal account. Warehouse warrants should be in the name of, or to the order of, the bank.

- *Arrange insurance*
  Insurance should be arranged for the cleared value of the goods, with a margin, against fire and any other risks stipulated by the customer, debiting him with the cost.

- *Release the warehouse warrants only against certain payment*
  This will involve endorsing the warehouse warrants or issuing delivery instructions: these actions should only be taken when payment is certain from the ultimate buyer direct to the bank. However, if the customer (importer) is considered sufficiently trustworthy, he may be allowed to obtain the goods for delivery to the ultimate buyer if he (the importer) signs a trust letter. This is a document by which the customer undertakes to hold the goods and the proceeds of their sale as trustee for the bank and to pay over the proceeds to the bank as and when received. Furthermore the customer agrees, pending receipt of sale proceeds, to keep the goods adequately stored and insured and to return any unsold goods to the bank on request. If required, the exporter also undertakes to give the bank an authority addressed to the buyers requiring them to pay the purchase price direct to the bank. A trust letter protects a bank against the claims of a liquidator or trustee in bankruptcy but, unlike a bill of sale, does not require registration. It is important to note that the bank loses physical control of its security and must ensure that its source of repayment is guaranteed.

- *Other considerations*
  A bank must be certain that the final proceeds of sale will be sufficient to cover the value of the goods and accrued charges, i.e. duty, insurance and warehousing, etc. It would be prudent for a bank to make status enquiries on the seller, the ultimate buyer, and the warehousing firm. Import licences, where appropriate, should be seen and, if the goods have already been sold by its importer customer, the contract of sale and/or sale invoices. The bank will also form an opinion of the ability of its own customer in such trading transactions. A consideration must also be made of the type of goods for which the loan is made: care should be exercised in granting facilities to cover perishable goods, or those in which market prices fluctuate, or which need special handling and storage facilities. Produce loans are usually made for basic commodities and raw materials for which buyers can be readily found.

❏ Accommodation finance/acceptance house credit

This method of finance (see fig. 13.1) might be used by an importer when the overseas seller has sent the documents covering the transaction on an 'at sight' collection basis. The importer will be required to make payment to the presenting bank at sight, but will not receive payment for the goods until they have been on-sold. It is possible for the importer to finance the 'gap' between paying for the imports and receiving the sale proceeds by drawing an accommodation bill on his/her bankers - often done through a merchant bank - for a time period (or tenor) slightly longer than the period within which the payment is to be received. The bank will accept the bill which is then discounted at the rate for that type of bank bill, the net discounting proceeds being used to pay for the inward collection. The importer can then sell the goods to customers and the sale proceeds will be used to pay the bill upon its maturity.

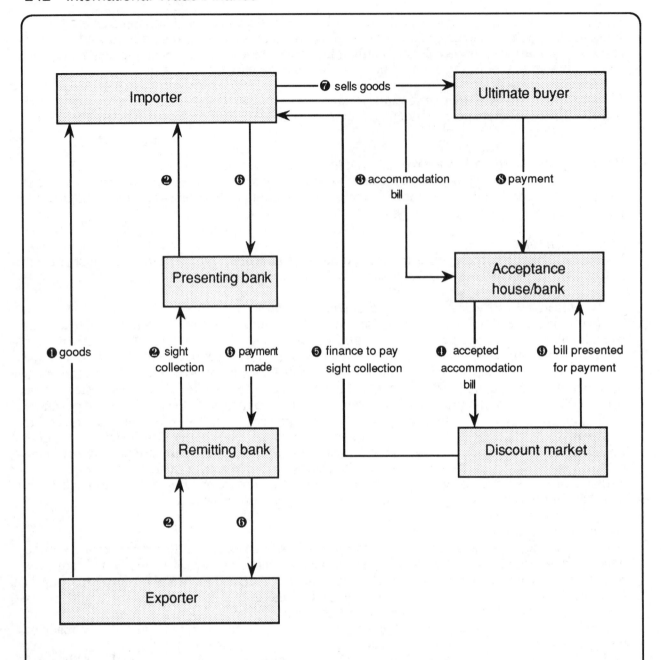

Fig. 13.1: Acceptance house finance for importers

Notes:

• The importer uses an accommodation bill (step 3) to raise the finance through the discount market (step 4) in order to pay the sight collection (step 5).

• The goods are sold (step 7) to the ultimate buyer, who makes payment (step 8) to the acceptance house/bank prior to presentation of the discounted bill (step 9), ie the accommodation bill is drawn for a tenor longer than the expected date of payment by the ultimate buyer. This gives the acceptance house the funds to meet payment of the accommodation bill; if funds are not received the acceptance house will seek recourse from the importer.

• The acceptance house will usually take a letter of hypothecation from the importer as security over the goods.

The bank concerned, whether a commercial or merchant bank, will normally require control of the documents covering the goods. The importer may be allowed to take possession of the documents to enable the goods to be delivered to the buyer, but will be asked to sign a letter of pledge and a trust receipt.

❏ Documentary acceptance credit

Where settlement between importer and exporter is to be by means of a documentary credit, a period of credit can be obtained from the exporter by seeking an acceptance credit rather than a sight credit. This means that, instead of receiving a payment when the required documentation is presented to the advising or confirming bank, the exporter will have a bill of exchange accepted for an agreed term. Thus the buyer of the goods will not have to make payment until maturity of the bill, so enabling the goods to be sold and, perhaps, also payment received. As we have seen in lesson 12, the exporter can, instead of providing finance to the buyer, discount the accepted bill of exchange.

❏ Documents against acceptance collection

When documents are handled on a documents against acceptance basis, the importer receives credit for the term of the bill of exchange (see lesson 9). An exporter might be persuaded to agree to these terms if the importer's bank was prepared to issue a standby letter of credit to guarantee its customer's trade debts. Under this letter of credit the issuing bank would undertake to pay any dishonoured bills of exchange drawn on, and payable by, the customer and duly protested for non-payment at maturity, under the stand-by letter of credit.

❏ Open account trading

Where an importer is buying goods on open account terms, the exporter is providing a measure of trade credit. Settlement will be made by the importer remitting funds on the agreed date to the supplier.

❏ Hire purchase and leasing

As already seen in lesson 12, hire purchase and leasing may be arranged to finance the acquisition of assets, although with leasing, the asset concerned remains the property of the leasing company while, with hire purchase, the asset is not legally acquired until the last payment has been made. We have seen that both of these forms of finance may be arranged either through a finance house in the exporter's country, or one in the importer's country.

❏ Forfaiting (avalisation) of bills of exchange

Forfaiting is the discounting of bank-guaranteed (avalised) trade bills (see pages 225-8). For an importer, forfaiting provides finance quickly and easily.

Advantages of forfaiting to an importer:
• Forfait finance is quick and easy to set up.

• As term bills of exchange and promissory notes are used, the buyer obtains credit for the imports.

Disadvantages of forfaiting to an importer:
• In the UK there is no statutory recognition of avalisation of bills of exchange. (Thus a UK bank would take an indemnity from the importer, allowing the bank to reclaim any monies paid out.)

- The bank guarantee will utilise part of the importer's credit facilities with the avalising bank.

- The importer will have to pay a fee for the guarantee.

- The obligation to pay under the bill of exchange or promissory note is clear and separate from the commercial contract: any dispute about the quality of the goods cannot be used to delay or stop payment.

❏ VAT deferment

When goods are imported into the UK from outside the European Union, Value Added Tax is payable by the importer before the goods can be cleared through customs. Regular importers can agree with HM Customs and Excise to defer payment of VAT. The usual arrangement is for the VAT to be paid in respect of a particular month's imports on the fifteenth day of the following month, eg VAT due on imports in January will be paid on 15 February. Thus between two and six weeks' credit is received by the importer. However, before they will agree to VAT deferment, HM Customs and Excise require the importer's bank to issue a bond (see page 250) guaranteeing payments on behalf of their customer.

As a method of finance, the importer must weigh up the benefits of deferring VAT payments with the charge made by their bank for the provision of the bond.

❏ Examination hints

- Questions on finance for importers may ask you to describe one or more methods, and to state the advantages to the importer.

- Produce loans are a particularly important financing method which have appeared regularly in recent papers.

- When a bank is lending to an importer, you should understand the paperwork necessary for a bank to safeguard its security, by way of access to the goods, or the sale proceeds of such goods.

- The wording of a question will often direct you to a produce loan with phrases such as 'the bank wishes to obtain maximum security from the transaction itself', or 'your customers' facilities are fully extended but you would like to assist them in financing this import'.

Know Your .... Finance for Importers

1. How can banks provide finance to an importer, using the goods as security?

2. Describe accommodation bill (acceptance house credit) finance.

3. Who provides the finance for an importer buying goods on a 'documents against acceptance' basis?

4. Who provides the finance for an importer buying goods on an open account basis?

5. In what two ways can hire purchase and leasing be arranged when providing finance to an importer?

6. What rights does a letter of hypothecation give to a bank?

7. Under what circumstances is a trust letter used in import finance?

Past Examination Questions

13.1*   Dockside Depositories Ltd is an importer and warehouse keeper which owns and manages a number of warehouses in your locality.

An appointment has been arranged for you to see one of its directors, Mr Pallett, who, you understand, will be accompanied by one of your customers, Mr Chest, who is an importer/broker and the Chairman/Managing Director of T Chests Ltd. You understand that Mr Pallett has suggested to Mr Chest that T Chests Ltd should take advantage of the value of the stock which it warehouses with Dockside Depositories Ltd. Your own records show that T Chests Ltd is a well managed company but it tends to have cash flow problems because of overtrading. The company's real asset is its standing in the commodity market and the stocks which it has deposited with Dockside Depositories Ltd.

The usual searches have been made on both companies. Dockside Depositories Ltd is a highly respectable company and T Chests Ltd has the necessary powers to charge any assets owned by the company. The stock held in the warehouse represents an acceptable range of commodities which can be readily valued, safely stored and, if necessary, sold on the open market.

REQUIRED in brief note form:
The points which you want to discuss with Mr Pallett and Mr Chest, working upon the assumption that you will be asked to provide facilities to T Chests Ltd. against the security of the goods.
(question 6, September 1986)

13.2   As Branch Manager you make arrangements to meet one of your customers, Junk Galore, which imports goods, principally from the Far East, for the UK seaside tourist industry. Their Finance Director, Andy Oldiron, tells you that he has had a discussions with his suppliers and they have suggested that he should arrange for his bank to avalise bills of exchange drawn on the company at 60 days sight. He agreed to this course of action and is now endeavouring to obtain your agreement to this arrangement.

REQUIRED:
Your explanation as to the obligation(s) your bank would enter into if you agreed to Mr Oldiron's proposal. As manager, would you agree to involve your bank in this arrangement? Give reasons for your answer?

What alternative would you suggest to Andy Oldiron which would protect the interests of your bank yet at the same time enable the customer to obtain 60 days credit after presentation of documents.
[Total marks for question - 20]
(question 5, September 1987)

13.3   Far Eastern Imports Ltd has contracts to purchase goods from a Japanese supplier. The Japanese are prepared to accept payment in sterling but insist upon payment on a cash against documents basis. Your customer, however, requires 90 days credit in order to clear the goods through customs and sell them to purchasers in the United Kingdom.

The Financial Director calls to see you. He says he has heard that the bank would be prepared to finance these operations.

REQUIRED:
Assuming that the bank will arrange to finance these operations:

(a)   State the two methods by which your bank could help Far Eastern Imports to resolve its problem.
[4]

(b)   Describe briefly the way in which these two methods operate, showing the steps the bank will take to protect its interest fully in the circumstances described in the question.   [16]
[Total marks for question - 20]
(question 6, October 1988)

13.4*   Fishy Business Ltd imports seafood products from Norway, Iceland and Canada. The company plans to expand rapidly. As their banker, you are asked to assist in the provision of facilities to finance this expansion.

You call to see Mr Shrimp, the Financial Director, to discuss the business plans. He tells you that the company has many first class buyers and shows you contracts from some of the top quality names who sell seafood to the public.

REQUIRED:
(a)   An explanation of the methods by which an overseas supplier could be paid against documentary evidence that the goods have been despatched to the UK.   [5]

(b)   Using the underlying transactions described in (a), explain the method by which you would make the bank as secure as possible and yet at the same time provide your customer, Fishy Business Ltd, with three months credit.   [15]
[Total marks for question - 20]
(question 8, May 1990)

13.5   *Scenario*
Time's Money PLC: see page 237

Question
The construction company in the group, Build in Time Ltd, imports building materials from the Far East and USA for use in time-share apartments under construction in the UK and in continental resorts.

The materials are stored in one of its warehouses in the UK, and can then be either used in the UK or re-exported to one of the sites on the continent.

Though these bulk shipments will be utilised within a six month period, they represent a substantial investment in stock.

The senior projects manager, Rodney Trotter, calls on you to see if the bank would be prepared to allow a short-term facility against the security of the goods.

The contracts with the suppliers are on a DDU any Build in Time warehouse in the UK basis to be settled in £ sterling or US$ 90 days after delivery.

Mr Trotter wants the goods to be released in up to 10 separate lots.

Repayment would come from the company's own resources.

REQUIRED:
(a)   What does the shipping term, or INCOTERM, quoted above mean?   [3]

(b)   Describe the means by which Build in Time Ltd might organise payments to its suppliers in the Far East and USA.   [6]

(c)   Explain how any bank finance might be structured and what documentation the bank might require.   [11]
[Total - 20 marks]
(question 6, Spring 1994)

Lesson Fourteen
Banking Services for the Exporter and Importer

This lesson considers firstly the services provided by most major banks for their exporter customers, secondly the services provided to importers, and thirdly some of the more specialised facilities available, including those of other financial institutions.

Within the European Union, banks are able to offer their services freely within all countries of the EU. Thus, for example:

- a UK exporter might consider using a French bank for export finance
- a German exporter with several customers in the UK could use a UK factoring company to collect debts
- a French branch of a UK bank could offer export finance to a UK exporter
- a UK hire purchase company offers to provide finance to the customers of a Dutch manufacturer of capital goods

The European Union offers both opportunities and threats to UK banks and financial institutions. The next few years are likely to see further development of *pan-european finance*.

❏ Services for the Exporter

All the major UK banks have international or overseas departments that are able to provide information to both established exporters and those who are considering exporting for the first time. All branches of the bank will have access to the international department and will thus be able to obtain required information.

Advisory and information services

Trade enquiries
Within an international department there will be a specialist department in contact with the bank's branches established overseas and correspondent banks, which can assist customers to find potential markets/agents for exported goods and which can effect introductions to overseas buyers, agents and banks.

Credit information
Banks are able to obtain up-to-date credit information on buyers and agents anywhere in the world.

Economic and political reports
Most large banks prepare reports on a wide range of countries and keep them regularly updated to show the current political and economic background. Also, specialist information is usually available on trading groups such as the European Union, the European Free Trade Association, the European Economic Area, and the North American Free Trade Area.

Import restrictions
Banks are able to give up-to-date information on tariffs and quotas imposed by countries.

Exchange control regulations
Banks can advise on the current exchange control regulations of countries.

Other information
This is available on a wide range of topics such as the various methods and risks of selling abroad; assistance and advice on documentation and shipping terms; information on the role and services of NCM, ECGD and other specialist agencies; marine insurance, etc.

Handling of payments
Banks are able to make collections on behalf of exporters or, if a documentary credit has been opened in favour of the exporter, will negotiate the exporter's bills with the advising/confirming bank. Alternatively, if the exporter's own bank is the advising/confirming bank, it will be able to make payment or accept his bills at the appropriate time. An exporter's bank will also receive mail transfers, telegraphic transfers and drafts on behalf of their customer in respect of settlements for open account trade.

The bank is able to exchange foreign currencies for the home currency and, where required, will enter into forward contracts, either fixed or option, in order to eliminate exchange risks. Foreign currency accounts - either current or deposit - can also be maintained for customers, subject to any exchange control regulations in force. Currency options can also be established.

Provision of finance
As we have already seen in lesson 12, banks are able to provide a range of ways in which finance may be provided. These include:

- ordinary loan/overdraft;
- advances against collections;
- negotiation/discount of bills/documents;
- accommodation finance/acceptance house credit;
- documentary credits;
- short-term finance, linked to credit insurance;
- ECGD-backed buyer and supplier finance;
- factoring;
- leasing and hire purchase (through the bank's subsidiary and associated companies);
- forfaiting.

Provision of guarantees
We have already seen in lesson 11 the four main types of guarantees or bonds which banks are requested to issue on behalf of contractors or suppliers for large overseas contracts. These are:

- bid or tender bond;
- performance bond;
- advance or progress payment bond;
- warranty or retention bond.

In addition a bank may be asked to provide an indemnity to an issuing bank under a letter of credit for discrepancies on documents presented. Banks will give guarantees in support of loans or overdrafts, usually to subsidiary companies abroad. See also 'average bond' under *Services for the Importer* (below).

A further type of bond or guarantee that a bank may be required to issue on behalf of exporter customers is a *countertrade bond*. This covers the penalties imposed in the counter trade where an exporter fails to make compensation purchases within a set time limit.

Travel services

These include the provision of foreign currency, travellers' cheques, credits opened, the remittance of funds abroad, and cheque and credit cards. Assistance can also be given with passport and visa applications. A letter of introduction can be provided, addressed to correspondent banks in countries that the exporter plans to visit, requesting them to give assistance by way of information and advice about possible buyers of his goods and about local trading terms and conditions.

Cash management systems

UK banks offer cash management systems to their corporate customers. Such a system allows a corporate treasurer, using electronic banking, to use a computer terminal in his/her office to obtain details of the company's accounts held with the bank anywhere in the world, at any time of the day. Balances held in different currencies can be checked, and the flow of funds can be watched as payments are debited or credited. The corporate treasurer is able to move funds from one bank account to another using the terminal in his/her office. In this way advantage can be taken of the best interest rates available in overseas countries, consistent with prudent currency exposure.

Using electronic banking (see also ED1 – page 93) a company can make SWIFT transfers to beneficiaries, arrange forward exchange contracts with the bank, and keep in touch with the progress of collections.

International trade consultancy service

In order to provide general advice on various aspects of international business, some UK banks provide an 'audit', or 'health check', of a company's export (and also import) activity, including advice on marketing. This service is provided in conjunction with the Department of Trade and Industry's *Business Links* scheme (see page 78) which aims to bring closer working relationships between banks and exporters.

❏ Services for the Importer

Advisory and information services

Some of the services listed for exporters will apply equally to importers. In addition assistance can be given in finding overseas sources of supply and the names of potential suppliers. Banks are able to obtain status reports on overseas suppliers: this ensures that an importer who considers entering into an overseas contract can ascertain beforehand whether the supplier is of sufficient standing and creditworthiness to carry out his side of the contract and supply the goods required.

Handling of payments

The methods of payment are, of course, the same as for exports except that the settlement flows are in the opposite direction. Where an importer is buying goods on open account the bank will be involved in making mail/telegraphic transfers or issuing drafts. With other methods of payment, an importer may request his bank to issue a letter of credit in favour of an overseas supplier; alternatively, the bank may receive inward collections for their customer.

An importer is almost always required to pay his supplier in a foreign currency and the bank is able to provide a means of eliminating the exchange risk in such settlements by entering into a forward contract, either fixed or option. Some importers will also operate foreign currency accounts.

Provision of finance

Financing facilities can be arranged through his bank as follows:

- ordinary loan/overdraft;
- produce loan;
- accommodation finance/acceptance house credit;
- hire purchase and leasing;
- forfaiting;
- VAT deferment.

See lesson 13 for further details of these.

Provision of guarantees

There are a number of types of bonds and guarantees that apply particularly to importers:

Indemnities
These are given to shipping companies where bills of lading are missing, either because they and the other documents have not yet arrived or are lost, and enable an importer to take delivery of the goods and avoid demurrage charges (the extra charge made by port authorities if the goods are not collected after clearance through customs).

Average bond
Lesson 6 discussed the meaning of the insurance word 'average' which could, under certain circumstances, be declared over a ship and its contents. When this happens, even though he is covered by insurance, the cargo owner has to contribute either by means of a cash deposit or by his bank giving an average bond, before his goods will be released. Where a bond is issued, it will be released after settlement under the insurance policy for the contribution payable, as determined by the average adjuster.

Avalisation
This is the practice, common in Europe, of a bank guaranteeing the payment of a bill of exchange. The bank usually endorses the bill 'pour aval' and thus makes itself primarily liable for payment at maturity.

VAT deferment
Value Added Tax is payable by importers when goods from outside the EU are imported into the UK. The goods cannot be cleared through customs until VAT has been paid. Regular importers are able to defer payment of VAT by arranging with HM Customs and Excise to pay the VAT due in a lump sum each month. The usual arrangement is for the VAT to be paid in respect of a particular month's imports on the fifteenth day of the following month, eg VAT due on imports in January will be paid on 15th February. The method of payment is by direct debit, and Customs and Excise require the importer's bank to issue a bond guaranteeing payments on behalf of their customer.

❏ Specialised Facilities

This part of the lesson is concerned with the following:

- Eurocurrency loans;
- Eurobond and foreign bond issues;
- certificates of deposit;
- merchant banks;
- consortium banks;
- the European Investment Bank.

Eurocurrency loans

For a currency to become 'Euro', it must be available for deposit or loan in a country in which it is not the domestic currency. Eurocurrency deposits are, therefore, deposits held by banks in one country but in the currency of another; similarly Eurocurrency loans are made by banks in one country in the currency of another. The Eurocurrency market involves bringing together those who have currencies to lend and those who wish to borrow in these currencies; it is essentially a 'wholesale' market dealing with large sums of money on a fairly short-term basis - most borrowing is for six months or less, although there is also a medium/long-term element in the market where borrowing can go up to five years or even longer. The market is inter-bank: a company with Eurocurrency funds cannot directly place them on the market but must deposit them with a bank and equally a company wishing to borrow must go through a bank.

What can a Eurocurrency loan be used for?
The importance of Eurocurrency borrowing as a source of finance for businesses and governments has developed rapidly in recent years. The following are some of the transactions for which a loan may be used:

- An exporter can invoice in a foreign currency and then borrow the currency amount which is immediately converted into the home currency; thus the exchange risk is eliminated. The currency loan will be repaid by the proceeds of the export. This is an alternative to entering into a forward exchange contract.

- Lending to overseas subsidiaries.

- Making investments in foreign currency securities/property.

- Financing the purchase of capital items, e.g. ships and aircraft, which, when built abroad, are usually priced in US dollars.

- Financing major capital projects, e.g. North Sea oil.

Note that, because it is obtained on an international market, a Eurocurrency loan is a way of avoiding tight credit restrictions in the home country. This is one of the reasons why the market has expanded enormously since its origins in the 1950s. The market is free from national restrictions on the transfer of funds and from differences of interest rate structures between countries.

Operation of a Eurocurrency Loan
Funds in the market are deposited for a fixed time and lending is usually matched to the maturity of deposits. Thus Eurocurrency loans normally take the form of term loans rather than overdrafts, although revolving loan facilities can be arranged. As with loans made in the home currency, normal banking considerations, such as creditworthiness and availability of security, will be applied.

Interest rates charged may be either fixed or floating. In the UK interest rates are quoted as a margin over the London Interbank Offered Rate (LIBOR), being the rate at which a bank can acquire matching funds for on-lending. Where fixed rate loans are negotiated they provide the borrower with security against rising interest rates. In addition to Eurocurrency loans, banks will enter into standby credits, whereby the bank will provide Eurocurrency funds if they are required. This has the effect of creating an overdraft facility on the foreign currency account. An additional charge will be made by banks for this facility and a commitment fee will be levied if the standby credit is not used.

The main danger for a Eurocurrency borrower is that of exposure to exchange rate fluctuations: this is particularly so when commitments are undertaken in a currency in which the borrower has no income. A prudent businessman would, wherever possible, cover this risk with a forward exchange contract. Alternatively a loan may incorporate, at extra cost, a multi-currency option clause which gives the borrower the option of converting his loan into one of a stated number of foreign currencies.

Eurocurrencies
Any currency can become 'Euro-', but the market in Eurodollars was the first and remains the most important. Besides the dollar, the other principal Eurocurrencies are sterling, Deutschemarks, Swiss francs, Dutch guilders and Canadian dollars. Thus Eurodollars are those dollars held on accounts in banks in the USA by non-residents of that country, and which have been, or are, available for lending to other non-residents by transfer to the borrower's account in the USA. You will appreciate that, if a

person has a bank account designated in US dollars in Britain, then those dollars will, in practice, be held in America. Similarly for other Eurocurrencies they never leave the country which uses them as a currency. The thing that is exchanged on the Eurocurrency market is ownership of these bank balances.

Eurocurrency syndicated loans

These are loans for larger amounts and longer terms than are the shorter-term Eurocurrency loans described earlier. They are organised by a bank or a multi-national group of banks (consortium) and the loan is syndicated - or 'shared out' - by a group of up to fifty international banks. The borrowers are governments, government-linked bodies and large companies who wish to finance a specific investment project for periods of up to ten years or more. Interest rates will be linked to the existing rate for Eurocurrency loans, plus a fixed premium. Being for longer terms, such loans 'bridge the gap' between shorter-term Eurocurrency loans and the long-term Eurobond issues (see below).

Eurobond and foreign bond issues

The Eurobond market has developed to provide longer-term (up to twenty years) international finance. To be 'Euro-' they are sold principally in countries other than the country of the currency in which the issue is denominated, e.g. a dollar-denominated bond issued by a US company in Europe. The first Eurobonds were issued in the mid-1960s and were designated in US dollars but were issued in Europe to avoid US taxation. Bonds are now issued in a range of currencies and are usually underwritten by an international syndicate of banks.

A foreign bond issue is, in theory, different from a Eurobond issue in that it is sold mainly in the domestic market of the country in whose currency the issue is denominated, and is normally underwritten by a national syndicate of banks, e.g. a Deutsche Mark-denominated bond issued in Germany by a US company. In practice, however, foreign bond issues are often largely taken up, like Eurobonds, outside that country. An international secondary market exists for subsequent sales and purchases which deals with both foreign and Eurobonds.

The borrowers on the foreign and Eurobond market are governments, nationalized industries, municipal authorities and multi-national corporations. The most common method of issue is for banks in the consortium handling the loan to place the bonds with their customers and other banks in their own country. When the issue has been successfully placed, an advertisement is put in various newspapers announcing it, as required by law: this describes the issue and lists the names of the participating banks. Some issues are publicly offered for sale and are listed on a stock exchange, usually either London or Luxembourg.

There are three forms in which international (Euro- and foreign) bonds are issued:
- fixed rate issues;
- floating rate notes (FRN);
- convertible, and so called 'drop lock' floating rate notes.

Fixed rate issues are by far the most common. Floating rate notes are becoming increasingly more used; they are in most respects the same as fixed rate issues except that the interest is calculated on the basis of a specified margin over a reference rate. This reference rate is often the three or six month LIBOR rate, usually subject to a minimum level. Floating rate notes are more often issued by international banks than by industrial companies, because this type of borrowing is particularly appropriate for funding loans. There are two other types of FRN issues: firstly FRNs which are convertible at the investor's option to fixed rate bonds within a predetermined period and, secondly, the so called 'drop lock' FRNs, which convert to fixed rate bonds automatically if LIBOR falls to a certain level. Other types of international bonds are convertible into equity shares.

Investors in international bond issues are usually central banks, off-shore pension funds of multi-national companies, insurance companies, investment and unit trusts, and individual investors.

Certificates of deposit

A certificate of deposit is a certificate issued by a bank acknowledging that a sum of money has been deposited with it for a fixed period of time. The important thing to note is that certificates are negotiable and payable to bearer, i.e. title to them passes freely from one person to another by delivery of the certificate. The rate of interest is fixed for the time period until maturity and certificates are usually issued for stated periods between three months and five years. Interest on certificates issued for a period of one year or less is paid on maturity with the capital sum; interest on certificates issued for longer periods is payable annually.

The advantage to a bank of the certificate of deposit system is that it has the use of the money for a fixed time period and only has to repay on maturity of the certificate; this helps it to plan its future medium-term lending as it knows what funds are available and when they are due for repayment. For the depositor there are two advantages: firstly, the fixed rate of interest payable for the time period of the deposit and, secondly, that should the funds be needed urgently, the certificate can be sold on the secondary certificate of deposit market. Thus, from the depositor's point of view, the certificate is more flexible than a term deposit, which a bank is not obliged to repay before the due date.

In the UK, banks issue certificates of deposit usually designated in either sterling and US dollars. The rates of interest paid are generally slightly below those offered on ordinary fixed term deposits.

Merchant banks

In essence these banks are financial institutions providing specialist services which generally include the acceptance of bills of exchange, corporate finance, portfolio management and other banking services. Most merchant banks are members of the British Merchant Banking and Securities Houses Association.

Merchant banks became established as a result of overseas trading. Several of the present-day merchant banks had, as their founders, merchants who traded abroad. As world trade expanded during the nineteenth century these merchants grew in reputation and soon found themselves being asked to lend their name to lesser-known traders by accepting bills of exchange. This enabled such bills to be discounted at finer rates of discount than commercial bills which bore only the acceptance of a trader. In the nineteenth century 'the bill on London' became the main instrument of payment for goods moving internationally. It was also the merchant bankers who developed the documentary letter of credit which, because it was a secure method of settlement, helped to bring about an increase in international trade.

By specialising in the financing of international trade, the merchant banks were able to build up a store of information on traders throughout the world which further enhanced their reputations in international trade.

Nowadays merchant banks have expanded into other areas such as corporate finance and portfolio management but are still able to offer a range of services to the importer and exporter. Like other banks, they are able to arrange finance for exporters, supported by credit insurance. Acceptance credits, as described in lesson 12, are also a speciality of merchant banks, providing short-term export finance. In particular, as a result of their close banking connections and associates abroad, merchant banks are able to offer Eurocurrency and Eurobond finance, and to put together 'packages' of finance as part of a banking consortia.

In the UK, during the last two decades, the major clearing banks have all developed an interest in merchant banking and each has either bought its way into an established merchant bank or set up a new one. Thus most of the specialist services of a merchant bank are available to the customers of a clearing bank.

Consortium banks

As the name suggests, a consortium bank is formed by a group of other banks usually from several different countries. In the UK, the Bank of England defines such a bank as one which is

> *owned by other banks but in which no one other bank has a direct shareholding of more than fifty per cent and in which at least one shareholder is an overseas bank.*

These banks are formed in order to be able to put together large loan 'packages' to meet the financial requirements of multi-national companies for long periods of time. As seen earlier in this lesson, they are able to arrange Eurocurrency Syndicated Loans by sharing out large loans amongst syndicates of banks. The bank that is organising the loan, called the *lead bank,* contacts up to fifty other banks inviting them to participate.

The European Investment Bank (EIB)

The EIB was created in 1958 by the Treaty of Rome with the object of furthering the balanced development of the European Community (now known as the European Union) by making or guaranteeing long-term loans. The bank's resources consist of capital subscribed by member states, and bonds issued on both the international capital markets and also the capital markets of individual member countries.

The EIB lends funds to public enterprises, public authorities with financial autonomy, financial institutions of any nationality provided the project for which finance is required is situated in a member state or in an associated country, and to private firms. The Treaty of Rome stipulates that there are three economic policy objectives for loans:

- regional development;
- modernisation and new technology;
- projects of common interest to several member countries.

All of the bank's loans are vetted to ensure that they are in accord with EU policies. Loans are made for periods between four and twelve years in the case of industrial projects, and up to twenty years (or more) if the loans are used to finance economic infrastructure projects. The loans are used to 'top up' finance already obtained from other sources and they rarely exceed forty per cent of the fixed assets in a project; loan amounts are normally between £0.5 million and £15 million. To help with smaller transactions, EIB is empowered to make lump sums available to financial institutions in member countries to be disbursed by them, e.g. the *3i's (Investors in Industry) Group* in the UK. These financial institutions are then able to make sub-loans to relatively small companies, usually for projects which are beneficial to regional development.

The bank's statutes stipulate that loans shall not exceed 250 per cent of its authorised capital.

❑ Examination hints

- Examination questions on this topic usually ask for the assistance that a bank can give to an exporter customer, given certain circumstances.

- Some questions call for information on more specialist areas, e.g. eurobond and foreign bond issues.

Know Your .... Banking Services for the Exporter and Importer

1. Define 'Eurocurrency'.

2. What is meant by 'Eurosterling'?

3. To whom is a letter of introduction addressed? How can it help an exporter?

4. What is an 'average bond'?

5. What is meant by the term 'avalisation'?

6. How might an importer be able to take delivery of goods prior to receipt of the bills of lading?

7. What is 'demurrage'?

8. Distinguish between a Eurobond issue and a foreign bond issue.

9. State two types of transaction for which a Eurocurrency loan might be appropriate.

10. What is the major disadvantage in borrowing in a Eurocurrency?

11. Define a consortium bank.

12. How is a certificate of deposit different from a fixed term deposit?

13. What are the present-day functions of merchant banks?

14. What is the objective of the European Investment Bank?

15. What function does a 'lead' bank perform?

Past Examination Questions

14.1*   One of your customers, Plant Propagations Limited, makes arrangements for a director, A Grafton, to call to see you to discuss an enquiry which the company has had from one of the Arabian Gulf States. The proposal is that your customer should supply a range of plants which will be used to landscape a new hotel, office and shopping arcade complex in the Gulf. The enquiry emanates from the main contractor, a resident company in the Middle Eastern country in question. Your customer does not necessarily need finance.

REQUIRED:
Brief notes showing the help, other than financial, which is available to the customer from yourself and other interested agencies.

(question 9, April 1985)

14.2*   You are taking part in a panel on the subject of banking at a combined meeting of the local Chamber of Commerce and Institute of Export. During the course of the evening the following question is posed and you are invited to answer it:

'What is the role of banks in international trade?'

REQUIRED:
A concise description under four main headings of the role of UK banks in the field of international trade.
Note: Long and detailed descriptions are not required.

(question 8, May 1987)

14.3*   Steponit Ltd sells braking systems to the top end of the motor industry as well as to the aerospace industry and to the ministries of defence of a number of overseas countries. It has a turnover of more than £3½ million per annum.

Your bank has recently won Steponit's account from a major competitor, and you have been asked by your regional office to enter into discussions with the company's Finance Director, Mr Brake-Fast, to ascertain how you can help the company — particularly in the development of its international business.

From preliminary discussions with Mr Brake-Fast you discover that the company always sells on open account terms, since it often receives orders by telex which have to be despatched within 24 hours.

These orders are for amounts of between £1,000 and £50,000 each. Steponit believes that it is selling only to top quality names, and so it has not been its practice to obtain status reports.

The company buys raw materials (which account for about a third of the total cost of the product) from the USA, and pays for them in US dollars. However, all sales are made in sterling on delivered price terms (CIP), though the company's forwarding agents invoice it in US dollars for the freight and forwarding costs of its exports, and it settles these invoices in US dollars. In effect, therefore, the sterling invoices presented to overseas buyers show an FOB price plus the costs of insurance and delivery. In other words, the difference between the CIP and FOB prices is shown separately on the invoice *in sterling*, notwithstanding the fact that the forwarding agents always claim and receive dollars from Steponit in respect of freight and insurance charges. It appears that the forwarding agents also arrange the insurance cover.

Mr Brake-Fast arranges to meet you to discuss the ways (other than the provision of financial assistance) in which your bank can help Steponit Ltd to develop its international business.

REQUIRED:
Brief notes on the matters you would wish to discuss with the company's Finance Director at the forthcoming meeting. Describe any problems which your bank could help to resolve and the solutions you would suggest.

(question 1, May 1989)

14.4* You have been asked by your Senior Manager to take over control of the account of Bright Sparks Plc, which manufactures high value electronic equipment, each unit costing £100,000 upwards.

You arrange to meet the company's Finance Director, Mr Damp-Squibb.

Mr Damp-Squibb is regarded as being somewhat difficult to deal with, and so you are advised by your Senior Manager to prepare some detailed notes covering the suggestions you would make to Mr Damp-Squibb during a forthcoming meeting.

1. The company has been selling throughout the EC, other European countries, the USA and Canada through subsidiary selling agents.

2. New markets are being sought, and an extremely large contract is being discussed with a potential Japanese buyer. If the negotiations with the Japanese buyer are successful, the company will expect to receive an advance payment and to obtain secure methods of payment under which they are prepared to give some 30 days credit after the date of shipment of the product.

3. Because of the value of the product, the company expects, and usually receives, an advance payment of 25% of the value of the product, against which their bankers are expected to issue a bank guarantee/bond.

REQUIRED:
Brief notes you would prepare for the meeting, covering the suggestions you think might be appropriate to the needs of Bright Sparks Plc.

(question 2, May 1989)

14.5 *Scenario*

Special Optics Ltd: see page 83

Question
In view of the effects of the UK recession on Special Optics Ltd, the managing director, Mr Glass, visits you to explore methods by which Special Optics might obtain more export orders.

Mr Glass knows, in general terms, that the main market potential is within the European Community.

REQUIRED:
(a) Advise Mr Glass of the main advisory/information services available from UK banks that would enable Special Optics to develop trade within the EC. *[10]*

(b) List ten services from sources other than UK banks that Special Optics might use to seek export orders within the EC. *[10]*

[Total marks for question - 20]

(question 7, Spring 1993)

Author's note: the EC is now usually referred to as the EU (European Union).

14.6 *Scenario*

Time's Money PLC: see page 237

Question
The construction company in the group, Build in Time Ltd, is to build a complex in Spain.

The project will be funded by the holding company, Time's Money PLC, which will take over and own the complex on completion.

UK based architects and a project management team will work on site.

A subsidiary will be formed in Spain to employ local building workers and purchase building materials.

Some equipment and materials will be exported from UK stocks or purchased elsewhere in Europe, particularly Sweden on an FCA Build in Time's warehouse in Malmo basis.

The senior projects manager, Rodney Trotter, is drawing up business plans, including those for the operations of the local subsidiary.

You visit the group's headquarters in South East London, where Mr Trotter tells you that Build in Time Ltd will not want to keep large balances in Spain but will need to send urgent bank transfers to cover Peseta payments to be made in Spain.

REQUIRED:

(a)   How may Pesetas be remitted urgently to Spain to provide cover for payments?   *[3]*

(b)   How may finance in Pesetas be arranged if required?   *[3]*

(c)   What other services can UK banks arrange to assist in the completion of the project?   *[4]*

(d)   What does the shipping term, or INCOTERM, quoted above mean?   *[3]*

(e)   Is it possible for the subsidiary in Spain to pay for the imports from Sweden on a Peseta basis?

Give reasons for your answer.   *[4]*

(f)   Explain whether the subsidiary in Spain would be able to arrange for documentary credits to be issued if suppliers insist on secure payment terms.   *[3]*

[Total – 20 marks]
(question 8, Spring 1994)

Multiple-Choice Questions: Set 8

Read each question carefully. Choose the *one* answer you think is correct.
Answers are given on page 318.

1.   The type of goods most likely to be the subject of a produce loan are:

A   fruit and vegetables
B   'production-line' goods
C   specialist 'one-off' goods
D   non-perishable raw materials

2.   For a produce loan to a UK importer, the bank takes as security:

A   letter of pledge/hypothecation
B   mortgage
C   assignment of a credit insurance policy
D   letter of introduction

3.   Demurrage is

A   an insurance term for the 'average' contribution
B   marked on a bill of lading to indicate a defective condition of the goods
C   a risk covered by an 'all risks' (ICC 'A') marine insurance policy
D   a charge made by port authorities for uncollected goods

4. Where a bill of lading is lost/delayed a bank can help an importer customer to obtain the goods by issuing:

    A   an indemnity
    B   a retention bond
    C   a cash cover certificate
    D   a reference

5. An average bond is issued by banks to:

    A   cover shortages in bulk cargo
    B   enable goods which are subject to average to be unloaded without payment of the average contribution
    C   enable goods to be unloaded without production of the bill of lading
    D   guarantee payment of a bill of exchange

6. Certificates of deposit are issued mainly by:

    A   the Bank of England
    B   banks
    C   government departments
    D   multi-national corporations

7. Eurocurrency deposits are:

    A   held by banks in one country in the currency of another
    B   held by banks in Europe
    C   bank deposits designated in the common currency of the European Union
    D   bank deposits in dollars

8. A US company wishes to raise sterling funds by selling a bond issue in the UK market. This is a:

    A   foreign bond issue
    B   Eurobond issue
    C   Eurocurrency issue
    D   ECU bond issue

9. A Eurocurrency loan is made available to one borrower by a number of banks. This is a:

    A   Eurobond issue
    B   certificate of deposit
    C   floating rate note
    D   syndicated loan

10. The European Investment Bank

    A   lends funds for development projects within the European Union
    B   is a consortium bank
    C   is the central bank of Europe
    D   maintains the reserves of member states within the European Union

Appendix A
Past Examination Questions: Rates and Calculations

- The questions contained in this Appendix comprise exchange rates questions involving calculations.
- Many of the questions also include aspects from several parts of the examination syllabus.
- Where appropriate, work answers to four decimal places.
- Answers are given in Appendix B.

1.   Sleeptite Plc manufacture bedroom furniture. On 30 March you call to see their Financial Director, Mr Eiderdown, to discuss renewal of their banking facilities. You are given to understand that the company has signed a contract with Norwegian suppliers to purchase sufficient materials to cover its next six months' requirements. The company has agreed to purchase 10,000 loads of timber at £100 a load, and payment will be effected in two equal amounts on 30 June and 30 September.

The rates of exchange for Norwegian kroner on the day of your visit are as follows:

30 March	11.03	11.05
1 month	3.5 ore discount	4.5 ore discount
3 months	11.75 ore discount	12.5 ore discount
6 months	23.5 ore discount	25.5 ore discount

Mr Eiderdown tells you of his pleasure at finding a reliable source of supply, and expresses his satisfaction at having obtained a sterling contract, as opposed to one whereby payment would have to be effected in Norwegian kroner. He believes that his company has benefited because the cost of the timber was originally quoted as 11.1 million Norwegian kroner, whereas in fact the company will only be paying £1m. You discuss this matter fully with your customer and explain to him that you would have been able to arrange forward cover for the company within its existing facilities, without a strain on its resources.

During your meeting, you discuss whether or not there would have been an advantage to the company in arranging to pay Norwegian kroner as opposed to sterling in respect of this contract.

REQUIRED:

(a)   Your calculations, based upon the rates quoted, showing arithmetically:

(i)   the advantage or disadvantage in annual percentage terms to the company if it had arranged to pay the two equal amounts, on 30 June and 30 September, in Norwegian kroner as opposed to sterling.

(ii)   the sterling amount which the company would have paid if it had agreed to pay Norwegian kroner 5,550,000 on 30 June and 30 September respectively, compared with the £1 million which the customer has now agreed. Show the possible saving (or cost) to the customer.

[10]

(b)   A definition and explanation of the obligations which the customer and your bank would have entered into if the customer had arranged to take out forward cover for the two payments described in (a) above.   [5]

(c)   A clear definition of an alternative method [to (b) above] by which Sleeptite Plc might have obtained protection from the exchange risk if the company had agreed to pay Norwegian kroner and had wished to base the exchange rate on 11.10 Norwegian kroner to the pound.   [5]

[Total marks for question - 20]

(question 4, May 1988)

2.   Hardup Ltd exports goods to many overseas markets. The company usually sells on open account terms and in the past has sold its goods for sterling. New markets have been developed recently in Germany, Japan and the United States but the buyers are insisting upon paying in local currency.

Some delays in settlement have occurred and the Financial Director, Mr Scrooge, calls to see you. He complains that the banks must be holding up settlement as he has been informed that all the German, Japanese and US buyers have settled their outstanding invoices 30 days after the date of the invoices. However, funds have been received by means of cheques issued by London banks, expressed in sterling, which have taken about 15 days to be cleared by the bank after presentation by the customer. Moreover, the cheques were received by Hardup Ltd some time after the date of payment indicated by the overseas buyers.

Further, the sterling sums which the company has actually received were much smaller than the sterling equivalent which Mr Scrooge estimated he would receive at the time the goods were invoiced. For example, in respect of export debts of Deutsche Marks 10,000, Yen 1,000,000 and Dollars 5,000 he tells you that, on the date of the invoice a couple of months ago, the rates quoted by the bank were as follows:

	Spot		1 Month		2 Months	
Deutsche Marks	2.9536	2.9749	1.44pf	1.33pfpm	2.74pf	2.59pfpm
Japanese Yen	228.2807	230.3372	1.0600y	0.8600ypm	1.9600y	1.6600ypm
US Dollars	1.8470	1.8635	0.29c	0.26cpm	0.53c	0.48cpm

On the actual dates that the sterling was credit to the company's account (ignoring bank charges) the following spot rates would have been applied by the bank:

	Spot	
Deutsche Marks	2.9807	3.0012
Japanese Yen	230.7125	232.7081
US Dollars	1.8455	1.8615

REQUIRED:

(a)   Explain to Mr Scrooge why the sterling sums expected by the company were not realised.

Indicate any specific risks which the company should have taken into account.

Using the rates and amounts quoted at the invoice and crediting dates, show arithmetically (i) the amount which your customer expected to receive, and (ii) the amount he would have received if currency cheques had been used as a means of settlement and had been sold to the bank on the crediting dates. Show the differences in each case.   [8]

Using the rates and amounts quoted at the invoice and crediting dates, show arithmetically (i) the amount which your customer expected to receive, and (ii) the amount he would have received if currency cheques had been used as a means of settlement and had been sold to the bank on the crediting dates. Show the differences in each case.   [8]

(b)   (i)   List the methods by which your customer could, in future, overcome the problems encountered in (a).   [4]

(ii)   Illustrate your answers by means of the forward rates quoted on the date the invoices were issued.   [5]

(c)   Give details of a method by which Hardup Ltd might overcome the delays in receiving proceeds in the future.   [3]

[Total marks for question - 20]
(question 1, October 1988)

3.   Plastic Products Ltd is a successful small company situated in the English countryside, well away from any seaport or airport. As the company's bankers, you are asked to meet their Managing Director, Mr X Trusion, to discuss importing plastic building materials direct from Finland. This will be the first time that the company has imported their supplies direct, as it normally buys them from large importers in the UK. The order will therefore be for a relatively small amount.

In the course of your discussions you are advised by Mr X Trusion that the price he has negotiated is a *'delivered price to his factory unit in the UK'*. He shows you a pro-forma invoice expressed in Finnish markka and you notice that the price quoted on the invoice is *'ex-works Helsinki'*. He asks you to explain to him what these terms mean and what the implications are of purchasing goods in Finnish markka.

You are advised that the goods will be despatched 30 days after the suppliers receive a bank guarantee or undertaking in their favour. Payment must then be effected within 30 days after the date of despatch of the goods.

On the day of your visit to Plastic Products the rates of exchange for Finnish markka were as follows:

	Spot 7.3410	7.4025
1 Month	0.85p pm	0.25p pm
2 Months	1.45p pm	0.60p pm
3 Months	1.80p pm	0.75p pm

REQUIRED:

(a)   An explanation, in note form, covering the meaning of, and the differences between, the terms of shipment mentioned in the course of your discussion with Mr X Trusion.   [9]

(b)   A brief description of any risks (other than credit risks) which the company will undertake if it confirms the order under discussion in the circumstances described in the question, and the ways in which it can reduce these risks.   [4]

(c)   The exchange rates which your bank would quote to Mr X Trusion in connection with your answer to (b).   [7]

[Total marks for question - 20]
(question 4, May 1989)

4.   One of your customers, Codswallop Ltd, is a fishing and fish-merchanting company. It wishes to buy an additional fishing vessel to add to its small fleet and has ascertained that a suitable vessel can be built to its specifications either in the UK or in the Netherlands. The company would be allowed only two years' credit by the UK shipbuilders, but the Dutch have offered up to five years' credit, providing payment is effected in Dutch guilders. Both shipbuilders would expect a pre-payment of about 20%, for which they would be willing and able to arrange a form of bank undertaking in favour of Codswallop Ltd. The Netherlands shipbuilding yard would also require a bank undertaking in respect of payments due during the whole of the period. The basic prices, and delivery dates, quoted by the two shipyards are broadly comparable.

Current interest rates are:

UK	12½%
The Netherlands	5⅞%

Current exchange rates for sterling/Dutch guilders are as follows:

Spot rate	3.6157
1 year's rate	3.3950

Although Codswallop Ltd is highly profitable, it borrows from the bank for its working capital requirements. It sells many of its fish and related products to the Netherlands and other parts of the EC through its fish-marketing division, but invoices are issued, and payments received, in sterling.

Mr Whiting, the financial director, has made an appointment to see you tomorrow to discuss the relative merits of the two quotations.

REQUIRED:
Brief notes showing the points you would cover in the discussion with Mr Whiting to help him to decide which quotation to accept.   *[20]*

Note:(i)   *Ignore lending considerations and security arrangements.*
(ii)   *Ignore any government or EC grants that may be available to the fishing industry.*
                                                              (question 1, October 1989)

5.   Wreckers Ltd are scrap metal merchants dealing in high value scrap. They have contracted to sell some scrap to buyers in Japan. Delivery is to be made in not more than six lots, with not more than two shipments in any one quarter, commencing some 90 days after 1 January, the date of signing the contract. Payment is to be made within 21 days of the date of shipment in US dollars by secure banking methods against presentation of correct documents.

On 3 January Mr Smashit, the Financial Director, calls to see you to discuss the payment methods for this contract. You are told that the scrap will be purchased from two separate sources, one in the UK and the other in Taiwan. The Japanese buyers have agreed to provide a bank undertaking in Wreckers favour, but the suppliers also insist upon some form of bank undertaking.

The UK suppliers are to be paid in sterling but they are quite prepared to accept an agreed dollar figure, to be converted into sterling, providing the conversion is not worse than the current spot price of 1.5740. The Taiwanese suppliers on the other hand are happy to receive US dollars upon presentation of documents.

You are satisfied from your discussions with Mr Smashit that shipments will be effected in accordance with the terms of the commercial contract.

On 3 January the following exchange rates apply:

Spot	1.5730	1.5740
3 months	1.89 cpm	1.87 cpm
6 months	3.64 cpm	3.61 cpm
9 months	5.66 cpm	5.60 cpm
12 months	7.60 cpm	7.50 cpm

UK interest rates are 14%
US dollar rates are 8⅞%

Cashflow considerations do cause you some concern and, although you are anxious to assist as far as possible your customer, Wreckers Ltd, in protecting their interests, you do not wish to increase their banking facilities to any great extent.

REQUIRED:

(a) Describe the appropriate banking instrument which will give protection to you and your customer without increasing their banking facilities to any great extent. [4]

(b) Give details of specific terms/conditions which you would expect to be included in such an instrument, and in relation to this particular contract. [4]

(c) Detail the method(s) by which your customer could be assured of the sterling value of any proceeds they will receive from this contract, in order to protect their profit margins. [4]

(d) Set out the rates of exchange which would apply if your customer decided to protect the sterling value of any receipts due to them and the UK suppliers. [6]

(e) Describe briefly the method by which Wreckers Ltd might have been able to arrange for a bank undertaking to be given in favour of the two suppliers if the company's cashflow considerations and banking facilities had not been stretched. [2]

Note: Assume that payment dates fall within the quarters in which shipments are effected.
[Total marks for question - 20]
(question 1, May 1990)

6. Skrapit Ltd is a UK sterling-based wholesale scrap merchant that buys ships and oil rigs which have reached the end of their useful working life. It has recently contracted to export 100,000 tonnes of high quality scrap at a price of ECU 135 per tonne to a buyer in the EC. Payment is to be made by means of an irrevocable letter of credit payable at your bank's counters. The drafts are to be drawn at 30 days' sight from the date of shipment, which would be evidenced by the date of a bill of lading. On 1 October you receive, advise and confirm an irrevocable letter of credit from a buyer based in Germany. Part of the terms of the letter of credit are:

- value of the letter of credit ABOUT ECUs 13,500,000;
- shipments to be effected in two lots of 50,000 tonnes, the first in the month of November and the second in the month of December;
- price ECU 135 per tonne CPT Dusseldorf, Germany.

On the same date that you receive and confirm the letter of credit, Mr Pigiron, the Financial Director of Skrapit, calls to see you to discuss the methods by which the company can protect its interests. You note from your foreign exchange dealers that the following rates of exchange apply:

1 October
ECU/£ sterling

Spot	1.3495	1.3554
1 month	0.48p	0.45p
2 month	0.87p	0.83p
3 month	1.20p	1.15p
4 month	1.61p	1.55p

The following interest rates also apply:

£ sterling	15% pa
ECU	11$\frac{9}{16}$%pa

Mr Pigiron advises you that his company has won this contract against fierce competition and its gross margins on the contract depend upon whether the company can sell currency to the bank at a rate not exceeding (worse than) ECUs 1.35 to the pound sterling.

REQUIRED:

(a)   In connection with this particular contract, what essential points should be considered by Skrapit Ltd in respect of presentations under the letter of credit?   *[11]*

(b)   What other risk must the company bear in mind?   *[2]*

(c)   What recommendations would you suggest to Mr Pigiron in respect of (b) above, indicating any advantages to his company in any or all of your recommendations?   *[7]*

[Total marks for question - 20]
(question 1 [amended], October 1990)

7.   Sporting Equipment Plc exports most of its turnover to many parts of the world, selling against irrevocable letters of credit or documentary collections. The company has been borrowing heavily from the bank at 2% over base rate which has remained at 15% for some time.

In a re-organisation the company has just appointed a new Finance Director, Mr Hyjump. On 15 May he calls to see you to discuss a loss of over £3,500 the company has suffered in a foreign exchange transaction arranged by your branch on 28 October last. He implies that the loss was due to incorrect advice on your part, and that any 'close-out' or extension was not the fault of the company and therefore it should be re-imbursed for any loss debited to the company's sterling account.

Investigations show that the company presented three sets of documents to your bank, each with a draft attached drawn payable on 28 April fixed: one draft was expressed in Deutschemarks, one in US dollars and one in ECUs. Of the three sets of documents two were under irrevocable letters of credit and one was a documentary collection. The following were therefore presented to the paying banks/drawees just prior to the due date, with specific remitting instructions.

(i)   A draft for DEM 300,000, drawn on and payable by yourselves as confirming bank.

(ii)   A draft for USD 300,000 drawn on and payable by a Taiwanese bank as issuing bank.

(iii)   A draft for XEU (ECU) 300,000 drawn on and accepted by a French buyer.

The customer received the funds as follows:

(i)   DEM 300,000 on 28 April, the correct due date.

(ii)   USD 300,000 on 2 May, some four days after the proceeds were expected by the customer.

(iii)   XEU (ECU) 300,000 on 12 May, some fourteen days after the customer expected the proceeds.

At the request of the customer, three 6 months fixed forward contracts had been established based upon the rates of exchange shown. No mention was made at that stage that the contracts were in respect of bills of exchange. When the currency was not made available on the due dates, the appropriate contracts were extended for another month *with the agreement of the previous Finance Director*, creating a one month's forward option contract. The spot and forward rates at the close-out date are shown below:

28 October				28 April		
Deutsche marks						
Spot	3.0111	3.0187	LIBOR 9¾%		2.8911	2.9032
5 mth	7.45 pm	7.10 pm	1 mth		1.72 pm	1.62 pm
6 mth	8.75 pm	8.40 pm				
7 mth	9.83 pm	9.38 pm				
US Dollars						
Spot	1.9475	1.9515	LIBOR 10%		1.8718	1.8768
5 mth	5.03 pm	4.96 pm	1 mth		1.10 pm	1.07 pm
6 mth	5.94 pm	5.84 pm				
7 mth	6.73 pm	6.63 pm				
Euro-Currency Units						
Spot	1.4524	1.4574	LIBOR 11.5%		1.4170	1.4232
5 mth	2.41 pm	2.33 pm	1 mth		0.60 pm	0.57 pm
6 mth	2.82 pm	2.74 pm				
7 mth	3.16 pm	3.06 pm				

REQUIRED:

(a)   Explain briefly the reason(s) why Sporting Equipment did not receive all the funds when expected, indicating whether you would accept the claim from your customer that the bank was responsible for the foreign exchange loss.   [5]

(b)   Explain any method by which the company could have made certain that it received not less than the sterling amount of the bills/drafts based upon the spot rates ruling on 28 October.   [3]

(c)   Assuming that on the date of the close-out you agreed to extend the contracts (if/where appropriate), show arithmetically the proceeds which the company received for each of the drafts: (i) DEM, (ii) USD and (iii) XEU above. Indicate the final loss, if any, which the company had to bear, giving an explanation as to why this situation arose.   [12]

[Total marks for question - 20]
(question 1, May 1991)

8.   Your customers, Financial Wizards Ltd, are in the investment business and have asked you to help them with a temporary cash-flow shortfall. They have lent £1,000,000 to a leisure complex and are receiving interest at $13^7/_{16}$% pa. As they need funds to tide them over until the loan falls due for repayment in thirty days time, they ask if you can lend them foreign currency to cover their current sterling requirements – until the leisure company settles in 30 days' time. They believe that this suggestion will be advantageous, but they do not wish to be exposed to foreign exchange risks. You are satisfied with the quality of the asset held by the company as well as the standing of your customer.

The current rates for the ECU, US dollars, D Marks and Swiss Francs applying in the market are, respectively, as follows:

Interest/Lending Rates		Spot Rates	One month Forward Rates/Margins
XEU	$10^7/_{16}$%	1.4066	.43c pm
USD	$7^{15}/_{16}$%	1.9475	.93c pm
DEM	$9^5/_{16}$%	2.8909	1.06pf pm
CHF	$8^3/_4$%	2.4657	.95c pm

REQUIRED:

(a)   The calculations your bank would make in each currency to ascertain whether the bank might assist Financial Wizards Ltd in the way suggested by them.   [16]

(b)   If the bank did assist, which currency (of those above) would be the most appropriate? Would there be any advantage/profit for the customer and, if so, how much in percentage terms?

[2]

(c)   Would your answer to (b) be different, if the customer had an income in foreign currency?   [2]

Note: Base your calculations on a 360 day year and ignore any charges or commissions.

[Total marks for question—20]
(question 1, October 1991)

9. Your customer, Primary Products Plc, trades in wholesale grain. On 1 May it contracts to buy 600 tons of long-grain rice from a supplier in the USA at a price of USD 600 per ton FOB Savannah, payment and shipment to be made on 1 August. The goods are re-sold on 1 June to buyers based in the Netherlands at a price of NLG 1500 per ton, CIF Rotterdam, this contract calling for payment to be made to Primary Products on 1 August. On 1 June Primary Products made a payment to the shipping company in respect of the freight at the rate of USD 40 per ton.

    As the payment terms under both contracts were that funds were to be paid on the agreed shipment date, Mr Oats, Primary Products' financial director, covered these transactions forward *immediately the commercial contracts were agreed*, i.e. on 1 May and 1 June respectively.

    On 1 August, the shipment date, Primary Products Plc also paid the insurance premium, for the CIF price plus 10% at a rate of 50 pence per cent. The insurance premium was based upon the sterling equivalent of the NLG CIF price.

    The following rates applied:

	USD		NLG		USD		NLG	
spot	1.7320	1.7410	3.3327	3.3483	1.6165	1.6255	3.3018	3.3172
1 mth	0.73	0.71pm	0.50	0.30pm	0.74	0.70pm	0.70	0.50pm
2 mth	1.35	1.15pm	1.05	0.95pm	1.42	1.37pm	1.18	0.93pm
3 mth	2.30	1.95pm	1.65	1.30pm	2.02	1.96pm	1.60	1.32pm

    REQUIRED:
    Your calculations showing the gross sterling proceeds on these contracts. [13]

    A description of any other method which Primary Products Plc could have employed with would have given some certainty as to the minimum amount of sterling the company would receive. [7]

    Note: for the purposes of your calculations assume that all the payments are effected on the correct dates.

    [Total marks for question - 20 marks]
    (question 1, May 1992)

10. Your bank is based in London and on 10 May you receive, and are asked to confirm, an irrevocable letter of credit on behalf of one of your German correspondent banks. The beneficiary is one of your own valued customers, Flash Harry Ltd. The main terms of the credit are as follows:

In favour of:	Flash Harry Ltd
For account of:	Deutsche Klauslamphaus
Expiring:	15 October 1992 in London
Amount:	About DEM 2,850,000 (two million eight hundred and fifty thousand deutsche marks)
Covering:	About 100,000 cases of 16 watt halogen bulbs to be shipped in two approximately equal instalments, one during the first half of July and one during the second half of September 1992
Price:	DEM 28.50 per case CIF Hamburg (liner terms)
Drawings:	To be made available against presentation of drafts drawn at sight on yourselves and accompanied by documents, showing Flash Harry Ltd as shippers, evidencing shipments from Tokyo to a European port

    On 15 May you confirm the letter of credit and at the same time Flash Harry asks you to arrange normal forward cover for the two instalments of DEM 1,425,000 each. On the same day you are told by Flash Harry that the goods are to be supplied by a Japanese manufacturer, Nippon Nightlights, against a firm contract for deliveries during early July and late September 1992. Payment to Nippon Nightlights is to be effected by direct telegraphic transfer/SWIFT payment orders within ten days of the delivery of the goods to Flash Harry's shipping agents in Tokyo. The price to be paid per case is JPY 2,000 FCA Tokyo. You are asked to cover these payments forward on 15 May.

Delivery will be as shown above. Flash Harry's agents have booked space on liner vessels scheduled to be loading in Tokyo on 10 July and 20 September.

The agents WILL obtain the bills of lading and other documents within five days of loading and these will be sent by courier to London, enabling presentation under the credit to be made ten days after the loading dates.

The rates for deutsche marks and yen on 15 May are:

	DEM		JPY	
Spot	2.8381	2.8528	229.93	231.48
1 mth	0.37	0.27 pm	0.70	0.60 pm
2 mth	0.85	0.65 pm	0.89	0.79 pm
3 mth	1.15	0.90 pm	2.60	2.35 pm
4 mth	1.40	1.10 pm	3.45	3.15 pm
5 mth	1.70	1.35 pm	4.30	4.00 pm

The rates for deutsche marks and yen on 20 July are:

	DEM		JPY	
Spot	2.8321	2.8483	228.23	229.93

Shipments were effected on 10 July and 20 September, as agreed, and the documents presented under the credit (as indicated above) and the SWIFT payments made on 20 July and 30 September.

Immediately upon receiving delivery of the first shipment, the Tokyo agent advised Flash Harry that the number of cases received from the suppliers was only 40,000.

The issuing bank was contacted immediately this was known and the buyer/applicant, Deutsche Klauslamphaus, agreed to accept documents showing a shipment of 40,000 cases only. The outstanding balance was to be ignored, meaning that the shipment of the shortfall of 10,000 cases was to be cancelled. The second shipment contained the full 50,000 cases.

REQUIRED:

(a)   Your calculations showing the sterling amounts passing through Flash Harry's account.   *[15]*

(b)   Explain briefly why it was necessary to seek the agreement of the German buyer to the cancellation of part of the shipment, ie the 10,000 missing cases.   *[5]*

NB: Assume that the bank effected payment for each presentation on the same dates that the documents were presented to them, ie the receipts and payments took place on 20 July and 30 September respectively.

[Total marks for question - 20]
(question 1, Autumn 1992)

11.   *Scenario*

EURO MULTINATIONAL CO LTD

Euro Multinational Co Ltd is the UK subsidiary of a US corporation, Worldwide Machinery Inc. Euro Multinational has a sterling account with your bank and is an important customer.

You handle regular urgent transfers in US dollars to the parent company in settlement of goods imported. Euro Multinational issues such instructions after notification of the arrival of the goods in the UK.

Up until now, the company has used spot rates, but the new finance director, Mr Money, is keen to explore other ways of fixing exchange rates.

The following market report with closing rates appeared in the *Financial Times* on Tuesday 26 January 1993:

'The dollar fell nearly two pfennigs against the D-Mark in European trading yesterday. After closing in London at DM 1.5900 on Friday night the US currency tumbled to a low of DM 1.5690 before closing at DM 1.5725.

Sterling consolidated against the D-Mark following last week's sharp fall. It closed at DM 2.4525, up $1^{1}/_{4}$ pfennigs on the day, helped by a report from the CBI [Confederation of British Industry] on business confidence.'

Pount spot – forward against the pound

	Close		
US dollars	1.5590 – 1.5600		
One month	0.56 – 0.54 cpm	4.23% pa	
Three months	1.46 – 1.43 cpm	3.71% pa	

Eurocurrency interest rates

	One month	*Three months*
Sterling	$7^{7}/_{16} - 7^{5}/_{16}$	$7^{1}/_{16} - 6^{15}/_{16}$
US dollars	$3^{3}/_{16} - 3^{1}/_{16}$	$3^{5}/_{16} - 3^{3}/_{16}$

Question

The finance director of Euro Multinational Co Ltd, Mr Money, visits you on 26 January to obtain information based on the FT market report (above).

REQUIRED:

(a)   An indication of the cost in sterling of remitting US$ 250,000 value in two working days' time by SWIFT transfer to the US parent company.

Calculate the cost to two places of decimals using the rates given in the FT market report.   *[2]*

(b)   Mr Money asks approximately how many US$ Euro Multinational could have remitted to its parent company if it had received DM 2,000,000 and converted it to US$ on 25 January.

Make your calculations using the closing rate from the FT report.   *[2]*

(c)   Mr Money asks what details are agreed in a forward exchange contract and what the conditions of such a contract are.

List the information he requires.   *[10]*

(d)   The company has a payment of US$ 2,000,000 to make to its parent company in three months' time. Mr Money requests an approximate cost of covering the transaction forward.

Calculate the cost in sterling to two places of decimals using the rates given in the FT market report.   *[2]*

(e)   Mr Money wants to know what is meant by '4.23% pa' quoted in the FT market report.

Give an explanation and show how the figure is calculated.   *[4]*

Note:

For the purposes of this question one year should be expressed as 360 days and each month as 30 days. Ignore any bank charges or commissions.

[Total marks for question - 20]
(question 1, Spring 1993)

12.   *Scenario*

NUTS ABOUT FOOD LTD

Nuts About Food Ltd is an import/export company run by Colonel K P Brazil and his wife, Hazel.

The Brazils trade as principals with approximately 200 shipments of nuts and dried fruit each year. The average value of each shipment is US$ 50,000.

Nuts About Food is a longstanding customer of your bank and has an overdraft facility of £100,000 (maximum) available in sterling and/or equivalent in US$.

The company enjoys an excellent reputation for quality produce and its business is demanding but steady.

The core of the business is with buyers who have maintained a good payment record over a number of years.

Question

At the end of October 1993, Nuts About Food Ltd signed a contract to sell produce to a new customer in the Republic of Ireland on sight irrevocable documentary credit terms.

The contract was for US$ 150,000 with three shipments, value US$ 50,000 each, required in December 1993, January 1994 and February 1994. (These facts were reflected in the letter of credit.)

On 29 November 1993 Colonel Brazil decided to cover the whole of the exchange risk with one forward exchange contract on an option three months' basis. The rates were:

	US$	
Spot (1 Dec)	1.5105 – 1.5115	
One Month Forward	0.37 –	0.35 cpm
Two Months Forward	0.73 –	0.71 cpm
Three Months Forward	1.04 –	1.01 cpm

The first two presentations under the letter of credit were made correctly. However, on 25 February Colonel Brazil called to see you to say that the final shipment was delayed and that he wished to extend the forward contract to cover delivery in April.

On 25 February the rates were:

	US$	
Spot (1 Mar)	1.4825 – 1.4835	
One Month Forward	0.35 –	0.33 cpm
Two Months Forward	0.69 –	0.67 cpm
Three Months Forward	0.99 –	0.96 cpm

REQUIRED:

(a)   What forward rate was agreed on 29 November?   *[2]*

(b)   (i)   Calculate as at 29 November the anticipated income in sterling from the letter of credit.

[3]

(ii)   Assuming that the final presentation was made correctly on 25 April, what would the accounting entries passed over the company's accounts have been in respect of:

–   the extension of the contract;

–   the utilisation of the extended portion of the contract on 25 April?   *[9]*

Notes:

Calculations should be to two places of decimals.

For the purposes of this question, the advising bank's charges are for the beneficiary's account and should be levied as follows:

advising fee – 0.125%

payment commission – 0.10%, payable on each presentation of documents

(c)   In accordance with Uniform Customs and Practice:

(i)   What was the position on 25 February regarding the remaining presentation under the documentary credit?   [3]

(ii)   If the first presentation had been delayed until January, what would have been the position regarding the second and third presentations under the documentary credit?   [3]

[Total marks for question - 20]

(question 2, Spring 1994)

Appendix B
Answers to Questions contained in Appendix A

- Where appropriate, answers have been calculated to four decimal places.
- See page 24 for the SWIFT nomenclatures for currencies.

1. (a) (i) *30 June payment*

$$\frac{0.1175 \times 4}{11.1475^*} \times 100 = 4.22\% \text{ p.a.}$$

* 11.03 spot rate + 0.1175 three-month forward discount.

30 September payment

$$\frac{0.2350 \times 2}{11.2650^{**}} \times 100 = 4.17\% \text{ p.a.}$$

** 11.03 spot rate + 0.2350 six-month forward discount.

Both of these represent an advantage to an importer, because the forward rate is cheaper than the spot rate.

(ii) *30 June*
N.Kr. 5 550 000 @ 11.1475   = £497 869.47

30 September
N.Kr. 5 550 000 @ 11.2650   = <u>£492 676.43</u>
                                           <u>£990 545.90</u>

Therefore, to pay N.Kr. (using fixed forward contracts) is cheaper by £9 454.10 than paying in sterling.

(b) Definition of a forward contract (see lesson 1), and obligations.

(c) Definition of a currency option (see lesson 2).

2. (a) •   The reason for the difference between the sterling amounts expected and actually received is the change in exchange rates from the invoice date to the date the proceeds were received on the date of settlement/crediting. Thus:

	Invoice date	*Settlement/crediting date*
DM	2.9749	3.0012
Yen	230.3372	232.7081
US$	1.8635	1.8615

•   Under a commercial contract in which the Hardup Ltd invoices in currency amounts, the exchange risk is the seller's from the moment the contract is signed. This risk should have been covered.

•   The method of payment and transfer of the currency does not appear to have been agreed in the commercial contract.

•   Using the rates above, the sterling amounts received by Hardup (ignoring bank charges) would have been:

	Invoice date	*Settlement/crediting date*
DM 10,000 =	£3,361.46	£3,332.00
• extra cost to Hardup Ltd =		£29.46
Yen 1,000,000 =	£4,341.46	£4,297.23
• extra cost to Hardup Ltd =		£44.23
US$ 5,000 =	£2,683.12	£2,686.01
• benefit to Hardup Ltd =		£2.89

(b) (i) *Exchange risk*
•   forward exchange contract
•   currency option
•   currency borrowing
•   the use of foreign currency bank accounts (particularly if Hardup Ltd has payments to make in the currencies concerned)

Note that the exchange risk commences on the date the commercial contract is signed, and not from the date of the invoice.

Other risks
•   the method of payment and transfer of the currency needs to be agreed
•   the use of credit insurance should be considered

(ii) Hardup Ltd could have entered into two month forward contracts, option month two. The rates used would have been:

DM	2.9749	spot rate
	0.0133	loss one* month premium
	2.9616	

Yen	230.3372	spot rate
	0.8600	less one* month premium
	229.4772	

US$	1.8635	spot rate
	0.0026	less one* month premium
	1.8609	

*   As all of the currencies are at a premium, and the bank is buying, the one month premium is deducted to calculate the forward rate.

(c) The buyers should be asked to instruct their bankers to remit the currency amounts direct to Hardup Ltd's bank by means of a telegraphic/cable transfer (or priority SWIFT transfer). A clause to this effect should be inserted in the commercial contract and also stated on the commercial invoice.

3.   (a) The two Incoterms quoted are:

EXW — ex-works Helsinki
CIP   — carriage and insurance paid to Plastic Products Ltd's warehouse in ... named place

See pages 85 to 93 for a list of the main responsibilities of the seller and buyer under these two Incoterms.

(b) The major risk, apart from the credit risk, is an *exchange risk:*

- The Finnish markka may fluctuate in value against sterling between the date of placing the order and making payment.

- Plastic Products Ltd should enter into a forward exchange contract for the bank to sell a specified quantity of Finnish markka at an agreed rate (fixed at the time of entering into the forward contract) for delivery on or between two specified dates.

- The most appropriate forward exchange contract for Plastic Products Ltd would be a three month forward contract, option month three entered into today. This will allow time for the bank guarantee or undertaking to be established in favour of the suppliers.

- A currency option is a possible alternative to a forward contract, but as the order is for a relatively small amount, it is unlikely to be appropriate.

Other risks to be considered are:

- The quality of the goods — Plastic Products Ltd should call for an inspection certificate (as a letter of credit is likely to be issued in favour of the suppliers, this should be one of the documents specified on the credit).

- The goods must be insured — under EXW this is the responsibility of the buyer; under CIP, the responsibility of the seller.

(c) Three month forward contract, option month three:

end of month two	*end of month three*
7.3410 spot selling rate	7.3410 spot selling rate
0.0145 two months premium	0.0180 three months premium
7.3265	7.3230

As the bank is selling, the bank will quote the lower rate of 7.3230.

Note that, by arranging the above forward contract, there is a time allowance to enable the bank guarantee or undertaking to be issued. The earliest that Plastic Products Ltd will have to pay is at the beginning of month three; the latest, towards the end of month three.

4.　　• The choices for Codswallop Ltd are:
　　　　— to buy from a UK shipyard on two years' credit
　　　　— to buy from a Dutch shipyard on five years' credit, with payment to be made in Dutch guilders

　　• Considerations must include:
　　　　— interest rate differentials (the company borrows from its bank)
　　　　— cashflow position of the company
　　　　— working capital requirements
　　　　— exchange risk if the vessel is purchased from the Netherlands

　　• Can the company sell its fish, etc priced in guilders? If so, part of the exchange risk can be relieved. Furthermore, borrowing in guilders is cheaper than in sterling: 5⅞%, plus margin, compared with 12½%, plus margin — a saving of 6⅝%.

　　• As guilders are at a premium, the company could take the benefit of this by generating guilder income (which is covered forward), and continuing to borrow in sterling. Forward exchange cover for 12 months, expressed as a percentage, is:

$$\frac{0.2207}{3.3950} \times \frac{100}{1} = 6.5007\% \text{ pa}$$

　　As Codswallop Ltd is receiving currency, this represents a benefit which must be deducted from the interest rate differential:

6.6250%	differential*
6.5007%	less forward cover
0.1243%	benefit of borrowing guilders

　　* Assumes the lending margin is the same for a guilder loan as for a sterling loan.

　　• The company should consider:
　　　　— if interest rates will fluctuate for the periods involved
　　　　— if fixed rate loans can be obtained

　　• The advance payment guarantee should be issued by a first-class British or Dutch bank (depending on which contract is signed).

　　• The 20% advance payment has to be made and this will utilise a part of the company's banking facilities. If the Dutch vessel is to be bought, the advance payment will be in guilders, so giving an exchange risk.

　　• The Dutch shipbuilders also require a bank guarantee, such as a stage payment guarantee for the five years; an alternative might be a standby letter of credit.

5.　(a)　• transferable letter of credit
　　　　— confirmed and irrevocable
　　　　— transferable in whole or in part
　　　　— issued in accordance with Uniform Customs and Practice for Documentary Credits

　　(b)　• documents to be issued in neutral names
　　　　• shipments to be from European or far Eastern ports to Japan
　　　　• partial shipments and partial drawings to be permitted
　　　　• documents to be presented within 21 days of shipment
　　　　• discrepant documents (supported by banker's indemnities) will not be accepted
　　　　• bank drafts to be drawn at sight in US dollars on the confirming bank (ourselves), with negotiation and payment at our counters in the UK

(c) • Currency borrowing of US dollars to cover the estimated gross profit of Wreckers Ltd. This will be especially advantageous if Wreckers Ltd are borrowing in the UK as the US dollar rate is 8⅞% (plus lending margin) compared with a UK rate of 14% (plus lending margin). The UK bank will buy the dollars at the current spot buying rate of 1.5740.

• Enter into a series of forward option contracts for the bank to buy US dollars. The amount will be for the estimated gross profit of Wreckers Ltd plus the amount due to the UK suppliers. The most likely contracts will be:
— six months forward, options months 4–6
— nine months forward, option months 7–9
— twelve months forward, option months 10–12

• Enter into a series of currency options ('American' options) at strike prices of 1.5740 (spot buying price), or at forward prices.

(d) • six months forward, option months 4–6:

US$	1.5740	spot buying rate
	0.0187	less three* months' premium
	1.5553	

• nine months forward, option months 7–9

US$	1.5740	spot buying rate
	0.0361	less six* months' premium
	1.5379	

• twelve months forward, option months 10–12:

US$	1.5740	spot buying rate
	0.0560	less nine* months' premium
	1.5180	

* As the currency is at a premium and the bank is buying, the rate used will be that at the beginning of the option period.

(e) Back-to-back letters of credit: our bank, as issuers of the letters of credit in favour of the suppliers, would have to ensure that these letters of credit were in line with the original letter of credit in favour of Wreckers Ltd.

6. (a) • Skrapit Ltd must be sure that it will be able to supply the goods and make the shipments during November and December.

• The company must understand the Incoterm CPT: either the company's own transport department or a freight forwarder must arrange dispatch of the goods in accordance with the terms of the credit, and produce the correct documentation.

• The company will need to carry out export customs formalities.

• The company will need to arrange and pay for the contract of carriage to Dusseldorf (the buyer is responsible for all risks of loss of or damage to the goods once they have been delivered to the carrier).

• Documents must be presented strictly in accordance with the terms of the credit — if they are not, payment will be delayed.

- The value of the credit is *about ECUs 13,500,000*: under Article 39 of UCP, this allows for a difference of ±5%, ie between 47,500 and 52,500 tonnes. As the price is ECU 135 per tonne, this makes the total value of shipments between ECUs 12,825,000 and 14,175,000.

- In accordance with Article 41, the company will need to comply with the terms of the letter of credit for the first shipment in order for the credit to be available for the second shipment.

(b) Exchange risk. Although the ECU is a basket of currencies, its value may fall in terms of sterling from the date the commercial contract is signed until the bill of exchange is paid.

(c) The customer can cover the exchange risk by one of the following methods:
— forward exchange contract
— currency option
— currency borrowing

Forward exchange contract
On 1 October the company can enter into two forward option contracts:

November shipment (payment to be received not later than end of December)
Bank to buy ECUs three months' forward, option month 3 at a rate of:

1.3554	spot rate
0.0083	less 2 month premium
1.3471	(a higher rate than 3 months' forward)

December shipment (payment to be received not later than end of January)
Bank to buy ECUs four months' forward, option month 4 at a rate of:

1.3554	spot rate
0.0115	less 3 month premium
1.3439	(a higher rate than 4 months' forward)

Currency option
Skrapit Ltd can request the bank to arrange a currency option allowing the customer to deliver the currency when it becomes available in December and January. The premium charged on the currency option will depend on the rate at which the customer asks the bank to cover; this may be close to the forward rates quoted above.

Currency borrowing
Here the company can borrow ECUs and convert them into sterling at the bank's spot buying rate of 1.3554. This is above the rate of 1.35 quoted by the financial director: however, borrowing will be based on a rate of 11%₁₆% compared with sterling rates of 15% (to both rates will be added the borrowing margin appropriate to Skrapit Ltd).

Conclusion
Both forward exchange contracts and currency options will give a better exchange rate than that mentioned by Mr Pigiron. Currency borrowing gives a worse rate but offers interest rate benefits.

7.   (a)   • The proceeds of the Deutschemark bill were paid on the due date.

   • The proceeds of the other two bills were received later because they were both payable outside the UK.

   • Allowance has to be made for 'transit time', ie the time it takes to remit the proceeds and for cleared funds to be received in the UK.

- The bank entered into three fixed forward contracts to buy currency. As the currency had not been received for the USD and XEU (ECU) contracts on the delivery date, the bank had to close out the contracts and extend them for a further month, on an option basis. Closing out a contract can result in either a gain or a loss for the customer.

- As the bank had no knowledge of the bills of exchange at the time the forward contracts were entered into, it could not advise the customer. Thus the bank is not liable for any loss incurred.

(b) • The company should have entered into currency borrowing on 28 October: this will reduce a part of their sterling borrowing.

- The bank would have arranged currency loans for the amounts of the bills of exchange: the borrowing would then have been bought back immediately at spot rates of DEM 3.0187, USD 1.9515, and XEU 1.4574.

- Sporting equipment would now have part of its borrowing based on the LIBOR rates of $9\frac{3}{4}\%$, 10%, 11.5% (all plus a margin of approximately 2%). This represents a considerable interest saving over sterling rates of 15% + 2% = 17%.

(c) (i) *DEM*
Bank to buy DEM 300,000 six months' fixed forward:

3.0187	spot rate (28 October)
0.0840	six month premium
2.9347	

No close out and extension required, so sterling proceeds of DEM 300,000 ÷ 2.9347 = £102,225.09 received on 28 April.

(ii) *USD*
Bank to buy USD 300,000 six months' fixed forward:

1.9515	spot rate (28 October)
0.0584	six month premium
1.8931	

Credit the customer with USD 300,000 at 1.8931	= £158,470.23
Debit the customer with USD 300,000 at 1.8718 (ie spot selling price)	= £160,273.53
Net debit to customer	= (£ 1,803.30)

The contract is now extended on a one-month option basis at 1.8718
(close-out rate used instead of the one month fixed forward rate).
Credit to customer when proceeds received:
USD 300,000 at 1.8718   = £160,273.53

(iii) *XEU (ECU)*
Bank to buy XEU 300,000 six months' fixed forward:

1.4574	spot rate (28 October)
0.0274	six month premium
1.4300	

Credit the customer with XEU 300,000 at 1.4300	= £209,790.20
Debit the customer with XEU 300,000 at 1.4170 (ie spot selling price)	= £211,714.89
Net debit to customer	= (£ 1,924.69)

The contract is now extended on a one-month option basis at 1.4170
(close-out rate).
Credit to customer when proceeds received:
XEU 300,000 at 1.4170   = £211,714.89

Summary

Comparison of proceeds received:

	Fixed forward contracts	*Fixed forward contracts, plus extension*	
	£	£	
DEM	102,225.09	102,225.09	no extension
USD	158,470.23	160,273.53	extended
XEU	<u>209,790.20</u>	<u>211,714.89</u>	extended
	470,485.52	474,213.51	

Less cost of close-out:

USD	–	(1,803.30)
XEU	<u>–</u>	<u>(1,924.69)</u>
	470,485.52	470,485.52

Because sterling has fallen against each currency the cost of the close-out has been eliminated. The company would, however, have incurred higher interest charges, but this is not the responsibility of the bank.

8. (a)   The cost of forward cover expressed as a percentage is calculated as follows:

$$\frac{\text{premium} \times 12^*}{\text{forward rate}} \quad \times \quad \frac{100}{1}$$

* number required to raise the period of forward cover to one year in this question.

The percentages are calculated as follows:

XEU $\quad \dfrac{0.0043 \times 12}{1.4066 - 0.0043} \quad \times \quad \dfrac{100}{1} \quad = 3.6797\% \text{ pa}$

USD $\quad \dfrac{0.0093 \times 12}{1.9475 - 0.0093} \quad \times \quad \dfrac{100}{1} \quad = 5.7579\% \text{ pa}$

DEM $\quad \dfrac{0.0106 \times 12}{2.8909 - 0.0106} \quad \times \quad \dfrac{100}{1} \quad = 4.4162\% \text{ pa}$

CHF $\quad \dfrac{0.0095 \times 12}{2.4657 - 0.0095} \quad \times \quad \dfrac{100}{1} \quad = 4.6413\% \text{ pa}$

The effective cost of borrowing the currencies with forward cover is:

	XEU	*USD*	*DEM*	*CHF*
actual rate	10.4375%	7.9375%	9.3125%	8.7500%
add forward cover	<u>3.6797%</u>	<u>5.7579%</u>	<u>4.4162%</u>	<u>4.6413%</u>
	14.1172%	13.6954%	13.7287%	13.3913%

Note: As the customers are borrowing currencies at a premium, the forward cover is a cost to them and is added to the actual interest/lending rates.

(b) As UK interest rates are 13.4375%, there is an advantage to the company of borrowing in Swiss francs (CHF). The benefit is:

UK interest rate	13.4375%
Effective cost of CHF	13.3913%
Benefit to customer	0.0462%

(c) If the company had income in any of the stated currencies, the benefits of borrowing in currency, instead of in sterling, increase. The most advantageous currency is USD where the benefit will be:

UK interest rate	13.4375%
US interest rate	7.9375%
Benefit to customer**	5.5000%

** The benefit to the customer is restricted to the amount of income in the particular currency during the next 30 days.

9. (a) (i) On 1 May the bank enters into a forward contract:
to sell USD 360 000 (600 tons @ USD 600 per ton)
three months' fixed forward at

1.7320
230 c.pm
1.7090

(ii) On 1 June the bank enters into a forward contract:
to buy NLG 900 000 (600 tons @ NLG 1500 per ton)
two months' fixed forward at

3.3172
093 c.pm
3.3079

Transactions are as follows: £

1 Jun.	Freight payment USD 24 000 (600 tons @ USD 40 per ton)	
	at spot rate of 1.6165	14 846.89 DR
1 Aug.	USD 360 000 @ 1.7090 (see above)	210,649.50 DR
1 Aug.	NLG 900 000 @ 3.3079 (see above)	272 075.93 CR
1 Aug.	Insurance @ 50p per cent on £272 075.93 + 10%	1,496.42 DR
	Sterling proceeds	45 083.12 CR

(b) Primary Products could use a currency option as an alternative to a forward exchange contract. (Definition of a currency option - see Lesson 2).

10. (a) On 15 May forward contracts will be arranged in respect of the following:

- second half of July (delivery of currency on 20 July)

  - receipt of DEM 1,425,000

  - payment of JPY 100,000,000 (100,000 cases x JPY 2,000 in two instalments)

- second half of September (delivery of currency on 30 September)

  - receipt of DEM 1,425,000

  - payment of JPY 100,000,000 (see above)

Forward contracts will be:

- bank to buy DEM

  - three months forward option month 3:
    rate at beginning of option period is 2.8528 – 0.0065 pm   = 2.8463
    rate at end of option period is 2.8528 – 0.0090 pm   = 2.8438

    As the bank is buying, it will use the higher rate of 2.8463.

  - five months forward, option month 5:
    rate at beginning of option period is 2.8528 – 0.0110 pm   = 2.8418
    rate at end of option period is 2.8528 – 0.0135 pm   = 2.8393

    As the bank is buying, it will use the higher rate of 2.8418.

- bank to sell JPY

  - three months forward, option month 3:
    rate at beginning of option period is 229.93 – 0.89   = 229.04
    rate at end of option period is 229.93 – 2.60   = 227.33

    As the bank is selling, it will use the lower rate of 227.33.

  - five months forward, option month 5:
    rate at beginning of option period is 229.93 – 3.45   = 226.48
    rate at end of option period is 229.93 – 4.30   = 225.63

    As the bank is selling, it will use the lower rate of 225.63.

Proceeds will be:

- 20 July
  DEM 1,425,000 @ 2.8463   = £500,649.96 CR
  JPY 100,000,000 @ 227.33   = £439,889.14 DR
  Close-out in respect of 10,000 cases not shipped:
  DEM 285,000 @ 2.8321 (bank's spot selling rate)   = £100,632.03 DR
  JPY 20,000,000 @ 229.93 (bank's spot buying rate)   = £ 86,982.99 CR

- 30 September
  DEM 1,425,000 @ 2.8418   = £501,442.74 CR
  JPY 100,000,000 @ 225.63   = £443,203.47 DR
  NET CREDIT   £105,351.05 CR

(b)
- The word 'about' in respect of the amount of the credit and the number of cases to be shipped allow a difference not to exceed 10% more or 10% less (Article 39 of UCP). As the first shipment is expected to be 50,000 cases, a shortfall of 10,000 is 20%.

- Article 41 of UCP states that "if drawings and/or shipments by instalments within given periods are stipulated in the credit and any instalment is not drawn and/or shipped within the period allowed for that instalment, the credit ceases to be available for that and any subsequent instalments, unless otherwise stipulated in the credit."

- As a result of these points, the credit became invalid and it was necessary to seek the agreement of the German buyer to the cancellation of part of the shipment.

11. (a) Bank to sell USD 250,000 @ 1.5590 (spot rate)   = £160,359.20

(b) Using the cross rate of DEM 1.5725:
DEM 2,000,000 @ 1.5725   = USD 1,271,860

(c)
- Details
  - date of contract
  - name of customer
  - currency being bought or sold
  - amount of currency being bought or sold

     – exchange rate (agreed at time contract established)

     – date currency is to be exchanged

       either on a fixed date

       or between two agreed future dates (at the customer's option)

- Conditions
  - a firm and binding contract between bank and customer
  - confirmation signed by the customer in accordance with mandate
  - one contract can be used to cover a number of separate commercial transactions
  - customer to give instructions two working days before utilisation
  - any unused balance left on the contract at maturity must be

    either closed out

    or extended

    which may result in a profit or loss to the customer
  - payments in sterling and currency to be made at maturity of contract
  - some banks write a facility limit of between 10% and 20% of the amount of the contract to the customer's account

(d) Bank to sell USD 2,000,000 in three months' time at a rate of

$$
\begin{array}{ll}
1.5590 & \text{spot rate} \\
\underline{146} & \text{pm} \\
1.5444 &
\end{array}
$$

USD 2,000,000 ÷ 1.5444   = £1,295,001.20

(e)
- '4.23% pa' is the one month's forward cover expressed as a percentage per annum.
- It is the cost or benefit against spot rate and is, in effect, the difference between interest rates in the US and UK.
- It is calculated by the formula:

$$\frac{\text{premium or discount} \times \text{number required to raise period of forward cover to one year}}{\text{forward rate}} \times \frac{100}{1}$$

bank selling:

$$\frac{0.0056 \times 12}{1.5534} \times \frac{100}{1} = 4.32 \quad \left.\begin{array}{l} \\ \\ \\ \\ \\ \\ \\ \\ \end{array}\right\}$$

bank buying:

$$\frac{0.0054 \times 12}{1.5546} \times \frac{100}{1} = 4.17$$

approximately 4.24%

11. (a) Bank to buy USD 150,000 three months' forward option at 1.5115:

           rate at beginning of option period is 1.5115

           rate at end of option period is 1.5115 – 1.01 c pm   = 1.5014

           As the bank is buying, it will use the higher rate of <u>1.5115</u>.

(b) (i)

USD 150,000 @ 1.5115 (see above)	= £99,239.17 CR
Advising bank fee £99,239 x 0.125%	= £ 124.05 DR
Payment commission £99,239 x 0.10%	= £ 99.24 DR
Net anticipated income	= £99,015.88 CR

(ii)   *Original option contract:*

USD 50,000 @ 1.5115   = £33,079.72 CR

Close-out on 1 March:

USD 50,000 @ 1.4825   = £ <u>33,726.81</u> DR

Net debit on extension of contract   = £   <u>647.09</u> DR

Extension of contract:

The contract is extended for two months on an option month two basis.

Applying the *diagonal rule*, the rates will be:

    rate at beginning of option period is 1.4825 – 0.33 c pm   = 1.4792
    rate at end of option period is 1.4825 – 0.67 c pm   = 1.4758

    As the bank is buying, it will use the higher rate of <u>1.4792</u>.

USD 50,000 @ 1.4792 (see above)   = £33,802.05 CR

Payment commission £33,802 x 0.10%   = £   <u>33.80</u> DR

Net credit on utilisation of extended portion of contract = £33,768.25 CR

(*Note:* the advising bank's fee will have been paid when the credit was advised to Nuts About Food Ltd)

(c) (i)   *Article 41, UCP 500*

- As the final shipment has been delayed beyond the period allowed in the credit, then the credit is no longer available for that shipment (unless otherwise stipulated in the credit).

- The exporter should see if the applicant for the credit will agree to a changed shipment date and perhaps the expiry date of the letter of credit.

(ii)

- Under *Article 41, UCP 500*, if the shipment is not made on time, then the credit ceases to be available for subsequent instalments.

- An amendment to the letter of credit or a new letter of credit may be necessary. (In view of the extra costs involved in amending the letter of credit, settlement may be considered outside the letter of credit.)

- If the shipment was made on time but there was late presentation, the second and third presentations may still be made.

- Under *Article 43, UCP500*, the credit may stipulate a time period after the date of shipment during which presentation must be made; if such a period is not stated then banks will not accept documents presented to them later than 21 days after the date of shipment.

Appendix C
Suggested Outline Answers

Note: 1. Answers to asterisked (*) questions from each lesson.
2. These are *outline* answers only, and are intended as a guide to a full answer.

1.1

- There is an interest advantage of investing in Italy of 2.375% p.a.

- However, if funds are invested in Italy, Mr Pylle must invest in lire at spot rate, and then cover the exchange risk by selling six months fixed forward.

- Spot rate for selling Italian lire is 2695; the six months fixed forward rate for the bank to buy back the lire is 2695 plus 35 lire discount = 2730 lire.

- The rates quoted are middle rates and, in practice, the buying and selling rates would be at a wider margin.

- As the rate is at a discount in the forward market, and as Mr Pylle is investing in lire, the discount represents a cost to him (i.e. the pound is more expensive against Italian lire in the forward markets).

- Cost of forward cover for six months is calculated as:
$$\frac{35 \times 2}{2730} \times \frac{100}{1} = \underline{2.564\% \text{ p.a.}}$$

- Investment in sterling is at a rate of 11.5% p.a.

- Investment in Italian lire is at a rate of   13.875%
  Less cost of forward cover   2.564%
                                      11.311%

- Thus an investment in sterling is more profitable to the customer than an investment in Italian lire by 11.5% minus 11.311% = 0.189% p.a.

2.1   (a)   • As Mr Scrooge is resident in the UK, and does not wish to set up residence in either Switzerland or Germany, it would not be in his interest to switch his mortgage from sterling to either Deutsche marks or Swiss francs.

• The reason for this is that, while the level of interest rates is lower in the two countries, Mr Scrooge would be faced with a major exchange risk.

• If sterling weakens against the two currencies, Mr Scrooge will have to pay more, in sterling terms, to make interest and capital repayments.

• In order to cover the exchange risk, Mr Scrooge would need to take some form of cover, eg forward exchange contract, or currency option. The cost of these would, effectively, negate the advantage of lower interest rates. Also, forward contracts and currency options are not normally available for more than one year ahead.

• As Mr Scrooge is wealthy, he could invest funds, or make deposits in currency amounts in order to generate currency income to meet loan interest and repayments. However, as interest rates are lower in the two countries being considered than in the UK, his income would similarly be reduced.

• Mr Scrooge could take out a forward exchange contract. However, as this is not normally available for periods of more than one year ahead, he would need to keep extending the contract to provide cover.

(b)

• The percentage cost of forward cover for Deutsche marks is:

	2.7213	spot selling rate
	2.5748	twelve months' forward
Therefore	0.1465 =	twelve month premium

$$\frac{0.1465}{2.5748} \times \frac{100}{1} = 5.6898\% \text{ pa}$$

Therefore the cost of Deutsche mark cover is:

8.5625	interest rate
5.6898	% cost of forward cover
14.2523% pa	

• The percentage cost of forward cover for Swiss francs is:

	2.4809	spot selling rate
	2.3489	twelve months' forward
Therefore	0.1320 =	twelve month premium

$$\frac{0.1320}{2.3489} \times \frac{100}{1} = 5.6197\% \text{ pa}$$

Therefore the cost of Swiss franc cover is:

8.6250	interest rate
5.6197	% cost of forward cover
14.2447% pa	

- As the cost of Mr Scrooge's UK mortgage is 14.375%, covering forward negates the interest benefits of a currency mortgage.

- Additionally, a margin might be added to the cost of the currency mortgage, so making it more expensive than a sterling mortgage.

(c) • If Mr Scrooge has income in Deutsche marks or Swiss francs he will be able to negate, or at least reduce, the exchange risk.

- The customer should open a Deutsche mark or Swiss franc currency account from which loan repayments and interest can be made. Currency income can be credited to this account. It may be necessary to arrange an overdraft to cover a temporary shortfall between payments and receipts.

2.2   (a) • Veterinary Sciences Plc has an exchange risk because
   — it receives amounts of currencies from overseas licence holders
   — it will have to pay the Spanish company a licence fee

- It seems likely that the currency amounts receivable and payable will vary from year to year.

- A range of currencies is involved, some of which may be in the Exchange Rate Mechanism of the European Monetary System. All currencies are subject to fluctuation against sterling.

- At present the company converts currency receipts at spot rate when received. Also, some London banks are receiving currency amounts, converting them into sterling and remitting the proceeds by sterling cheque to the company.

- As no steps are taken to reduce its foreign exchange exposure, the company does not know in advance how much sterling they will receive, and the sterling cost of the Spanish payments.

- The company can reduce its foreign exchange exposure by
   — agreeing to pay the Spanish company in a currency that the company already receives, ie matching receipts against payments as closely as possible — a foreign currency bank account will be needed for this
   — establishing forward contracts for expected receipts and payments
   — establishing currency options for expected receipts and payments
   — the use of currency borrowing in currencies in which receipts are expected (such borrowing is converted into sterling at spot rate, or at rates fixed by forward contracts and/or currency options): much depends on the company's cash flow position, the currencies involved, and overseas interest rates.

(b) *Currency account*
   - The normal bank/customer relationship applies.

   - There is an exchange risk for the customer if the balance of the currency account had to be switched into sterling.

(c) *Forward contract*
   - An immediately firm and binding contract between a bank and its customer for the purchase, or sale, of a specified quantity of a stated foreign currency at a rate of exchange fixed at the time that the forward contract is made, for performance by delivery of and payment for the stated foreign currency at an agreed future time, or between two agreed future dates.

   - A forward contract is a facility arranged by the bank for the customer: many banks regard this as the equivalent of lending between 10% and 20% of the contract value.

Currency option

- An agreement whereby the purchaser of an option purchases the right, upon payment of a premium, to buy from or sell to a bank a specified amount of any underlying foreign currency at an agreed rate against delivery of a counter-currency either at any time during a given period, or on a fixed future date.

- The agreed rate (or 'strike price') is chosen by the customer, with reference to the current spot rate or forward rates.

- Premium payable in advance.

- With an *American option* the buyer can exercise the option at any time up to the expiry date; with a *European option*, the buyer can exercise the option on the expiry date only.

- Banks do not normally regard a currency option as a liability, although there is a risk that, if the customer decides to exercise the option, the customer may not deliver the underlying currency.

Currency borrowing

- The customer has a liability with the bank for the amount of the borrowing.

- There is an exchange risk for the customer.

2.3　(a)　(i)

- As the dollar has weakened against the pound, Euro Multinational will be able to buy more USD to the pound.

- Thus the sterling cost of remittances to the US holding company will be cheaper.

(ii)　*Speculation*

- Speculators moving 'hot money' from one currency to another seeking future currency movements, eg selling weak currencies and buying/holding strong currencies.

- 'Leads' and 'lags' by businesses anticipating exchange rate movements in their favour.

Interest rates

- Investors buy and sell currencies so as to ensure the best returns.

- The value of a country's currency is generally strengthened by an increase in interest rates and weakened by a fall in interest rates.

Central bank support

- A country's central bank may buy or sell its own currency in order to stabilise exchange rates (selling will replenish its reserves of foreign currency).

- Sometimes a number of central banks will act in concert to support a particular currency.

- Where currencies have relatively fixed exchange rates (such as the Exchange Rate Mechanism of the European Monetary System), a country's central bank may realign (revalue/devalue) its currency against others.

Other factors

- Economic and political news, either world or home news, is likely to have an effect on exchange rates, eg balance of payments, money supply figures, inflation rates, government borrowing, world prices (such as oil), political events, civil war and disobedience, etc.

- Bad news will unsettle the markets and there will be a flow of funds into safer currencies.

- Supply and demand for trading purposes will have a general effect on exchange rates.

(iii)
- Both currencies are part of the European Monetary System.
- While sterling is not currently in the Exchange Rate Mechanism of the EMS, there is nevertheless a general aim of exchange rate stability within the EMS.
- Generally, within the EMS, central banks would act in concert to prevent instability in exchange rates.
- Future development of the EMS is for convergence of economic performance in EU countries.

(b) (i)
- Open a USD bank account in order to match dollar receipts and payments.
- Arrange a USD overdraft so that expected receipts can be converted into sterling on the day the invoice is issued. The overdraft is repaid when payment is made by Regional Distribution plc. Note that there is an exchange risk if Regional Distribution fails to pay.

(ii)
- Regional Distribution will obtain details of Euro Multinational's USD bank account and will then make a SWIFT transfer (or priority SWIFT transfer if the funds are needed quickly) into this account.
- Alternatively the payment can be made by means of a bank draft or, if Regional Distribution has a USD account, by cheque.
- With a SWIFT transfer, payment will be made on a value date and will be cleared funds. With a bank draft, or Regional Distribution cheque, the instrument will have to be presented for payment (and the cheque cleared through the currency clearing in London).
- Regional Distribution will probably make use of a forward contract, or currency option, to provide the USD, or will use funds on their USD bank account. It is possible that they may decide to buy the USD at spot rate.

3.2 (a) The methods of payment (starting with the most preferred) available to these exporter customers are:
- payment in advance
- confirmed irrevocable letter of credit
- irrevocable letter of credit (not confirmed)
- revocable letter of credit
- documentary collection
- open account

(i) *Payment in advance* — safest method

Risks:
- Almost none, although the buyers might insist on a bank advance payment guarantee (see lesson 11) which could utilise part of Orkward and Meen's bank facilities.
- If a part-payment was received, Orkward and Meen could suffer loss if the contract was cancelled by the buyers.

Advantages:
- Orkward and Meen's cash flow is assisted.

(ii) *Open account* — least safe method

Risks:
- Full risk taken by Orkward and Meen, as the goods and documents of title will be despatched to the buyer before payment can be requested.

Advantages:
- In competitive markets, this method of payment may have to be offered in order to gain business.

(c) A compromise method is likely to be a documentary collection using bills of exchange, and presented through a bank.

(d) *Documentary collection*

<u>Risks for the exporter</u>:
- The overseas buyer may accept the bill of exchange in order to obtain documents of title, but the bill may be unpaid on maturity.

- The overseas buyer may not take up the documents — this would lead to Orkward and Meen having to arrange and pay for warehouse and insurance costs and then either selling the goods at a lower price/loss to another buyer, or shipping the goods back to the UK.

- In the event of non-acceptance or non-payment of the bill of exchange, Orkward and Meen will become involved in suing the buyers in a foreign court.

<u>Risks for the importer</u>:
- The goods despatched may not be as ordered.

- The goods cannot be inspected until the exporter's bill of exchange has been either paid or accepted.

- If the goods are faulty, the importer's business could suffer, eg sales could be lost or a production line halted.

4.1 (a) Sterling notes should **not** be taken, other than a small number sufficient for expenses at UK airports. US dollar notes should be ordered, and Mr Ring Culture's bank account will be debited when he collects them a few days before departure.

(b) Sterling travellers cheques are not normally acceptable in the US. Instead, dollar travellers cheques should be taken. These can be ordered (if not held in stock at the branch) and he can collect them a few days before departure. His bank account will not be debited until the travellers cheques are sold to him (he will be debited at the then rate of exchange).

(c) The remittance should be in US dollars by priority SWIFT transfer (or telegraphic transfer). The funds must be sent immediately for them to be available to the hotel at the required time. Mr Ring Culture should be asked for the name of the bank with which the hotel has an account, together with the account number. If this information is not known, the funds should be dispatched to a correspondent (or branch of the bank, if appropriate) requesting them urgently to advise and pay the hotel. Mr Ring Culture's bank account will be debited with the cost of the remittance immediately.

In view of the timescale, the customer should be given the bank's reference number and should be advised to send a telegram immediately to the hotel indicating that the funds have been sent.

(d) He should be advised to contact us by cable, telex or telephone requesting an immediate telegraphic/priority SWIFT transfer to a *named bank and branch*. Alternatively he should be advised to call at a bank in California (advise him of our correspondent bank) and request them to telex us urgently for funds.

Also advise him to take his credit card(s) with him.

4.5 (a) *US cheques*
- As these are expressed in US dollars, they should be negotiated, ie the bank purchases the cheques immediately and Mr Shirt's account will be credited either the same day or within a few days (quicker than the 30-40 days for a collection).

- With negotiation, the bank sends the US dollar cheques in bulk to its main correspondent bank in America (or its US subsidiary company). This bank will then put the cheques through the local clearing system.

- With negotiation, the cheques are accepted from Mr Shirt on a with recourse basis, ie if any cheques are subsequently unpaid, Mr Shirt's account will be debited. Also, the clearance time will be much greater than under UK Clearing House rules and an unpaid cheque might be returned after several weeks. (Note that it is a criminal offence in America to tender a cheque in payment that subsequently 'bounces'.)

- As bankers to Mr Shirt, we need to establish a negotiation limit so that lending against the uncleared effects is formalised.

EU cheques
- These should be drawn in sterling under the Uniform Eurocheque scheme.

- Cheques accepted within the limits and under the conditions of the Eurocheque scheme (£200 per cheque at present for goods and services; £100 when cheques are cashed by banks) are guaranteed, with no recourse to Mr Shirt. His account is credited immediately, the funds being treated as cleared in four working days (quicker than the collection time).

(b) • Mr Shirt should consider entering into a forward exchange contract (or a series of contracts) for the bank to buy US dollars (or, indeed, other currencies). This will fix the exchange rate but is subject to Mr Shirt being able to generate sufficient foreign business to meet his liabilities under the forward contract: he will need to use his past experience/sales to help him establish his forward contract needs.

- Also, forward exchange contracts are part of the customer's total borrowing facilities — usually taken as being between 10% and 20% of the sterling value of the contract. Thus Mr Shirt's borrowing facilities may be curtailed somewhat.

- If business warrants, he could consider the use of currency options.

- Mr Shirt will need to keep up-to-date with daily exchange rates. If business warrants, he might wish to use a cash management system whereby his computer can link with the bank's — this would enable him to call up the latest exchange rates, and to book forward contracts.

(c) • Mr Shirt should consider encouraging the use of credit cards: he would claim amounts in sterling from the credit card company, so avoiding the need to arrange foreign exchange cover. Proceeds will be received either immediately, or within a few days — certainly much quicker than with collections.

- He might consider opening a US dollar bank account to which his dollar cheques could be credited. This would be appropriate if he has expenses in US dollars which could be paid from the account. If not, there will be no saving in costs or time over his bank negotiating the cheques, as in (a).

5.2 (a) The only practical method is to sell on open account terms. The quality of the US buyers precludes advance payment, letters of credit and collections.

US buying houses
- The buying houses are based in London and will be responsible for collecting the goods on an ex-works basis from Uniform Products Ltd.

- They will buy on open account terms with payment in sterling.

- Effectively, for Uniform Products Ltd, this is the equivalent of a home sale.

Selling to the US main agents

- As the main agents are situated in America, Uniform Products Ltd are selling on delivered duty paid terms, ie they must dispatch the goods to a named point.

- Their invoice price will be higher than EXW to allow for the following costs for which they are responsible under DDP Incoterms:

  — arranging for appropriate documents and customs clearance (a forwarding agent should be used, as the company has no previous experience of the export trade)
  — insurance to the named point (an insurance broker, or the bank's insurance service will provide or issue the correct insurance documents

- In addition, the customer should be advised to take out credit insurance (eg through NCM), together with foreign currency cover. Credit insurance could be linked with the bank's finance scheme for smaller exporters — this will offer finance at favourable interest rates (see lesson 12).

- A factoring company (see lesson 12) could be considered — this would cover exchange risks, credit risks, and could be used to provide finance.

(b) • The major risk is a foreign exchange risk from the moment the orders are accepted.

- This is best covered by a forward exchange contract or, if amounts are large enough, by a currency option.

- Definition of a forward exchange contract — see page 9.

- Definition of a currency option — see page 38.

- A forward option contract, or an 'American' currency option would seem to offer Uniform Products Ltd the most flexibility: in both cases the bank (or writer of the option) will buy US dollars.

- With a forward exchange contract, the customer has the obligation to complete, otherwise the contract must be closed out at a possible cost to the customer.

- With a currency option, the customer must pay the 'up front' premium, and the agreed strike price must be acceptable.

6.1 (a) CFR Felixstowe means that the seller must pay the costs and freight charges to the named port of destination, ie Felixstowe.

The responsibilities of the buyer and the seller are detailed in lesson 6.

(b) *Advantage to the buyer paying in sterling:*
- No exchange risk

Disadvantages to the buyer paying in sterling:
- As the exchange risk is passed to the supplier, there may be reluctance to maintain continuity of supply if other customers can be found who will pay in the supplier's currency.

- The supplier may try to pass back the exchange risk to Much Wallop Ltd by fixing an exchange rate in the commercial contract.

(c) *Advantages to the buyer paying in Deutsche marks*
- By paying in the currency of the supplier, the buyer may be able to ensure continuity of supply.

- It might be possible to obtain an advantageous exchange rate by using forward contracts (but, with DEM, the currency is usually at a premium in the forward markets). This would protect the costs and profit margins of Much Wallop Ltd.

Disadvantages to the buyer paying in Deutsche marks
- Exchange risk borne by the buyer.

- Must arrange forward contracts (or other facilities) which may restrict the company's borrowing facilities with the bank.

(d) • Enter into a forward exchange contract for the bank to sell Deutsche marks, either on a fixed or an option basis.

- Enter into a currency option (provided the currency amounts are large enough) for the holder (Much Wallop Ltd) to call Deutsche marks from the bank (the writer of the option) at an agreed strike price.

- A forward option contract, or an 'American' currency option would seem to offer Much Wallop Ltd more flexibility as to the payment date.

- With a currency option, the customer would be able to take advantage of currency movements (if any) in the customer's favour and settle at the then spot rate.

- By arranging to cover the exchange risk, the company is protecting its costs and profit.

6.3 (a) Incoterms, issued by the International Chamber of Commerce.

(b) (i) *FOB Manila* — Free On Board, Manila; used for sea or inland waterway transport.

(ii) *CFR Southampton* — Cost and Freight, Southampton; used for sea or inland waterway transport.

(iii) *CIF Southampton* — Cost, Insurance and Freight, Southampton; used for sea or inland waterway transport.

	Carriage	Insurance	Risks transferred
(i)	• buyer	• buyer	• when goods pass over ship's rail at port of shipment
(ii)	• seller	• buyer	• when goods pass over ship's rail at port of shipment
(iii)	• seller	• seller	• when goods pass over ship's rail at port of shipment

Fuller details of the responsibilities of the buyer and seller for these Incoterms are given in lesson 6.

(c) As the act of goods passing over the ship's rail is not relevant for roll-on/roll-off or container transport, the equivalent terms are:

(i) FCA (Free Carrier . . . named place)
(ii) CPT (Carriage Paid To . . . named place of destination)
(iii) CIP (Carriage and Insurance Paid To . . . named place of destination)

(d) The terms shown in (c) are appropriate, depending on who is responsible for arranging and paying for the insurance and/or freight.

7.5   (a)   • An alternative payment method is an irrevocable letter of credit — possibly confirmed by a German bank.

• The letter of credit would provide for payment at sight upon presentation of specified documents which comply strictly with the terms of the credit. If the customer wishes a period of credit then a term bill could be discounted, with Tintinnabulum Ltd paying the discount charges, ie the German supplier receives the face value of the bill.

• Amongst the documents called for by the credit should be an inspection certificate provided by a third party acceptable to both buyer and seller.

(b)   • Tintinnabulum Ltd must arrange a forward contract for the bank to sell the amount of deutschemarks. The forward contract can be either fixed or, more likely, option.

• As an alternative, subject to the contract being large enough, Tintinnabulum Ltd could arrange a currency option under which the bank will deliver deutschemarks at an agreed strike price. This could be either a European option or, more likely, an American option.

• In order to establish all the costs of the transaction, the customer will need to know the bank's charges for establishing the letter of credit, payment/acceptance charges, and discounting charges, as well as charges likely to be levied by the advising/confirming bank in Germany.

• There will also be charges for the forward contract, and the premium on the currency option.

(c)   *Forward contract*
• Definition of a forward contract – see page 9.

• The customer is entering into a legal contract which must be completed either at a fixed date, or for an option contract, between two specified dates.

• If the forward contract cannot be completed, it will either have to be closed out or extended.

Currency option
• Definition of a currency option – see page 38.

• With a currency option, there is no obligation for the customer to take delivery (in this case) of the currency. Generally, if the spot rate has moved in the purchaser's favour, he or she will 'walk away' from the option without exercising his or her rights. In these circumstances, the bank, as writer of the option, will seek to ensure that the premium paid will cover the exchange risk that it has to bear.

• The bank will wish to be sure that, if the customer exercises its option, it can deliver the agreed currency (in this case, sterling) to the bank.

Other risks
• Commercial risks, ie ability of the supplier to deliver the goods in accordance with the terms of the contract, together with correct documentation to enable the buyer to take delivery.

• Documentary credit costs will be charged on issue of the credit whether or not it is used.

7.6   (a)   • As the issuing bank, we can only make payment against documents which conform strictly to the terms of the credit. To do otherwise, would make the bank guilty of negligence.

• Discrepant documents cannot be honoured without the authority of the customer, and it is in the customer's interests that discrepancies should be investigated fully.

(i)
- The credit calls for drafts drawn at ninety days' sight, drawn on the bank, for the full invoice value.

- However, the drafts presented are at sight, drawn on the customer, and for the net invoice value.

- This means that
  — the customer will not receive ninety days' credit
  — the draft will not be the equivalent of an eligible bill because it is not drawn on the bank
  — the draft is for an amount different from that called for in the credit

(ii)
- The credit calls for invoices showing the full CIP value.

- However, the only invoice presented is for the net amount after deducting 5%.

- This means that
  — the customer, presumably, required more than one invoice
  — as the price has been reduced, the goods may not be of the quality ordered

(iii)
- The credit calls for an insurance policy/certificate, transferable, in the same currency as the credit, for 110% of the CIP price, and which covers specified risks.

- The insurance certificate presented is not transferable, is expressed in sterling and does not cover the specified risks.

- This means that
  — the insurance is not readily available for the bank's protection (a condition under which the bank agreed to open the credit)
  — neither bank nor customer are fully protected

(iv)
- The credit calls for a full set of clean, 'on board', shipping company's bills of lading, freight paid, with the goods consigned to Toolcraft Ltd.

- Only two out of three 'received for shipment' bills of lading have been presented, marked 'freight prepayable', and the goods consigned to the order of the shipper.

- This means that
  — full sets of 'on board' bills of lading are required (see Article 23)
  — the bank and customer are not fully protected as the missing bills of lading could be used by another person
  — the bills of lading do not show that freight has been paid (see Article 33)

(v)
- The indemnity from the negotiating bank *may* be acceptable; however, in the event of a dispute, the negotiating bank may disagree about the validity of a discrepancy raised by the issuing bank or the customer.

- The indemnity should be *specific*, rather than general; ideally it should be capable of being enforceable according to English laws.

(b)   The solutions to points (i) to (v), above, are:

(i)
- As the suppliers want immediate payment, and the customers want 90 days' credit, the bills should be discounted. It must be agreed between supplier and customer as to who is to pay the discounting charges.

- The bills of exchange should be drawn on the bank: this will make them into bank bills which will then be eligible for the finest rates of discount.

(ii)
- The customer should specify the exact number of invoices required.

- If it is agreed that invoices are to be for a net amount (with bills of exchange drawn for the same amount), then it should be incorporated as a term of the credit.

(iii) • The terms of insurance must be agreed between the parties, with the beneficiary providing the correct document. (If they cannot agree, then the terms for the transaction should be changed to CPT — the customer will then arrange and pay for insurance.)

• The insurance must be in the same currency as the credit — any loss will be in that currency.

(iv) • The shipping documents must be as called for in the credit.

• There should be a full set of shipping documents showing that the goods have been loaded on board.

• The shipping documents should show the goods consigned to the order of the buyer.

• The shipping documents must show that freight has been paid — unless the terms are altered so that the buyer is to pay freight charges.

• The shipping documents do not need to be a shipping company's bill of lading — other transport documents could be used.

(v) • The credit should state that discrepant documents and banker's indemnities are not acceptable.

The above will cover future transactions. For this transaction, however, the presenting bank should be advised that the documents are being held pending the arrival of the ship, with the request to release the documents in trust to the customer. Additionally, the presenting bank could be asked for new drafts, new insurance documents and details of the missing bills of lading. The customer should not pay for the goods until these aspects have been clarified.

7.7 (a) • Status enquiry to be taken out on the new supplier.

• Trade references to be taken up.

(b) • Exchange risk from the moment the order is placed until the date of payment.

• Some form of forward cover should be taken from the date of the order to the likely date of payment:
— forward exchange contract, either fixed or option
— currency option (if the amount is large enough)

(c) • Irrevocable letter of credit (possibly a re-instatement credit — see Lesson 8).

• Issued in accordance with Uniform Customs and Practice for Documentary Credits.

• The credit should call for drafts drawn at 90 days' sight (or date) on and payable at the bank's counters in the UK.

• Stoneface plc and the overseas supplier must agree who is to pay the discount charges, and the credit should specify this. (Thus the beneficiary will be able to discount the bill at eligible bill rates.)

• The letter of credit should specify an inspection certificate, issued by a third party acceptable to both buyer and seller.

(d) • The supplier is referring to FCA (Free Carrier . . . named place) terms.

• The buyer is expecting DDU, VAT unpaid (Delivered Duty and VAT Unpaid . . . named place of destination).

The responsibilities of buyer and seller for these Incoterms are given in lesson 6.

As the terms are completely opposite, the buyer and seller need to resolve this difference as a matter of urgency.

(e)   *FCA*
- Invoice (or equivalent electronic message).

- Transport document, eg freight forwarder's receipt, waybill, bill of lading (or equivalent electronic message) — freight payable at destination.

- Bill of exchange at 90 days' sight.

- Certificate of inspection, issued by a third party acceptable to buyer and seller.

Note: the bank will wish to ensure that Stoneface plc has arranged insurance cover (this protects the bank's interest, as issuing bank).

DDU
- Documents as above, except that the transport document will show the place of delivery, and will indicate that the freight has been paid.

(f)   The issuing bank is responsible to the

- applicant (its customer) for carrying out the customer's instructions and for making payment against the stipulated documents, provided the terms and conditions of the credit are complied with (Articles 2, 9, 13 and 14).

- beneficiary that claims are honoured against presentation of the stipulated documents, provided the terms and conditions of the credit are complied with. The credit cannot be amended or cancelled without the agreement of all parties (Articles 9 and 10).

- advising or confirming bank — the same responsibilities as to the beneficiary.

7.8   (a)   *Irrevocable letter of credit*
- While the letter of credit is irrevocable, it is not confirmed; thus Telecom Exports is reliant on the standing of the issuing bank and the country of issue, there being no engagement on the part of the UK bank.

Performance bond
- Under the performance bond, Telecom Exports' bank will take a counter indemnity from the customer.

- The overseas buyer may claim back the 10% paid to Telecom Exports against the performance bond.

- If the bond is unconditional, there is the risk of unfair calling.

Shipping documents
- In order to obtain payment, Telecom Exports must present precise documents specified in the letter of credit.

Acceptance certificate
- To receive the final payment, Telecom Exports is dependent on the overseas buyer providing the acceptance certificate before the expiry of the credit.

(b)   *Performance bond*
- Telecom Exports will request the issue of a performance bond – this will utilise part of their banking facilities.

- On presentation of the performance bond under the letter of credit, they will receive 10% of the contract value.

Pre-shipment finance
- Telecom Exports' bank, on the strength of the expected proceeds under the letter of credit, may be prepared to provide pre-shipment finance by means of a loan or an overdraft.

Export finance
- If drafts are to be drawn on the advising bank, it may be possible to discount them, subject to the shipping documents being in order.

- It may be possible to obtain forfait finance from a bank (even though the letter of credit is not confirmed), subject to the shipping documents being in order.

(c) • Each of the three discrepancies is material and prevents Telecom Exports from obtaining payment of the 80%.

- Without presentation of correct documents, export finance by discounting or forfaiting will not be possible.

- The final 10% payment cannot be obtained until the shipping documents are in order.

- Possible action:

  – incorrect description of goods can be corrected by Telecom Exports amending the invoices or providing new invoices before the expiry of the letter of credit and within the period specified for presentation of documents (see also Article 43, UCP);

  – missing bill of lading should be obtained and submitted before the expiry of the credit and within the period specified for presentation of documents.

- Other possible actions include:

  – contacting the applicant of the credit to seek agreement to the discrepancies;

  – asking the advising bank to contact the issuing bank to seek acceptance of the discrepancies;

  – sending the documents to the issuing bank on a collection basis.

8.4   *Note:* This question involves the use of letters of credit between buyers and sellers, both of whom are UK-based.

(a) The financial package can include the use of
   — either letters of credit
   — or bills of exchange/promissory notes

Letters of credit
- New World Computers Ltd should request the ultimate buyers to establish a letter of credit.

- The credit should allow New World to draw 15% of the contract value from the advisory/confirming bank upon presentation of documentation such as an advance payment guarantee in favour of the buyers (such guarantee could well be issued by ourselves, as bankers to New World).

- The credit should be established from the date of signing the commercial contract, or as soon as possible thereafter.

- The credit must allow for drawings of up to 50% of the contract value against presentation of documents to the advising/confirming bank showing that appropriate parts have been received by New World. The documentation might comprise a bill of lading, or a freight forwarder's receipt, or other documentation.

- The credit will allow for the balance of the contract monies to be drawn upon completion of the contract. The documentation might comprise a receipt for the goods issued by the buyers.

- New World Computers Ltd may be required to provide a performance bond or a retention monies bond to support other documentation before drawings can be made under the credit. Any such bonds which are issued by the bank on the customer's behalf form a contingent liability and will affect the customer's facilities.

Bills of exchange/promissory notes

- If the ultimate buyers do not wish to establish a letter of credit, an alternative solution is for them to accept a series of bills of exchange drawn on them by New World. The bills can be drawn to meet the three payment amounts. (Instead of bills of exchange, promissory notes could be issued by the ultimate buyer.)

- With bills of exchange and promissory notes the ultimate buyers will, almost certainly, require an advance payment guarantee, performance bond, and retention monies bond to be issued in their favour.

- The accepted bills/signed promissory notes could be discounted/purchased by ourselves, so providing a means of finance for New World.

- If the bills/notes are avalised (see Lesson 12) by the buyer's bank they can be purchased by a forfaitor without recourse to New World.

(b)
- A stand-by letter of credit issued in favour of the ultimate buyers might be an alternative to an advance payment guarantee. However, any undertaking issued by the bank on behalf of New World will incur a contingent liability, so affecting the customer's facilities.

- If the buyers are known to be first-class, the bank may be prepared to advance part of the contract value to allow New World to import the required parts from the EU suppliers. The bank would need to examine the commercial contract, and be sure of the commercial ability and financial standing of its customer, and of the financial standing of the ultimate buyers.

8.5 (a)
- The banking instruments would be documentary letters of credit or guarantees/bonds issued by the bank on behalf of the customer in favour of the suppliers.

- The letters of credit could be:
  — documentary credits covering one or two months' supply
  — reinstatement or revolving letters of credit covering one or two months' supply
  — standby letters of credit under which, if the customer fails to honour obligations, the beneficiary could make a claim and receive payment.

- Letters of credit will be issued subject to Uniform Customs and Practice for Documentary Credits (ICC Publication no 500).

- A performance bond could be issued by the bank in favour of the suppliers: under this, the UK bank will guarantee that the overseas suppliers will be paid in the event of the customer failing to make payment.

- The performance bond, being issued by a UK bank, should, ideally, be subject to UK law and banking practice.

- Both letters of credit and guarantees/bonds may have to be issued in foreign currency, i.e. there will be an exchange risk for Bric-à-Brac Ltd.

(b) (i) *the customer*
- Any form of letter of credit and guarantee/bond will utilise part of the customer's facilities with the bank, ie the facility to borrow for other purposes will be reduced.

- Reinstatement and standby letters of credit are possible ways of reducing the use of overall facilities.

- With both letters of credit and guarantees/bonds, the bank will require a counter-indemnity or undertaking to be signed by the customer. The bank will not issue letters of credit or guarantees/bonds until it is satisfied with the standing of the customer and the counter-indemnity or undertaking issued in its favour.

- Under the terms of the counter-indemnity or undertaking, the bank can debit the customer with
  — the value of documents (and expenses incurred) presented under the terms and conditions of the credit
  — claims made under the guarantee/bond
  without regard to the quality or otherwise of the goods.

- If an on demand/unconditional bond is issued (as seems will be required by the suppliers), the customer will be responsible to the bank for any calls made under the bond, even if they are fraudulent.

- If settlement is to be in a foreign currency, the customer must consider the exchange risk implications. This may require forward exchange cover, which will further utilise the customer's banking facilities.

(ii) *the bank*

- With both letters of credit and guarantees/bonds, the bank gives an undertaking to make payment
  — subject to the terms and conditions of the credit
  — in accordance with the conditions of the guarantee/bond

- A letter of credit will have a fixed expiry date, so the bank's obligations will cease on that date.

- A guarantee/bond issued under UK law usually has a fixed liability and a fixed expiry date. However, if it is issued in accordance with Far Eastern law, it may not be limited either to amount or time; also, the responsibility of the bank to pay may be difficult to establish if the wording of the guarantee/bond is ambiguous.

- The customer may wish to take out forward cover for the bank to sell currency at a future date. This creates a delivery risk for the bank if it has to close out the forward contract.

- With a currency option, the bank still takes a delivery risk, although this should be covered by the premium paid by the customer when entering into the option.

8.6 (a) • As Surgical Products Ltd has a small asset base, the transaction can be arranged by means of:
  — either a transferable letter of credit
  — or a back-to-back letter of credit
  Both of these use the creditworthiness of the issuing bank to make up for the shortfall in resources of Surgical Products Ltd.

- With a transferable letter of credit, Surgical Products Ltd must ask the overseas buyer to open the credit as transferable. It is preferable that the credit is confirmed and payable at the confirming bank's counters in the UK. Upon receipt of the credit, Surgical Products Ltd will instruct the advising/confirming bank to transfer a reduced amount of the credit in favour of the UK manufacturer.

  The transferred credit will be for:
  — a shorter expiry date
  — a shorter shipment date
  — a reduced unit price (if appropriate)
  than the original credit.

  The goods will be shipped direct from the manufacturer to the overseas buyer. Upon presentation of the required documents to the advising/confirming bank, and subject to the terms and conditions of the credit, the manufacturer will receive payment. Surgical Products Ltd will substitute its own invoices at the higher value to receive its profit. Surgical Products will need to arrange additional insurance to bring the insured value to CIF plus 10%; alternatively it could call for the required insurance value in the transferred part of the credit.

- With a back-to-back credit, the overseas buyer would arrange for an irrevocable letter of credit to be opened in favour of Surgical Products Ltd, preferably confirmed and payable at the confirming bank's counters in the UK. On the strength of this first credit, Surgical Products Ltd will ask its bank to open a second letter of credit in favour of the UK manufacturer. The amount of the second credit will be for a lower amount than the first and will also have a shorter expiry date, a shorter shipment date, and a reduced unit price (if appropriate). When the UK manufacturer presents the correct documents, subject to the terms and conditions of the credit, Surgical Products Ltd will substitute its own invoices, arrange any additional insurance cover, and present the documents under the first credit, so taking its profit.

(b) All credits should be subject to Uniform Customs and Practice for Documentary Credits (ICC Publication No 500).

Transferable credit
- The credit will be designated 'transferable' and will be subject to Article 48 of Uniform Customs and Practice.

- If part shipments are required, the credit must state that it is transferable in whole or in part; it should state that partial drawings are unacceptable against partial shipments.

- All documents should be issued either in neutral names, or in the name of Surgical Products Ltd.

- Shipments should be from a UK port (unless the manufacturer is producing goods in another country) to the destination.

- Surgical Products Ltd must ensure that the insurance value is correct, ie CIF plus 10%: this can be done by either calling on the second beneficiary to present insurance documents for the required value in the name of Surgical Products Ltd or in a neutral name; alternatively, Surgical Products Ltd can increase the amount of insurance cover to the required amount.

- If possible, the transferred credit should show that discrepant documents and banker's indemnities are unacceptable.

Back-to-back credit
- The same requirements as for a transferable credit must be met. However, the insurance document could be substituted completely, provided the new document complies with Articles 34–36 of UCP.

- The second letter of credit must show that discrepant documents and banker's indemnities are unacceptable.

(c) - As bankers to Surgical Products Ltd the transferable letter of credit is much preferable. This is because, unlike the back-to-back credit, it will not use facilities which the customer has with the bank.

- It is most unlikely that, as bankers to the company, we would wish to issue a second letter of credit based solely on the strength of the first one — other security would be required, which the company clearly does not have.

- Only if the first letter of credit was issued by a first-class bank situated in a low-risk country, confirmed by a first-class UK bank and payable in the UK, would the risk be considered — for a fee.

8.7 (a) - An irrevocable credit "can neither be amended nor cancelled without the agreement of the issuing bank, the confirming bank, if any, and the beneficiary" (Article 9, UCP). Thus, an amendment can be sought, but may be rejected by the beneficiary.

- "In credit operations all parties concerned deal with documents, and not with goods, services and/or other performances to which the documents may relate" (Article 4, UCP). Thus, if the documents are in order, payment, or an undertaking to pay, must be made.

(b) The credit will be worded to include:

  - expiry date and latest shipment date
  - partial shipments allowed (Article 40, unless the credit stipulates otherwise)

Alternatives include:

  - shipment by instalments within given periods (see Article 41)
  - use of revolving credits
  - use of reinstatement credits

(c) *Note:* no documents will guarantee the quality of the goods; the applicant should be sure of the reputation of the supplier

  - certificate of inspection, showing a clean report
  - certificate of weight, to show weight expected
  - certificate of origin, to show correct origin
  - certificate of analysis (where appropriate), to show correct make-up
  - full set of clean, on-board, shipping company bills of lading
  - cargo insurance to cover risks during transportation

All certificates should be issued by an independent third party, not the beneficiary of the credit.

(d)
  - The letter of credit could be issued for a smaller amount, such as the first shipment. If the goods are found to be acceptable, the credit can be increased/extended to cover further shipments.
  - A reinstatement credit could be issued which gives the intention to increase/extend the value of the credit, provided that the goods are of acceptable quality.
  - The letter of credit could include a retention clause whereby a percentage of the value is paid once the goods have been accepted, or against a retention monies guarantee (see lesson 11).
  - There is also the possibility of:
    - using a revocable credit (unlikely to be acceptable to the beneficiary)
    - requiring a performance bond

8.8 (a) *Transferable letter of credit*
  - If the applicant for the letter of credit is agreeable, the credit can be opened in transferable form.
  - Part of the credit can then be transferred by Telecom Exports to one or more second beneficiaries.

  Back-to-back letter of credit
  - On the strength of the first letter of credit, the beneficiary becomes the applicant of a second credit in favour of the ultimate supplier of the goods.

  Assignment of credit
  - The beneficiary instructs the advising/confirming bank to assign part of the credit in favour of the ultimate supplier of the goods.
  - The supplier receives a letter from the advising/confirming bank which states that the bank holds the beneficiary's instructions to make payment.

(b) *Transferable letter of credit*
  - The standing of the issuing bank (and its country), and the confirming bank (if appropriate).
  - The requirement to present precise documents in order to obtain payment.
  - Possible exchange risk – the credit is payable in USD.

Back-to-back letter of credit
- The standing of the issuing bank for the second credit.

- The requirement to obtain precise documents under the second credit which will also meet the requirements of the first credit.

- Possible exchange risk – the credit is payable in USD.

Assignment of credit
- The standing of the issuing bank (and its country), and the assigning bank.

- The ultimate supplier receives an assignment and not a letter of credit – this may be unacceptable.

- The ultimate supplier is not party to the letter of credit or its terms and may not produce requirement documents.

- The ultimate supplier is reliant on the beneficiary being paid under the credit before they are paid.

- Possible exchange risk – the credit is payable in USD.

(c) *Transferable letter of credit*
- The beneficiary must purchase from the second beneficiary(ies) on FOB UK Port terms.

Back-to-back credit
- The second credit should be issued on FOB UK Port terms, or other appropriate terms.

Assignment of credit
- The beneficiary should purchase from the ultimate supplier on FOB UK Port terms, or other appropriate terms.

(d) *Transferable letter of credit*
- As the credit is payable in USD, this is the currency that will be paid to the second beneficiary(ies), who would have to cover the exchange risk.

Back-to-back credit
- The second credit can be opened in sterling. However, this leaves the exchange risk with Telecom Exports; the issuing bank of the second credit will have to be sure that there is a sufficient margin between the two credits to allow for potential currency movements.

Assignment of credit
- The assignment can only be in USD, and the supplier of the goods will have to cover the exchange risk.

9.7 (a) The collection is to be handled in accordance with Uniform Rules for Collections — publication no 322.

- This international set of rules, issued by the International Chamber of Commerce, lays down a uniform code so that banks follow standard practices and procedures when handling collections.

- All parties to a collection know that the practices and procedures set down in the code will be applied by banks and countries which have accepted the URC.

- The use of URC lessens the difficulties of different phraseology and practice throughout the world.

- Only if local or national law is different, or the parties to the collection agree, can the rules be varied.

- If a bank cannot (or will not) comply with the instructions in the collection order, it must immediately advise the remitting bank (or the party from whom the collection was received).

(b) • The bank will act in accordance with the instructions contained in the collection order, provided these do not conflict with UK banking practice.

• The 50% should be accepted and placed on a separate interest-bearing account.

• The bill should be noted or protested (under section 94 of the Bills of Exchange Act 1882) for the full amount of the bill. The bill should be retained by the presenting bank pending further instructions from the principal or remitting bank.

• The remitting bank should be advised by cable/telex of the dishonour and our action; further instructions should be requested.

• The case-of-need, Good Samaritans Ltd, should be advised but, as we have not been told their powers (Article 18 of URC) we cannot follow any instructions from them unless/until the remitting bank gives further instructions.

(c) • The documents cannot be released to the buyer, and should be retained.

• The remitting bank must be advised of the non-acceptance by the method stated in the collection order, e.g. telex or cable.

• The case-of-need must be advised, but for information only. Without authority from the remitting bank, the instructions from the case-of-need cannot be followed.

• If the documents include a bill of lading, the bank must retain control of the goods and follow the instructions in the collection order to protect the goods at the expense of the principal. (In the absence of instructions in the collection order, the presenting bank can, under Article 19, take action to protect the goods at the principal's expense.)

• If the documents include a waybill, which is not a document of title, the goods will be delivered to the consignee. If the consignee is the customer, the seller has lost control of the goods.

• The presenting bank will await instructions from the remitting bank. If these are not received within a reasonable time (say, 90 days maximum), the documents can be returned to the remitting bank subject to the payment of expenses incurred by the presenting bank.

9.8 (a) • The amount of 100,000 Norwegian kroner (NOK) will be sent by cable transfer/priority SWIFT to our correspondent bank, Viking Bank A/S, Oslo.

• The customer must complete an instruction form giving us details of the transaction, and giving us authority to debit their account with the sterling equivalent (or, if Willnotpay Ltd has a NOK account, to debit this).

• The settlement instructions will state that charges are to be for the account of the recipient. This does mean that the recipient, Thor A/S, will not receive the amount of NOK 100,000. In accordance with Mr Hardup's instructions, UK bank charges will also have to be borne by the recipient.

• If Willnotpay Ltd has an electronic link with us, the instructions to remit the money could be received in electronic form.

(b) The accounting procedures are:

• *UK bank*
— Debit Willnotpay Ltd with the sterling equivalent at the bank's spot selling price of NOK 100,000.
— Credit the mirror of the nostro account which we hold with Viking Bank A/S in Oslo.

• *Norwegian bank*
— Debit the vostro account that they hold in our name.
— Credit the account of the recipient, Thor A/S, with the Norwegian kroner amount, less charges.

• If Willnotpay Ltd has a Norwegian kroner account, the accounting entries will be the same, except that the UK bank will debit this account with NOK 100,000 (instead of the sterling account).

(c) For a collection order addressed to a bank, with the following instructions:

Documents to be released against acceptance
- The presenting bank can only release the documents upon acceptance of the bill of exchange.

- By accepting the bill of exchange, Willnotpay Ltd undertakes to make payment on the due date.

- The bill of exchange is subject to the Bills of Exchange Act 1882. If the bill is not paid on the due date, Thor A/S can take action on the bill, separately from the terms of the commercial contract.

Collect all charges . . .
- The presenting bank is instructed to collect from the drawee the bank charges of both the Norwegian and UK banks.

- If the drawee refuses to pay the charges, the presenting bank (ourselves) must seek further instructions on the collection order. If the collection order states that such charges may not be waived, then the documents cannot be released – see Article 22 of Uniform Rules for Collections.

- When payment of charges is refused, the presenting bank must inform the bank from which the collection order was received.

- If the drawee refuses to pay the charges and they are waived, they are for the account of the principal, and may be deducted from the proceeds (Article 22).

Protest if unaccepted or unpaid
- If the drawee refuses to accept, or pay, the bill on the due date, the UK bank must note or protest the bill within 24 hours of dishonour. This is in accordance with s.51 of the Bills of Exchange Act 1882.

- The dishonoured bill will be either noted by a notary public, or protested by means of a householder's protest. A notice of protest is lodged with the High Court.

- The credit rating of Willnotpay Ltd will suffer if it is in the habit of dishonouring bills.

(d) • A banking method which will give protection to Thor A/S, the suppliers, is the use of a standby letter of credit.

- Documents would continue to be presented on a collection basis. Only if a bill was dishonoured would the suppliers claim payment under the letter of credit. In order to receive payment, they would need to produce evidence of the shipment to Willnotpay Ltd, eg copies of commercial documents, together with the unpaid bill duly noted or protested.

- A standby letter of credit would be issued by ourselves to cover, say one or two months' shipments by Thor A/S. In this way, the issue of the credit would not impinge too much on the banking facilities of Willnotpay Ltd.

9.11 (a)

	ECU 700,000

Pay at 120 days' sight this ...(first)... bill of exchange to the order of MDI Italiana SRL for the sum of ECU seven hundred thousand for value received.

To: Euro Multinational Co Ltd

For and on behalf of
MDI Italiana SRL

.........(signed).........

Note:
- Euro Multinational Co Ltd is the drawee
- MDI Italiana SRL is the drawer

(b) • 'D/A' means documents against acceptance of the bill of exchange (Article 10 of Uniform Rules for Collections).

 • This means that the collecting or presenting bank will release the commercial documents only against acceptance of the bill of exchange.

 • Euro Multinational Co Ltd may examine the documents but can only have the documents upon acceptance of the bill of exchange, ie MDI Italiana SRL is retaining control of the goods until acceptance.

 • The procedures will be:

  – the drawee examines the documents

  – if the drawee wishes to commit themselves to payment in 120 days' time, they will accept the bill of exchange by signing it across the face

  – the documents are released, so enabling the importer to obtain the goods using the bill of lading

  – the due date for payment will be calculated by the collecting or presenting bank and advised to the remitting bank

  – the collecting or presenting bank will usually retain the bill of exchange until maturity (the drawee may wish to arrange a forward contract or currency option)

  – on the date of maturity, if funds are available, the collecting or presenting bank will make a bank transfer to the remitting bank in accordance with the latter's instructions

 • If the bill is unaccepted, or unpaid at maturity, the collecting or presenting bank will follow the instructions in the collection order – these might be to protest the bill, and to advise the remitting bank

 • If the bill is unaccepted, the collecting or presenting bank will need to follow instructions in the collection order about taking care of the goods and contacting a 'case of need'; the remitting bank will need to be informed.

(c) *Quality of goods*
 • The importer is unable to inspect the goods prior to acceptance of the bill of exchange.

 • After acceptance of the bill of exchange, the importer is in the position of having agreed to pay for the goods, without being able to check the quality.

 • A possible solution is to have the goods inspected prior to shipment.

 • Cargo insurance should be taken out to cover against damage to the goods in transit.

Demurrage
 • Because of the short sea journey from Italy, the goods have just arrived at the port. Urgent action is needed to avoid demurrage (port costs for uncollected goods).

 • If the bill of exchange is accepted, Euro Multinational can use the bill of lading to collect the goods from the port, although some demurrage may still be payable.

 • If the bill of exchange is unaccepted, MDI Italiana SRL will need to take urgent action to move the goods in order to avoid demurrage costs.

Foreign exchange risk
 • As payment is due in ECUs in 120 days' time, Euro Multinational must consider covering the exchange risk, eg

  – spot purchase and holding the currency on an account

  – forward contract, or currency option

  – currency already held on a currency account

 • The company may decide to 'lag' in the hope that the exchange rate will move in their favour; however, the risk is that exchange rates will move against them.

(d)   Under Uniform Rules for Collections:

- the collecting or presenting bank must act in accordance with the remitting bank's instructions in the collection order (General Provisions and Definitions: C).

- Unless otherwise instructed, the collecting or presenting bank must release the documents only against acceptance of the bill of exchange without delay (Articles 9 and 10).

- However, copies of the documents can be handed or sent to the customer for inspection; also, as the customer appears to be undoubted, and the clearance of the goods from the port is urgent, the bank may consider releasing the documents in trust to the customer.

11.1   (a)   (i) The banking instrument that would give Ancient Mariners Ltd. the security it is seeking is a confirmed irrevocable letter of credit. Provided that the correct documents, as called for in the letter of credit, are presented at each of the three stages, payment will be made.

(ii) The banking instrument which will satisfy the requirements of Neptune Inc. is an advance payment guarantee issued by a UK bank or insurance company. It is likely that Neptune Inc. will seek an on-demand unconditional guarantee.

(b)   The letter of credit will allow for payment to be made in three stages against presentation of specified documents:

(i)   *Advance payment* - against presentation of the claim, together with the advance payment guarantee.

(ii) *Second stage payment* - claimed by presenting a certificate from the ship's master stating that the vessel has sailed to Savannah and that payment is now due.

(iii) *Third stage payment* - claimed by presenting a certificate issued by agents of the owners, Neptune Inc., stating that the vessel has arrived in Savannah and that the final payment is now due.

(c)   The liability which the bank and Ancient Mariners Ltd. will enter into in connection with the advance payment guarantee is:

- By establishing an advance payment guarantee the bank is entering into a commitment to pay the amount of the advance payment back to the owners of the vessel, Neptune Inc., if the customer fails to deliver the vessel in accordance with the contract.

- The customer will have to sign a counter indemnity to reimburse the bank in the event of a claim being made.

The conditions which could be included in the advance payment guarantee in order to minimise liability are:

- The advance payment guarantee only becomes operative when Ancient Mariners Ltd. receives the irrevocable letter of credit, and it is acceptable both in wording and terms to the customer and the bank.

- The guarantee should be subject to English law (if possible).

- It should bear an expiry date.

11.3   (a)   (i)   • Status enquiry to be taken on the French supplier. A trade reference should also be taken to ensure that the supplier can undertake the work to the required standards.

• Exchange risk — see (b) below.

• The secure method of payment will be an irrevocable letter of credit, which the French supplier may require to be confirmed by a French bank.

• The letter of credit should allow for an advance payment of 30% to the French boatyard against the issue of an advance payment guarantee issued by a French bank in our customer's favour.

• The balance of the letter of credit, ie 70%, will be payable against documentation showing that the boat is ready for collection/delivery in accordance with the terms of the commercial contract. The documentation should include an inspection certificate from a reputable ship broker indicating that the vessel has been completed in accordance with the terms of the commercial contract.

• Unless both the vessels are to be ready together the credit must allow for partial delivery, and drawings against appropriate percentages. The credit must also state a last date for delivery and an expiry date.

• The customer may be able to negotiate, on the grounds of providing a secure means of payment to the supplier, that all bank charges are for the supplier, and an estimate of total bank charges can be given.

(ii)   • The buyer should consider the retention of 10% of the contract price until the vessels have been found to be satisfactory. Alternatively, the suppliers can be requested to provide a retention monies guarantee from their bank.

• The supplier should be requested to provide a performance bond from their bank. Preferably, this should be unconditional, issued under English law, and allow for claims to be made at the buyer's bank.

(b)   • Some form of exchange risk cover to meet exchange risks is essential.

• A forward option contract should be arranged to meet the 30% advance payment to be made in January. A second forward option contract should be arranged to meet the payment of the balance in April. If 10% is to be retained, then the second contract must be reduced to allow for this.

• Instead of forward contracts, the buyer may prefer to use call currency options.

• The amount of exchange risk cover can be reduced if the buyer has any French franc income, which should be placed into a currency account.

• If any monies have to be refunded, eg under the advance payment guarantee, there will be an exchange risk.

• If the commercial contract cannot be completed, there will be the cost of closing out unutilised forward contracts; there will be no additional cost in allowing currency options to lapse — the up-front premium will have been paid already.

• Additionally the buyer must

— agree delivery terms with the supplier, in accordance with Incoterms

— agree with the supplier the documentation against which payment will be made under the letter of credit

— establish the costs of the credit

— establish the costs of an independent inspection of the vessels

12.4   Finance methods to meet the requirements of a customer exporting on short-term credit include:

- Overdraft, in sterling or foreign currencies:
  — unsecured
  — secured, using either usual bank security, or the assignment to the bank of the customer's credit insurance policy

  Note: for normal bank security, the UK assets of the manufacturing enterprise could be taken; alternatively a guarantee or standby letter of credit could be issued in our favour by the bankers of Blanc et Blanc SA.

- Advance against collections (sterling or foreign currency), supported by a letter of hypothecation and/or assignment of the customer's credit insurance policy.

- Export finance schemes:
  — linked to either the customer's own credit insurance policy, or an 'umbrella' credit insurance policy taken out by the bank
  — post-shipment finance of up to 90% (100% for some bank schemes) in sterling or foreign currencies
  — generally without recourse, subject to the customer not breaking the terms of the commercial contract

- ECGD-backed lines of credit might be available to the customer.

- Discounting of bills of exchange:
  — presented under credits in the UK
  — accepted by the confirming bank
  — without recourse to the customer

  Note: such bills would be eligible bank bills and would thus command fine rates of discount.

- Forfaiting, in sterling, or a range of foreign currencies:
  — the purchase of bills of exchange which have been guaranteed (avalised) by the buyer's bank
  — without recourse to the customer

- Factoring, in sterling or foreign currencies:
  — finance up to 80% of the invoice value for sales made to approved customers
  — other services, ie sales ledger accounting and credit insurance
  — non-recourse finance

- Acceptance house finance might be available.

- Leasing and hire purchase (available from the bank's finance company) may be appropriate for the finance of machinery, vehicles, etc.

12.5   Two methods of finance are:
  — factoring
  — short-term export finance schemes, using a credit insurance policy

Factoring
- Available from the factoring department of a finance company — often a bank's subsidiary company.

- Export sales of over £250,000 pa are usually required.

- Services provided include:
  — sales ledger accounting
  — credit insurance
  — finance, usually without recourse

  The first two services will reduce the administration costs of Frame-Up Ltd.

- Post-shipment finance is, initially, up to 80% of the invoice value for sales made to approved customers. The balance, less charges and interest, is payable on collection of the debt, or a maximum of 90 days after the due date for payment.

- Methods of payment can be either open account or collections.

- The factoring company will undertake status enquiries on buyers before approving the buyers. Only sales made to approved buyers and within agreed limits will be underwritten by the factoring company.

- Costs:
  — administration charges of between 0.75% and 2.5% for sales ledger accounting and credit insurance
  — bank collection charges where the method of payment used in a collection
  — finance costs of between 3% and 4% over bank base rate

- Other services:
  — where sales are made in a foreign currency, the factor will require the exporter to cover the exchange risk
  — undisclosed factoring, where the use of a factoring company is not revealed to buyers
  — invoice discounting, where finance is provided against particular invoices thus providing for temporary finance

Short-term export finance schemes
- Various schemes available from banks using as security either the customer's credit insurance policy or an 'umbrella' credit insurance policy taken out by the bank.

- Post-shipment finance of up to 90% (100% for some bank schemes) is available for approved exporter customers, usually at preferential interest rates.

- Any balance is paid when the debt is collected.

- Methods of payment can be either collections or open account.

- Usually lending under such schemes is considered to be 'without recourse', subject to the customer not breaking the terms of the commercial contract. Therefore, such finance is usually 'off-balance sheet', but subject to the agreement of the company's auditors.

- Costs:
  — bank administration charges and credit insurance, premiums (with an 'umbrella' policy both of these will be payable to the bank)
  — bank collection charges, where the method of payment used is a collection
  — finance costs at favourable rates, e.g. 1.5% over the bank's base rates, although the lending is usually made on a separate loan account

- In the event of a claim under the credit insurance, the exporter will claim direct, unless the bank's 'umbrella' policy is being used in which case the claim will be handled by the bank.

- Other services:
  — where sales are made in a foreign currency, the bank will require the exporter to cover the exchange risk (this could also include taking out additional cover under a credit insurance policy).

12.6   (a) • The bank would arrange to have the exporter's rights under the credit insurance policies assigned to the bank.

• The credit insurance company would acknowledge notice of assignment.

(b) Under these circumstances, it would not be good practice to advance 100% of the value of the exports:

• The insurance cover is not 100%; the amount paid out is
— insolvency of the buyer, 90%
— buyer's failure to pay within six months, 90%
— buyer's failure to take up goods, 90% of 80%, ie 72% for total loss
— other risks, 95%

• Insurance cover is subject to the exporter complying with the commercial contract, and the terms of the credit insurance. Thus the bank cannot be certain that, in the event of loss, payment will be due to it.

(c) • An alternative is for the exporter to use the credit insurance policy in conjunction with the bank's smaller exports scheme or finance for exports scheme (most banks offer these facilities under a variety of names).

• Under such schemes, banks will lend up to 90% of the invoice value (sometimes up to 100%) at favourable interest rates.

• Lending is generally considered to be 'without recourse' provided that the exporter has complied with the commercial contract and the credit insurance policy. In the event of non-compliance, the lending is 'with recourse'.

• In accounting terms, such lending is not considered to be 'off balance sheet', therefore the amount lent will be shown on the customer's balance sheet.

(d) *Smaller Exports Schemes*
• Some banks, under smaller exports schemes, use their own 'umbrella' credit insurance policies.

• Here, the exporter customer does not need to concern himself/herself with negotiations with the credit insurer — the bank will manage the policy.

• Post-shipment finance of up to 100% of the invoice value is available under such schemes, usually at favourable interest rates.

• Usually such lending is considered to be 'without recourse', subject to the customer not breaking the terms of the commercial contract.

• Therefore such finance is usually 'off balance sheet', but subject to the agreement of the company's auditors.

Factoring
• Finance is available from the factoring department of the bank's specialist finance company.

• Services provided include:
— sales ledger accounting
— credit insurance
— finance, usually without recourse

Post-shipment finance is, initially, up to 80% of the invoice value, with the balance (less charges and interest) payable on collection, or a maximum of 90 days after the due date for payment.

• Available where export sales are over £250,000 pa.

(e) • Facilities, as described above, will be available when invoices are in foreign currency.

• It would be advisable for the company to take out additional cover on its standard credit insurance policy to cover goods invoiced in a range of foreign currencies. It is also possible to arrange that, where an exporter has used the forward exchange market, claims (within limits) can take account of any additional losses in meeting the forward exchange commitment.

12.8   (a)   the exporter should check that:
- the letter of credit is irrevocable, and the creditworthiness of the issuing bank.
- the letter of credit is confirmed and, if appropriate, the creditworthiness of the issuing bank.
- the letter of credit is in accordance with the terms of the commercial contract, in particular:
  - amount of the credit
  - currency of the credit
  - description of the goods
  - shipping terms (including reference to Incoterms)
  - shipping details
  - whether or not partial shipments are allowed
  - whether or not transhipment is allowed
  - the payment terms
  - the payment of bank charges
- whether the transaction can be completed within the timescale of the credit:
  - whether the goods can be shipped by the latest date of shipment
  - whether the specified documents can be presented before the expiry date for presentation (21 days after shipment unless stated otherwise – see UCP Article 43)
  - whether the specified documents can be presented before the expiry date of the letter of credit
- there will be no problems in obtaining the required documents:
  - the name and address of the exporter is stated correctly in the credit
  - the documentation is consistent with the shipping terms
  - specialist documents, such as certificates of inspection, can be obtained within the timescale

If there are any points that the exporter considers unacceptable, an amendment should be sought to the letter of credit.

(b)
- If the letter of credit is confirmed by a UK bank and the letter of credit calls for bills to be drawn on the UK bank, it may be possible to discount the accepted bill.
- If the letter of credit calls for bills to be drawn on the issuing bank or the applicant, it may be possible for the bills to be negotiated on a non-recourse basis.
- With an irrevocable letter of credit, it may be possible to obtain finance by means of forfaiting, using the irrevocable undertaking of the issuing bank.
- Finance can also be provided by
  - overdraft or loan
  - negotiation of the bills of exchange on a recourse basis
  - the issuing of a letter of credit in favour of suppliers (a back-to-back credit)
- The credit might
  - be opened as transferable in which case part of the credit can be transferred to a supplier (second beneficiary(ies))
  - allow pre-shipment finance

12.9   The two choices for Special Optics are:
- collection direct to the presenting bank (see pages 174-5)
- avalised promissory note

(a)   <u>Collection direct to the presenting bank</u>
Advantages
- Not required to produce as precise a set of documents as with a letter of credit.
- Marketing point for importer customers
  - cheaper than a letter of credit
  - no administration work in setting up a letter of credit
  - no bank facilities utilised as with letters of credit

- Payment may well be required faster than with a letter of credit.

Disadvantages
- Risk of non-compliance and/or non-payment of the bill of exchange (a letter of credit gives an undertaking by the issuing bank to pay).
- Finance may be easier to raise with a letter of credit.
- As the collection is sent direct to the presenting bank, there is no document check by the remitting bank.

Avalised promissory note
Advantages
- As the avalised promissory note is received prior to shipment, Special Optics receives bank commitment to pay in advance.
- No requirement, in this case, to present correct documentation (contrast with a letter of credit).
- Finance can be obtained pre- or post-shipment, subject to the standing of the avalising bank (finance against a letter of credit is usually post-shipment).

Disadvantages
- The importer customers will not favour this method of payment because
  - they are agreeing an advance payment
  - the availisation will utilise part of their bank facilities
  - costs will be at least as high as for a letter of credit

(b) #### Collection direct to the presenting bank
- UK bank not involved in handling the documents as they are sent direct to the presenting bank by the UK exporter.
- Presenting bank makes presentation to the importer for acceptance of the bill of exchange.
- Presenting bank holds bill until maturity and then seeks authority from drawee to make payment
- Presenting bank acts as agent of UK exporter in order to collect payment from the importer.
- Any correspondence and advice of payment is sent direct to the UK exporter by the presenting bank.

Avalised promissory note
- Promissory note is held by UK exporter and sent for collection in time for maturity.
- UK bank collects the proceeds of the avalised promissory note.
- As the promissory note has been avalised, the avalising bank must make payment at maturity, whether or not its customer can pay.
- Advice of payment sent to either the UK collecting bank or the exporter.

(c)
- UK exporter prepares the collection order on their bank's paper, using the UK bank's reference numbers.
- Collection sent direct by the UK exporter to the presenting bank.
- Details of the transaction passed to the UK bank – either a copy of the collection order, or the details may be sent electronically.
- Any subsequent correspondence is handled by the UK bank, and the exporter can check on the progress of the collection with this bank – if the exporter has a computer link with the bank, this can be used to access information.
- Payment is received by the UK bank through the international banking system, and passed to the customer's account.
- For the exporter the principal benefits are:
  - a reduction in processing time (which means that payment should be received more quickly)
  - a reduction in bank charges

12.10 (a)   *Payment in advance*
- The exporter is paid before shipment either in full or a percentage payment.
- The importer has to be sure that the exporter will ship the correct goods at the right time.

Collections
- The exporter hands the collection to its bank and the proceeds are collected through the banking system.
- The collection will be either documents against payment (D/P), or documents against acceptance (D/A) of a bill of exchange – for D/A, the importer's bank might be asked to avalise the bill of exchange.
- Alternatively, a clean collection could be used where financial documents are presented without shipping documents.

(b)
- Payment in advance, or against an accepted bill of exchange or promissory note which has been avalised in advance.
- Collections where there is
  - payment, or acceptance and avalisation prior to delivery of documents which include a bill of lading, or
  - credit insurance, or
  - a standby letter of credit, or
  - non-recourse finance

(c)
- Payment in advance, or an accepted bill of exchange or promissory note which has been avalised in advance: the documents would be sent direct to the importer.
- Clean collections: the documents would be sent direct to the importer (if the bill of exchange is avalised prior to shipment, the exporter should be prepared to use non-negotiable sea waybills – these will lessen delays in the movement of paperwork)

12.11 (a)
- Risk of non-acceptance of the bills of exchange, giving problems of what to do with the goods, ie warehousing, insurance, and reshipment.
- Risk of non-payment of the bills at maturity.
- Country risks, eg political and economic events.
- In practice these risks are relatively low in view of the small invoice values, and the one buyer who is known to Telecom Exports.

(b)
- The collection order will specify the action to be taken in event of dishonour. This action could be:
  - protest the bill of exchange for non-acceptance, or non-payment
  - instructions for taking care of the goods, eg warehousing and insurance
  - name and address of 'case of need', together with their powers 'follow their instructions' or 'for assistance only'
- In practice, Telecom Exports is unlikely to follow measures such as protesting the bill in view of the relationship built up with the buyer and the relatively small invoice values. Instead, they could call for advice of non-acceptance or non-payment by telex or SWIFT – this will stop further shipments from being made.
- The goods are likely to have been dispatched by air direct to the buyers, so there will be no need for instructions on taking care of the goods.
- As the buyers are already distributors of Telecom Exports, it seems unlikely that a case of need will be stated.

(c)
- Negotiation of bills – the bank purchases bills of exchange, with recourse to the exporter.
- Advances against collections – the bank advances with recourse an agreed percentage (often 85%) against outstanding collections.
- Short-term finance, linked to credit insurance – eg 'smaller exports scheme' or 'finance for exports scheme', whereby the bank advances 90% (sometimes 100%) of the amount of the bills, generally on a without recourse basis, and subject to credit insurance, either the bank's own policy or assignment of the customer's policy in favour of the bank.

13.1
- A produce loan/merchandising advance can be arranged, secured on the goods warehoused by Dockside Depositories Ltd.
- Lending will be carried out on a separate loan account.
- The amount of the loan will be for no more than 40% or 50%.
- The goods are to be kept under the control of the bank at all times.
- When commodities arrive at the warehouse, the warehouse warrant will be either endorsed over to the order of the bank or issued in the bank's name and deposited with the bank as security. No lending will take place prior to receipt of warehouse warrants.
- The warehouse warrant must be in a transferable form and must indicate that all charges are for the account of the customer, T. Chests Ltd.
- The goods are to be easily identifiable and the bank or its agent must ensure that they are stored separately away from other goods and are marked as being owned by the bank.
- The goods must be adequately insured against fire and theft, the insurance being in transferable form; all charges are for the account of T. Chests Ltd.
- When the goods are sold at auction, they will be released to the purchasers against payment; either the warehouse warrant will be endorsed in favour of the purchaser, or a delivery order issued. Payment is to be made directly to the bank and applied to the separate produce loan account.
- T. Chests Ltd. will have to agree to regular independent valuations of the goods held by Dockside Depositories Ltd. If the goods fall below an agreed market value, say 50% of the value of the goods, the company must agree to sell sufficient goods to clear the loan.
- Dockside Depositories Ltd. must give an undertaking to hold all goods to the order of the bank, and only release goods against the bank's endorsement of warehouse warrants, or the issue of delivery orders.
- The warehouse should be examined to ensure that the goods will be adequately stored.
- The searches on both companies should be monitored continually to ensure that the companies do not charge any assets to other institutions which might be to the detriment of the bank.

13.4   (a)   *Letter of credit*
- An irrevocable letter of credit can be issued in favour of the overseas supplier.
- The letter of credit can call for a documentary draft, payable at sight and drawn on the bank.
- Fishy Business Ltd will specify the commercial documents to be presented for payment to be made under the letter of credit.
- The normal commercial documents will be invoice, document of movement (eg bill of lading), insurance certificate. In the circumstances of these shipments, the buyers might also call for an inspection certificate or a health certificate, together with documentary evidence that the goods have been packed in refrigerated containers with appropriate maximum/minimum temperatures.

Documentary collection
- The sellers could send the documents on a collection basis.
- A sight bill of exchange drawn on Fishy Business Ltd will be included, with documents to be released against payment.
- The same commercial documents as detailed above will form the documentary collection.

(b)   Fishy Business requires three months' credit. This can be arranged as follows:
- A documentary credit can be arranged in favour of the supplier calling for drafts drawn on the bank at three months sight/date. If the beneficiary (supplier) requires sight payment, the documentary credit should allow for the bill of exchange to be discounted. Thus the supplier will receive either the face value of the bill or the face value less discounting charges — it will be for the buyer and seller to agree beforehand who is to pay these charges.

- With both a documentary credit and a documentary collection, accommodation house finance can be arranged. Here the buyer draws an accommodation bill on the bank at three months' sight. This bill is then discounted at fine rates of discount in order to provide the customer with funds to meet the credit or collection. The goods will then be sold in order that the customer has funds to pay the bank in three months' time just prior to presentation of the accommodation bill.

- With both accommodation finance and a produce loan, the bank requires the customer to sign a letter of hypothecation/pledge, incorporating a power of sale. Lending is on a separate loan account.

- The bank will require documents of title either in the bank's name or endorsed over to it.

- The goods will be warehoused and insured in the bank's name at the customer's expense. Warehouse receipts and insurance documents will be in the bank's name and will be in transferable form. In view of the nature of the goods, the insurance policy must cover the risk of breakdown of refrigeration plant.

- A status enquiry will be taken out on the warehouse company, and a search made on both warehouse company and customer to ensure that assets charged cannot be claimed by third parties.

- The goods must be inspected by the bank or its agent.

- The goods can be released to the ultimate buyers provided that they agree to pay the bank direct. If the customer is considered trustworthy, the goods can be released against signature of a trust letter. This specifies that the sale proceeds will be paid to the bank (and credited to the loan account), and any unsold goods will be returned to the warehouse in the bank's name.

14.1   Assuming that Plant Propagations Ltd. are able to supply the plants, the following assistance is available:

(i)   Information on the overseas country, e.g. bank economic reports, details of exchange control regulations, if any.

(ii)   Creditworthiness and business acumen of buyer - status reports through bank, general reports through British Overseas Trade Board.

(iii) Methods of payment - advice from banks.

(iv)   Advice on export documentation, packing and shipping; introduction to a freight forwarder.

(v)   Credit insurance.

(vi)   Possible that overseas buyer may require finance - buyer credit, supported by ECGD.

(vii) Possibility of bonds, e.g. tender bonds, performance bonds, advance payment bonds, retention money bonds, if large orders are received; available from the bank.

(viii) Possible visit to the overseas country: bank to supply a letter of introduction; trade mission organised through BOTB.

14.2   Four main headings:
- Provision of foreign exchange facilities.
- Transfer of funds and collection of proceeds.
- Information regarding economic reports, and specific information on potential contacts/contracts.
- Banking facilities for financing exports and imports.

Foreign exchange facilities
- Buying and selling currencies, both spot and forward
- Currency loans and currency deposits
- Travel facilities

Transfer of funds and collection of proceeds
- Transfer of funds using either branches abroad, or correspondent banks
- The use of nostro and vostro accounts to facilitate international payments
- Membership of SWIFT
- Telegraphic transfers, mail transfers, SWIFT payments, bank drafts
- Inwards and outwards collections

Information
- Economic reports on world markets and on particular countries
- Status reports on creditworthiness of overseas buyers
- Assistance in finding overseas buyers
- Assistance in finding agents abroad
- General information on documentation, shipping terms, and marketing

Provision of finance
- Overdrafts
- Advances against collections
- Export finance schemes linked to credit insurance
- Documentary credits
- Acceptance credits
- Produce loans
- Guarantees, bonding, and stand-by letters of credit

14.3   Points to discuss with the company's finance director include:

- The company sells on open-account terms — other methods of payment should be discussed. In particular Steponit Ltd should consider asking some existing and new customers to open standby letters of credit. This would enable customers to continue with open account terms, but would give some measure of security to Steponit Ltd. Can the bank assist with status enquiries?

- Pricing policy — how does the company calculate the sterling cost for sales when it buys raw materials in US dollars and pays for freight and insurance in dollars?

- Exchange risks — the company pays for raw materials in US dollars. Is the exchange risk covered? Does the company make any sales to America which could be receivable in USD so as to partly offset the payments? Would it be appropriate for the company to borrow dollars?

- Is it appropriate to invoice all sales in sterling? The company's export turnover may well improve if it invoices in the local currency of the buyer, although there would be exchange risk implications.

- Is Steponit Ltd satisfied with the services of the forwarding agent? What insurance cover is provided? Is Steponit Ltd protected by transit risks insurance? The bank's insurance company may be able to help. (Note also the exchange risk of invoicing buyers in sterling for freight and insurance, whilst Steponit Ltd pays for these in dollars.)

- Does the company understand the INCOTERMS, including the responsibilities of parties? Is the company selling on CIP or FOB terms? Under what terms does it buy goods?

- Steponit Ltd needs to consider credit insurance, to cover both buyer and political/country risks — eg NCM or ECGD insurance.

- The company may wish to use the bank's finance for exports scheme, linked to credit insurance. Alternatively, an overdraft facility could be offered, with assignment of the company's credit insurance policy.

- Another finance shceme that the company should consider is export factoring. The other services of factoring companies — sales ledger accounting and bad debt protection — should be considered by the company.

- It would also be useful for the bank to arrange an international trade seminar for the staff of the company.

14.4
- To develop new markets the company should contact the British Overseas Trade Board (BOTB) and make use of the DTI's Export Intelligence Service.

- If the company expands by establishing subsidiary companies in new markets, the bank can:
  — provide economic information, exchange control regulations (if any), legal background, banking restrictions
  — introductions to correspondent banks/overseas branches of the bank
  — provide guarantees to correspondent banks/overseas branches offering facilities to new subsidiaries

- For sales to non-subsidiaries, the bank can provide status reports — either through a correspondent bank or a credit reference agency. Credit risk insurance should be considered for sales to non-subsidiaries.

- Political and country risks should also be considered for the future, although sales are, at present, to low-risk countries.

- With regard to the potential Japanese contract, the terms of the advance payment bond should be discussed. Ideally this should be:
  — subject to English law
  — bear an expiry date
  — in the bank's standard text

  If it is to be a conditional bond, an arbitration clause can be used to protect the interests of the customer. The bank will require the customer to sign a counter-indemnity in respect of the bond, and this may affect the company's total facilities with the bank.

  An alternative to an advance payment bond could be a standby letter of credit.

- The secure method of payment for the potential Japanese contract is an irrevocable letter of credit, which should be confirmed by our bank and payable at our counters. The credit should call for documents, together with a bill of exchange drawn at 30 days in order to give the buyers a period of credit. In order to give Bright Sparks Plc immediate finance, such bills could be discounted: if they were drawn on and accepted by a major bank (eg ourselves) in sterling, they could be discounted as eligible bank bills at the finest rates of discount.

  The advance payment bond should be incorporated into the letter of credit, so that it does not commence until payment has been effected.

- The company should consider the exchange risk aspects of its trading, including the potential Japanese order. Are invoices in sterling or foreign currency? The company should consider foreign currency borrowing — with the possibility of lower interest rates — if proceeds are to be received in currency. The usual forms of exchange risk cover — forward contracts and currency options — should be discussed.

- Credit insurance for the Japanese and other non-subsidiary customers should be considered. If invoices are in currency, then additional cover for foreign currency invoices may be appropriate.

- Finance schemes should be considered, such as:
  — the bank's finance for exports scheme, linked to credit insurance
  — forfaiting
  — export factoring

  The company should consider offering longer credit terms than 30 days to its potential customers — this might increase its export turnover.

APPENDIX D

Answers to Multiple-Choice Questions

Question number:	1	2	3	4	5	6	7	8	9	10
Set number 1:	C	B	B	C	D	A	D	D	C	A
2:	C	A	D	C	C	C	B	D	A	B
3:	B	A	B	D	B	A	B	B	D	D
4:	C	A	C	B	A	C	B	D	C	B
5:	B	B	B	A	C	C	D	B	D	B
6:	B	C	A	C	D	B	C	C	A	B
7:	C	D	B	A	B	C	D	A	C	A
8:	D	A	D	A	B	B	A	A	D	A

APPENDIX E

Examination Topics Frequency Table
The Chartered Institute of Bankers

	May 89	Oct 89	May 90	Oct 90	May 91	Oct 91	May 92	Oct 92	May 93	Oct 93	May 94	Oct 94
Foreign exchange/forward contracts/ currency options	✔	✔	✔	✔	✔	✔	✔	✔	✔	✔	✔	
Methods of payment			✔		✔		✔	✔	✔	✔	✔	
Nostro and vostro accounts	✔			✔		✔			✔	✔	✔	
Travel facilities	✔	✔				✔	✔		✔			
Incoterms and documents	✔	✔	✔	✔	✔			✔			✔	
Documentary letters of credit	✔	✔	✔	✔	✔	✔	✔	✔	✔	✔	✔	
Collections	✔	✔	✔	✔		✔		✔	✔	✔	✔	
Credit insurance; bank guarantees; bonds	✔	✔	✔	✔	✔	✔	✔	✔	✔		✔	
Finance for exporters and importers	✔	✔	✔	✔	✔	✔	✔	✔	✔	✔	✔	
Bank Services			✔		✔				✔		✔	

The above are *main* topic areas only – some questions consist of a mixture of topics.

Index